MATERIAL ECOCRI

MATERIAL ECOCRITICISM

Edited by
Serenella Iovino
and Serpil Oppermann

Indiana University Press

Bloomington and Indianapolis

This book is a publication of

Indiana University Press
Office of Scholarly Publishing
Herman B Wells Library 350
1320 East 10th Street
Bloomington, Indiana 47405 USA

iupress.indiana.edu

Telephone   800-842-6796
Fax   812-855-7931

© 2014 by Indiana University Press

All rights reserved

No part of this book may be reproduced or utilized in any form or by any means, electronic or mechanical, including photocopying and recording, or by any information storage and retrieval system, without permission in writing from the publisher. The Association of American University Presses' Resolution on Permissions constitutes the only exception to this prohibition.

⊖ The paper used in this publication meets the minimum requirements of the American National Standard for Information Sciences—Permanence of Paper for Printed Library Materials, ANSI Z39.48–1992.

Manufactured in the United States of America

Library of Congress Cataloging-in-Publication Data

Material Ecocriticism / edited by Serenella Iovino and Serpil Oppermann.
    pages cm
  Includes bibliographical references and index.
  ISBN 978-0-253-01395-8 (hardback) — ISBN 978-0-253-01398-9 (pb) — ISBN 978-0-253-01400-9 (eb) 1. Ecocriticism. 2. Materialism. 3. Ecology in literature. I. Iovino, Serenella, [date–] editor. II. Oppermann, Serpil, editor.
  PN98.E36M38 2014
  809'.9336—dc23

2014007338

to those who matter

Contents

Foreword: Storied Matter \ Jeffrey Jerome Cohen — ix

Acknowledgments — xiii

Introduction: Stories Come to Matter \ Serenella Iovino and Serpil Oppermann — 1

Part 1. Theories and Relations

1. From Ecological Postmodernism to Material Ecocriticism: Creative Materiality and Narrative Agency \ Serpil Oppermann — 21

2. Limits of Agency: Notes on the Material Turn from a Systems-Theoretical Perspective \ Hannes Bergthaller — 37

3. Creative Matter and Creative Mind: Cultural Ecology and Literary Creativity \ Hubert Zapf — 51

4. Natural Play, Natural Metaphor, and Natural Stories: Biosemiotic Realism \ Wendy Wheeler — 67

5. The Ecology of Colors: Goethe's Materialist Optics and Ecological Posthumanism \ Heather I. Sullivan — 80

Part 2. Narratives of Matter

6. Bodies of Naples: Stories, Matter, and the Landscapes of Porosity \ Serenella Iovino — 97

7. When It Rains \ Lowell Duckert — 114

8. Painful Material Realities, Tragedy, Ecophobia \ Simon C. Estok — 130

9. Semiotization of Matter: A Hybrid Zone between Biosemiotics and Material Ecocriticism \ Timo Maran — 141

Part 3. Politics of Matter

10 Pro/Polis: Three Forays into the Political Lives of Bees \ Catriona Sandilands — *157*

11 Excremental Ecocriticism and the Global Sanitation Crisis \ Dana Phillips — *172*

12 Oceanic Origins, Plastic Activism, and New Materialism at Sea \ Stacy Alaimo — *186*

13 Meditations on Natural Worlds, Disabled Bodies, and a Politics of Cure \ Eli Clare — *204*

Part 4. Poetics of Matter

14 Corporeal Fieldwork and Risky Art: Peter Goin and the Making of *Nuclear Landscapes* \ Cheryll Glotfelty — *221*

15 Of Material Sympathies, Paracelsus, and Whitman \ Jane Bennett — *239*

16 Source of Life: *Avatar, Amazonia,* and an Ecology of Selves \ Joni Adamson — *253*

17 The Liminal Space between Things: Epiphany and the Physical \ Timothy Morton — *269*

Coda. Open Closure
A Diptych on Material Spirituality

18 Spirits That Matter: Pathways toward a Rematerialization of Religion and Spirituality \ Kate Rigby — *283*

19 Mindful New Materialisms: Buddhist Roots for Material Ecocriticism's Flourishing \ Greta Gaard — *291*

Afterword: The Commonwealth of Breath \ David Abram — *301*

Works Cited — *315*
List of Contributors — *339*
Index — *345*

Foreword

Storied Matter

Jeffrey Jerome Cohen

A ROCK JUMPS. EVERY hiker has had the experience. The quiet woods or sweep of desert is empty and still when a snake that seemed a twig writhes, a skink that was bark scurries, leaves wriggle with insectile activity. This world coming to animal life reveals the elemental vibrancy already within green pine, arid sand, vagrant mist, and plodding hiker alike. When a toad that seemed a stone leaps into unexpected vivacity, its lively arc hints that rocks and toads share animacy, even if their movements unfold across vastly different temporalities. Just as the flitting hummingbird judges hiker and toad lithic in their stillness, a rock is within its properly geologic duration a wayfarer, a holder of stories of mountains that undulate and continents that journey the sea. The stone-like toad discloses its intimacy to toad-like stone. Both are part of a material world that challenges the organic bias of the adjective "alive."

Though slow moving and often disregarded, toads are instructive animals to follow in their irregular lines of travel. Mel Y. Chen begins her recent book *Animacies* with a story of these tailless amphibians. Her book examines how sorting the environment into anthropocentric hierarchies of life ignores the hybridity, slipperiness, and vitality of the nonhuman. The tangible childhood presence of toads, writes Chen, spurred her thinking and feeling:

> I begin with heartfelt thanks to the toads: literally grubby and ponderous yet lightning fast.... Toads infused my lifelong experience with their peculiar, but resolute, grace, with a style of creatureliness that I could and could not occupy. And though they were only sporadically visible, I could be certain a toad was somewhere nearby. (vii)

Frogs and toads are now vanishing from the world, victims of a lethal fungus distributed globally through the laboratory use, commercial trade, and domestic keeping of aquatic frogs. Though the toads of Chen's Illinois youth are important, it is the "style of their disappearance" that becomes the spur to the subject of the book, with its emphasis upon toxicity, unexpected animacy, and "retrospective temporalities and affects" (vii). The toxic network formed by a fungus, aquatic frogs, laboratories, humans, and systems of global exchange has materialized certain catastrophic effects, but mourning those results will not alter the future for backyard toads. The extinction of these jumping amphibians is not inevitable.

The leap into movement of Chen's story-laden toads resonates with the possibilities within what Serenella Iovino and Serpil Oppermann have described as a new "material ecocriticism."[1] With passion, beauty, and rigor, Iovino and Oppermann urge the contemplation of

> matter's "narrative" power of creating configurations of meanings and substances, which enter with human lives into a field of co-emerging interactions. ... [M]atter itself becomes a text where dynamics of "diffuse" agency and nonlinear causality are inscribed and produced. ("Material Ecocriticism" 79–80)

What has too often been accounted inert materiality becomes in the works gathered beneath this rubric "a site of narrativity, a storied matter, a corporeal palimpsest in which stories are inscribed" (Iovino, "Stories" 451). The world burgeons with unexpected life and astonishing textualities. Material ecocriticism is a story-laden mode of reenchantment.[2] It demands an ethics of relation, entanglement, and wonder. As the essays in this collection make clear, matter and its dynamic, diffusive meshworks generate strange stories and demand participations that move beyond the certainties of closure: not a study *of* so much as movement *with*.

A fungus threatening amphibian extinction is one of very many ecological calamities we now face. It is by no means the worst. Yet if we convince ourselves of inhabiting a historical cul-de-sac, then we should also recognize that resignation to calamity is far less demanding than an embrace of the ethics of relationality that bind us to living creatures like toads and fungi as well as to inorganic compounds and the rest of the material world. Despair is easy. Composing with hope requires work. We live in catastrophe's wide wake, but that does not mean that we will not sometimes be surprised when an immobile stone darts to sudden life. Other than a tragically familiar narrative of species decline at anthropogenic environmental change that they bear along with thousands of other plants and animals, what ecomaterial tales might toads offer? Can we imagine these amphibians as possessing a future in which we are perilously coimplicated, companions rather than elegists for the disappeared?[3] Might toads possess a unique materiality, an agency, and even an inscrutability that demand that their story not be merely human, not be familiar, not be a text written without their participation?

A wondrously catalytic toad that brings to life "storied matter" was discovered in the North of England eight hundred years ago. Encased in the geological, blurring the lines between living and inanimate, beautiful and lethal, nature and culture, the sudden advent of this medieval toad is queer. Writing just before the year 1200, historian William of Newburgh provides the contemporary account.

Foreword | xi

An attractive stone that some unknown artist seems to have fashioned by conjoining two lithic pieces is cracked open to reveal the living creature within. Workers in a quarry are excavating building materials when they discover the perplexing object:

> There was found a beautiful double stone, that is, a stone composed of two stones, joined with some very adhesive matter. Being shown by the wondering workmen to the bishop, who was at hand, it was ordered to be split, that its mystery (if any) might be developed. In the cavity, a little animal called a toad, having a small gold chain around its neck, was discovered. When the bystanders were lost in amazement at such an unusual occurrence, the bishop ordered the stone to be closed again, thrown into the quarry, and covered up with rubbish forever. (*The History of English Affairs* 28)[4]

William narrates the story because its inexplicability haunts him. He does not know what to make of an animal emerging from a rock to announce its strange intimacy to human dwelling (the stones are being quarried to fashion buildings, after all). The enmeshment of stone-toad-chain seems to exist beyond the dualisms that order the world. The gold around the creature's neck is a precious token of artistry and humane care (William's Latin word is *cathenula*, a pet's leash). The toad is natural, startling, vivacious, toxic (they were held to be venomous in the Middle Ages). The conjoined rock is a cementing together of the disparate into a beautiful if incongruous whole, a union of geology and art. No totality emerges from the discovery. William cannot render the episode an allegory for something else. The stone-toad-chain is *parabolic* in a double sense: it demands story, and it curves epistemologies into new orbits, warps knowing into swift but novel coursings. The excavated and opened objects have an undeniable materiality, a heft. They also possess agency, causing the quarry men to become lost in astonishment, lost in the realization that the world is wider than they had imagined, enlivened by stories that meld the human and the inhuman, stories that are fragments seeking greater connection. Perhaps that dangerous expansiveness explains why the bishop reassembles the stone (but how?) and consigns the toad and its golden chain to the earth's depths, to the rubbish heap of history (a fertile place, in the end: the toad surely must be awaiting rediscovery). Despite the episcopal command, the work of the toad has been set into unstoppable motion. The laborers at the quarry are already enraptured by amphibious wonder. William of Newburgh is infected by the same wonder, an astonishment irreducible to a moral. Ever since reading the passage, I have wondered at its lithic toad, at its hold on me, how it makes me dream of childhood toads uncovered in their winter stillness while digging in my family's yard, creatures and their cold earth suspended between life and death, full of agency all the same. I remember a toad in my hand as I write these words, its heft and its chill, and realize that the toad-rock-chain is a material manifestation of a storied world that is more than I can ever hold or know. Toads are humbling.

Inspired by this collection of essays that plumb the beauty, the agency, the danger, and the complicated multiplicity within material ecocriticism, I pass along that wonder—and that rock that is a work of art, and that gold chain that is a work of love, and that beautiful toxic amphibian—to you.

Notes

I thank Serenella Iovino and Serpil Oppermann for their invitation, their inspiration, and their companionship.

1. In addition to this collection, see Iovino and Oppermann, "Material Ecocriticism" and the two segments of their "Theorizing Material Ecocriticism: A Diptych."

2. "Its intention to 're-enchant' reality, claiming that all material entities, even atoms and subatomic particles have some degree of sentient experience and that all living things have agency of their own, is essential in the making of the new materialist approaches" (Iovino and Oppermann, "Material Ecocriticism" 78).

3. I take "coimplicated" as a term for environmental entanglement and composition from Duckert 274.

4. I am grateful to the students in my graduate seminar "Environ Body Object Veer" at the George Washington University (2013) for talking through the apposition of Mel Y. Chen's and William of Newburgh's toads with me.

Acknowledgments

THERE IS NOTHING less personal than a book. In our case, this has a double meaning: *Material Ecocriticism* is an ensemble of many different voices, and it is itself the outcome of a complex and ramified ecology of ideas, which, to use Gregory Bateson's image, forms the collective mind hosted in these pages.

Many subjects created the conditions for these ideas to materialize into a volume. In the first place, we would like to thank the Alexander-von-Humboldt Foundation and the Fulbright Program, whose generous support enabled us to spend long periods of research, respectively, in Germany (Serenella Iovino) and in the United States (Serpil Oppermann). Without the opportunity given to us by those prestigious grants, many of the material-discursive realizations of this project would simply be unthinkable. We would like to acknowledge the people and the institutions that, in the framework of those grants, first considered with us the concepts related to material ecocriticism: the students and colleagues at the Elitestudienkolleg "Ethik der Textkulturen" at the University of Augsburg, Germany, who participated in the Oberseminar on Material Ecocriticism, in the fall of 2011, and those in the Literature and Environment Program at the University of Nevada, Reno, who were among the first to discuss these subjects, in the same period.

Friends and colleagues at EASLCE and ASLE, with whom we exchanged ideas about material ecocriticism at conferences, gave us crucial feedback, constructive criticisms, and enlightening suggestions. A constant presence in these pages, Karen Barad has encouraged our enterprise with generous words and warm support. We also wish to acknowledge Christian Arpaia, Mike Branch, Margarita Carretero González, Daniela Fargione, José Manuel Marrero Henríquez, Elena Margarita Past, Dan Philippon, Christopher Schliephake, Maurizio Valsania, Alexa Weik von Mossner, and our students and cross-species families in Italy and Turkey.

A particularly profound appreciation is due to Anne Elvey and Scott Slovic, who acted as editorial reviewers for this book. Their favorable reports and perceptive advice have invigorated this collection in the most delicate moment of its "worldly becoming." The editorial team at Indiana University Press (Sarah Jacobi, June Silay, and Annette Wenda) did the rest with its meticulous and resourceful work on the texts, illustrations, and captions.

Jeffrey Cohen and David Abram, who wrote, respectively, the foreword and the afterword of this volume, deserve a special recognition: if this book could speak like a human, it would say how comforting it is to be surrounded by their ideas and words. Finally, we are grateful to the contributors, all stars themselves, who have helped us to map this new constellation of visions for ecocritical studies. Each one of them, in her or his unique way, has amplified our little universe much more than this page can tell.

The exciting journey of *Material Ecocriticism* started in Bloomington, Indiana, at the 2011 ASLE conference, where we met Dee Mortensen, our sponsoring editor at Indiana University Press. We extend our heartfelt gratitude to Dee, who has from the outset believed in our project and provided invaluable backing in the preparation of this volume. We thank her immensely, not only for her unwavering assistance and unique professionalism, but also for her warm friendship, precious insights, and collegiality in this journey. She has constantly accompanied us, sharing stories of bees and dogs, chickens and lavender. This has made our steps more stable, and our minds happier.

MATERIAL ECOCRITICISM

Introduction

Stories Come to Matter

Serenella Iovino and Serpil Oppermann

> After three and a half centuries spent charting and measuring material nature as though it were a pure exterior, we've at last begun to notice that the world we inhabit (from the ocean floor to the upper atmosphere) is alive.
> —David Abram, *Becoming Animal*

> We are a part of that nature that we seek to understand.
> —Karen Barad, *Meeting the Universe Halfway*

AN ANCIENT MEDITERRANEAN landscape; an endangered species in the Amazon; the Library of Congress; the Gulf Stream; carcinogenic cells, DNA, dioxin; a volcano, a school, a city, a factory farm; the outbreak of a virus, a toxic plume; bioluminescent water; your eyes, our hands, this book: what do all these things have in common? The answer to this question is simple. Whether visible or invisible, socialized or wild, they are all material forms emerging in combination with forces, agencies, and other matter. Entangled in endless ways, their "more-than-human" materiality is a constant process of shared becoming that tells us something about the "world we inhabit." This world, we understand through them, is far from being a "pure exterior," as the first epigraph says, and it is also far from being "pure." It is filled instead with intermingling agencies and forces that persist and change over eons, producing new forms, bodies, and natures. It is through all these natures, agencies, and bodies that "the world we inhabit," with all its stories, is "alive."

The conceptual argument of *Material Ecocriticism* is simple in its outlines: the world's material phenomena are knots in a vast network of agencies, which can be "read" and interpreted as forming narratives, stories. Developing in bodily forms and in discursive formulations, and arising in coevolutionary landscapes of natures and signs, the stories of matter are everywhere: in the air we breathe, the food we eat, in the things and beings of this world, within and beyond the human realm. All matter, in other words, is a "storied matter." It is a material "mesh" of meanings, properties, and processes, in which human and nonhuman players are interlocked in networks that produce undeniable signifying forces.

In the past years, the activities and properties of these networks of bodies and discourses, which Donna Haraway has called our "material-semiotic reality" (*Haraway* 2), have captured unprecedented attention in many areas of research, generating a powerful "turn to the material" in the environmental debate. Clarifying the position of the environmental literary criticism in this scenery, *Material Ecocriticism* aims to open an interpretive horizon for the complex interrelations between discourse and matter and to intensify the dialogue with authors who have brought "the materiality of the human body and the natural world into the forefront" of analysis (Alaimo and Hekman 1). The ecocritical vision proposed in this volume explores such a dimension in literary texts as well as in the forms this materiality assumes in the "material-semiotic" world. As the approaches taken by the featured authors clearly indicate, a *material* ecocriticism examines matter both *in* texts and *as* a text, trying to shed light on the way bodily natures and discursive forces *express* their interaction whether in representations or in their concrete reality.

The idea here is to couple ecocriticism's interest in revealing the bonds between text and world with the insights of the new materialist wave of thought. This is not an easy task, if we consider the breadth of such a conceptual debate. The "material turn" is an extensive conversation across the territories of the sciences and the humanities and embraces such fields as philosophy, quantum physics, biology, sociology, feminist theories, anthropology, archaeology, and cultural studies, just to name a few.[1] Whether one labels it "new materialisms" or "the material turn," this emerging paradigm elicits not only new nonanthropocentric approaches, but also possible ways to analyze language and reality, human and nonhuman life, mind and matter, without falling into dichotomous patterns of thinking.

The goals here at stake are ambitious and deserve a closer examination, which will be essential to understand the scope of our ecocritical discourse. As Diana Coole and Samantha Frost note in their introduction to *New Materialisms,* at the very heart of the debate is "a challenge to some of the most basic assumptions that have underpinned the modern world, including its normative sense of the human and its beliefs about human agency, but also regarding its material practices, such as the ways we labor on, exploit, and interact with nature" ("Introducing" 4). The first of these "most basic assumptions" is the chasm between the human and the nonhuman world in terms of agency. Compared to a human endowed with mind and agentic determinations, the material world—a world that includes "inanimate" matter as well as all nonhuman forms of living—has always been considered as passive, inert, unable to convey any independent expression of meaning. The drawbacks of this vision are considerable. Besides restricting the latitude of ethics to our species, this dichotomous ontology has also reinforced other common misunderstandings, including the "break-it-and-fix-it mentality of some environmental rhetoric, a mentality informed by the assumption that human agents (knowingly or inadvertently) create ecological problems, but can readily solve all of them at will with the right technology" (Phillips and Sullivan 446). But how does such mentality deal with the complex phenomena in which human agency is only a part of the picture? How does it conciliate with the entanglements of more-than-human forces and substances, which, visibly or imperceptibly, merge with the life of our bodies and places? Are we really in control of the many worlds—the worlds of electricity, toxins, fungi, climate patterns—inhabiting our world, when even the simple use of an antibiotic can exert a long-term interference on the complex balances of our microbiome, and therefore on our health? To overlook the complexity of this landscape of forces and all the "nonhuman powers circulating around and within human bodies" (Bennett, *Vibrant* ix) leads not only to a very partial vision of the world's processes, but also to behaviors whose consequences might affect the entire biosphere. It is quite arduous for humans to declare their agentic independence in a hybrid, vibrant, and *living* world.

Bridging the current developments in sciences and technology with motives borrowed from a tradition of immanent thinking that "breaks through . . . the mind-matter and culture-nature divides of transcendental humanist thought" (Dolphijn and van der Tuin 96), the new materialist thinkers invite us to reconsider the categories of this world. Their main claim is that discourses about the *living* world, though necessary, are per se insufficient, if separated from their broader material substratum of inanimate substances and apersonal agencies. In other words, not everything that happens in this world and interferes with living systems is "alive" in the biological sense. Agency assumes many forms, all of which are characterized by an important feature: they are *material*, and the meanings they produce influence in various ways the existence of both human and nonhuman natures. Agency, therefore, is not to be necessarily and exclusively associated with human beings and with human intentionality, but it is a pervasive and inbuilt property of matter, as part and parcel of its generative dynamism. From this dynamism, reality emerges as an intertwined flux of material and discursive forces, rather than as complex of hierarchically organized individual players.

Seeking to provide a more accurate (and also more ontologically generous) picture of reality, the new materialists argue for a "theory of distributive agency." Accordingly, the "root or cause of an effect" (Bennett, *Vibrant* 31) is not a human subject—posited in isolation from the nonhuman—but a material-semiotic network of human and nonhuman agents incessantly generating the world's embodiments and events. "Nonhuman" here denotes "a community of expressive presences" (Abram, *Becoming* 173): not only sentient animals or other biological organisms, but also impersonal agents, ranging from electricity to hurricanes, from metals to bacteria, from nuclear plants to information networks. Contrary to the vision fixed on human supremacy, a different approach based on a confederation of agencies implies that things and nonhumans in general are no longer seen as mere objects, statically depending on a subject, but as "full-fledged actors" (Latour, *Pandora's* 174). Whether materializing in species extinction, climate patterns, racial discriminations, health policies, in the practices of extraction, transformation, and consumption of natural resources, or in the many voices and experiences of a more-than-human mind, the world's phenomena are segments of a conversation between human and manifold nonhuman beings, which act together and "exchange properties" in indissoluble "collectives," as Bruno Latour insists (*Politics* 61).

The term "conversation" here is not simply a metaphor. The new materialisms suggest that things (or matter) draw their agentic power from their relation to discourses that in turn structure human relations to materiality. Resisting the emphasis on linguistic constructions of the world, formulated by some trends of postmodern thought, the new materialist paradigm is premised on the integral ways of thinking language and reality, meaning and matter together. A key point, provided by Karen Barad's theory of agential realism, is that phenomena result from the intra-actions of material and discursive practices and agencies, which coemerge at once (hence *intra-* and not *inter*action), thus constituting the world "in its ongoing becoming." Matter and meaning, Barad states, are "inextricably fused together, and no event, no matter how energetic, can tear them asunder.... Mattering is simultaneously a matter of substance and significance" (*Meeting* 3). Meaning, she maintains, is "an ongoing performance of the world in its differential intelligibility" (335).

This is a crucial theme in the discourse of the new materialisms, and it has been stressed from different but concurring perspectives. The power of matter to build dynamics of meaning in and across bodies can be detected, for example, in the biosemiotic assumption that "the natural world is perfused with signs, meanings, and purposes which are material and which evolve" (Wheeler, "The Biosemiotic" 279), making life an embodied process of understanding (or, in Barad's terms, "differential intelligibility") that engages all beings "from the humblest forms of single-cell life upwards" (271). As Wendy Wheeler writes, "What goes on *inside* an organism, and *between* an organism and its environment (the two processes being intimately connected) always involves what ... we must call interpretations—however minimal" ("The Biosemiotic" 271).[2] In other words, the borders between meaning and matter are constitutionally porous, making the "intimate" material-semiotic connection between the "inside" and "outside" of organisms recognizable at smaller as well as larger levels of organization. Such dynamics are also visible, in fact, in the complex pathways of trans-corporeality—the transits of substances and discursive practices within and across bodies—insightfully conceptualized and explored by Stacy Alaimo in *Bodily Natures*. Illustrating the mutual interferences of places, sociopolitical practices, and the health of all living organisms, trans-corporeal dynamics reflect the way bodies "interpret" the ecologies of discourses and forces with which they interact, reconfiguring subjectivity as interfaced with landscapes of risks, biological materialities, and "power structures" (86).[3] Finally, the coemergence of matter and meaning and the permeability between the inside and the outside are also present in the elemental embodiments of the "more-than-human world" as examined by David Abram.[4] In tune with the biosemiotic insight of a universe "perfused with signs" in which mind is "immanent in all things" (Wheeler, "The Biosemiotic" 272), and also in terms that resonate with Alaimo's trans-corporeality as a "bodily immersion" within "a landscape of interactions" (*Bodily* 70), Abram draws an ecophenomenological vision of natural life as a congealing of imaginative and biological processes, as the "state of mind" of a storied world, in which humans and nonhumans are "carnally immersed" (*Becoming* 123). In all these cases, the porosity of biosphere and semiosphere, the trajectories of toxins and discourses across living bodies, and the fact that the world's imagination is "an ever-unfolding story" embedding "our variously sensitive bodies" (Abram, *Becoming* 270–72) exist in a dimension where meaning and matter are inextricably entangled, constituting life's narratives and life itself.

On this conceptual horizon, the world's vibrant materiality appears as a "web teeming with meanings" (Wheeler, "The Biosemiotic" 270), in which humans, nonhumans, and their stories are tied together. The emerging dynamics of matter and meaning, body and identity, being and knowing, nature and culture, *bios* and society are therefore to be examined and thought not in isolation from each other, but *through* one another, matter being an ongoing process of embodiment that involves and mutually determines cognitions, social constructions, scientific practices, and ethical attitudes. In this perspective, there is no simple juxtaposition or *mirroring* between nature and culture, but a combined "mesh." Here culture and nature become a hybrid compound, congealing, to use Haraway's term, into *naturecultures*. This natural-cultural plexus is the cypher of our world, and therefore the necessary terrain of every critical analysis.

* * *

All these ideas—a distributive vision of agency, the emergent nature of the world's phenomena, the awareness that we inhabit a dimension crisscrossed by vibrant forces that hybridize human and nonhuman matters, and finally the persuasion that matter and meaning constitute the fabric of our storied world—are the basic premises of material ecocriticism. In this volume we explore this landscape of "swarming" agencies, with the conviction that ecocriticism can adopt and fruitfully develop on the perspective provided by the new materialisms. What lies behind the nodes of the ecological crisis—pollution, mass extinctions, poverty, enslavement of humans and animals, and many other forms of oppression—are tangles of natures and cultures that can be unraveled only by interpreting them as narratives about the way humans and their agentic partners intersect in the making of the world.

At first glance, these points are not new in ecocritical studies. If ecocriticism has a grounding assumption at its origin, it is the tight connection between literature and the natural-cultural dynamics of the material world. More specifically, and despite its increasingly varied and multivalent definitions, analytical strategies, and theoretical standpoints, ecocriticism's initial objective stands intact: seeking "to restore the significance to the world beyond the page" (Rigby, "Ecocriticism" 154–55).[5] In her memorable introduction to *The Ecocriticism Reader*, Cheryll Glotfelty posits that "literature does not float above the material world in some aesthetic ether, but, rather, plays a part in an immensely complex global system in which energy, matter, *and ideas* interact" (xix). Framing these insights within the new conceptual premises, material ecocriticism traces the trajectories of natural-cultural interactions by reading them as "material narratives." In other words, it analyzes the interlacements of matter and discourses not only as they are re-created by literature and other cultural forms, but also as they emerge in material expressions. Its particularity, as previously stated, is that it heeds matter not solely as it appears in texts, but as a text itself. This extension of the realm of textuality beyond the margins of canonical texts and, as we will see, the elaboration of a "diffractive" methodology resulting from the intra-action (or, using Glotfelty's famous metaphor, "cross-pollination") between human interpreter and material textuality are, in our opinion, the main additions of this new paradigm to the field of ecocritical studies.

Bodies, both human and nonhuman, provide an eloquent example of the way matter can be read as a text. Being the "middle place" where matter enmeshes in the discursive forces of politics, society, technology, biology, bodies are compounds of flesh, elemental properties, and symbolic imaginaries. Whether performing their narratives as statues in a square, teachers in a classroom, plankton in the ocean, fossils trapped in a stone wall, or chickens in industrial factory farms, bodies are living texts that recount *naturalcultural* stories. The key point in this argument is that all things and beings, as David Abram reminds us, "have the ability to communicate something of themselves to other beings" (*Becoming* 172). The recognition of their agency as an intrinsic property "steadily bodying forth [their] own active creativity and sentience" (170) not only insinuates new conceptions of nature, life, and materiality, but also relocates the human in a larger material-semiotic "collective."

Material ecocriticism argues that there is an implicit textuality in the becoming of material formations, and this textuality resides in the way the agentic dimension of matter expresses itself, as well as in the way bodies emerge in the combined and simultaneous action of material dynamics and discursive practices. Whether a thing or a living creature, "every being that matters" is, to quote Haraway, "a congeries of its formative histories" (*Haraway* 2). In the way it "joins text and body in . . . material semiosis and semiotic materiality"—whether in transcorporeal, biosemiotic, or evolutionary terms—every being has a story to tell; it is "semiotically active" (*When Species* 163, 250). Its inner interplay of agencies has a spatiotemporal trajectory; set within this world, its materiality is punctuated over time with meanings. It is a *storied* matter.

Material ecocriticism, in this broad framework, is the study of the way material forms—bodies, things, elements, toxic substances, chemicals, organic and inorganic matter, landscapes, and biological entities—intra-act with each other and with the human dimension, producing configurations of meanings and discourses that we can interpret as stories. Even though no preordered plot can rigorously distinguish these stories of matter, what characterizes them is a narrative performance, a dynamic process of material expressions seen in bodies, things, and phenomena coemerging from these networks of intra-acting forces and entities. Seen in this light, every living creature, from humans to fungi, tells evolutionary stories of coexistence, interdependence, adaptation and hybridization, extinctions and survivals. Whether perceived or interpreted by the human mind or not, these stories shape trajectories that have a formative, enactive power. Think of our planet: the transformative stories built by telluric powers, magnetic forces, clashing and melting elements, and dawning forms of life extend the past of the earth into our present, determining the way all beings articulate their relationships to the world. In the same way, all matter—even the one that we do not see, sense, or suspect—constantly interacts with other matter, whether in human or nonhuman forms. Far from being a naive concession to animism or any mythos, framing this interplay in a narrative dimension is essential in the economy of ecological discourse. As Jeffrey Cohen has written,

> to believe that rivers compose might be to project human qualities on indifferent things. . . . Yet what is at stake in limiting agency to an origin in human volition—as if we intend much of what we accomplish? The profundity of climate change in the Anthropocene argues against such easy alignment. Causes tend to be known retroactively when they are known at all, traced back . . . through volatile knots of human and inhuman actors operating in alliance as well as at odds with each other. ("Ecology's Rainbow" xxiv)

Reading into the "thick of things," material ecocriticism aims to explore not only the agentic properties of material forms, whether living or not, whether organic, "natural" or not, but also how these properties act in combination with other material forms and their properties and with discourses, evolutionary paths, political decisions, pollution, and other stories. The "volatile knots" of human and nonhuman agents, as Cohen insists, thus not only are crucial to "apprehend the environment dis-anthropocentrically" (xxiv), but also invite us to read their stories in the way they induce a transformation in plotting "dis-anthropocentric" disciplinary discourses and political, cultural, and ethical models. How would, for instance, "the maps of sustainability change, if we read 'through bodies' the stories of these encounters? How would we deal with waste . . . if we followed the narrative patterns that matter, in visible and invisible forms, draws across bodies?" (Iovino, "Steps" 144). We need to read *through* all these stories if we want to encourage new visions that have less harmful effects on the world of bodily natures.

This form of "material narrativity" also leads to a different and less human-centered idea of literature. Framed as material-discursive encounters, literary stories emerge from the intra-action of human creativity and the narrative agency of matter. Playing together, *this* shared creativity of human and nonhuman agents generates new narratives and discourses that give voice to the complexity of our collective, highlighting its multiple and "fractal" causal connections and enlarging our horizon of meanings. In other words, narrative agency and human creativity coemerge in new and more complex levels of reality. Here human and nonhuman players produce narrative emergences that amplify reality, also affecting our cognitive response to this reality.

We are well aware that "stories" or "narratives," if applied to matter, might be read as a metaphor. We want, however, to challenge the criticisms of anthropomorphizing matter and use this human lens as a heuristic strategy aimed at reducing the (linguistic, perceptive, and ethical) distance between the human and the nonhuman. So understood, anthropomorphism can even act against dualistic ontologies and be a "dis-anthropocentric" stratagem meant to reveal the similarities and symmetries existing between humans and nonhumans. As Jane Bennett has compellingly argued:

> A touch of anthropomorphism . . . can catalyze a sensibility that finds a world filled not with ontologically distinct categories of beings (subjects and objects) but with variously composed materiality that form confederations. In revealing similarities across categorical divides and lighting up parallels between material forms in "nature" and those in "culture," anthropomorphism can reveal isomorphism. (*Vibrant* 99)

More basically, however, we can explore this "narrativity" of matter—bodies, natures, cultural forms—because the meanings it conveys are not separated from us. As a part of these "confederations" of "variously composed materiality," we are entangled with their material agency and emerge *together* as storied beings. If humans are fruits of the world's becoming, this interpretation is a way to take part "in bringing forth the world in its specificity, including ourselves" (Barad,

Meeting 352). This is our way, as Barad would say, "to meet the universe halfway, to move toward what may come to be in ways that are accountable for our part in the world's differential becoming" (353). In material-ecocritical terms, the human agency meets the narrative agency of matter halfway, generating material-discursive phenomena in the forms of literature and other cultural creations, including literary criticism. Also the way we interpret the world's narratives is evidently a mode of intra-action, a phenomenon emerging from the world's creativity. In other words, this is one of the endless ways of being "a part of that nature that we seek to understand" (67).

Ecocritics have long talked about "narrative scholarship."[6] Material ecocriticism is a way to give the adjective "narrative" a more ontologically complex meaning. "Narrative" in this sense means the way our interpretation is itself intermingled with what it considers, in a material and discursive way. In this material "narrative scholarship," the interpreter and the interpreted emerge together, in intra-action. This critical practice is therefore a further development—and, in a way, a completion—of traditional narrative scholarship, with the difference that the emanating point of the narrative is no longer the human self, but the human-nonhuman complex of interrelated agencies.

In this conceptual framework, the project of material ecocriticism can, therefore, be understood as an approach that entails a critical self-reflection on our part as humans and on the constitutive engagement of human discursive systems with the material world. Integrally situated in this dance of matter and meanings, our cognitive practices participate in the world's "differential intelligibility." As Barad explains: "We are not outside observers of the world. Neither are we simply located at particular places *in* the world; rather, we are part of the world in its ongoing intra-activity" (184). Interpretation, therefore, "is an ontological performance of the world in its ongoing articulation. . . . Knowing is a matter of intra-acting" (149). But in a storied world, every cognitive appropriation creates "interference patterns"; it happens by way of "diffractions." As Barad, again, writes:

> Diffraction is a material-discursive phenomenon that challenges the presumed inherent separability of subject and object, nature and culture, fact and value, human and nonhuman, organic and inorganic, epistemology and ontology, materiality and discursivity. . . . *Diffraction is a material practice for making a difference, for topologically reconfiguring connections.* (381; emphasis in the original)

One of the basic insights of material ecocriticism consists in turning this "diffractive" reading into an interpretive methodology to be applied in the fields of literary and cultural studies and to conceive textual interpretation as a "practice of entanglement." Reading the discursive and the material, the cultural and the natural *diffractively,* not in separation, means reading them through one another. Instead of concentrating on texts and seeing how they "reflect" the world's phenomena—natural life or a society's cultural practices—such an interpretation reads world and text as an agentic entanglement. This involves a reconceptualization of both the idea of text (as distinct from other nontextual material formations) and the idea of world (as "the outside of text"). According to this vision, text and world can be read as "circulating references,"[7] the same way that nature and culture can be *read and thought* through one another in laboratories, gender politics, or hybrid collectives of humans and nonhumans. In all the fields of life, the materiality of beings and of substances that support their existence is deeply related to the ways this materiality is conceptualized and discursively formulated. Therefore, instead of transforming "nature" into an endless series of interpretations, the "diffractive" method allows us to actively participate in a creative process in which material levels and levels of meanings emerge together, contributing to the world's becoming a web teeming with collective stories.

* * *

Like all the entanglements of material and discursive agencies at work in the world's becoming, material ecocriticism is a "collective" effort. Even though, with essays and conference presentations, we might have been instrumental for its first explicit developments, material ecocriticism articulates motives traced by authors and texts that, within and across the field of the new materialisms, continue to trigger the creativity of ecocritics involved in reinforcing this new paradigm. The material ecocritical approaches presented here should, thus, be read in dialogue with the authors who are frequently quoted (and, in some fortunate cases, even materially present) in the pages of this volume, but they also engage a lively conversation with thinkers such as Gregory Bateson, David Bohm, Deleuze and Guattari, Antonio Damasio, Bruno Latour, Rosi Braidotti, Vicki Kirby, Bill Brown, Manuel De Landa, Andrew Pickering, and Joseph Rouse, to name just a few. The theoretical territories explored here are heterogeneous and mix their boundaries with several fields, ranging from biosemiotics to the ecology of mind, from ecological postmodernism to posthumanism, from "thing theory" to object-oriented ontology (OOO). A relationship of particular intensity is the one that connects material ecocriticism with all the trends and figures of material feminisms, especially where the exploration of the agency of matter meets the categories of ecocultural and feminist discourses, as exemplified in the works of Stacy Alaimo, Karen Barad, Susan Hekman, Catriona Sandilands, and Nancy Tuana. A powerful conversation is also set up with posthumanism and the posthuman approach to cultural and literary texts, with such authors as Donna Haraway, Cary Wolfe, N. Katherine Hayles, Giorgio Agamben, Jeffrey J. Cohen, and Roberto Marchesini. And, though the passage of the new materialisms to the field of ecocritical studies would have hardly happened without the influence of books such as David Abram's *Becoming Animal,* Stacy Alaimo's *Bodily Natures,* Karen Barad's *Meeting the Universe Halfway,* Jane Bennett's *Vibrant Matter,* and Wendy Wheeler's *The Whole Creature,* it is interesting to see how their conceptual lines are developing in many autonomous ecocritical pathways.

The fast-growing literature and the limits of this introduction make it impossible for us to map all the emergences and coemergences of this field of research. In previously published essays we have tried to provide a detailed sketch of the genealogy and morphology of material ecocriticism.[8] Because these writings are all materially available in the virtual sphere, we have chosen not to repeat their argumentative outlines in this introduction. We cannot, however, omit from this bird's-eye overview a reference to some of the publications that, though in some cases not explicitly connoted as "material ecocriticism," have contributed to shape the theoretical horizon in which this book is situated. The first of these publications is the *ISLE* special cluster titled *Material Ecocriticism: Dirt, Waste, Bodies, Food, and Other Matter* (2012), edited by Heather Sullivan and Dana Phillips, an inspiring collection of essays that, being the first concerted articulation of these topics, is an indispensable reference for our area of study. Remarkable examples of material ecocriticism *avant la lettre* can also be listed in some of the essays published in *Ecocritical Theory: New European Approaches,* edited by Axel Goodbody and Kate Rigby (2011). In particular, Heather Sullivan's interpretation of Goethe's *Faust* in the diffractive key of affinity studies, Laura Dassow Walls's contribution subtitled "Latour on Walden Pond," and Anne Elvey's explicit emphasis on the "matter of texts" openly call into question the necessity to consider materiality and textuality together, theorizing their relationship as a "chiasm" in which "boundaries are not frontiers but rather contact surfaces."[9] A noteworthy consonant approach can also be traced in the way Rob Nixon (*Slow Violence and the Environmentalism of the Poor* [2011]) pits the interlacements of politics, global pollution, and environmental justice against a temporal horizon in which bodies and places become expressive sites of neocolonial forms of violence. Finally, it is very important to us to stress the crucial convergence that material ecocriticism has with the ecocritical projects led by Jeffrey J. Cohen. With their emphasis on hybrid agencies, material narrativity, and "dis-anthropocentrism," his collections *Animal, Vegetable, and Mineral* (2012), *Prismatic Ecology* (2014), a special issue of *postmedieval* titled *Ecomaterialism* (2012), and the now forthcoming *Elemental Ecocriticism* (these last two publications edited with Lowell Duckert) clearly belong to the same creative and conceptual atmosphere of this volume and of our research.[10]

It is necessary to note that, like the new materialisms, material ecocriticism does not acknowledge or require any "overall orthodoxy" (Coole and Frost, "Introducing" 4). Thematically and stylistically, "material ecocritics" are still exploring their personal ways into this ecocritical paradigm, making material ecocriticism a polyphonic chorus, which addresses the issues at stake from various but complementary angles. This reflects in the way our volume is organized and in the approaches here represented.

By opening the book with "Theories and Relations," comprising five chapters, we aim to expose the ways in which material ecocriticism can be theorized. Starting with the insights of ecological postmodernism, integrating the new materialist conceptualization of agency with the perspectives of systems theory, and moving to the viewpoints of cultural ecology, biosemiotics, and posthumanism, these essays demonstrate that a theory of material ecocriticism can begin in multiple pathways. The opening chapter, Serpil Oppermann's "From Ecological Postmodernism to Material Ecocriticism: Creative Materiality and Narrative Agency," acknowledges a genealogical lineage between these two fields, especially visible in the way they describe matter in terms of its internal experience, agentic creativity, and vitality. Visible at all levels of the natural world (from atoms to complex structures here called "compound individuals"), the power of matter to create and transmit "stories" through the interchange of forces and forms resonates, in Oppermann's interpretation, with the postmodern emphasis on the reenchantment of nature. From a quite different angle, Hannes Bergthaller's "Limits of Agency: Notes on the Material Turn from a Systems-Theoretical Perspective" illustrates both the potentialities and the risks of the new materialist vision of agency. By examining the developments of these ideas in biology (as described by Francisco Varela and Humberto Maturana) and in social studies (as in Niklas Luhmann's social systems theory), Bergthaller proposes to integrate autopoiesis in the ontology and ethics of the new materialisms. In the third chapter, "Creative Matter and Creative Mind," Hubert Zapf scrutinizes the question of cultural and natural creativity from the combined perspective of material ecocriticism and cultural ecology. A nondualistic analysis of material-discursive dynamics, cultural ecology—of which Zapf is one of the major exponents—is set in a dialogue with biosemiotics and mind theories and proposed as a tool to bridge the materiality of the world's agency with the apparent "disembodiment" of discursive constructions in literary texts. "Laterally" introduced in Zapf's essay, biosemiotics is a discipline that, being a privileged interlocutor for material ecocriticism, is present in our volume with two dedicated studies. The first of these essays, included in this section, is Wendy Wheeler's "Natural Play, Natural Metaphor, and Natural Stories: Biosemiotic Realism." Giving an account of biosemiotics as a discipline that challenges a "simple" materialism, the author shows how the homologies existing between aesthetic and natural forms actually disprove the old distinctions between culture and nature, mind and body, "essenzialized" human self and natural others. The essay that completes "Theories and Relations" is Heather

Sullivan's "The Ecology of Colors: Goethe's Material Optics and Ecological Posthumanism." Reading Goethe's *Theory of Color* through the new materialisms, the author argues that his anti-Newtonian stance displays striking similarity to Barad's notions of diffractions and intra-action. Focusing on the way colors emerge via the intra-action of light, energy, bodily natures, and technological enactments, Goethe's optics offers, in Sullivan's interpretation, a precursory form of ecological posthumanism, which is here developed by the author as an integral part of material ecocriticism.

"Narratives of Matter," examining the ways meanings, stories, signs, and discourses are embedded in material forms, intra-acting with the lives and landscapes of humans and nonhumans, is the title of the second section of *Material Ecocriticism*. In the opening essay, "Bodies of Naples: Stories, Matter, and the Landscapes of Porosity," Serenella Iovino analyzes the material-discursive entanglements of her "porous city" (as Walter Benjamin defined it), by discussing two examples of "storied matter": the plaster casts created by archaeologists in excavating Pompeii's ruins and the "war on the bodies of Naples," as represented in Curzio Malaparte's novel *The Skin* (1949). Considering the way the diffractive dynamics of nature and memory are embodied in Naples's reality, Iovino argues that interpretation participates in the "differential becoming" of this reality, adding new levels to the place's mind. In the second chapter, "When It Rains," Lowell Duckert discusses the impersonal agency of rain, describing it as a vital materiality that resists the binaries between in/human, in/organic, and climate/culture. When it rains, he maintains, we recognize reality as a system in cascade: networks of in/human things that, in their random swerves and collisions, *precipitate* ("bring about") alliances, stories, and desires. Finally, by putting modern travel literature into conversation with actor-network theorists, the essay considers new ways of narrating embodied experience. The third chapter is Simon Estok's "Painful Material Realities, Tragedy, Ecophobia." Drawing from his idea of "ecophobia," Estok considers how conceptual and discursive displacements of pain measure and manifest our delusions about human exceptionalism and anxieties about death. The author argues that theorizing ecophobia through discussions and narratives about pain allows us to see the thick materiality of our embeddedness, which, in many ways, is synonymous with *involvement* in processes of interacting agencies. This section concludes with Timo Maran's "Semiotization of Matter: A Hybrid Zone between Biosemiotics and Material Ecocriticism." Addressing the notion of "storied matter," Maran analyzes what he calls the "semiotization of matter," a process by which the environment is materially and semiotically shaped by humans. The way humans "semiotize" matter, he argues, can interfere with the ability of many nonhuman species to perceive and interpret these environments. The degradation of the habitats of many nonhuman species can therefore be framed in terms that are not only ecological, but also semiotic: it is a material-semiotic practice, whose consequences are difficult to predict but nevertheless crucial for the survival of our "collective."

The third part, "Politics of Matter," concentrates on cutting-edge topics of ecocritical studies—biopolitics, detritus, pain, and disability—shedding light on the way material-discursive dynamics concur to shape the human, nonhuman, and environmental political dimension. The sections opens with "Pro/Polis: Three Forays into the Political Lives of Bees" by Catriona Sandilands, an essay in which the interspecies bond between humans and bees is exposed as a biopolitical one. Via three theoretical and zoosemiotical "forays" into the possibilities of bee politics, and a material-ecocritical reading of Sean Borodale's *Bee Journal,* Sandilands demonstrates that beekeeping may ground a practice of human attentiveness to bees that allows a more deeply egalitarian politics to emerge. The second chapter, Dana Phillips's "Excremental Ecocriticism and the Global Sanitation Crisis," articulates what he calls a "subsidiary" discourse of material ecocriticism. Displaced from the sight, and more often from the consciousness, excrement embodies, for Phillips, the way modern societies both produce and suppress the environmental crisis. Developing his "excremental ecocriticism" through texts that deal with the chaotic and "recalcitrant agency of shit," the author interprets the "global sanitation crisis" as an entanglement of material emergences, cultural-technological practices, and historical-political factors that involve both colonial and postcolonial ecologies. In the third chapter, "Oceanic Origins, Plastic Activism, and New Materialism at Sea," Stacy Alaimo elaborates a "marine" version of her foundational concept of trans-corporeality. Retracing the evolutionary, economic, and ecological exchanges and entanglements of human life and the life of the seas, Alaimo demonstrates how a trans-corporeality extended to the seas links humans to global political networks of consumption, waste, and pollution. The last chapter of this section is Eli Clare's "Meditations on Natural Worlds, Disabled Bodies, and a Politics of Cure." In this narrative prose, Clare explores the tangle of *normal* and *natural, abnormal* and *unnatural* and the use of medical technology to preserve life and to reshape bodies. Creating a parallel between the ecological restoration of a prairie ecosystem and the politics of cure as the "restoration" of the health of human bodies, the author turns to disability and discusses the contradictions emerging from the medical industrial complex and the biopolitical categories of human and natural "normality."

The fourth section of the volume is titled "Poetics of Matter." This title not only is due to the relevance that the aesthetic dimension has in this section, but—more profoundly—also resonates with the Greek root of "poiesis," implying a literal sense of "making." In our perspective, participating "diffractively" in the world's becoming, the creative entanglements of agencies are not only ways of world mirroring but coemerging "ways of worldmaking" (see Goodman, *Ways of*

Worldmaking). The "poetical" dimension of material ecocriticism is here explored by turning particular attention to art, poetry, and philosophy. The opening essay, Cheryll Glotfelty's "Corporeal Fieldwork and Risky Art: Peter Goin and the Making of *Nuclear Landscapes,*" instantiates this "mutual making" between human and nonhuman agency via artistic creation. Engaging a conceptual and personal conversation with the landscape photographer Peter Goin, Glotfelty examines his work *Nuclear Landscapes* (1991), a project documenting several American nuclear test sites. By analyzing Goin's artistic intra-action with the landscape as it materializes in his photos, Glotfelty sheds light on the way his art discloses many co-emerging levels, which include not only the ecological, political, and technological agencies at work in the material making of America's nuclear landscapes, but also the artist's own body, which intra-acts with all these material-discursive processes in a trans-corporeal way. In the second chapter, "Of Material Sympathies, Paracelsus, and Whitman," Jane Bennett proposes a "vibrant-materialist" theory of "sympathy"—the presence of affecting affinities between bodies—taking her cue from two literal arts of world making: alchemy and poetry. The author concentrates on Paracelsus's attunement to the sensuous specificities of bodies and Walt Whitman's invocations of "sympathy" in *Leaves of Grass,* exploring how both authors conceive the affective bonds at work between the bodies of people and the bodies of animals or landscapes. She also considers another kind of "sympathy": the one between some bodily postures (tilted head, bent back, open mouth) and democratic moods or ethical dispositions (nonchalance, industriousness, civic affection). Joni Adamson's "Source of Life: *Avatar, Amazonia,* and an Ecology of Selves" constitutes the third chapter of this section. By analyzing Juan Carlos Galeano's *The Trees Have Mothers* (2008) and James Cameron's *Avatar* (2009), Adamson scrutinizes the cooperation of agencies between these films and the cosmologies of Amazonian oral traditions. The author argues that the Amazonian concepts of boundary crossing, dreaming, and an "ecology of selves" in which trees have "mothers" and all sentient beings are considered "persons" or "selves" open a way to "multinatural worlds" and to a mutual creation of humans and nonhumans by way of ethical-aesthetical encounters. Timothy Morton's essay "The Liminal Space between Things: Epiphany and the Physical" completes this section. Drawing from object-oriented ontology, Morton analyzes causality not as a mechanical grinding underneath things, but as an aesthetic emanation of them. A phenomenology of causality is thus necessary for understanding what Morton calls "epiphany," which is how things come into being and contribute to the making of the world. The essay achieves this by examining *Twilight Epiphany,* an artwork by James Turrell that puts human construction in dialogue with the sky.

Material Ecocriticism concludes with a short final section composed of "Diptych on Material Spirituality" and a lyrical-philosophical afterword composed by David Abram. In the diptych—two independent but thematically related short essays—Kate Rigby and Greta Gaard sketch their proposals for a possible dialogue between material ecocriticism and nondualistic forms of "material spirituality." In her part, Rigby contends that material ecocriticism could be considerably enriched by taking account of older forms of nonreductive materialism, such as that which pertains to Aboriginal narratives and practices of country and their ontopoetic understanding of reality as a dynamic order of mutual arising. Combining the insights of Buddhism with her ecofeminist activism, Gaard argues for what she calls a "mindful" material ecocriticism: an ecocriticism able to bridge Buddhism's three characteristics of existence—impermanence, no-self, and dependent origination—with the material ethics of contemporary movements such as climate justice, interspecies justice, and indigenous rights.

Finally, David Abram's piece, "The Commonwealth of Breath," accompanies us through the transformations of air, a material spirituality and an elemental medium that binds our awareness to that of countless other creatures, congealing in the embodied stories of the more-than-human world.

David also suggested the heading of this last section, "Open Closure." We take it as a good wish, while, closing this introduction, we invite the readers to open the door of material ecocriticism and to join the authors of this book along the pathways through which stories come to matter.

Notes

1. For a panorama of this debate, see Coole and Frost, *New Materialisms*; Dolphijn and van der Tuin, *New Materialism*; and Hicks and Beaudry, *Oxford Handbook of Material Culture*.

2. As Timo Maran has also stressed, "Sign processes take place not only in human culture but also everywhere in nature.... *Meaning is the organising principle of nature*." Therefore, "semiotic and communicative processes [are]an indispensable part of living nature" ("Where?" 455, 461, 458).

3. On the topic of ecological health, its use in ecocritical discourse, and its narrative metaphors, also in connection to material ecocriticism, see Garrard, "Nature Cures?"

4. The phrase "more-than-human" was introduced in 1996 by Abram in *The Spell of the Sensuous*. Abram used it as a way to overcome the nature-culture bifurcation, suggesting that the human world should be considered a subset of the more-than-human world, as the subset of a material collective that contains, yet exceeds, all our human designs.

5. In *The Future of Environmental Criticism*, Lawrence Buell has provided a canonical description about the development of ecocritical studies based on the "wave" metaphor. While the "first wave" of ecocriticism focused mostly on nature writing, the "second wave," he argues, has taken a more "sociocentric direction," moving "toward substantive engagement with issues of environmental welfare and equity of more pressing concern to the impoverished and socially marginalized" (112). Buell's theorization has been recently complemented with the addition of a third wave, which, according to Joni Adamson and Scott Slovic, "recognizes ethnic and national particularities and yet transcends ethnic and national boundaries" ("Shoulders" 6). We have many branches of ecocriticism today, such as postcolonial, environmental justice, urban,

bioregional, place-based, transnational, and feminist ecocriticisms with various methodologies and perspectives that converge only on the general agreement of construing more egalitarian, nonanthropocentric discursive formations. Therefore, with its many definitions, ecocriticism forms a rhizomatic network of diverse approaches to literature, culture, and the more-than-human world (see Oppermann, "Rhizomatic Trajectory"). In our view, material ecocriticism, with its material-semiotic and posthumanist liaisons, might be intended as a further "wave" of ecocriticism, which expands rather than confronts the initial premises of the field (see also Slovic, "Editor's Note" 619).

6. Scott Slovic can be considered the most prominent exponent of this ecocritical methodology. See, among his many works, *Going Away to Think: Engagement, Retreat, and Ecocritical Responsibility*. John Elder's *Pilgrimage to Vallombrosa: From Vermont to Italy in the Footsteps of George Perkins Marsh* also deserves an important mention.

7. "Circulating References" is the title of a chapter of Latour's *Pandora's Hope*. For an application of this model to ecocriticism, see Laura Dassow Walls's excellent essay "From the Modern to the Ecological: Latour on Walden Pond."

8. See in particular our *ISLE* diptych "Theorizing Material Ecocriticism" and our essay "Material Ecocriticism: Materiality, Agency, and Models of Narrativity." See also Iovino, "Steps to a Material Ecocriticism" and our individual essays: Iovino, "Material Ecocriticism: Matter, Text and Posthuman Ethics"; and Oppermann, "Rethinking Ecocriticism in an Ecological Postmodern Framework."

9. The quotation is taken from Louise Westling's description of Maurice Merleau-Ponty's "bodily phenomenology" of the world, in the same book (135). The quoted essays are Heather I. Sullivan's "Affinity Studies and Open Systems: A Nonequilibrium, Ecocritical Reading of Goethe's *Faust*," Laura Dassow Walls's "From the Modern to the Ecological," and Anne Elvey's "The Matter of Texts: A Material Intertextuality and Ecocritical Engagements with the Bible."

10. Without explicitly using ecocritical categories, the special issue *Things* of the *European Journal of English Studies* 15.1 (2011), edited by Maurizio Calbi and Marilena Parlati, delineates interesting convergences with the project of material ecocriticism. Also worth mention are some inspirational essays by Patricia Yaeger, appeared in *PMLA* ("The Death of Nature and the Apotheosis of Trash" [2008], "Sea Trash, Dark Pools, and the Tragedy of Commons" [2010], and "Literature in the Ages of Wood, Tallow, Coal, Whale Oil, Gasoline, Atomic Power, and Other Energy Sources" [2011]).

PART 1
THEORIES AND RELATIONS

1 From Ecological Postmodernism to Material Ecocriticism
Creative Materiality and Narrative Agency

Serpil Oppermann

THE CONCEPTION OF physical reality within the framework of ecological postmodern thought and the nature of the material world described by quantum theory have recently been given new life by the emergence of the new materialist paradigm. The radical revisions of our ideas about the description of physical entities, chemical and biological processes, and their ethical, political, and cultural implications represented in recent discourses of feminist science studies, posthumanism, and the environmental humanities have also occasioned considerable interest among ecocritics, leading to the emergence of material ecocriticism. Proposing that we can read the world as matter endowed with stories, material ecocriticism speaks of a new mode of description designated as "storied matter," or "material expressions" constituting an agency with signs and meanings. The idea that all material life experience is implicated in creative expressions contriving a creative ontology is a reworking of ecological postmodernism's emphasis on material processes intersecting with human systems, producing epistemic configurations of life, discourses, texts, and narratives. Because ecological postmodernism perceives matter equipped with internal experience, agentic creativity, and vitality, it is important to acknowledge it as one of the roots upon which material ecocriticism constructs its theoretical premises, as this chapter aims to show.

Relational Materiality

Although material ecocriticism moves its focus beyond the perimeter of ecological postmodernism, there are plenty of ecological postmodern ideas within its radius. The postmodern discussions on the basic units of nature, such as atoms and molecules, as well as nature's individual units, such as rocks and minerals, conceived as material entities with varying degrees of agency, for example, are implicated in material ecocriticism's reflections on matter's creativity. This creativity can be interpreted as a form of narrative transmitted through the interchanges of organic and inorganic matter, the continuity of human and nonhuman forces, and the interplay of bodily natures, all forming active composites.

Standing at the intersection of ecological postmodern ideas that converge on the new ontologies of matter and agency, material ecocriticism advances the understanding that composites, as noted by Jane Bennett in *Vibrant Matter*, are "inextricably enmeshed in a dense network of relations" (13). The premise that the world is "a dense network" of agencies constitutes the leading idea of both the new materialisms and ecological postmodernism. The sustained attention to interconnected processes that operate as composite agentic assemblies in networks is complemented by the keyword "relation." A vision of the world's phenomena as being in constant "relation" with each other is in fact what connects ecological postmodernism, material ecocriticism, and the new materialist theories.

Ecological postmodern thinkers such as Charles Hartshorne, David Ray Griffin, and Charlene Spretnak, among others, have repeatedly argued that the exponential escalation of the ecological crisis necessitates a radical epistemic shift in perspective from a mechanistic to an ecocentric paradigm. The solution to the highly problematized relationships between the human and the nonhuman spheres of existence for them lies in replacing mechanistic models of nature grounded in Cartesian dualisms with a relational ontology. In order to provide an adequate framework for more ethically and ecologically accountable interpretations of the more-than-human world, ecological postmodernists have proposed a new worldview, one that recognizes the vitality of things in all natural-cultural processes and cultivates the idea of restoring "health and aliveness through an empowered new vision" (Gablic 179). Ecological postmodernism, in other words, has made a clarion call for an integral relationship between humanity and the more-than-human world (on this point, see also Oppermann, "Rethinking"). In his "Introduction to SUNY Series in Constructive Postmodern Thought," David Ray Griffin, the major exponent of ecological postmodernism, for example, calls attention to the "ecological devastation of the modern world" and compellingly argues that this devastation "is providing an unprecedented impetus for people to see the evidence for a postmodern worldview and to envisage postmodern ways of relating to each other, the rest of nature, and the cosmos as a whole" (*Sacred* xii). Similarly, Charlene Spretnak emphasizes the significance of embracing the ecological postmodern paradigm, as it provides the best "understanding of the deeply relational nature of reality" (*Relational* 1). According to Spretnak, "The failure to notice that reality is inherently dynamic and interrelated at all levels . . . has caused a vast range of suffering" (1). In such a critical climate, ecological postmodernism rigorously contests the Cartesian model of rationalism with its mind-matter dualism, its modernist legacy of subject-object splits, and its social, cultural, and linguistic models of constructivism. Ecological postmodernists aver that at a fundamental level, dualist models define the basic constituents of nature as objects that "are devoid of all experience, intrinsic value, internal purpose, and internal relations" (Griffin, *Whitehead's* 8). One of the destructive practical consequences of anthropocentric models of knowledge that describe nature either as a lifeless mechanism or as a mere textual construct is the capitalization of local ecosystems in the name of economic progress. Another related consequence is the oppressive social practices such as racism, sexism, and speciesism. In short, all manner of familiar ramifications follow from these anthropocentric models. Its most tragic outcome, however, as Charlene Spretnak points out, can be seen in the planetary disequilibrium:

> the entire planet is now imperiled by climate destabilization and ecological degradation, resulting from the modern assumption that highly advanced societies could throw toxic substances "away" somewhere and could exude staggeringly unnatural levels of carbon dioxide and other greenhouse gases into our atmosphere without ill effect. (*Relational* 1–2)

Spretnak highlights how the illogical view "that all entities in the natural world, including us, are essentially separate and that they function through mechanistic ways of interacting" (4) continues to inform worldwide modes of consumption and production, and thus "*threatens the survival of life on our planet*," as Griffin also points out ("Introduction to SUNY" xii; emphasis in the original).

Ecological postmodernism offers an alternative to this view of nature with its main objective of "re-enchanting nature."[1] As Griffin explains, the "disenchantment of nature" meant "the denial to nature of all subjectivity, all experience, all feeling" ("Introduction: The Reenchantment" 2), which created alienation and instrumental positioning of human practices and discourses. The major legacy of this approach is what quantum physicist David Bohm calls fragmentary perception of reality. Indicating the limitations of this view, Bohm states that fragmentation "is an attempt to divide what is really indivisible" (*Wholeness* 15–16), whereas the experimental confirmation of the true nature of reality is that "both observer and observed are merging and interpenetrating aspects of one whole reality" (9). In his chapter "Postmodern Science and a Postmodern World" in Griffin's edited collection *The Reenchantment of Science*, Bohm further clarifies this point by calling attention to the findings of "postmechanistic physics," or "*quantum mechanical field theories*" (64; emphasis in the original), which reveal an "unbroken wholeness" (65). In concord with Griffin's claim of internal relations in matter, the more fundamental truth, Bohm argues, "is the truth of internal relatedness . . . which I call implicate order" (66).

Ecological postmodernism places a concerted emphasis on "internal relations" (Griffin, "Introduction: The Reenchantment" 2), or acting in response to the environment. Biologist Charles Birch defines internal relations in terms of having a "compelling purpose" to respond to external relations:

> The idea of internal relations is that a human being, let us say, is not the same person independent of his or her environment. The human being is a subject and

> not simply an object pushed around by external relations. To be a subject is to be responsive, to constitute oneself purposefully in response to one's environment. The postmodern view that makes most sense to me is the one that takes human experience as a high-level exemplification of entities in general, be they cells or atoms or electrons. All are subjects. All have internal relations. (70–71)

As explicitly underlined by Birch and others, such a postmodern approach is not dependent on teleological explanations; rather, it aims to show that all organisms "exercise at least some iota of purposeful causation" (Griffin, "Introduction: The Reenchantment" 22). This idea is particularly foregrounded by another ecological postmodern thinker and proponent of process philosophy, Charles Hartshorne. Anticipating the new materialist conceptualizations of matter as being "affective, and signaling" (Bennett, *Vibrant* 117), and imagining "the universe as a vast system of experiencing individuals" (6), Hartshorne points to nonhuman entities as possessing creative experience and some degree of feeling. He explains the "creative freedom that is found on this planet" (190) in terms of what Whitehead has called "compound individuals" (individuals compounded out of simpler entities). A compound individual can be high-grade, such as an animal, or low-grade, such as a molecule. More complex life forms have a higher degree of cohering experience, which enables them to express a unity of feeling or purpose. Hartshorne extends the concept of experience into less complex entities, such as molecules and cells, which do not have consciousness, but nevertheless have internal relations as they respond to their environment. In his vision, "the cells of one's body are . . . constantly furnishing their little experiences or feelings which, being pooled in our more comprehensive experience, constitute what we call our sensations" (7). Against the objections raised to this claim that molecules and atoms also possess creative experience and some degree of feeling, Hartshorne responds by stating, "If atoms respond to stimuli (and they do), how else could they show that they sense and feel? And if you say, they have no sense organs, the reply is: neither do one-celled animals, yet they seem to perceive their environments" (6). Because, according to him "atoms, molecules, and still more nerve cells, seem to exhibit signs of spontaneous activity" (8), Hartshorne concludes that "we have no conceivable ground for limiting feeling to our kind of individual, say the vertebrates, or even to animals" (144). Considering reality as a "creative becoming" (13), Hartshorne suggests that we sympathize "with the universal 'life of things,' the 'ocean of feelings,' which is reality in its concrete character" (144). This is in fact something that the new materialists have consistently insisted upon, increasingly acknowledging the idea of creative becoming as the most conspicuous characteristics of material entities. This emphasis on creativity locates agency as a property "inherent in nature itself" (Coole and Frost, "Introducing" 20). In other words, concepts developed by ecological postmodern thinkers complement "ontologies of immanently productive matter" (20)—a matter that is defined today as unpredictable, self-creative, generative, active, and expressive by the new materialists. In this regard, the influence of ecological postmodernism on some of these accounts of matter is far from speculative, because it does underpin the shifting definitions of matter, life, nature, and agency. The ecological postmodern idea that nonhumans should be regarded as enlivened, or animated, beings in interacting with what the new materialists, such as Jane Bennett, call the "vibrant matter" itself is an obvious example.

Bennett's aim to "theorize a vitality intrinsic to materiality" (*Vibrant* xiii), and "material vitality" (55) of all nonhuman forces, clearly evokes ecological postmodern sentiments,[2] developed, for instance, by Charlene Spretnak regarding life processes: "Animate or inanimate, our relatives are all around us, lighting the sky, rushing through a river bed, thrusting upward through Earth's crust" (*Resurgence* 183). Spretnak alleges that postmodernism's ecological orientation "acknowledges our constitutive embeddedness in subtle bodily, ecological, and cosmological processes" (73). Likewise, the work of such postmodern environmental thinkers as J. Baird Callicott, Jim Cheney, Michael E. Zimmermann, Carolyn Merchant, Daniel R. White, and Arran E. Gare indicates that in dismantling the binaries of language-reality, culture-nature, discourse-matter, human-nonhuman, ecological postmodernism sets in motion a nonanthropocentric paradigm. Postmodern theoretical approaches are also consonant with material ecocriticism's similar contestation of the distorting dichotomies between the human and the nonhuman realms, between realism and constructivism, and between discourse and matter.

In summary, postmodern thought is far from emphasizing the discursive to the exclusion of the material. Postmodernism today is intensely involved in challenging the old conceptualizations of nature, matter, reality, and discourse within a hierarchy of relations. It is precisely this vision that brings postmodernism into alliance with the new materialisms and material ecocriticism, as they all contest theories of the world as linguistic constructions disconnected from the material world, hence the lateral continuum of postmodernism, the new materialisms, and material ecocriticism (see Oppermann, "A Lateral").

The ecological postmodern conceptualization of matter is in fact a comportment that scientists (molecular biologists and quantum physicists in particular) consider as an underlying reality. It is also consonant with the new materialist theorizing of material agency in terms of matter's "expressive" dimension. Being perspicuously efficacious and morphogenetic, animate matter, both parties agree, exhibits a considerable degree of experience. Similarly, inanimate matter, though lacking morphogenetic quality, is performative and produces significant material effects in social processes and induces changes in corporeal forms or, in Stacy Alaimo's words, trans-corporeal interchanges. This, in other words, is a "reenchanted world" where every entity, living or nonliving, macro or micro, enacts causal structures, which Karen Barad calls "differential responsiveness" and "differential articulations" (*Meeting* 335), with emergent patterns of intelligibility. The only way to cultivate this new discernment, as Jane Bennett reminds us, is to "elide the question of the human" (*Vibrant* 120) and thus, in a way, bypass the hierarchy of subjects over objects. Similar to Griffin, Bennett contends that the image of the nonhuman world as inert, passive, and inanimate "feeds human hubris and our earth-destroying fantasies of conquest and consumption," whereas acknowledging the vitality, creativity, and effectivity of nonhuman entities enables us to detect "a fuller range of the nonhuman powers circulating around and within human bodies" (ix). Bennett evokes "bacteria colonies in the human elbow" (120) to express the obvious interchanges of human and nonhuman natures and to display the human as an assemblage of microbes and other substances. "If human culture is inextricably enmeshed with vibrant, nonhuman agencies," she writes, then we need to devise new "regimes of perception that enable us to consult nonhumans more closely, or to listen and respond more carefully to their outbreaks, objections, testimonies, and propositions" (108).

Is it possible to consult the nonhuman world, or "listen" to it in a way that does not presume that humans are separate observers who translate this world's stories into *comprehensible narrative format,* to quote Vicki Kirby? Because any answer to such questions will inevitably lead us "down the anthropocentric garden path," as Bennett concedes (120), maybe asking the question differently might offer an outlet, as Kirby does: "Does Nature require a human scribe to represent itself, to mediate or translate its identity?" (*Quantum* 86). Taking the notion of agency in terms proposed by Bruno Latour (actors emerging in agential networks) and Jane Bennett (distributive agency), and using Karen Barad's notion of intra-activity as a model, Kirby's response is that "nature does not require human literary skills to write its complexity into comprehensible format" (*Quantum* 87), because we are, as human scribes, part of the collective expressions (83). This statement can be understood within the broader onto-epistemology of Karen Barad, a wider framework that connects "human *and* nonhuman, material *and* discursive, and natural *and* cultural factors" (*Meeting* 26) in an undivided field of existence called "phenomena." To resolve the subject-object split and related dichotomies, Barad offers a compelling account of an agential-realist ontology where "*mutual constitution of entangled agencies*" (*Meeting* 33; emphasis in the original) emerges through specific "intra-actions." Intra-action designates the world's radical aliveness, its vitality, dynamism, and agency (*Meeting* 33), but, more important, it also refers to a dynamic topology where nothing precedes another thing, nor do humans preexist relations. There is no before or after, but an ongoing process of intra-acting agencies generating the world's "exuberant creativeness" (*Meeting* 177). This understanding—being wholly consonant with the postmodern proposal of relational ontologies and the ideas of unbroken wholeness, or of an undivided universe in quantum physics—is truly postmodern, in my view, and is crucial for material ecocriticism because interesting creative possibilities emerge from the coconstitution of matter and meaning, culture and nature, or "naturecultures," to use Donna Haraway's expression.[3]

In fact, I would suggest that the leading new materialist theorists—Karen Barad, Jane Bennett, Vicki Kirby, and Stacy Alaimo—recast postmodern thought and its arguments and categories from more forceful material perspectives. Stacy Alaimo, for instance, argues for new "conceptions of materiality that are neither biologically reductive nor strictly social constructionist" (*Bodily* 7). Even though Alaimo does not count herself a postmodernist, what can be a better postmodern approach than this? Making a similar point, and indicating the mutual emergence of ontology of life and its representations, Vicki Kirby claims, "The difference between ideality and matter, models and what they purportedly represent, or signs of life and life itself, is certainly difficult to separate here" (*Quantum* 75). Indeed, as these theorists emphatically express it, "the very ontology of the entities emerges *through* relationality" (*Quantum* 76), that is, through kinship and the human-nonhuman entanglements. "Entanglement" means that everything in life comes into being through a *relational* process. Jane Bennett suggests that we should consider seriously the implications of this view, that "the environment is actually inside human bodies and minds," making us "inextricably bound" with every possible life form (*Vibrant* 116). In other words, there can never be any divide between cultural forces and natural processes. In Bennett's perception, this is a world of "lively matter" where "biochemical and biochemical-social systems" (112) form a complex whole. In Karen Barad's compelling formulation, "We are part of the world in its differential becoming" (*Meeting* 185). In ecological postmodern terms, we exist in a "relational web," which is an "image for the intricate intercrossing, interlacing strands that web us into a corporate destiny" (Lee 53). This polysemic reality, like a large sponge, displays a giant grid of porous existence, in which all life forms and matter exhibit a kind of incipient self-articulation and communicate via internal relations.

Similar to the major premises of ecological postmodernism, then, the new materialists intrinsically entail a radical trajectory for environmental thought in order to open up the reenchantment of the world in its relationality, heterogeneity, productivity, agency, and vitality. Material ecocriticism adds expressive creativity to the list of capacities, to consider anew the process of reenchantment. This approach invites feeling empathy with all objects, human and nonhuman entities, and forces that constitute the matter of Earth within which human and nonhuman natures intertwine in complex ways. Vicki Kirby, for example, encourages us to "embrace the notion that Nature is articulate, communicative, and in a very real sense—intentional" (*Quantum* 82). In their revealing introduction to *New Materialisms,* Diana Coole and Samantha Frost state that we should understand "materiality in a relational, emergent sense of contingent materialization—a process within which more or less enduring structures and assemblages sediment and congeal" (29). A further example of the way matter emerges as a congealing assembly of agencies is provided by Andrew Pickering's concept of the mangle as "constitutive *intertwining*... between material and human agency" (*Mangle* 15). The metaphor of the mangle is also important in explaining the reciprocal interchanges between matter and meaning, a central matter of concern in material ecocriticism.

Seen from this vantage point, mangled matter and meaning, as interrelated forces, imply that there are no boundaries between human semiotic processes, knowledge practices, and the very material world itself. The material entities of this world produce multiple constellations, and whether these are geological, biological, social, or linguistic, they seem to map our discursive as well as material reality. In this perspective, materiality becomes, to use Katherine Hayles's words, "an emergent property created through dynamic interactions between physical characteristics and signifying strategies" (*My Mother* 3). In such a radical rethinking of the environment as a dynamic commingling of discursive and material flows, the world comes to be seen as a multiplicity of complex interchanges between innumerable agentic forces. Acknowledgment of such multiplicity and of heterogenesis that is now recognized as the defining property of the world connects the new materialist paradigm more closely with ecological postmodernism. What emerges from this constellation is the fact that "the linguistic, social, political and biological are inseparable" (Hekman, *The Material* 25), and in some profound sense the biological and the textual, the ecological and the sociocultural, are engaged in what Timothy Morton calls "an enactive dance" ("The Mesh" 28), a dynamic coming together in which the nonhuman is intimately instated into the human fields. In light of these views and following Derrida, we can say—perhaps also with a hint of irony—that ecological postmodernism is at the heart of the new materialist theorizing as an *absent presence,* for it is yet to be acknowledged. It is also axiomatic for material ecocriticism, which focuses on the expressive agencies of the storied world, ascribing "narrative agency" to creative materiality.

Narrative Agency and Storied Matter

Proposing a premise about agentic materiality generating meanings and stories in which both microscopic and macroscopic and even cosmic bodies display *eloquence,* material ecocriticism enhances the postmodern concept of reenchantment. It holds that these material agencies are self-representational, interlocked with human social practices, and compounded of each other, like "the partners in infoldings of the flesh," as Donna Haraway puts it (*When Species* 250). What material ecocriticism specifically underlines here is the point that all nonhuman agencies—including the deviant xenobiotic substances—are "meaning-producing embodiments of the world" (Iovino, "Stories" 454). Therefore, they are theorized in terms of their "dynamic self-articulation," which demonstrates the vitality of storied matter, or matter as text, where the "script is encoded into matter" (Morton, "Ecology" 4), as much as matter is encoded into script.

This point stresses the existence of an active creativity in all agential factors of material composites, producing what Serenella Iovino calls "configurations of meanings and discourses that we can interpret as 'stories,' as 'narratives'" ("Narrative" n.p.). What is crucial here is the dynamism inherent in materials of life encompassing a tremendously broad range of biological and material expressions that can admittedly generate complex narratives. "There are many ways nature can be *loquens,* eloquent, speaking, telling," Iovino claims ("Narrative" n.p.). Think of the porous bodies of Naples she discusses in her chapter in this volume. They are commendable examples of telling matter onto which "stories, memories, and meanings are materially carved." For Iovino, "the lively matter of these bodies" is a palpable example of narrative agency, which she presents as "a palimpsest for the stories of this region, a narrative agency, a 'storied matter.'" These are "articulations of meanings in matter" that contain narrative trajectories, efficacy, and unfolding stories for examining the complementary relationships between the human and the nonhuman forces.

With its creative energy, matter emerges in meaningfully articulate forms of becoming that can be interpreted as storied matter, even though this claim carries a heavy dose of anthropomorphism. This is, however, a nonanthropocentric conceptualization of materiality that acknowledges a creative disclosing of processes where materiality projects a lively impetus. In other words, this is what Charles Hartshorne was underlining as "creative becoming" to highlight matter's expressive potentials. For material ecocriticism, the creative becoming is the storied world, "a terrain filled with imagination" (Abram, *Becoming* 270), filled with narrative agencies that restore the world's immanent capacity of enchantment and creativity.

Although speaking of the world in terms of narratives is a human perspective, the concept of narrative helps explain the performativity exercised by material agencies in what Iovino calls "worldly emergences." Material ecocriticism, Iovino notes, "amplifies and enhances the narrative potentialities of reality in terms of an intrinsic performativity of elements" ("Material" 58). With its intersecting stories and composite agencies, the universe of materiality is a crossroad of compound bodyminds,[4] evoking copresence and evolution that invite a foray into the world of storytelling and creative narratives. In this regard, narrative agency discloses concretely the internal relations in a storied world.

Whether it appears as a meshwork, a process, an enactment, or a performative practice, narrative agency is the world's reenchanting property, characteristic not only of biological organisms, as Griffin would say, but also of the most elementary physical units. Different from personification, which attributes human traits to objects or ideas, narrative agency does not purport to enhance human qualities in fictive or material domains; rather, it denotes the vitality, autonomy, agency, and other signs that designate an expressive dimension in nonhuman entities. It becomes more avowedly manifest in the interchanges, fusions, and collisions of the human and more-than-human natures and environments. Therefore, narrative agency can be defined as a nonlinguistic performance of matter manifesting itself often in expressive collectives. Like entangled rhizomes, narrative agencies are coemergent and ontologically hybrid forms of expressions, ensembles of many elements. Because they are semiotically and materially interrelated, the scripters of narratives are material-semiotic actors who can be resembled to "a swarm of vitalities at play" (Bennett, *Vibrant* 32).

Framed by an engaged communicative process, nonhuman narratives are specific enactments of creativity and vitality, making language "a property of animate earth itself" (Abram, *Becoming* 171). Seen this way, narrative becomes intrinsic to matter, ranging from electrons to cells, all of which are regarded as bearers of meaning within a shared universe of discourse and matter. To understand narrative agency as such, we must first attempt to bring our view of reality into as close an alignment as possible with developing meanings in nonhuman reality. If, as Barad claims, meaning is "an ontological performance of the world in its ongoing articulation" (*Meeting* 149), narrative agency can be recognized in the world's creative expressions. Just like codes that biologists have discovered in the world of organic life similar to those in the world of culture, narrative agency is a display of "nature's literacy" (Kirby, *Telling* 127), a poetic panorama of dynamism. In cosmologist Brian Swimme's consideration, it includes expressive animals, trees,[5] lakes, rivers, mountains, hurricanes, earthquakes, "rocks, soils, waves, stars." They all "tell their story in 10,000 languages throughout the planet" (56), fostering an ecological vision of an animate reality. This "ever-unfolding story" is principally the narrative revelation of a storied world in which "we—along with the other animals, plants, and landforms—are all characters" (Abram, *Becoming* 270).

Telling stories and reading the storied world are means of understanding the creative experience that characterizes both humans and nonhuman natures. The storied world engenders an "epic of being" within which, Swimme pinpoints, "each creature is story" (48). Not only that, but the whole universe according to Swimme is a story. In his recent book *Journey of the Universe*, co-authored with Mary Evelyn Tucker, this vision is elaborated more poetically:

> The great discovery of contemporary science is that the universe is not simply a place, but a story—a story in which we are immersed, to which we belong, and out of which we arose. This story has the power to awaken us more deeply

to who we are. For just as the Milky Way is the universe in the form of a galaxy, and orchid is the universe in the form of a flower, we are the universe in the form of a human. (2)

Gregory Bateson also makes a similar point in *Mind and Nature* when he claims that "thinking in terms of stories does not isolate human beings as something separate from the starfish and the sea anemones, the coconut palms and the primroses" (13). Rather, he continues, *"thinking in terms of stories* must be shared by all mind or minds, whether ours or those of redwood forests and sea anemones" (13). Ultimately, Bateson argues, "we are parts of a living world" (17) interconnected via stories; the embryology of sea anemones, for instance, must be made of stories: "The evolutionary process through millions of generations whereby the sea anemone, like you and me, came to be—that process, too, must be of the stuff of stories. There must be relevance in every step of phylogeny and among the steps" (14). This implies that in this world where matter performs its narratives, "the human is essentially co-opted, hybridized, and entangled with alien beings, always in negotiations with other agencies, other bodies, and other natures" (Iovino and Oppermann, "Onword" 333). The point is to acknowledge the fact that agency signifies a "co-operative communication" among entities (Wheeler, *The Whole* 13) as well as some degree of intelligibility. Because matter, as Karen Barad argues, has an intelligible dimension that cannot be framed as a specific "human-dependent characteristic," intelligibility needs to be understood as "an ongoing flow of agency through which part of the world makes itself differentially intelligible to another part of the world" (*Meeting* 140). It is in this sense that matter is perceived as a site of narrativity in material ecocriticism, a site where the world reveals its creative becoming, its dynamism, and its reenchantment. It is not enough, however, to claim that matter has narrative agency producing creative expressions we can read as stories. The proposal that matter has narrative agency must take into account not merely the communicative capacity of entities from the cell upward but materiality itself as "a desiring dynamism, a reiterative reconfiguring, energized and energizing, enlivened and enlivening," as Karen Barad eloquently articulates it in an interview with Rick Dolphijn and Iris van der Tuin. Barad perceives matter's dynamism as a life force when she says:

> Eros, desire, life forces run through everything, not only specific body parts or specific kinds of engagements among body parts. Matter itself is not a substrate or a medium for the flow of desire . . . I have been particularly interested in how matter comes to matter. How matter makes itself felt. . . . Vicki Kirby is notable in this regard—feeling, desiring and experiencing are not singular characteristics or capacities of human consciousness. Matter feels, converses, suffers, desires, yearns and remembers. ("Interview" 59)

The last statement quite visibly echoes the central claims of ecological postmodernism that perceives "memory" and "decision," to quote Griffin again, in matter ranging from DNA and RNA macromolecules to atoms. In his words, "Matter . . . has internal movement or experience . . . properties called *perceptions, volitions, feelings* and sometimes *conscious thoughts*" as "emergent properties" ("Of Minds" 147). Thinking along with Barad and Griffin, I would say, matter produces stories, evolutionary histories, climate narratives, biological memories, geological narratives, and histories of earth movements, making meaning the necessary complement of matter. This account enables one to describe productively the expressive aspect of matter that cannot be accommodated by standard anthropocentric theories. Take the example of stones with manifest narrative agency, as Jeffrey Cohen brings to attention. Stone, he observes, is a "protean substance" and can be interestingly expressive: "Stone moves. Stone desires. Stone creates: architectures, novelties, art." He explains that stones possess "an agency, a desire, posing a blunt challenge to anthropocentric histories." This is matter's creative power, disclosing an *"anthropodiscentered"* vision ("Stories" 57, 58, 57).

Creativity of Matter: Examples of Bacteria and Photons

Perhaps the best instances of this creativity are provided by the stories of bacteria. Among these is the famous story of the natural nuclear reactor in the uranium mine in Franceville Basin, Gabon, Africa. In 1972 when the first ore shipments were prepared for processing in a French nuclear fuel processing plant (see Blake, "Fission in Gabon," they were discovered to have been emptied of the fissionable isotope U-235. Upon further investigations of the low concentration of U-235, it was understood that the so-called theft had taken place about 2.5 billion years earlier, when a natural nuclear fission of U-235 had occurred, causing uranium deposits to go critical. The insoluble uranium ore was oxidized, dissolved into the groundwater, and then ran into the streams. Surprisingly, some bacteria were found out to be responsible for the unexpectedly low concentration of U-235. The bacteria had learned how to collect and process it and had accumulated a critical mass of U-235 to start a chain reaction at the kilowatt level for millions of years. By distributing the waste harmlessly as stable fission products throughout the environment, those bacteria had learned to operate a nuclear reactor. They were, in effect, acting as "autonomous agents," to quote biologist Stuart Kauffman, slowly but effectively writing their story in the physical environment to animate the earth. They were, in other words, players "within an expansive, ever-unfolding story" (Abram, *Becoming* 271).

Bacteria also have cell-to-cell communication. Molecular biologists observe that bacteria use chemical signaling molecules as "words" to communicate with one another (Schauder and Bassler 1468). They "release, detect, and respond to the accumulation of these molecules, which are called autoinducers" (1468). Termed as quorum sensing, this process allows bacteria "to coordinately control the gene expression of the entire community" (1468). As such, bacteria can monitor the environment to detect the presence of other bacteria and respond to changes occurring in the community. Molecular biologists Stephan Schauder and Bonnie L. Bassler write that quorum sensing allows

> bacteria to behave as multicellular organisms, and to reap benefits that would be unattainable to them as individuals. Many bacterial behaviors are regulated by quorum sensing, including symbiosis, virulence, antibiotic production, and biofilm formation. Recent studies show that highly specific as well as universal quorum sensing languages exist which enable bacteria to communicate within and between species. (1468)

Most bacteria communicate using signal molecules to respond to other chemical signals, and, more important, "the signal-detection apparatuses are highly varied and appear precisely tuned for optimized communication in specialized niches. These findings indicate that quorum sensing enables bacteria to talk to each other, and in many cases, to be multilingual" (Schauder and Bassler 1469). In his insightful study *Investigations,* Stuart Kauffman gives another cogent example: "Consider a bacterium swimming upstream in a glucose gradient. We readily say that the bacterium is going to get food, that is, bacterium is acting on its own behalf in an environment. Call a system able to act on its own behalf in an environment an 'autonomous agent.' All free living cells and organisms are autonomous agents" (x). Kauffman suggests that all autonomous agents "reach out and manipulate the universe on their own behalf" (x). All complex life systems, he concedes, display agentic capacity: "It is utterly remarkable that agency has arisen in the universe—systems that are able to act on their own behalf. Systems that modify the universe on their own behalf " ("Beyond" n.p.).[6]

If bacteria can learn how to operate a nuclear plant, establish communication networks, and move toward their favorite food, they exemplify the narrative agency of storied matter, pointing to the world's dynamic performativity. Similar to bacteria, all organisms, and matter's fundamental constituents, subatomic particles, also affect their environment and display creativity. For example, in the delayed-choice experiment proposed by quantum physicist John A. Wheeler, photons act both as a wave and as a particle, responding to the experimenter's delayed choice instantly and retroactively, traveling one path or both paths, exactly in harmony with the observer's choice. Wheeler claims that a photon in the "double slit" experiment would know in advance whether an observation was going to be made and change its behavior to that of a wave or particle accordingly. In 2007 French physicists from the École Normale Supérieure de Cachan tested Wheeler's thought experiment (see Jacques et al., "Experimental") and demonstrated that photons seemed to infer the presence of an observer before they were emitted. Evidently, then, the photons were quite self-creative, proving matter's inherent vitality with their "immanent modes of self-transformation" (Coole and Frost, "Introducing"

9). This is true on all levels, as Ilya Prigogine concurs. "It is true in the case of the elementary particles; it is true for living systems and, of course, for our brain," he states, claiming that in the evolving self-articulate universe, "everywhere we see narrative stages" (8).

The new understanding of nature as an articulate force impels us to consider the question of "what exactly is alive," also addressed by biologists like Lawrence E. Hunter. "The mere presence of any particular material (including DNA)," says Hunter, "doesn't make something alive. The materials of life, it turns out, are just fairly ordinary chemicals, in particular combinations. What makes something alive is not what it *is,* but what it *does*" (17). Or, as Barad aptly puts it, echoing ecological postmodernism's focus on matter's internal relations, "agency is about response-ability, about the possibilities of mutual response" ("Interview" 55). This explains why stone, like any other matter, moves, desires, and creates. As Cohen allows, "Stones frequently trouble the divide between that which lives, breathes and reproduces and that which is supposed to be too insensate to exhibit such liveliness" ("Stories" 60). Stones "are neither inert nor mute, but like all life are forever flowing, forever filled with stories" (62). They have "response-ability."

As should already be clear, dismantling the binary distinctions between organic and inorganic matter, material ecocriticism interprets all physicochemical processes[7] as "living matter" in terms of their dynamic articulations. The basic reason is simple. As Rosi Braidotti writes, "Living matter itself becomes the subject and not the object of inquiry, and this shift toward a biocentered perspective affects the very fiber and structure of social subjects" ("The Politics" 201). That is to say, everything in the physical environment enacts a complex dynamic between social subjects and material processes not reducible to a subject-object binary. Although the human agency is radically different from material agency, they significantly entail each other in an intersubjective way. It is in this sense that the concept of narrative agency becomes paradigmatic to material ecocriticism, always instigating entangled relations that are often conflictual but always already rich with interpenetration of various beings, discourses, meanings, and materiality. As a result, all material life experience is implicated in creative expressions contriving a creative ontology. Storied matter, thus, is inseparable from the storied human in existential ways, producing epistemic configurations of life, discourses, texts, and narratives with ethico-political meanings. In this conjecture, material ecocriticism seeks to analyze meanings and agency disseminated across this storied world, across the stories of material flows, substances, and forces that form a web of entangled relations with the human reality. On this fusion of horizons, we find creative materiality encoded in a collective poetry of life.

What is important here is to be radically open to the ultimate "Other." Val Plumwood's ideas are very illustrative on this issue. Similar to Cohen's apprehension, Plumwood focuses on stones that present themselves as active partners in daily experience and argues that we can really recognize "the speaking and acting stone that is all around us" ("Journey" 34). That is to say, the liveliness of matter has liberating effects of moving the human vision from the language of otherness to that of differential coemergence. In this reciprocity, the entanglements of humans and nonhumans create an interplay of multiple agentic force fields where everything becomes an active participant in the world's "intra-active becoming" (Barad, *Meeting* 180).

* * *

What is significant in this reenchanted vision of the more-than-human world is that it clears away, in Val Plumwood's words, "oppressive forms and narratives that have made use of the culture/nature or reason/nature dualisms" ("Nature" 3). I want to note here that acknowledging nonhuman agency as an active player in shaping the world does not mean backgrounding the moral accountability of the human agent. We cannot, after all, refrain from "accounting for our part of the tangled webs we weave," as Barad makes clear (*Meeting* 384). It means remaking our cultural codes and changing our basic conceptual structures so that we become more sensitive to the radical liveliness of the world, which points to the significance of proximal relations between embodied, performative entities. Such a recognition not only urges us to act responsibly as part of the world, and develop a better "response-ability," but also underlines the importance of the ethical subject as "an embodied sensibility," the embodied self whose "ethical relations extend to the other-than-human" (Barad, *Meeting* 391–92). This world of coconstituted beings necessitates a different ethical stance, one that implies obligations for the world. Underlying this radical rethinking of human and nonhuman relations is the attempt to dehierarchize our conceptual categories that structure dualisms and to reconfigure our social, cultural, and political practices. Material ecocriticism is mainly concerned with amending artificially naturalized systems of meaning that precipitated anthropocentric epistemologies.

Discovering now how the world's stories convey meanings and how the communication of bacteria or photons, among many other examples, would be helpful in rewriting our own narratives and reinterpreting the world itself in ways that can transform our discursive formations opens up multiple intersections between the processes of materiality and discursive practices that shape social ideas, cultural artifacts, artworks, literature, ethics, and epistemology. This is worth striving for, because narratives and discourses have the power to change the world.

Notes

1. Taking its cue from Max Weber's term for disenchantment of nature, *Entzauberung* (taking the magic out), which Weber used to denote the mechanistic vision of reality, ecological postmodernism has proposed "the reenchantment of nature." The disenchantment of na-

ture was first introduced by Friedrich Schiller who used the term *Entgötterung* (dedivinization). See David Ray Griffin's "Introduction" in *The Reenchantment of Science* (1988).

2. Jane Bennett actually builds her idea of vibrant matter on the "reenchantment" of the world, explicitly acknowledging her debt toward postmodern thought, and reenchantment-agentic materiality correlations. See *The Enchantment of Modern Life* (2001).

3. In order to dissolve the epistemological division between nature and culture and to break down the boundaries of the animal and the human, Donna Haraway proposes the concept of "naturecultures." See *When Species Meet* (2008).

4. Wendy Wheeler uses the term "bodymind" to signify "whole creatures embodied in an environment which also is really a part of us" (*The Whole* 18).

5. See the video *Do Trees Communicate?* by Dan McKinney, a short documentary that explains the communication between trees and their intra-actions. http://www.youtube.com/watch?v=s8VoIJ11CoE. Dr. Suzanne Simard and her team of researchers "discovered that trees were connected via an underground web of fungi. This network allows trees to communicate and transfer carbon, nutrients and water to one another, while bigger trees can help smaller trees to survive." See http://www.imdb.com/title/tt2139811. See also Joni Adamson's chapter in this volume.

6. For his argument on "emergence and radical creativity in the biosphere and human world," see Kauffman, "Beyond." This emerging view, Kauffman writes, "places us as co-creators of the enormous web of emerging complexity that is the evolving biosphere and human economics and culture." He continues this argument in *Reinventing the Sacred*: "My purpose in attributing actions (or perhaps better, proto-actions) to a bacterium is to try to trace the origin of action, value, and meaning as close as I can to the origin of life itself" (78).

7. Diana Coole and Samantha Frost argue that everything is material "inasmuch as it is composed of physicochemical processes" ("Introducing" 9), substances formed by the chemical combination of two or more atoms of the elements.

2 Limits of Agency
Notes on the Material Turn from a Systems-Theoretical Perspective

Hannes Bergthaller

> If those arrangements were to disappear as they appeared, if some event of which we can at the moment do no more than sense the possibility—without knowing either what its form will be or what it promises—were to cause them to crumble, as the ground of classical thought did, at the end of the eighteenth century, then one can certainly wager that man would be erased, like a face drawn in sand at the edge of the sea.
> —Michel Foucault, *The Order of Things*

> The buck stops here!
> —Harry Truman

Lines in the Sand

If one had to choose an epigraph for the new materialisms, one could do worse than settle for the closing lines of *The Order of Things*. The new materialist thought takes as a given the "crumbling" of the conceptual foundations of modern humanism that Foucault anticipated; its intellectual project is a redescription of the world that dissolves the singular figure of the human subject, distinguished by unique properties (soul, reason, mind, free will, or intentionality), into the dense web of material relations in which all beings are enmeshed. This move cuts two ways. On the one hand, the new materialists point out that human beings are far less sovereign than the humanist tradition would have us believe; on the other, they insist that matter is much more than the inert *res extensa* of old-style materialism, that it is endowed with many of the same qualities that were formerly seen as exclusive to human beings: complex self-organization, reflexivity, consciousness, and the capacity to act *spontaneously*, that is, in a manner not reducible to external determination. This insight can be summed up by saying that *matter has agency*. Agency, the new materialists argue, is *emergent* and *distributed*—that is, it is not the property of concrete, isolable entities, but manifests itself only as distributed throughout the networks in which these entities are embedded.

In making this case, the new materialists are, in a sense, merely trying to articulate the consequences for the humanistic disciplines of some of the major transformations that the scientific understanding of the world has undergone over the past few decades, in the name of such new fields of research as complexity studies, systems biology, and cognitive science, to name only some of the more obvious candidates (Coole and Frost, "Introducing" 5–7). The new materialists are trying to coax the humanities out of their willful ignorance toward these developments, an ignorance licensed by the crude linguistic idealism into which postmodernist theory sometimes devolved after having achieved dominance in the 1980s. In this respect, the new materialists share an intellectual impulse with ecocriticism. However, ecocriticism continues to rely on outdated conceptions of nature (and ecology) that the newer scientific models favored by the new materialists have demolished (Phillips 42ff). In the new materialist account, nature is stripped of its metaphysical halo—that heirloom of natural theology and Indo-European grammar that seduced us into thinking of nature as a goal-oriented, value-charged "whole." The new materialist thought makes manifest the patent absurdity of lamenting an abstract alienation from nature when human beings are everywhere and ineluctably enmeshed in material processes that elude human mastery in their irreducible multiplicity, unpredictability, and sheer generative excess.

This alone would be enough to make a new materialist overhaul of ecocriticism a worthwhile undertaking. In pursuing this path, however, one should not underestimate the challenges that new materialist thought poses to traditional environmentalism. It is especially important not to assimilate it too quickly into the "biocentric" worldview prevalent in much of contemporary ecocriticism, to simply replace "nature" with "matter" and leave the rest of the conceptual edifice undisturbed. This temptation is especially great because when they speak of the ethical implications of their project, the new materialists sometimes do sound a lot like deep ecologists: they recommend the new materialist thought as an antidote to the anthropocentric hubris that has brought on the ecological crisis; they argue that it instills a salutary humility and allows us to grasp the scope of our dependency on the material world. Thus, Jane Bennett concludes her book *Vibrant Matter* with a "Nicene Creed for would-be vital materialists": "I believe it is wrong to deny vitality to nonhuman bodies, forces, and forms. . . . I believe that encounters with lively matter can chasten my fantasies of human mastery, highlight the common materiality of all that is, expose a wider distribution of agency, and reshape the self and its interests" (122).

There are good reasons Bennett offers these thoughts not in the form of straightforward assertions but as a profession of faith, because the ethical implications of the material turn are much less clear and a good deal more unsettling than her upbeat rhetoric sometimes suggests. As such, the realization that all matter has agency offers no more ethical guidance than the attribution of intrinsic value to all living beings—it merely begs the question how exactly, then, human value and human agency are to be weighed on the onto-ethical scales. But while the new materialists frequently point out the need of reconsidering social accountabilities from the perspective of such an expanded view, their efforts in this regard have, for the most part, remained as tantalizingly vague as William E. Connolly's call for "ontological affirmation" (197). Most of their energy has been expended on the "blurring of clear boundaries or distinctions between bodies, objects, and contexts" (Coole and Frost, "Introducing" 16). Yet most forms of discourse function *only* on the basis of exclusions and clear distinctions. This is especially true of those forms to which the new materialist thought appeals most often when it proclaims its own transformative potential—namely, ethical, legal, and political discourse. A lawsuit, for example, necessitates that at some point a sharp cut is made through the causative tissue of the world so as to apportion responsibility. It requires that somewhere, somehow, a line be drawn in the sand that allows one to say, "The buck stops here!"

Foucault's little allegory of the end of humanism does not ask how the figure of the human came to be drawn onto that beach, and it leaves open how a new configuration of lines could take its place. Risking a polemic hyperbole, one might say that the new materialists too often allow themselves to be transfixed by Foucault's allegory. They prefer to ponder the sand rather than examining the line. Yet when we speak about the world in ethical, legal, or political terms, everything hinges on how that line gets drawn. It is very well to assert that the difference between the agency of humans and the agency of other material entities is one in degree rather than in kind (Coole and Frost, "Introducing" 10) and that we therefore need a "flat" ontology to replace the ontological hierarchy of traditional humanism. From such a perspective, the clear-cut distinctions imposed on the world by discourse, which ceaselessly transforms differences in degree into differences in kind, must always appear arbitrary; this does not mean, however, that they are therefore illegitimate or that much could be won by erasing them. The problem is at once an ethical and an ontological one, because as the boundaries between different types of agency are blurred, so are the boundaries between things. If "coal, sweat, electromagnetic fields, computer programs, electron streams, profit motives, heat, . . . fantasies of mastery, static, legislation, water, . . . and wood" all count as "actants," and all actants are "heterogeneous assemblages" (Bennett, *Vibrant* 23–25), themselves decomposable into networks of other actants, then it becomes very difficult to privilege particular assemblages within the general flux. If humans are "little more than contingent and provisional forms or processes within a broader cosmic or evolutionary productivity" (Coole and Frost, "Introducing" 20), efforts to promote human welfare can easily appear like a form of cosmic egotism, and because what holds for the human species also holds for other biological species, it would be next to impossible to come up with a principled reason that any particular species or habitat ought to be protected.

The new materialists have not ignored this problem, but in their effort to overturn the old anthropocentric and mechanistic ontologies, they have pushed into the background the problem of how sharp ontological and ethical distinctions can emerge *immanently*, as a result of material self-organization. My contention in this chapter is that the most convincing and conceptually coherent account of how such distinctions are generated can be found in the theory of autopoiesis, as developed by Francisco Varela and Humberto Maturana and in Niklas Luhmann's generalization of the latter into a theory of society. Theories of autopoiesis, I argue, allow one to determine the limits of agency in a double sense: they foreground the constitutive function of boundaries and offer an account of their emergence compatible with the ontological premises of the new materialisms; by the same token, they expose the limitations of an expanded concept of agency that does not take the full measure of this problem. In the following section of this chapter, I use the example of an ant hill to parse the concept of expanded agency in such a manner as to highlight that in living beings, *self-organization* is predicated on *self-limitation*. By way of amplifying this point, the third section provides an overview of the theory of autopoiesis, while the concluding part briefly outlines Luhmann's application of this concept to social phenomena and spells out their implications for a material ecocriticism.

Ants and Letters

To my mind, one of the most stunning examples for distributed agency is the ability of ants to determine the shortest path between a food source and their nest. If one examines only individual ants, this is utterly baffling—their cognitive capacity is simply insufficient to accomplish such a complex task. Only as a collective do they acquire this remarkable ability, through the mechanism of evaporating pheromone trails: as shorter paths are reimpregnated at briefer intervals, their scent is stronger and they become more attractive to the ants; therefore, paths are impregnated more heavily and eventually prevail in a quasi-evolutionary competition between ant trails of different lengths. In this process, there is clearly no central locus of agency—there is no "hive brain" directing the ants to their goal. Rather, it is the entire assemblage, composed of thousands of foraging ant bodies *plus* the chemical trails they lay, that generates the highly complex, seemingly goal-oriented behavior that sustains the ant hill (Bonabeau et al. 8–14).

According to Gerald Edelman and the "neural Darwinists," similar processes of self-organization underpin cognition in humans and all other animals in possession of a brain. How they inform human social organization is the question driving much of contemporary research into swarm intelligence. That they are indeed essential to it is suggested by the simple fact that human society presents us with a problem analogous to that posed by the ant hill: if one examined only individual human beings, the existence of most of our more complex artifacts would be inexplicable—individual human beings do not have the cognitive capacity to design a modern code of law or an entire airplane. Human collectives have seen an exponential rise in complexity over the past ten thousand years, whereas the individual units of which they seem to be composed have changed very little. What has allowed for this increase of social complexity is not a corresponding increase in the complexity of individual humans, but an ever-expanding assemblage of technologies that have made it possible to aggregate the activities of ever-larger numbers of people. As in the case of the ant hill, it makes little sense to single out within this assemblage one kind of element as the "prime mover" of the entire process. The airplane has not sprung fully formed from an engineer's brain, like Athena from the brow of Zeus. It is the work of a host of engineers, past and present, whose efforts are coordinated through texts, drawings, CAD software, and so forth—devices functionally equivalent to the pheromone trails of ants. If we are to explain the existence of the airplane, what we need to consider is not the agency of individual engineers, but the entire assemblage of engineers *plus* texts *plus* drawings *plus* CAD software *plus* the computers running that software, and so on. But perhaps we are not casting our web wide enough. After all, engineers also need functioning brains, which require considerable amounts of energy. Engineers thus need to eat, and if they are to have time to think about their airplanes, we need a social system that relieves them of the need to hunt, gather, or farm. This social system depends for its functioning on a host of other complex, self-organizing processes—the growth of the organisms humans consume and the geobiological conditions that allow that growth to occur in the first place.

I offer this as a (somewhat simplified) example of the manner in which the new materialisms proliferate connections, point out that entities that seemed to be self-contained are in fact enmeshed in a tangle of relations to other entities, and demonstrate that they acquire their seemingly "intrinsic" qualities only within these relations. That is why Bruno Latour's recipe for dispelling the illusion of an ontological gap between humans and nonhumans can be summarized in a single imperative: "*extend* the repertory of actions through a longer list than the one that had been available up to now" (*The Politics* 76; emphasis in the original). And here is how Bennett, reflecting on the transitory coalition of agentic forces that brought forth *Vibrant Matter*, acts on Latour's maxim: "[This] book also emerged . . . from 'my' memories, intentions, contentions, intestinal bacteria, eyeglasses, and blood sugar, as well as from the plastic computer keyboard, the bird songs from the open window, or the air or particulates in the room, to name only a few of the participants" (23).

This playful expansiveness is one of the most compelling features of the new materialism, as it brings into view a range of interdependencies that are crucial if we wish to understand the contemporary environmental crisis. However, it leaves us with a theoretical and practical conundrum unless we also articulate a set of rules that would make it possible to draw distinctions between particular assemblages and between different types of assemblages and to specify the conditions under which they can persist through time. In many new materialist texts, the logic of assemblages is described as if it were purely additive: "Complex bodies ... congregate with each other in the pursuit of the enhancement of their power" (Bennett, *Vibrant* 22). But as anyone familiar with illness and injury knows, the congregation of bodies can also result in a dramatic loss of power. If we grant that agency is emergent and distributed, we must also account for the obvious fact that it is not distributed evenly and that it does not seem to emerge from any old convergence of matter.

Let me return to my earlier example to further illustrate this point. If one pours a glass of whiskey on an ant trail, the agency of the ant hill is not "enhanced" but disrupted, if only temporarily. In this case, adding another actant to the assemblage leads to a breakdown of the process of self-ordering. It is not difficult to see why this should be so: the system of pheromone trails works as well as it does *not* because it freely mingles with other material forces in its environment, but because it radically filters out everything but a narrow spectrum of stimuli and transforms the latter into a simple chemical code. The ant hill acquires its emergent properties because it imposes a strict limitation on the types of actants that can come into play. Its logic cannot be that of an open-ended list, because such a list would not allow for the kind of recursive processing by which the system builds up internal, ordered complexity. It is only because of this restriction that the chemical code can be *turned in on itself*: it is about ants laying trails following trails laid by other ants, who laid these trails following the trails laid by other ants ... and so forth. Any substance that is *not* on the short list of chemical signatures that the ants can recognize is out—it can make no positive contribution to the process of recursive self-organization, but can only disturb it—and it makes little difference, then, whether that substance is whiskey or bleach (except with regard to the severity of the disturbance).

By way of anticipating what I will say about Luhmann's concept of communication, let me already point out that the same logic also applies to Bennett's example: The "animal-vegetable-mineral-sonority cluster" (*Vibrant* 23) she describes may have figured in the creation of the book as a material object; however, the book functions *as a book* precisely because the entities she lists do *not* matter in my effort to understand it. *As a book,* it is composed not of blood sugar or birdsong, but only of a distinct series of letters—and that series of letters is largely indifferent to the particulars of its material instantiation: no matter whether they are printed on paper, displayed by an electronic reading device, or handwritten with a pencil, we still recognize them as versions of the *same* book (see Michaels 3ff). Surely, the material form in which a reader encounters a text affects the reading experience, yet in the act of reading, the materiality of the text is relegated to the cognitive background. If I focus my attention on qualities of the typeset, I am not reading the text, but looking at it. If an ant was squashed between the pages of a letter, this would not change the meaning of the letter because, like the pheromone trails of ants, written communication is coded in such a way that the number of permissible elements is strictly circumscribed—in most Western languages, the twenty-six letters of the alphabet, the ten arabic numbers, and a few other typographic symbols. If I decided that the dead ant did not get into the letter by accident but instead interpreted it as a message from the sender and wished to respond to it, I would probably do so in written letters, rather than by putting a dead ant of my own into the envelope. It is only this strict coding that allows written communication to build up complexity through recursive iteration (there are only so many things one can say with a dead ant).

Autopoiesis; or, How Matter Ceases to Matter

In my foregoing account, I have tried to describe the ant hill as an *autopoietic system*.[1] The theory of autopoiesis was originally developed in the 1970s by Chilean biologists Humberto Maturana and Francisco Varela to describe the organizational structure of cellular life, but later elaborated into a general theory of cognition in living systems. An autopoietic system is a system that (re)produces itself. What this means, before anything else, is that it is what it is because it can distinguish between itself and its environment, between inside and outside. It is only on the basis of this primary distinction that it can generate internal ordered complexity, maintain its own structure, and achieve a degree of autonomy from the environment. The properties of such a system cannot be explained by analyzing its components in isolation from the network of feedback loops through which these components regenerate themselves (Maturana and Varela, *Autopoiesis* 78–79). This process is circular and self-referential, in that the system's structure is produced by its own operations, which are themselves conditioned by the structure. Self-referentiality means that the system, as long as it persists, can refer to its environment only by *simultaneously* referring to itself, that is, by regenerating its own constitutive elements and thus continuing its autopoiesis: the system of pheromone trails reacts to changes in its environment *only* with *more* pheromone trails.

Autopoietic systems can therefore be described as *operationally closed*. How such a system responds to changes in the environment depends on the system's own evolved structure rather than on external determinants. The system itself "decides" which aspects of its environment are relevant to it. As Pier Luigi Luisi points out, Maturana and Varela's conception here is so close to Merleau-Ponty's phenomenology that a quotation from *The Structure of Behavior* can summarize their view of the way in which the organism projects its environment: "[It] is the organism itself—according to the proper nature of its receptors, the thresholds of its nerve centers and the movements of the organs—which chooses the stimuli in the physical world to which it will be sensitive. The environment emerges from the world through the actualization or the being of the organism" (qtd. in Luisi 55). Operational closure in an autopoietic system thus does not mean that it becomes entirely independent from its environment, and it must not be confused with the concept of "closed systems" in traditional thermodynamics, which was supervened by Ilya Prigogine's concept of dissipative open systems (see Sullivan, "Affinity" 244). Indeed, operational closure should be seen as *complementary* to energetic or material openness; as Evan Thompson describes autopoiesis on the level of cellular life:

> Metabolism is . . . the biochemical instantiation of the autopoietic organization. That organization must remain invariant, otherwise the organism dies, but the only way autopoiesis can stay in place is through the incessant material flux of metabolism. In other words, the operational *closure* of autopoiesis demands that the organism be an *open system*. (389; emphasis in the original).[2]

In this view, system and environment are mutually constitutive or *coemergent*; they come into being as two sides of a single process, paradoxically entwined like the mythical Ouroboros, which Varela often invoked to illustrate this point (cf. Kauffmann 58). It makes sense to speak of an environment only once an entity exists that is able to distinguish itself from it, and such an entity could not be conceived without presupposing an environment. As Maturana and Varela have stressed, the theory of autopoiesis is at the same time a theory of embodied cognition (or "enaction," as elaborated in Varela, Thompson, and Rosch) because the process of material self-organization through operational closure is essentially indistinguishable from the process of cognition. Significantly, the nervous system of complex organisms is also structured in this fashion: events external to it are translated into the radically reductive code of electrochemical impulses, and the system responds to changes in the environment only by the further processing of such impulses. Nowhere is the system in "direct" contact with its environment. Warmth, light, or smell never "enter" the nervous system—they are internal reconstructions of external events. Thus, autopoiesis makes obsolete both the traditional distinction between mind and matter and representationalist theories of knowledge, because an environment is strictly correlated to the embodied perceptual apparatus of a cognizing system. To quote Maturana and Varela's pithy summary: "*Every act of knowing brings forth a world*" (*The Tree* 26; emphasis in the original).

As should be clear from the above, the theory of autopoiesis is fundamentally consonant with the ontological premises of the new materialisms. It is monist in the sense that phenomena such as selfhood, intentionality, and agency are assumed to emanate from the same "stuff" that everything else is made of and do not require a dualism of substances for their explanation. The theory of autopoiesis does not consider cognition as the exclusive province of human beings, but conceives of it as an emergent property pervading the whole biosphere. However, it provides a more specific account of the formal structure that allows particular types of material assemblages—namely, living things—to acquire autonomy, to persist through time, and to elaborate a "self" distinct from their environments. Following Maturana and Varela, we are able to distinguish between autopoietic systems and "allopoietic" systems, that is, material assemblages that do not reproduce the elements of which they are composed and whose structural integrity depends on processes that are "independent of [their] organization . . . and operation" (*Autopoiesis* 79). Although this distinction, in itself, is hardly sufficient to ground an environmental ethic, it at least provides a certain baseline: as Maturana himself suggested, autopoiesis constitutes a minimal requirement for an entity to warrant ethical consideration (xiv–xxx). An ant hill may be said to have an "interest" in preserving its own structural integrity because the actions that constitute it are geared toward that outcome. If we let it, an ant hill repairs itself after a disturbance. The same is not true for an airplane or a stone.

At the same time, the constructivist epistemology implied by the concept of operational closure also presents a deeper challenge to new materialist ontologies, for it entails sharp and specifiable limitations to what an observer can know about its environment. Of course, the observer dependence of reality is a principle whose validity is acknowledged by most exponents of the new materialism and to which one of its leading thinkers, Karen Barad, has accorded central importance. My sense is that Barad's account of materiality as emerging from local discursive practices of boundary making is essentially congruent with the kind of constructivism advocated by the "Santiago School" (as Maturana and Varela's thought is also known) and by social systems theory. However, it seems to me that the facility with which she extrapolates concepts from quantum physics into general ontological claims underplays the theoretical consequences of observer dependence and therefore lends itself to misunderstanding. At the heart of both the Copenhagen interpretation of quantum physics and the Santiago School's theory of embodied cognition is the insight that the traditional scientific principle of self-exemption, according to which "the properties of the observer must not enter into the descriptions of his observations" (von Foerster 7), is no longer tenable. This means that any theory that would take the principle of observer dependence seriously must first of all apply this principle *to itself.* It must preface its account of the world with the admission that it is necessarily incomplete and specify the particular distinctions it employs in its observations (put differently, it needs to allow for its own deconstruction). For the new materialisms, and for a material ecocriticism informed by it, this entails, among other things, that their work must be viewed within the academic context from which it emerged (which surely did as much to shape it as the various material forces Bennett lists in describing her own writing process). Admittedly, such a form of self-reflexivity may devolve into self-crippling pedantry; however, it is indispensable if we do not want to delude ourselves about the possible effects of our work—an issue to which I will return in the concluding section of this chapter.

To bring this discussion back to a more general level, one can summarize the epistemological consequences of the theory of autopoietic systems by saying that all distinctions such systems draw in their environments are elaborations of the primary distinction by which they are constituted, in the first place, that is, the distinction between system and environment. Therefore, "coal, sweat, electromagnetic fields, computer programs, electron streams, profit motives" (Bennett, *Vibrant* 25), and so forth are distinct entities not in and of themselves, but only for an observer.[3] The distinctions through which they can be treated as coherent objects are not "ontological" features proper to them, but are, as it were, "internal" to the observer (although from the perspective of the observer, they are "external" features of its environment). They are ways in which the cognizing system reduces the overwhelming complexity of its environment and reinscribes the boundary between itself and everything else, preserving its operational autonomy by selecting which aspects of the environment matter to it. In order to understand the limits of agency, we must describe the autopoietic organization of a system so as to understand how the system limits *itself*.

Let me illustrate these assertions, once more, with the example of the ant hill. It models its environment on the basis of a highly reductive chemical code that circumscribes the domain of differences in the environment that are relevant to it (for example, food and not food). It is blind for everything that cannot be rendered in terms of that code. Presumably, both whiskey and bleach will register simply as obstacles to be avoided. For the ant hill, the distinction between these two actants is a difference that does not make a difference. The system of pheromone trails can react to them (with more pheromone trails), but cannot be integrated into its autopoiesis (which consists *only* of pheromone trails). They do not "matter" to the system—as long as they are not applied in quantities that destroy it. As an external observer, I can see that the ant hill cannot see what it cannot see, because I can observe the ant hill *and* its environment at the same time—I can describe all the material flows that the ant hill might be hitched to (including, perhaps, whiskey and bleach). But that I can describe the ant hill in this way should not distract from the fact that the ant hill is (and persists in being) what it is only because it cannot see its relationship to its environment in a like manner—and that, ceteris paribus, the same holds true for me: my own observation of the ant hill is conditioned by the distinctions I use and that, *in the act of observation*, I cannot observe; I, too, can see only because I cannot see what I cannot see—although another observer may observe how I observe the ant hill, what distinctions I use, and describe the specific blindness on which my (limited and local) insight is predicated.[4]

The upshot of this is that when we are dealing with an autopoietic (living, cognizing, observing) system, understanding how matter comes to matter (to use Karen Barad's formulation) is only half of our task; it is just as important to understand how for such a system, matter *ceases* to matter, because it attains whatever autonomy it possesses *only* by becoming to some extent *indifferent* to its environment, by decoupling itself from external determinants and, through the circular causality of autopoietic structuration, determining *itself*. It is only because it does not need to respond to every feature of its total environment, but can select which aspects are relevant to it, that it is able to cohere and reproduce itself. The system determines *which* matter matters to it—it functions by homogenizing both the elements that constitute it (pheromone trails, electrochemical impulses, or written letters) and, in the process of cognition, the environment (whiskey and bleach are perceived only as obstacles; for the receptor cells in our skin, the difference between 1.000°C and 10.000°C does not make a difference). The system creates a boundary between itself and the environment that shuts out the undifferentiated complexity of the environment and allows it to build up ordered complexity within. This boundary is *at once* material and cognitive. If it is decisively breached, the system disintegrates. When some new materialists aspire to provide a "view from everywhere" (Connolly 186) or urge the assimilation of epistemology into ontology (in the singular; Hekman "Constructing" 97), they underestimate the problem that in order to observe the world at all, an observer must distinguish itself from its environment and that through this distinction, the world *as a totality* is occluded.

Limits of Control

If all this is to make a difference for a material ecocriticism, the question that needs to be asked is: how do human collectives observe the world, and how do they draw the distinctions that determine the limits of agency? As already indicated, I believe that the most comprehensive attempt to answer this question is Niklas Luhmann's theory of social systems. Luhmann proposes that society should be understood as an autopoietic system not unlike the ant hill I have used as my example. Whereas the self-organization of the ant hill occurs through the recursive processing of pheromone trails, the self-organization of society occurs through the recursive processing of communication.[5] Communication itself, by elaborating the fundamental distinction between communication and environment, brings forth the categorical grids through which the ambient flux of material forces is sorted into distinct entities. These patterns of meaning may be more versatile than pheromone trails, but their coding is every bit as reductive as that by which the ant hill achieves operational closure: communication consists *only* of communication, nothing else, and the manifold distinctions that it draws in its environment are all ramifications of the fundamental distinction between communication and environment (including the distinction between communication and environment; Luhmann, *Die Gesellschaft* 50–54).

Luhmann insists that the "human individual" is itself one of the semantic patterns generated by communication. It is a semantic schema by which communication observes human minds, providing them with a stable "address," to use Peter Fuchs's term, thereby reducing environmental complexity—because both human minds and human bodies are not "parts" of society, but belong to its environment (it is difficult to imagine how a conversation could attain any sort of coherency if every change in the minds and bodies of its participants would directly register in communication).[6] The new materialists rightly remind us that humans are not really "individuals," that they are not "indivisible" units but temporary confederacies of material agents of different kinds and sizes (many of which, one should add, constitute autopoietic systems in their own right). Yet communication makes it possible to ignore the exigencies of our material existence—for example, to identify the son born to my parents several decades ago with the person now writing this essay, despite the fact that the infant and the adult share hardly a single atom. As in the example of the ant hill, the system's autopoiesis is predicated on its ability to make itself *indifferent* to the material agency of its environment. (Again, this does not mean that such a system is not *affected* by conditions in its environment—only that their relation becomes nondeterministic.) The kind of agency traditionally attributed to individual human beings (for example, under the title of "free will") is, from this perspective, entirely a construct of communication—its reality is inseparable from the reality of communication. It cannot be reduced to or deduced from an "underlying" set of material forces, but must be understood in terms of its internal formal organization, that is, its autopoiesis. This, one must presume, is the import of the sentence from Spinoza's *Ethics* that Luhmann chose as the epigraph for the capstone of his work *Die Gesellschaft der Gesellschaft*: "Id quod per aliud non potest concipi, per se concipi debet."[7] What distinguishes modern society from earlier social formations, according to Luhmann, is that it is differentiated into several distinct function systems, each observing the world according to its own code and thus generating its own reality. In this hypercomplex arrangement, no system can determine the reality of any of the other systems—for example, political communication can no more determine the outcomes of scientific communication than scientific communication can determine the outcomes of political communication.

The foregoing has far-reaching ethical and practical implications—implications that, again, are consistent with the new materialist thought, but add a further level of self-reflexivity. The insight that matter has agency has been understood as imposing limits to human control of the world: that the ant hill is an emergent, self-organizing entity means that it is not possible for me to redesign it at will or to predict the consequences of external interventions with any precision. Likewise, the hypercomplex system of circular feedback loops that constitutes the planetary biosphere is not amenable to direct external control (cf. Clarke 65–66). Human interaction with such systems is more similar to the interactions between a human being and an animal, say, than to the interactions between an engineer and an airplane. If we are to arrive at a form of social organization that does not destroy the environmental conditions that support it, we need to accept these limits of control and respect the tenuous autonomy of autopoietic systems. However, social systems theory insists that the same insight be applied to society itself—and thus also to our own work as literary scholars. We may have good theoretical reasons to decry the invidious effects of dualist thinking on the way in which societies conceptualize their relationship to the natural world, yet we cannot hope to simply replace it, like a faulty engine, with a better ontology, because such semantic patterns are themselves products of social evolution and deeply ingrained in the autopoiesis of communication.

Scientific theories, such as the new materialisms and social systems theory, are highly specialized products of academic communication. Their effects are measurable chiefly in the amount of further academic communication they instigate. By their very nature, the resonance they produce outside of the system of science is limited, and it is not possible to predict or control their effects on nonscientific communication. Quantum physics, for example, made for a lot of good science and a surprising amount of New Age obscurantism, and it has had no appreciable impact on everyday ontology. Material ecocriticism is not about the replacement of a false ontology with a true one—rather, it offers a *redescription* of the world from a new observer position. The best we can hope for is that it will nudge our angle of vision so that some of the interdependencies ordinarily occluded in communication swing into view—always keeping in mind that the blindness of society's systems to these interdependencies is to some extent congenital and that our own observer position is itself predicated on a blind spot. By doing so, material ecocriticism can play a part in redrawing those ever-shifting lines in the sand that demarcate the boundary between the human and the nonhuman, between things we do (and for which we are responsible) and things that merely happen. For us, that's where the buck must stop.

Notes

1. Whether insect colonies do in fact meet the criteria for autopoiesis is an open question; for a more extensive discussion of this problem, see Bourgine and Stewart, "Autopoiesis and Cognition."

2. For an extensive summary of this problem, see also Capra 15–32.

3. Unless, of course, we believe that they themselves constitute autopoietic, observing systems. The claim that *all* things can be understood in this way is the assumption on which Levi Bryant bases his argument in *The Democracy of Objects*. I hope that in light of the foregoing discussion of the theory of autopoiesis, it will be clear why I consider such an approach implausible.

4. For a detailed discussion of the paradox that "one can only see because one cannot see," see Luhmann, "The Cognitive" 67.

5. It must be emphasized that communication is not the same as language, although historically, language was that medium of communication that enabled the original takeoff of social autopoiesis. However, the various social function systems have developed specialized forms of communication that are, within their particular domains, much more efficient than language, such as money (in the economy), grades (in education), or votes (in politics).

6. This distinction between bodies and minds should not be mistaken for a reiteration of the traditional Cartesian dualism; as Hans-Georg Moeller has pointed out, Luhmann's solution to the mind-body problem is a kind of "systemic triadism" (62): he describes humans as a complexly nested arrangement of autopoietic systems in which the biological body constitutes the environment of consciousness, consciousness constitutes the environment of communication, and both the body and communication constitute the environment of consciousness.

7. "That which cannot be conceived through something else must be conceived through itself" (qtd. in Luhmann, *Die Gesellschaft* 10).

3 Creative Matter and Creative Mind
Cultural Ecology and Literary Creativity

Hubert Zapf

I WOULD LIKE TO focus in my chapter on the question of creativity, which after long neglect in literary and cultural studies is reemerging on the agenda of scholarship, especially within recent directions of ecocriticism. For a long time, the concept of creativity appeared to be inextricably bound up with a notion of radical individualism and of the quasi-godlike creative genius of the human mind, which seemed to represent a classic case of an anthropocentric metaphysics. In ecocritical perspective, however, creativity is beginning to newly move into the focus of attention not alone as an exclusionary feature of human culture but as a property of life and, to an extent, of the material world itself. The latter aspect is especially emphasized in the paradigm of a material ecocriticism, which provides the framework for the present collection of essays. I will address this question of creativity, however, not alone from the perspective of a material ecocriticism, but from the related and complementary perspective of cultural ecology (see Zapf, "Literary"; *Literatur*). In the first part of my chapter, I will structure my argument accordingly in the following steps, which reflect evolutionary stages of emergence and differentiation of creativity between matter and mind, nature and culture: creative matter, creative biosphere, and creative mind. In the second part of the chapter, I will specifically turn to the question of *literary* creativity, combining insights of material ecocriticism with cultural ecology, with contemporary creativity research, and with literary theories of creativity. In the third part, I will show that the creative potential of imaginative literature is intrinsically related to its power to actualize in always new forms the fundamental relationship between matter and mind, nature and culture, as a source of its creative processes. As will be demonstrated in various examples from literary history, specifically from American poems and novels, literary creativity can be described in one important sense as a self-reflexive staging and aesthetic transformation of those processes of emergence and creativity that characterize the sphere of material nature itself. This self-reflexive, transformative power of imaginative texts, however, marks both the interconnectedness and the difference between natural and cultural forms of creativity, of which literature surely is one of the most remarkable manifestations.

Creative Matter

From the very beginning of time after the big bang, matter started to self-organize in increasingly complex forms on the microlevel of molecules, atoms, and nuclear particles as well as on the macrolevel of cosmic forces and phenomena. Electromagnetic forces, chemical substances, geological processes, atmospheric conditions constantly interact across different scales in processes between chaos and order, stabilizing and destabilizing effects, entropy and emergence. In this wider meaning, creativity is a feature not only of cultural evolution or of the biotic sphere of living nature, but of the world of nonliving matter itself, which is not merely inert or passive but dynamic and agentive: "The true dimension of matter is not a static being, but a generative becoming. . . . [I]ts all-encompassing generativity justifies the etymological bond between the Latin words 'mater' ('mother') and 'materia' ('matter')" (Iovino, "Stories" 453). Matter in this sense is an indispensable part and medium of ecosemiotic and ecocultural processes, representing not merely passive conditions but co-agentive substances and energy fields on which all natural and cultural life depends.

On this fundamental level, creativity as a general feature of material nature is newly acknowledged, in different ways, by ecocritics from deep ecology to science studies. According to physicist David Bohm, the "latent creativity of the human mind" corresponds to the "presence of creativity in nature and the universe at large" (*On Creativity* i); philosopher Manuel De Landa evokes "matter's inherent creativity" (16); Jane Bennett speaks of reality as an "'onto-tale' in which everything is, in a sense, alive" (*Vibrant* 117); Serenella Iovino considers "matter as a text, as a site of narrativity" ("Stories" 451), which has its own onto-semiotic dynamics and productivity. In a more ecopoetic manner, David Abram describes how the "wild mind of the planet" expresses itself in all things—for example, in the "creativity of wind and weather" that carve the shape of mountains, which "carve the wind in turn, coaxing spores out of the breeze and conjuring clouds out of the fathomless blue" (*Becoming* 271). It should be kept in mind that such anthropomorphizing descriptions of the material environment, which can be helpful in pointing out "isomorphisms" between human and nonhuman forms of existence (Bennett, *Vibrant* 98–100), are nevertheless deliberate textual strategies and that, in a more general sense, any narrative of matter is always also the cultural, textual construct of such a narrative. However, this new attention to matter as an important agency in human culture and discourse is highly useful and productive, offering a wider and more comprehensive perspective on the phenomenon of human creativity as well.

Creative Biosphere

Within a related framework, the creative, generative processes of nature are an explicit or implicit point of reference in the natural life sciences from biology to complexity science. The transformation of primary matter and energy into manifold forms of life, the emergence and precarious self-maintenance of ever-new living beings and ecosystems, their symbiotic diversity and complex self-organization, and their adaptation to changing environments and their evolutionary intelligence of survival are all evidence of that enormous, life-sustaining creative potential of nature.

This potential has been elaborated recently in particularly illuminating ways by Wendy Wheeler, who proposes biosemiotics as a "thoroughly interdisciplinary proto-discipline" ("The Biosemiotic" 270), to which ecocritical theory can turn to explore the connection between nature's semiotic emergences and human creativity. Human creativity and nonhuman creativity are linked by the basic insight of biosemiotics that "*all* life—from the cell all the way up to us—is characterized by communication, or semiosis" (270). This semiotic dimension of life is evidenced in the functional cycles of semiotic loops "flowing ceaselessly between the *Umwelten* (semiotic environments) and *Innenwelten* (semiotic 'inner worlds') of creatures" (272). Creative processes in nature and culture share an element of agency and improvisational flexibility, with which they respond to changing demands of their environments by rearranging and recombining existing patterns of life, communication, and interpretation. On the level of human creativity, semiotician Charles Sanders Peirce calls this activity "abduction," which is different from the classical logical operations of both induction and deduction: it contains an irreducible degree of intuition and unconscious reasoning, and it involves an interpretive leap that brings together otherwise separated domains in new combinations. In such a nondeterministic form of biosemiotics, Wheeler maintains, "improvisation is the key to both natural and cultural creative evolution" (273). It is a recursive form of creativity in a "ceaseless cycle of feedback and change between creatures and environments" (273). Former layers of evolution remain present in later forms in a kind of biosemiotic deep structure, in which the new is always a "recycling" and adaptive readjustment of the old. As in the "reading" of the DNA structure by proteins, signs are constantly read in bodily natures within a survival-oriented process, which transforms itself into the various semiotic communication levels of organisms and ecosystems. The play of identity and difference is a decisive element in these biosemiotic transformations. Hence, the similarity between different forms, patterns, and phenomena is a "source of evolution in both organisms and languages" (274).

What is of special significance in our context is that this transference of similarities across different scales of living systems in their survival-oriented forms of self-organization suggests that, as Wheeler points out, processes of creativity in life can be likened to the operation of metaphors on the level of language, discourse, and art. The "meta-phorical" reading of one form or pattern and its transference to another are at the core of creative activity both in processes of life and in processes of literature and art, and "creation via metaphor" (275) constitutes a common ground between them. In this sense, the (auto)poiesis of life (in the sense of Maturana and Varela) becomes an analogue for the (auto)poiesis of the aesthetic, because in fact the "human grasp of the world is essentially aesthetic" (276). Art is thus also always implicitly self-reflexive, constituting a cultural medium that thematizes the "mysteries of human meaning-making itself" (276). This means that "art, and especially art in language, remains the best place of our hopes of self-understanding" (276).

Creative Mind

With such observations from the field of biosemiotics, we are already quite close to an approach that I would like to connect here with the question of creativity within a material ecocritical framework: the approach of cultural ecology. Indeed, Wheeler mentions Jakob von Uexküll and Gregory Bateson, along with Peirce, among the theoretical sources on which biosemiotics draws. Uexküll's notions of *Umwelten* and *Innenwelten,* as well as Bateson's ecology of mind, are likewise crucial influences on contemporary cultural ecology. The assumption that the evolution of inner worlds is not limited to human culture and that "'mind' and 'ideas' are not properties of humans alone, but are immanent in all living things" (Wheeler, "The Biosemiotic" 272) is shared by biosemiotics, material ecocriticism, and cultural ecology. In fact, it was Bateson's key theoretical move to relate mind and nature, mental process and biological evolution, to each other in terms of their constitutive interdependence and their mutual illumination. The mind is placed "in the very heart of natural history, in the self-generating grammar of living processes and of their incessant, remarkable metamorphoses" (Manghi xi). But the mind is also placed in the heart of cultural history, as a fluid, open, dynamic field of complex feedback relations within and between individual minds, forming interpersonal circuits of communication that are continually driving, transmitting, and balancing processes of cultural evolution and survival. Communicative networks, feedback relations, and connecting patterns between life and mind, natural and cultural evolution, move into the focus from this perspective. As in biosemiotics, metaphor emerges as a mode of biological, mental, and textual-semiotic operation that translates these processes into language and cultural discourse. Ecological thinking, according to Bateson, is therefore akin to metaphorical thinking, and because metaphor is used in the most intense, complex, and self-reflexive ways in poetic language, the discourse of ecology and the discourse of poetry and literature are intrinsically related to each other through the shared relevance of metaphor.

In the context of the epistemic paradigm shift in the humanities in general and in literary and cultural studies in particular, which becomes visible in these reflections on creativity, one conspicuous aspect of both material ecocriticism and of cultural ecology is that they emphasize relationality and interconnectedness on all levels and in all areas of study. In a way, they thus represent an opposite development to the dominant tendency of the antecedent paradigm of postmodernism, in which notions of difference, heterogeneity, and incommensurability were axiomatic assumptions. Instead of insuperable differences and alterities, the sense of a shared and complex world is the fundamental impulse of ecological thought, both in terms of a shared existence of all beings on Earth from the perspective of a planetary consciousness and in terms of the concepts and categories within which attributes of human and nonhuman life, of cultural and personal identity, of ethical values, or of aesthetic artifacts are analyzed and interpreted. Differences remain vital and important, but they are newly assessed as part of a shared material world of mind-body relations, as relational forms of diversity that are integrated into the universal connectivity of life and matter. What extreme versions of radical postmodernism and radical ecocentrism have in common, however, is a tendency to abolish all boundaries—one in the name of an endless play of differences, the other in the name of a fundamental sameness, which highlights universal interconnectedness but downplays or even neglects the differences and boundaries that nevertheless exist both on the material-semiotic level between cells, organisms, and ecosystems and on the cultural-semiotic level between cultures, social systems and subsystems, identities, forms of knowledge, and genres of texts.

Cultural ecology is inspired by but also distinct from both postmodernism and ecocentrism, in that it thinks together the two fundamental aspects of an ecological onto-epistemology, *connectivity* and *diversity, relationality* and *difference*. The ecological principle of diversity entails awareness and recognition, both in an epistemological and in an ethical sense, of the uniqueness and singularity of natural and cultural beings and phenomena as they have evolved in specific space-time contexts, while the inextricable interconnectedness of these beings and phenomena within complex networks of material and mental-cultural relations is equally acknowledged. Indeed, in this view, the uniqueness, individuality, and singularity of life forms emerge from and consist in precisely the specific ways in which they are interconnected with the natural and cultural forces that make up the process of being-as-continuous-becoming in which all life participates.

What this implies is that while cultural ecology highlights the indissoluble interconnectedness and dynamic feedback relations between culture and nature, mind and matter, text and life, it also remains aware of the fluid and ever-shifting but nevertheless real differences and boundaries that have emerged within and between them in the long and ever-accelerating history of cultural evolution. This hybrid copresence of connectivity and difference relates to the various phases of evolution: the emergence of life from matter, of animal life from plants, of human from nonhuman life, of the cultural from the natural evolution. In all these cases, the former stage of evolution remains present in the later stage, which, however, develops its own new forms of self-organization. Human culture and consciousness have evolved from but cannot be reduced to matter and bodily natures: they are matter or nature becoming self-aware. In this sense, Peter Finke, in his "Die Evolutionäre Kulturökologie" (evolutionary cultural ecology), interprets the approach of cultural ecology not simply as a deterministic application of biological ecology to human culture and society, but as a complex form of mutual transformation between culture and nature, which takes into account the semiautonomous dynamics and increasing internal differentiation of culture, consciousness, and the human mind. Drawing on concepts from evolutionary biology, on the one hand, and from social systems theory and linguistics, on the other, Finke develops the notion of "cultural ecosystems." Cultural ecosystems, according to Finke, have emerged in coevolution with natural energy cycles but have generated their own rules of selection and self-renewal, of production, consumption, and reduction of energy, along with their functionally differentiated tasks within society and culture. Language, economics, politics, law, religion, administration, science, as well as art and literature are such cultural ecosystems, which have been increasingly differentiated especially in the process of modernization since the eighteenth century and have produced their own forms of autopoiesis and self-reproduction. However, cultural ecosystems are not only collective entities, but each individual being is a cultural ecosystem in its own right, which coexists in its irreducible singularity with other individualities within a complex field of multiple interrelations. The characteristic environments of human beings are not just external but internal environments, the inner worlds and landscapes of the mind, the psyche, and the cultural imagination that make up the habitats of humans as much as their external natural and material environments.

Cultural Ecology and Literary Creativity

In all cultural ecosystems, creativity is an important element, even though the modes and degrees of creativity are quite different in different fields. What seems clear, however, is that art and literature constitute a cultural ecosystem in which creativity is given a central place. They are an "experimental field of cultural possibilities" and a "storehouse and innovational space for all sorts of creative processes, which are needed everywhere in cultural systems for the renewal of their dynamics and continued evolutionary force, but which can be relatively freely performed only in art" (Finke, "Kulturökologie" 272; my translation). This is, at least in part, due to the "de-pragmatized" status of literary discourse, as Wolfgang Iser puts it, which distinguishes it from pragmatic forms of discourse such as the discourses of economy, law, politics, and the technological sciences, in which an immediate, often highly standardized relation exists between text and meaning, knowledge and action, discourse and power (see *The Fictive*). In the aesthetic space of art and literature, this immediate relation is suspended, opening up an independent dimension of creativity within language, discourse, and the text. In this self-reflexive imaginative space of cultural creativity, processes of radical deconventionalization, defamiliarization, and deconfiguration, but also of creative reconstruction, recombination, and reconfiguration, are employed to renew ossified and conventionalized forms of thought, perception, communication, and imagination. (See the textual examples below.)

From its beginnings in mythical storytelling and oral narratives, literature has been a medium of cultural ecology in the sense that literature has symbolically expressed the fundamental interconnectedness between culture and nature in tales of human genesis, of metamorphosis, of symbiotic coevolution between different life forms. It has presented human experience as part of a shared world of bodily natures and embodied minds, as epitomized in the motif of the "human-animal dance," which has, as Louise Westling demonstrates, pervaded literary narratives from archaic to modern times, from the Gilgamesh epic to Virginia Woolf (see Westling, "Darwin"). However, in the more recent evolution of modern civilization, not only the accelerating differentiation of modern society since the eighteenth century, as described by Niklas Luhmann and others, but also growing asymmetries of power and imbalances in the culture-nature relationship have changed the status and functions of literature. As an increasingly autonomized cultural subsystem in its own right, literature, especially since the romantic period, has provided a discursive space for articulating those dimensions of human life that were marginalized, neglected, or repressed in dominant discourses and forms of civilizational organization (for example, emotions, eros, the body, nonhuman nature). Literature became a cultural medium that developed a special sensibility for the ecopsychological and ecocultural impoverishment caused by conformist, standardized structures of a one-sided economic and technocentric modernization. In reintegrating culturally separated spheres, literature restores diversity-within-connectivity as a creative potential of cultural ecosystems. However, in this very act of continually renewing cultural creativity, literature always remains aware of the former stages of its own evolution and of the deep history of culture-nature-coevolution, the biosemiotic memory that has been part of literature's generative potential from its very beginnings. Through imaginative transitions and metamorphoses between nonhuman and human life, natural and cultural ecologies, this evolutionary memory remains present in the symbolic forms and codes of literary creativity.

If we look back from here to the beginnings of literary theory in classical antiquity, we already notice the tension between the creative energies of art and the rational concepts and normative conventions of a logocentric—and, I would argue, an anthropocentric—social and political order. Plato's famous verdict, especially in *Ion* and *The Republic,* that art and literature should be excluded from his ideal state because of the uncontrollable power released by imaginative works of art over the human mind, soul, and body, at the same time contains a first theoretical description of the phenomenon of artistic creativity. Plato recognizes the strange intensity and fascination of invented worlds of the imagination: they transformed their authors, performers, and audiences into states of mental rapture and emotional ecstasy in which the rational self-control required from responsible citizens was radically suspended and the rule of ideas was replaced by the reign of the senses, reason by magic, mind by body, order by chaos, the human by the nonhuman, culture by nature. The creative energy associated with the literary imagination was thus linked by Plato to an inexplicable and rationally unavailable but culturally subversive and transformative power whose world-creating magic was ascribed to the influence of "inspiration." This transformative imaginative capacity was bestowed on man by a power that Plato variously calls the "gods," demonic forces, and spirits, clearly referring not to the new God of his transcendental idealism but to the old gods of preclassical Greek mythology. Inspiration in this sense involves the stepping outside of the individual mind and consciousness in the encounter with a more-than-human sphere and agency that lend the poetic self a rare power of speech and insight into the human world precisely by opening itself toward the force fields and energies of the culturally unavailable and excluded.

These force fields, however, are the source and medium of the mythopoetic narratives from which Plato tried to liberate his logocentric world order. They embody the very energies of creative metamorphosis between mind and body, human and nonhuman nature, personal self and transpersonal communication that Plato associated with artistic creativity, but for moral and educational reasons tried to expurgate from his well-ordered anthropocentric civilization. Even though he never fully succeeded in this attempt, a fundamental tension remained between dominant cultural discourses and the discourse of art and literature, which was again and again taken to synecdochally represent dimensions that were or ought to be excluded from the cultural order of power—emotions, the senses, the body, pleasure, eros, nature. Puritanism was only one extreme form in which this conflict between cultural order and literary creativity was enacted, but its stigmatizing and exclusionary attitude to fictional, imaginative literature—which was dramatized in Hawthorne's allegory of power and creativity, *The Scarlet Letter*—remained an important factor in American literary history far beyond Puritan times. Throughout different cultural formations, literature represented the discursive sphere of an intracultural "other" that was profoundly disturbing, but at the same time apparently indispensable for the ecologies of historically changing cultural worlds.

Aristotle's concept of artistic production as "composition," which he developed in response to Plato in his *Poetics*, rehabilitated art as the well-structured mimesis of human action in words, that is, as serious, carefully crafted work and artful mastery of form and material, which had its own inherent norms and rules. In this way, Aristotle helped to integrate the creative-transformative potential of art into the sphere of culturally respectable activities. Yet even though his view of artistic creation as composition shaped literary theory from Horace through Renaissance and modern classicism, it never fully resolved the tension between reason and art, civilization and literature, cultural and natural creativity. Instead, this tension was incorporated into the internal dynamics of the literary works themselves. Indeed, it seems that the traditional opposition between inspiration and composition has been translated in modern and postmodern literary texts into two kinds of interrelated metaphorical fields and imaginative spaces: metaphors of creative energy and metaphors of connecting patterns. The former is a chaotic, explosive, disruptive, and radically defamiliarizing textual force, the latter a connective, integrative, pattern-building, web-making, intertextual, and integrational textual force. Rather than an exclusionary opposition, an often conflictive yet also complementary interaction between the two poles is characteristic of how creative processes work and are staged in literary texts.

This open, dynamic structure of literary creativity corresponds in interesting ways to the findings of creativity research in other disciplines, such as psychology, social psychology, pedagogy, philosophy, or cognitive science (Holm-Hadulla). Human creativity is not an ahistorical autonomous property and product of isolated individual minds but originates from a complex field of factors involving cultural conditions, intersubjective networks of collaboration and communication, media- and genre-specific codes and repertoires. An ecology of human creativity, as David M. Harrington has outlined it, foregrounds the cooperative networks and "creative ecosystems" (147) through which the acts, products, and circulation of cultural creativity are enabled. These transpersonal "ecosystem resources" are, however, a necessary yet insufficient precondition of creative processes, and what creativity research also shows throughout its various branches is that human creativity cannot be understood unless the "personal resources" (Harrington 155) and productive agency of individual subjects are taken into account.

Characteristic features of the creative mind on which most theories agree are originality, spontaneity, and "divergent thinking," which requires a high degree of autotelic motivation and an ability to think laterally across conventional categories and separation lines. The creative act involves the ability to combine opposites and bring together contradictory mental domains—rationality *and* emotion, planning *and* spontaneity, distance *and* empathy, a sense of order *and* a tolerance of chaos. In this light, literary creativity appears as a cultural form that partakes of and combines elements from both sides of existing dualisms. It is a mode of cultural textuality whose generative matrix consists in bringing together what is habitually or culturally separated, opening up closed systems of thought toward complex dynamic interactions between rational and prerational, abstract and concrete, analytic and holistic modes of language and experience.

The Relationship between Mind and Matter as a Source of Literary Creativity

Metaphors centrally contribute not only to the production of literary narratives but also to the ways in which they stage their own sources of creativity. These sources, and this is one of the main points of interest for a cultural ecology of literature, are typically derived from the reflexive interactivity between mind and matter, biosemiotic and ecocultural processes.

One especially significant source domain for tropes of creativity are the four elements, which in the ancient worldview made up the material cosmos: fire, water, air, earth. Some of the most ancient metaphors of creative inspiration and energy, which have been countlessly recycled in later literary history, are related to the four elements. The element of fire is an inspirational force that is both destructive and creative, a sign of radical discontinuity yet also of new beginnings, of liberation and rebirth. It is connected with heat, light, intensity, and productive yet also self-consuming creative energy, as personified in archaic mythological figures such as Phoenix, the mythical firebird who dies in the fire and is reborn from the ashes, or Prometheus, the bringer of fire and creator of humans.

Air and wind, as the sound and energy of moving air, equally have been signifiers translating natural into cultural creativity, as in the myth of the Aeolian harp whose sounds are produced not by human hands but by the air itself. Well-known examples include Shakespeare's Ariel in *The Tempest,* representing the merging of wind, music, and art, and Shelley's "Ode to the West Wind," which invokes the wind as the "creator and destroyer" that renews the creative imagination of the poetic self.

Water is a source domain for metaphors of literary creativity in many different forms. Springs and fountains as symbolic sites of origins are analogues of poetical creativity—for example, in a Gothic-romantic conception, in Coleridge's "Kubla Khan," whose mighty pleasure dome is built on a "savage place" from whose

> chasm, with ceaseless turmoil seething,
> As if this earth in fast thick pants were breathing,
> A mighty fountain momently was forced. (355)

Rivers, too, are frequent sites of literary inspiration, as in Toni Morrison's *Beloved,* where the personified imaginative energy of the text, the ghost of the dead daughter, emerges from a river: "A fully dressed woman walked out of the water" (168). This scene blends images from nature and culture in a symbolic rising from the dead that initiates a polyphonic process of storytelling and remembering of a traumatizing past.

Of course, the earth itself is an almost omnipresent metaphor and source of creativity: in the myth of the Magna Mater, in its cycles of fertility, of growth and decay, of death and rebirth, of day and night, of the seasons and the weather, of seascapes and landscapes—all of them representing generative sites of the literary imagination throughout Western and non-Western literatures alike. Plants and vegetation are signifiers of poetic productivity, such as the spears of grass as "so many uttering tongues" in Whitman's poetry; the unfolding curls of leaves as semiotic markers of emerging natural as well as poetic forms in William Carlos Williams's "Spring and All": "One by one objects are defined" (264); or the soot-stained sunflower in Allen Ginsberg's poem "Sunflower Sutra," which in its black external shabbiness but beautiful yellow inside represents the shared creative potential of human and nonhuman life in the midst of an industrial wasteland:

> we're all beautiful golden sunflowers inside, we're blessed by our own seed &
> golden hairy naked
> accomplishment bodies growing into mad black
> formal sunflowers in the sunset.... (183)

Another recurrent source domain of creativity metaphors is the animal world. Birds especially are frequent dialogic others of poets and incarnate the transformative power of poetic discourse, such as the classical nightingale in Keats, the mockingbird and spotted hawk in Whitman, the white heron in Sarah Orne Jewett, the oven bird in Robert Frost, the vulture in Robinson Jeffers, or the eagle in Joy Harjo. Elisabeth A. Lawrence calls this metaphorical affinity to animals a form of "cognitive biophilia." Such biophilic affinity can be employed both in a sublime way, as in Melville's *Moby-Dick*, with the white whale as a monumental phenomenon of wild nature turning into a creative principle of the novel's style and process, or in a minimalist way, as in Emily Dickinson's poems of birds and snakes or in Marianne Moore's science-inspired nature poems, where the inconspicuous organisms of toads, sea mollusks, and snails become biomorphic models for her modernist economy of words.

The Staging of Creativity in American Poetry: Walt Whitman's "Song of Myself" and Elizabeth Bishop's "The Fish"

In order to demonstrate the textual dynamics of this reflexive interactivity between nature and culture, matter and mind, as a creative matrix of literary texts, I would like to focus here specifically on two poems, Walt Whitman's "Song of Myself" and a poem by the American modernist writer Elizabeth Bishop, "The Fish." In "Song of Myself," Whitman places the individual human self at the center of textual creativity, but he immediately includes the "you" of the reader in his celebration of life and emphasizes their interconnection on the basis of a shared material microworld: "For every atom belonging to me as good belongs to you" (25).

The creative source of his poem is explicitly identified as "Nature without check with original energy" (25), and the transformations of this energy include the material, biospheric, cultural, interpersonal, and personal dimensions of life in an ongoing process of metaphoric translation and metamorphosis, which, however, at the same time preserves the individuality and singularity of the human and nonhuman beings that make up the cosmos of the poem. Whitman's famous catalogs of facts, events, names, things, plants, and materials highlight both the connectivity and the multiplicity, the diversity and the singularity, of phenomena within the human-nonhuman coexistence. The poem is the translation of these different phenomena into human language, but it is a translation that remains aware of its own limitations, of its necessity yet also its ultimate impossibility. This paradox becomes obvious at the end when the voice of the poetic self merges with the voice of wild nature incarnated in the spotted hawk, whose "barbaric yawp" becomes an analogue to the poet's "Song of Myself." As such, the poem activates wild nature as a source of literary creativity, but simultaneously recognizes the difference and singularity of each individual being:

> The spotted hawk swoops by and accuses me, he complains of my gab and my loitering.
> I too am not a bit tamed. I too am untranslatable,
> I sound my barbaric yawp over the roofs of the world. (77)

The speaker likens himself to the bird, making the very untranslatability of life the subject and aesthetic principle of his text.

In Bishop's poem, the poetic self has caught a huge fish, which is, however, quite passive and almost immobile, a very old specimen that has apparently escaped many previous attempts to catch him, since his mouth and body are mutilated by various angle hooks and torn ropes, but seems to have ceased fighting. To the speaker, the material traces of the fish's numerous successful struggles for survival are like medals won in glorious battles, but they are also signatures of his tragic abuse and disfiguration. His skin is covered with natural biotic creatures (barnacles, sealice, green weed), and the grave silence of the fish is like a challenge to the speaker, a challenge that opens up a meditative space of shared reflection on human and nonhuman life. This reflexive mutuality is epitomized in the fish's eye, which seems to look into an open space beyond the vision of the human observer:

> I looked into his eyes
> Which were far larger than mine
> But shallower, and yellowed,
> the irises backed and packed
> with tarnished tinfoil
> seen through the lenses

of old isinglass.
They shifted a little, but not
To return my stare. (2259)

The fish's eyes seem to be deeply akin yet alien to the human gaze, and the strangeness of its look is described in a metaphoric blending between the cultural-technocentric and the biocentric domains—"with tarnished tinfoil seen through the lenses of old scratched isinglass." The poet's perception of the fish is shaped by material images from the cultural use of nature. In a striking reversal of perspectives, the fish seems to be looking at himself from the culturally transformed material of his own body, the isinglass, which is made from fish bladder. In the partially blind reflection of the "scratched isinglass," the strange familiarity and the familiar strangeness of this other living being are highlighted in the poetic depiction of the fish's self-knowledge, which is included as an intimately related yet also untranslatable phenomenon in the creative act of the text. At the end, a rainbow of bright colors connects the old, rusty boat and the ancient fish in a prismatic reflection of light, and from this recognition of the shared existence and dignity of human culture and nature, the speaker decides to let the fish go and returns it to the water.

The Staging of Creativity in American Novels: Herman Melville's *Moby-Dick* and Don DeLillo's *Underworld*

As these poems show, tropes of interaction and mutual transformation between nature and culture, ego and eco, pervade the imaginative texture of literature. They form intertextual fields of metaphors in which a deep ecological consciousness manifests itself in the texts as a culturally regenerative form of cognitive biophilia. As has been seen, these transformative metaphors are not limited to the language and microstructure of literature but extend to the generative processes of imaginative texts as a whole. Let me demonstrate, in the concluding part of this essay, the larger significance of tropes of culture-nature interaction as self-reflexive modes of literary creativity in the example of two American novels from different historical periods. The first case in point is a scene from Melville's *Moby-Dick* in which the narrator, Ishmael, who leaves the depressing routines of civilized life to embark on his sea journey, immerses himself in the relationship with the sea's more-than-human world in an imaginative experience that opens up an unknown world of discovery and self-discovery. At the point of his entry into the underworld of his half-real, half-dreamlike sea journey, Ishmael encounters the white whale, the demonized object of Ahab's anthropocentric biophobia, as the living center of his own deeper self:

> The great flood-gates of the wonder-world swung open, and in the wild conceits that swayed me to my purpose, two and two there floated into my inmost

soul, endless processions of the whale, and, mid most of them all, one grand hooded phantom, like a snow hill in the air. (5)

In this ur-scene of the emergence of the novel's creative energy, images from nature and self, external and internal worlds, are translated into each other. The influx of wild images of elemental nature flooding the narrator's consciousness generates an irresistible flow that propels the self toward its own becoming. The amorphous stream of chaotic energies simultaneously takes on strangely ritual forms of order, oscillating between the poles of bustle and tranquillity, unsteadiness and balance, movement and stasis, oneness and doubling, animality and sacredness. At their center is the white whale, who appears as the unavailable ground and highest manifestation of this world, which hides itself in the very act of its revelation. The creative energy, which drives the human self toward its aesthetic purpose, turns out to be the same force that underlies the forms and metamorphoses of more-than-human life.

My second example is Don DeLillo's *Underworld*, which examines the global implications of nuclear power in an age of computer and information technology and particularly of the radioactive and other waste of civilization. The threat of atomic war that overshadowed the period of the Cold War functions as a death-in-life motif that runs through the text and is emphasized in the intermedial reference to Pieter Brueghel's painting *The Triumph of Death*. The fantasies of power manifested in the atomic bomb produced not only reductive binary worldviews but also a growing amount of military and technological waste. Indeed, with the progress of civilization, the wastelands it produces seem to have moved out of Fitzgerald's Valley of the Ashes to become an omnipresent symptom of modern society's social and ecological underside, of its "underworld" in many different senses. Structurally, the novel oscillates between two poles: On the one hand, the principle that "everything is connected" is the thematic and aesthetic principle of the text, which not only corresponds to one of the fundamental assumptions of ecology but also reflects the growing interdependence and intermingling of public events and private lives in a virtual space of globalized information circuits. On the other hand, in its radically nonlinear and fragmented form of narration, the novel reflects the chaotic arbitrariness of the waste that is its theme—historical, social, personal, commercial, technological waste. From this double perspective, the interconnections of global processes and events with local places and personal forms of experience are explored. This is highlighted in the land art/waste art project of Klara Sax, the central artist figure in the novel. Klara paints nuclear warplanes that had been circling the globe during the years of the Cold War and are now deposited as waste in the Arizona desert, thereby foregrounding the tension and interaction of this technological war machinery with the concrete individuality of the artists and with the local natural environment: "See, we are hand-painting in some cases, putting our puny hands to great weapons systems, to systems that came out of the factories and assembly halls as near alike as possible, millions of components stamped out, repeated endlessly" (77). The project is both a collaborative effort and an expression of the individual singularity of the persons involved. To Nick Shay, the narrator, the project conveys the following impression:

> The painted aircraft took on sunlight and pulse.... The air was color-scrubbed, coppers and ochers burning off the metal skin of the aircraft to exchange with the framing desert. But these colors did not simply draw down power from the sky of lift it from the landforms around us. They pushed and pulled. They were in conflict with each other, to be read emotionally, skin pigments and industrial grays and a rampant red appearing repeatedly through the piece—the red of something released, a burst sac, all blood-pus thickness and runny underyellow. And the other planes, decolored, still wearing spooky fabric over the windscreen panels and engines, dead-souled, waiting to be primed. (83)

Clearly, art here becomes a force that returns life to a death culture symbolized by the planes and their Cold War past. The apparently dead material is transformed into a living energy field in which the exchange between technological civilization and environment, culture and nature, becomes the primary focus of aesthetic production and reception. An excessive imagery of wildness, color, conflict, sickness, and the grotesque opens up a space of aesthetic possibilities that are generated in the liminal, intensely charged boundary zone between nonhuman nature and the artifacts of human civilization, staging the artistic transformation of the waste products of a life-threatening technology as a monstrous form of birth. Klara Sax's project is an intermedial representation of that postmodern "waste art" that characterizes DeLillo's novel as a whole. Reconnecting culture to nature, civilizational structures to vital energies of life, the transforming power of art represents an ecological force within culture, which simultaneously acts as an ethical force of cultural criticism and self-renewal.

* * *

The examples cited indicate the transformative ecological function of literary texts, which perform the self-reflexive staging of their own sources of creativity in multiple scenarios of culture-nature interaction. They suggest that phenomena and processes of matter, the biosphere, the body, and intense emotional states in their relation to processes of human culture are used as particularly frequent sources of literary creativity. Biosemiotic images from natural evolution are mapped onto and blended with images of a modern economic and technocentric culture. Thereby, metaphors of physical energy are translated into metaphors of psychic and cultural energy, and this translation process is one important form that literary creativity assumes. The fundamental ecological relation between mind and matter, culture and nature, thus emerges as a particularly powerful generative signature of literature. Its metaphorical transformations generate ever-new emergent spaces in texts, in which conventional dichotomies of thought are dissolved and new ways of perceiving the vital interconnectedness between culture and nature are envisioned. As an ecological force within culture, literature is a medium that represents the exclusions of the cultural system and symbolically reintegrates the nonintegrated into language and discourse. The neglected relationship between culture and nature is one of these exclusions, and its symbolic empowerment is a major function of literary creativity and of the larger process of cultural criticism and cultural self-renewal that literary texts perform.

4 Natural Play, Natural Metaphor, and Natural Stories
Biosemiotic Realism

Wendy Wheeler

> It seems a strange thing, when one comes to ponder over it, that a sign should leave its interpreter to supply a part of its meaning; but the explanation of the phenomenon lies in the fact that the entire universe,—not merely the universe of existents, but all that wider universe, embracing the universe of existents as a part, the universe which we are all accustomed to refer to as "the truth,"— that all this universe is perfused with signs, if it is not composed exclusively of signs.
> —Charles Sanders Peirce, "The Basis of Pragmaticism in the Normative Sciences"

> Our willingness to accept scientific claims that are against common sense is the key to an understanding of the real struggle between science and the supernatural. We take the side of science *in spite* of the patent absurdity of some of its constructs ... because we have a prior commitment ... to materialism. It is not that the methods and institutions of science somehow compel us to accept a material explanation of the phenomenal world, but ... that we are forced by our *a priori* adherence to material causes to create an apparatus of investigation and a set of concepts that produce material explanations. ... Moreover, that materialism is absolute, for we cannot allow a Divine Foot in the door.
> —Richard C. Lewontin, "Billions and Billions of Demons"

> Art is the nearest thing to life.
> —George Eliot, "The Natural History of German Life"

Materialism: An Incomplete Account

As philosopher Thomas Nagel writes in his 2012 book, *Mind and Cosmos: Why the Materialist Neo-Darwinian Conception of Nature Is Almost Certainly False,* the three-hundred-year grip of materialism and reductionism in evolutionary biology seems to be weakening. Not only is this—Nagel calls it "physico-chemical reductionism in biology" (5)—because the ability of such a widely held position convincingly to explain the evolution of mind from physico-chemical nature has failed, but it is also because the difference between "ontological dependence upon" and "reduction to" has in recent years been addressed by the concept of emergence, or emergent features in complex systems that cannot be explained by reduction to individual components.[1] In addition, the gene-centric reductionist idea of a mechanically effective gene for every function has taken a serious knock with the completion of the Human Genome Project in 2003 (see Sapp). This latter indicated not only far fewer gene sequences than mechanical reductionists had predicted, but also the puzzling and widely noted fact that identical gene sequences code for different outcomes depending upon context (see Hoffmeyer, *Biosemiotics* 129–31; and Shapiro, *Evolution*). As Jesper Hoffmeyer writes:

> Genes do not—as previously supposed—correspond to distinct functions within the organism. Rather—and both embryological and neurobiological research bears this out overwhelmingly—genes function as signposts in a dynamic interplay with each other and with the network of proteins and membranes in the growing embryo. It is not the genes per se, but their interplay and *interpretation* in the cell that counts. (*Biosemiotics* 131)

Similarly, in an article entitled "DNA as Poetry: Multiple Messages in a Single Sequence," James A. Shapiro points out that what he calls "coincident messages," that is, multiple messages written within the same DNA coding sequence, cause tremendous problems for a mechanistic account of biological functions. In fact, we understand perfectly well that the same words in human languages can have different meanings according to the contextual interpretation; it appears that DNA code is, like human language, indeed, not a mechanical but a semiotic, and thus interpretive, phenomenon in which cells (and bodies and organisms) have learned to make many meanings.

The shifting critical terrain in relation to materialism and reductionism is now all around us. A NASA-sponsored conference at Princeton University in early 2013, for example, confirmed the general shift in origin-of-life studies away from gene-centric linear-descent models and toward multimodal, including lateral and epigenetic, information-transfer models (see Mazur; Dupré). But nonetheless, and unsurprisingly, Nagel's book (as with Shapiro's similar skepticism regarding psychophysical reductionism and unmediated materialism in biology in his *Evolution: A View from the Twenty-First Century*) has met with a widespread hostility from orthodox materialists in science and philosophy of science. In *Mind and Cosmos,* Nagel himself notes that "physico-chemical reductionism in biology is the orthodox view, and any resistance to it is regarded as not only scientifically but politically incorrect" (5). This latter fact should be a cause for alarm. As biologist Richard Lewontin has noted (see the epigraph above), there is nothing in science to compel a materialist explanation other than an a priori commitment to keeping the "Divine Foot" out of the door. It now appears that the commitment to a materialist view to the exclusion of all other perspectives is assuming the features of a dogma and is working much as the commitment to a theological view worked four hundred years ago: as a potential barrier to ongoing processes of scientific inquiry and human understanding more widely. That such an exclusive materialism in science might also have wider implications in encouraging a materialist culture in the broader sense, and that this might be a cause of difficulty for the well-being of humans and of other life on this planet, makes antidogmatism ever more urgent.

This, broadly speaking, is the context in which biosemiotics has developed in theoretical biology with its proposal that all life, not just human life and culture, is semiotic and interpretive. Not only does this put humans and human poiesis and techne back in nature where they belong as evolutionary developments, but it also erases the false sharp modern distinction between mind and body, nature and nurture, and materialism and idealism (on these topics, see Evelyn F. Keller; and Deely, *Purely*). Perhaps most important, it also obliges us radically to reconsider what we might mean when we talk about mind, consciousness, and intentionality. As Hoffmeyer argues, the taboo against anthropomorphism carries a secret anthropocentrism at its heart—a point also noted by Karl Popper (see Hoffmeyer, "The Natural" 98). Maxine Sheets-Johnstone, too, warns against this *"reading humanness out of nature"*: "By such an act, nonhuman creaturely life is interpreted in ways that consistently exalt the measure of humans: humans become special creations" (125).

In order for such antidogmatic inquiry to begin to develop a proper purchase in discussions of materialism (both scientific and cultural) and its limits, what is needed is more than a philosophical and scientific description (which Nagel explores) of the problem. This is especially the case as these questions are raised in relation to the ontological status of information. As Norbert Wiener observed in *Cybernetics; or, Control and Communication in the Animal and the Machine* in 1948, "Information is information, not matter or energy. No materialism which does not admit this can survive at the present day" (132). Two things that might prove helpful in thinking through the meaning of these changes are, first, a sense of the historical cultural conditions under which a nonsemiotic materialism was shaped out of both the semiotic theology of the Middle Ages and the semiotically costive Protestant Reformation that followed and, second, an insight into the ways in which homological patterns and behaviors cross the false distinction between human and nonhuman nature and human culture. This will illustrate the biosemiotic point about the natural evolution of cultural forms and help us to see that the "old" materialist doctrine is in part both the inheritance of theology and, in itself, an increasingly outdated metaphysics (see Davies). Certainly, for some, the ecological insight is radically opposed to most of the assumptions born of Enlightenment modernity and requires serious "metaphysical reform" (on this point, see Ulanowicz).

In this chapter I shall thus attempt three main things. The first will be a very brief sketch of the biosemiotic trajectory that has done so much to provide a scientific underpinning of a wider semiotic understanding. Second will be an equally brief sketch of the semiotic disavowal upon which the Protestant Reformation, and the seventeenth-century scientific revolution that grew from it, was based. Third, I will discuss the semiotic growth of meanings in literature while noting that this growth in meanings and knowledge exemplifies the wider structurations of knowledge growth generally—particularly as described in the semiotic philosophy of Charles Sanders Peirce (1839–1914) (on this point, see Hanson). I shall argue that metaphor and metonymy, the means by which meanings grow in the meeting of reader and aesthetic text, are not simply interesting but unimportant literary devices, but are the real means by which both natural and cultural semiosis drives natural and cultural evolution and development (see Bateson and Bateson; Hofstadter and Sander). The recognition of similarity in difference (metaphor) is a real causal factor in both natural and cultural evolution. But notice that *difference* is not a thing but a *relation*. Peirce, and Gregory Bateson after him, called the conscious or nonconscious recognition of such difference in similarity "abduction": the movement based on iconic signs (resemblance) whereby development is possible in the shift of meaning (or biological function) from one form to another similar one whereby difference is introduced (see Ricoeur, "The Work of Resemblance").[2] Paul Ricoeur's discussion of metaphor in verbal language can also help us to understand that the human use of metaphor, which is one of the engines of all creativity in the sciences, humanities, and arts, is descended from metaphoric processes—Bateson called these "syllogisms in grass" (*Angels* 26)—in nature. The assertion that nature is meaningless and random is, thus, incorrect. It is a work of meaning making and purposes from which our own human meaning making and purposes have evolved. This, plus the central ecological insight that life is relationship, and that relationship (information, semiosis) is carried by matter but is not reducible to it, can be seen very readily in a consideration of the growth of meaning in aesthetic experience. Matter, we can say, is not merely a passive substratum, but a *meaning-bearing* field of agency. In the fourth section of this chapter, I shall discuss Gregory Bateson and Jesper Hoffmeyer's idea of "natural metaphor" (abduction), "natural play," and "natural stories" and will indicate the ways in which we can see these at work over time as processual experience in the reading of aesthetic forms.

A Brief Biosemiotic Background

Biosemiotics has a long prehistory in the work of biologists who have not been wholly convinced by absolutely all the orthodox Darwinian assumptions (on this point, see Favareau). In its present form it arose, on the one hand and largely in Europe, with the recognition by a number of theoretical biologists that the semiotic language they were using—of codes, transcription, messengers, reinscription, translation, transduction, genetic information, chemical signals, cell signaling, and so on—was not, as convention had it, in fact just a metaphor (see Queiroz, Emmeche, and Niño El-Hania). On the other hand, a similar idea of a general "biosemiotics" ("an ecumenical semiotics," as Thomas Sebeok called it) incorporating dynamic systems theory arose among semioticians (largely North American) influenced by the zoosemiotic work of Hungarian American semiotician Thomas A. Sebeok. In 1984 Sebeok and fellow semioticians published a "manifesto" exploring

> the possibility of semiotics providing a new paradigm or framework in terms of which it will be possible to overcome the divide between the so-called two cultures, and pointing out a direction for the overdue reintegration of the human and natural sciences at a level of synthesis beyond the false dichotomy which has bred the multifarious, stale oppositions of realism and idealism. (Anderson et al. 35)

This 1984 essay specifically rejected (as have biosemioticians subsequently) the reductionist mechanistic sociobiology (and "evolutionary psychology") associated with thinkers such as Edward O. Wilson (*Sociobiology* [1975]) and Jerome Barkow, Leda Cosmides, and John Tooby (*The Adapted Mind* [1992]).

Eventually, throughout the 1980s and 1990s, these disparate groups of researchers were gradually brought together at various conferences and seminars, culminating in the foundation of the International Society for Biosemiotic Studies in 2005 (see Favareau, in particular, "Introduction" 1–77). In effect, what these various scientists and semioticians realized was that human language is just the most recent evolutionary part of a vast global web of semiosis encompassing all living things—from the smallest cell to the most complex multicellular organism (Sebeok and Umiker-Sebeok; Hoffmeyer, *Biosemiotics*). An early reference, by Hoffmeyer and his colleague at Copenhagen University Claus Emmeche ("Code Duality and the Semiotics of Nature" [1991]), to the anthropocentric and glottocentric dyadic semiology of Saussure proved (unsurprisingly) unproductive. In its place Charles Sanders Peirce's triadic more-than-human semiotic answered closely to the biological phenomena that they were attempting to describe via a theory of semiosis. As the quote at the beginning of this chapter indicates, Peirce's philosophy was not anthropocentric but involved the much wider conception of a universal cosmic, evolutionary and open-ended, developmental semiosis. It was (and is) intended to show how both natural and cultural evolution is possible as a nonmechanical, nondualistic emergent process of quasi-Mind, intelligence, and scientific discovery in this universe.[3]

Semiosis is always open-ended and, teleologically, future directed toward more complex and overdetermined formations. We can take literary uses of language as a model here. An immediate meaning-generating object can be later understood as part of a larger meaning-generating process at a more developed level. This more developed sign was in fact the implicit dynamical object initially encountered in the immediate object: the "figure" that, retrospectively as our narrative knowledge progresses, we come to understand as "standing for" a host of more complex meanings that subsequent reading reveals.[4] This is also a model for Peirce's central concern, the development of knowledge. The scientist (as Michael Polanyi also put it) is directed toward a whole set of as yet hidden implications even as he grasps some sign that "stands for" them in advance:

> Such is the true sense of objectivity in science. . . . I called it the discovery of rationality in nature, a name which was meant to say that the kind of order which the discoverer claims to see in nature goes far beyond his understanding; so that his triumph lies precisely in his foreknowledge of a host of yet hidden implications which his discovery will reveal in later days to other eyes. (64)

In other words, for Peirce (as for Polanyi, who had read him), the fact of natural, then human cultural, meaning making guarantees a homology of semiotic structurations across nature and culture. The experienced scientist is grasped by a significant detail, without yet understanding its full implications, just as the experienced reader is similarly grasped by a symbol of some kind that equally seems significant. Both are on the lookout for emergent patterns.

The Desemiotization of Modernity: The Medieval Nominalist Turn, the Reformation, and Modern Science

In order to understand how the strange case of a materialist modernity came about—unable to account for the richly communicative world all human and nonhuman organisms manifestly live in—it is necessary to travel back in history. Perhaps surprisingly, the modernity impasse, in which some influential philosophers and scientists of an eliminativist persuasion actually deny the reality of mind, which they reduce to physics and chemistry, and count it an illusion that we must just *pretend* to believe in (see Favareau 33), has its roots in the medieval theology of nominalism in the thirteenth and fourteenth centuries. Despite the "information turn" and the very qualified materialism of nearly a century of quantum physics in which, as Karl Popper noted, "materialism transcended itself" (Popper and Eccles 5),[5] plus some unease with the modern Darwinian synthesis, both reductive materialism and its close relative determinism (opposed to the idea of free will—a central gnostic theme of modernity "earth-hatred" [see

Poole 17–18; Taubes; Jonas])[6] remain firmly planted in both public and (most) scientific imaginations. Of course, the very radical Cartesian cleaving of the eliminative materialists cannot survive the discovery that *living* nature is semiotically, and not mechanically, causal.

The story of biosemiotics, and its profound implications for how we think about the relationship between human and nonhuman selves and world, and between culture and nature, is thus, and at the same time, a story about the odd pathway taken by Western modernity and modern science between the fourteenth and twentieth centuries. The depths of this story touch upon the biosemiotic unconscious, the limits (and even dangers) of the elevation of conscious human reason in its capacity successfully to manipulate natural and cultural systems (on this point, see Bateson, "Conscious"), and on our understandings of the sacred and animistic patterns of meaning making that still live on within us just as our biological evolutionary history does.

From Augustine of Hippo (354–430) in the fifth century AD to Thomas Aquinas (1225–74) in the thirteenth, the integration of Greek knowledge with Christian doctrine had produced a developing semiotic philosophy of creation in which divine truth was legible in God's two great books of nature and of scripture (Harrison, *The Bible* and *The Fall*). This idea of legible revelation via interpretation would begin to be undone in the nominalist arguments developed first partially by John Duns Scotus (1265–1308) and then in all their fullness by William of Ockham (1288–1348) in the thirteenth and fourteenth centuries. These centered on God's omnipotence and on the question of whether he was bound by the natural laws he had created. Aquinas (an Aristotelian realist) thought he was; the nominalists believed otherwise. In the nominalist view, this meant that there was no *essential* order to being and beings. God could make creation any way he wished, and all perceptions of order and legibility were, thus, simply human fictions that were imposed upon an indecipherably random creation for human convenience alone. The effect of this was to shift theological discussion away from the goodness (and hence legibility) of God's creation and toward the problem of Adam's Fall and human error. It was in this context, of a fallen and hateful world full of uncertainty, that both Reformation theology and modern science (Martin Luther and Francis Bacon were both nominalists) took hold in the grip of gnostic intimations of the sinfully despicable unreliability both of world and of human knowledge. This affirmation of a senseless universe would inform both modern science and philosophy and would lead inevitably from Pyrrhonian skepticism to modern nihilism. In other words, modern science was founded in the gnostic-influenced theological conviction of the randomness and meaninglessness of nature and of human beings' "thrown-ness" into the world.

What had been wanting in the pagan philosophy that the church fathers had inherited from Greek philosophy "was a science of interpretation, a hermeneutical method by which natural things could be made to yield up their secret meanings" (Harrison, *The Bible* 15). It was Origen (ca. 185–ca. 254) who began most fully first to develop this semiotic philosophy of a relationship between the visible and the invisible:

> In principle, this Platonic understanding of the created order made possible an elaborate semiotics of the natural world, in which every visible feature of creation corresponded to some reality in the unseen, heavenly realm. "Each of the manifest things," said Origen, "is to be related to one of those that are hidden . . . all things visible have some invisible likeness and pattern." For his successors, Origen had demonstrated how the physical world could be rendered intelligible through a process of laying bare the spiritual realities which material things signified. By the fourth century there was general agreement among Christian theologians from both East and West that the world was indeed designed to be a school for souls, and that the things of this world, for all their transience and imperfections, could serve to edify the soul in search of salvation. . . . The things of nature, in this latter role, were regarded as signs. (Harrison, *The Bible* 17)

Although the full scientific import of this idea—that there is a hidden significance in pattern, in repetition and difference (abduction and metaphor), as *information* understood as *semiosis* in biosemiotic nature—would not reappear in all its fullness until more than sixteen hundred years had passed (that is, in the semiotic philosophy of Charles Sanders Peirce and, following him, in the semiotic ethology of Jakob von Uexküll, in the protosemiotic work of Gregory Bateson inspired by biocybernetic understandings, and in biosemiotics itself), a semiotic understanding continued to be developed throughout the medieval Latin period. It finally found its fullest articulation in the 1632 publication of John Poinsot's *Tractatus de Signis* in which Poinsot, in asking what a sign has to be to function, recognized that a sign is not a thing but a suprasubjective relation that works (that is, is meaningful and causally efficacious) regardless of whether what is signified is material or imagined (Deely, *Four Ages* 430–31). Too late, however. By the time of Poinsot's writing, nominalist doctrine was secure.

In other words, the medieval philosophy that got pushed aside by the Reformation (itself a full-blown triumph of nominalism) was a *semiotic* theology; it drew upon the "two books" of nature and of scripture (see Harrison, *The Bible* 44–45). This was replaced by a sort of Protestant literalism in relation to "reading" and interpretation (see Simpson). Thus, whereas early modern science was nominalist, its empiricism retained a very qualified sort of realism; the realism it hung onto remained stuck on the side of Cartesian *res extensa*, but with no way of accounting for *res cogitans* other to than to say it was either unknowable or entirely insubstantial and idealist.

Natural Play, Natural Metaphor, and Natural Stories

In the work of Gregory Bateson, and in biosemiotics itself, however, we can trace the theme of a realist reanimation and agency in nature in the articulation of the idea of *natural play* and *natural stories*. As Hoffmeyer writes:

> There is an aspect of *play* in the evolutionary process . . . which has been more or less overshadowed . . . by the Cyclopsian focus on selection. . . ."What is characteristic of 'play,'" writes Gregory Bateson, "is that this is a name for contexts in which the constituent acts have a different sort of relevance or organization from that which they would have had in non-play." Bateson also suggests the definition of play as "the establishment and exploration of relationship." . . . Thus, to the extent that the living world is engaged in an open-ended and non-settled exploration of relationships between systems . . . it can truly be said that nature does, in fact, exhibit play-like behavior. It therefore will be as legitimate to talk about *natural play* as a force in the evolution of life-forms, as it is to talk about *natural selection*. Selection acts to settle things thereby . . . putting an end to some element of ongoing play in the system while simultaneously providing for the beginning of whole new kinds of play. (*Biosemiotics* 196–97)

In the introduction to *A Legacy for Living Systems: Gregory Bateson as Precursor to Biosemiotics*, Hoffmeyer discusses the reality of biological "stories" and the importance of natural play (2). These two things (stories and play) seem clearly related. I discuss this below with reference to Roman Jakobson's model of (poetic) language (see Jakobson). The point I derive is that the development of literary meanings in narratives—which readers must *play* with to discover—imitates the processes of natural evolution. In a reworking of Jakobson's schema, I suggest that the paradigmatic patterns that are selected (thus forming the genre, or form, of a story) are, themselves, the subject of playful recombination in and from new contexts, thus providing new articulations of patterns for selection. As Terrence Deacon says, "I believe that the experience of being alive and sentient is what it feels like to *be* evolution" ("How I" 153). Living systems, we might say, are their own creative readers (see Kull, "Organism").

Thinking about the growth of meaning in literature, one can use Jakobson's model of the two axes of association: the vertical axis of paradigmatic (that is, metaphoric) association and potential substitution via similarity and the horizontal axis of association via metonymic contiguity. Jakobson expressed this in his formula (in regard to the poetic function—although it surely goes wider) that the relation between the two axes consists in the projection of the principle of equivalence from the axis of selection to the axis of combination (358). But, as Terence S. Turner argues, a persistent narrative (metonymical) association repeated *over time* hints at metonymy's metaphoric potential and constitutes the patterned basis for *metaphoric* substitution.

Thus, we need not say that Jakobson's two axes are wrong, but that they are more closely interrelated such that "the universe of relations comprising the narrative as a whole [is transformed] into a set of dynamic principles with the power to generate and control the order manifested by that universe: in a word, to reproduce itself" in narrative time and "memory" (T. S. Turner, 141–42). Although Jakobson is associated with structuralism (that is, the attempt to identify structures of meaning production), it is clear that what his axes actually model is not static structure but, rather, the evolution of structuration both *as form* and as formal semiotic constraint (or Aristotelian formal cause). In literary analyses, we recognize these things as the formation (via paradigmatic choices and their combination) of choices that both structure and determine specific discourses, or genres, in culture and also develop (final cause) constraints on interpretation in narratives. Nonetheless, and while formal and final causes put limits on semiotic freedom of interpretance by "low-level agents" (individual "cells" of meaning or metaphor and metonym organization), at the higher level of narrative and story ("multicellular") organization, they make complex "high-level" interpretants of natural and cultural "surroundings" both possible and evolutionarily useful.

As Turner argues, repeated pattern of paradigmatic structure at a "higher" narrative level "is really a syntactic or combinatorial device" such that "the principle of combination is reciprocally projected onto the axis of selection" (145). Far from being mutually exclusive, there is a creative and complementary tension between the two axes. In "Dante... Bruno. Vico.. Joyce," Samuel Beckett gives an example of the evolution of language via both kinds of association in the Latin word for "law" (*lex*):

1. Lex = Crop of acorns.
2. Ilex = Tree that produces acorns [the *Quercus ilex*: Holm oak or Holly oak].
3. Legere = To gather [acorns or people for a village meet under an oak tree].
4. Aquilex = He that gathers the waters.
5. Lex = Gathering together of peoples, public assembly.
6. Lex = Law.
7. Legere = To gather together letters into a word, to read.

The root of any word whatsoever can be traced back to some pre-lingual symbol. (114–15)

A visual representation of this process looks strikingly like the growth of a complex multicellular organism.[7]

Imagine the two axes: an original selection is made on the basis of a significant difference; this paradigmatic selection is thus "placed" on the syntagmatic axis of combination. Another paradigmatic (that is, metaphorical) selection is added, and a syntagmatic (association via stable combination) relation is established. Following Turner's suggestion, this persistent association is now capable of, itself, becoming the basis of further paradigmatic selection. The processes are repeated, with further associations moved up and down (so to speak) from the axis of combination to the axis of selection. The result is ever-growing and more complex "cellular" clusters of combination and selection. The effect is very similar to Lynn Margulis's description of the evolution of complex cellular forms via symbiosis (see *Symbiotic*). Thus, we can say that the growth of complex organisms via symbiogenesis is strikingly like the growth of complex symbolic meanings in literature. As hinted earlier in relation to Peirce's conception of immediate and dynamical semiotic objects, subsequent formations of meaning retrospectively alter antecedent intimations of meaning. In biology, this is known as "downward causation" (Emmeche et al.); humanities scholars are likely to have encountered this idea in Freud's idea of *Nachträglichkeit*, "secondary revision" ("afterwardsness"), or deferred action. The movement is of a dynamic process in which the enfleshed and enminded analogic world of the reader both gives new life to and is given life by the life of the aesthetic organism. The reader, from her subsequent point in time, revivifies and (at best) gives new meanings to the dynamical semiotic object that is the text.

It is surely right to say that biological, as well as aesthetic, life is made of stories. Just as a reader plays with resonant patterns in order to discover (recursively and in narrative time) the growth of poetic meanings, so evolutionary life—on the basis of a primordial difference initiated by the coming into being of a membrane—plays with patterns of similarity and difference metonymically encoded, recursively in*form*ed, and shifting (as Denis Noble puts it) "from one metaphor to another" (104). As Laura Shintani has noted, Jakobson was fully aware of the correspondences between the genetic code and encoding in language. Introducing "the idea that the linguistic model can be in some respects mapped on to the problem of molecular heredity" (109), Jakobson continues, she tells us, with the observation that

> biologists and linguists as well have observed an impressive set of attributes common to life and language since their consecutive emergence.... The makeup of the two codes—the genetic one, discovered and deciphered by molecular biology in our time, and the verbal one, scrutinized by several generations of linguists—has displayed a series of noticeable analogies. (110)

"Selection," as Hoffmeyer writes, "acts to settle things" (*Biosemiotics* 197). But combination, allowing the possibility of new metaphors emergent from the evolution of hierarchically nested meanings, provides "for the beginning of whole new kinds of play." Such abductions, as Bateson drawing on Peirce observed, are the basis of creative evolution in biology and in human culture. In introducing the idea of *natural play* and stories alongside *natural selection,* Hoffmeyer (and biosemiotics) reminds us of Bateson's idea of the "necessary unity" between mind and nature and of the *living* nature of the patterns that connect them.

As in many other growing fields, there has never been complete agreement about what ecocriticism means. However, seen with the eyes of a biosemiotician, ecocriticism—and material ecocriticism in particular—must mean a keen awareness of the layers and *the growth of meanings.* Such awareness can be achieved by turning to a new semiotic materialist perspective, in which causal powers inhere in all semiotic objects (regardless of whether these objects are also things [on this point, see Deely, *Purely*]) and all nature and all culture are thus capable of bearing meaning. This is what Jesper Hoffmeyer calls "semiotic freedom," a concept that I have also explored in my book *The Whole Creature.* Establishing a conversation between biosemiotics and material ecocriticism, Serenella Iovino writes that "the horizon of material ecocriticism is that of a material-semiotic freedom, of an ecology of mind and of imagination as embodied processes that are created and re-created in the essential co-implication with nonhuman subjects and forms" ("Material" 61). This is, I believe, a fruitful start for a combined perspective.

Although an artifact's meaning is not contained by its author but is grown in relationship with subsequent interpreters, it is also the case that every thoughtful, creative person is involved in a lifelong abductive project of understanding and poiesis. Where this project captures the imaginative engagement of a reader, there we find the possibility for growth of new knowledge and the handing on of a system's "mind" and a culture's inheritance: its only stock for the future. This means that art exercises, at best, a kind of freedom and ruthlessness in the mind of a receptive reader. Poems, novels, paintings, and so on are not doctrinal advertisements for the promotion of whatever local virtues are currently approved; rather, they constitute relationships and serious demands for the light of other minds and room to grow.

Standing in front of Barnett Newman's *Vir Heroicus Sublimis* in the Museum of Modern Art in New York, Peter de Bolla tried to frame a few questions to get into dialogue with the painting. After dismissing a couple of clichéd false starts, he finally hit on what, for Michael Wood (8) who is reporting the incident for me, is the really interesting question: what does this painting *know*? This assumption, that the work is like an organism that knows something—no matter how potentially alien the knowing belonging to this way of life—is the *productive* question, the question that might bear fruit, because it recognizes that the work has a life of its own, that minds and knowledges are not confined to humans, and that we can (and perhaps should) get into conversation and relationship with *all* the life and mindedness we encounter around and about us, whatever form it takes. From such differences—themselves nonmaterial—new semiotic objects (some as ideas and some as things) and new ways of knowing become possible.

Notes

1. Nagel's preferred position is "neutral monism": "Consciousness is in that case not, as in the emergent account, an effect of the brain processes that are its physical conditions; rather, those brain processes are in themselves more than physical, and the incompleteness of the physical description of the world is exemplified by the incompleteness of their purely physical description" (57). Because biosemiotics contends that every cell has what we must call a "cognitive" element, and despite the fact that biosemioticians often invoke emergentism as a description of the relation between what in Nagel's terms is the "physical" and the "psychic," neutral monism seems compatible with the biosemiotic view that life involves both material (physical) and immaterial (psychic) elements right from the start.

2. Ricoeur discusses the primary importance of iconic signs in the work of metaphor but also the ways, certainly assimilable to biology, in which "a family resemblance first brings individuals together before the rule of a logical class dominates them. Metaphor, a figure of speech, presents in an *open* fashion, by means of a conflict between identity and difference, the process that, in a *covert* manner, generates semantic grids by fusion of differences into identity" (235).

3. For all references to Peirce's use of "quasi-mind," "quasi-interpreter," and so on, see http://www.helsinki.fi/science/commens/terms/quasimind.html.

4. As Albert Atkin points out, Peirce was primarily concerned with the evolution of knowledge (science). This led him, toward the end of his life, to divide the object into two (the *immediate* object and the *dynamic* object) and the interpretant into three (*the immediate, dynamic,* and *final* interpretants). The *immediate* object is the object as we know it at any point; the *dynamic* object is the object as it will be understood when our scientific knowledge is complete. See Atkin, "Peirce's Final."

5. Popper continues, "Matter turns out to be highly packed energy, transformable into other forms of energy; and therefore something in the nature of a process, since it can be converted into other processes, such as light and, of course, motion and heat. Thus one may say that the results of modern physics suggest that we should give up *the idea of a substance or essence.* They suggest that there is no self-identical entity persisting during all changes in time.... The universe now appears to be not a collection of things, but an interacting set of events or processes (as stressed especially by A. N. Whitehead)" (Popper and Eccles 7).

6. David Bentley Hart writes, "However hostile ... Heidegger's own diagnosis of the 'oblivion of being' may be to Christian thought, it nevertheless proceeds from a sadness quite familiar to theology in the post-Christian era. Heidegger recognises that the particular pathology of modernity lies—to some very large degree—in the loss of a certain kind of wonder or perplexity, a sense of the abiding strangeness of being within the very ordinariness of beings. Not, it must be said, that he really wishes to reverse the course of this decline; for him the nihilistic dissolution of every transcendental structure of being—every metaphysics—is something both good and bad, both a promise and a risk, and something that must be followed to its end. Following Nietzsche, he reads the history of nihilism as the story of the Western will to positive truth, which must—before it can be transcended—exhaust itself, and so bring metaphysics to its ultimate collapse" (258). The idea that truth can never be grasped in this *positive* way, because the world is real, but always mediated by signs, is fundamental to C. S. Peirce's semiotic philosophy. Signs are "open" and *unfinished* and always capable of growth in the process of semiosis.

7. We can thus perhaps understand literary texts as what Hubert Zapf, in his essay in this collection, calls a "translation process" between biosemiotic nature and semiotic culture. And, as one would expect, the cultural translation mimics the form of the natural original quite closely.

5 The Ecology of Colors
Goethe's Materialist Optics and Ecological Posthumanism

Heather I. Sullivan

Locating "Nature" in the Matter of Color and Light

The primary goal of this chapter is to unsettle our basic assumptions regarding nature as a "place" separate from the human realm and to posit it instead as natural-cultural processes continually occurring *all around, through,* and *in us.* With the ecology of colors, I therefore explore nature in terms of dynamic material and informational exchanges. There is no doubt that the scenic places traditionally viewed as "nature" are rapidly being transformed—destroyed, developed, logged, mined, polluted. Yet bounded *places* are not the trope here. Instead, nature is unbounded by material ecocriticism and reconfigured in an inclusive, natural-cultural sense of energy and light, that is, of optical colors emerging from the solar input into the biosphere. In this view, the *sensory perception* of living beings functions as the site of natural-cultural interfaces. The visual, auditory, tactile, taste, and smell sensory processes are bodily interactions with our material environment that guide our actions. Locating "nature" in this small-scale process-oriented view requires tracing the patterns of our perceptions and processing of the elements without the subject-object dichotomy. The ecology of colors highlights the reciprocity of our bodily materiality with energy forms, discursive information, and the other-than-human materiality of many species, or the "mesh," as Timothy Morton describes it. The vast yet often overlooked extinction of species ongoing today and the impacts of our "risk society" producing unknown quantities of chemical substances flowing through all biotic and abiotic forms in the biosphere require, literally, an eye-opening process or enhanced perception. With the "ecology of color" and light, I work toward an increased awareness of natural-cultural processes through sensory attentiveness to our ecological immersion in the material world.

Paying attention to color and light awakens us to our inextricable engagements with nature's vibrant materiality in potentially surprising ways, as Johann Wolfgang Goethe's *Theory of Color* (1810) demonstrates. This optical treatise portrays nature as a realm of active matter in a manner with striking similarity to the work in the new materialisms. Color, according to Goethe, is the embodiment of nature's metamorphic forms: when light, objects, eyes, and perceiving beings engage, then colors emerge. Rather than being static states, colors are representative for nature's fluctuating processes continually fueled by solar energy. Colors embody the exchanges of living things utilizing light. Their appearance in our visual processes occurs as bodily life-energy interfaces. On a broader scale, colors reveal the earth's reliance on transforming solar energy. This Goethean view of colors is "ecological" not in terms of population counts or predation and parasitical relationships but rather in its contextualization of human bodies and practices within the biotic and abiotic processes of material environments; there is no sense of the separation of the human from the elemental realm. The ostensibly subject-object quality of our relationship to "matter" is colorfully reshaped with attention to the processes of our sensory systems deriving and creating information through the continual exchange of energy and matter across our bodily boundaries. We cannot walk away from this "place" of light, shadows, and color as we might depart from a lovely landscape. An ecology of colors based on light and solar energy may initially seem nonecological or disconcertingly abstract, yet these elements are very much a constant part of our physical surroundings, if not the most significantly determining factors. In fact, light and color determine such key ecological issues as photosynthesis and pollination and hence almost all of terrestrial life, particularly the greenery upon which the very notion of a "green" environmental perspective derives.

The ecology of colors sheds light on the mesh of human and other-than-human materiality. It is thus an ecocritical strategy much like Kate Rigby's work on auditory aspects of lyric poetry. Rigby emphasizes how the poetic *sounds* in romantic and modern poetry evoke the more-than-human environment in which we are immersed. As she notes regarding the extensive use of "Rauschen" (rustling or murmuring) in Joseph von Eichendorff's poetry: "What murmurs and rustles in Eichendorff's *Waldlieder* no less than in [Theodor] Storm's verse is not, in the first place, the inner voice of a human subject, but rather the other-than-human sounds of outer nature" ("[K]ein Klang" 149). We are surrounded by vibrant "other-than-human" sounds in the *auditory realm* in the same manner that we exist within the *visual and energetic spectrum* of light's energy. Turning our attention to visual and auditory perceptual processes brings attention to the material surroundings in which there is, in Rigby's terms, "much astir" (149). Sensory perception is the environmental engagement of every organism at its most basic, and that includes both anticipation and response. For human beings, as with most large and mobile organisms, this occurs as a combined biological and subjective process. Our brains ceaselessly assess our material surroundings through and with personal and cultural frameworks, as William E. Connolly has also argued:

"Visual perception involves a complex mixing—during the half second delay between the reception of sensory experience and the formation of an image—of language, affect, feeling, touch, and anticipation" (181). Consciousness emerges from our mobile engagement with the world building on past experience as much as it derives from our abilities both to structure and to filter out the endless information from sensory perception. Matter's energies and our perception and awareness of them are, as Goethe repeatedly notes, active processes on both sides. Goethe is not alone in making such assertions in the nineteenth century: he stands in good stead with many of the *Naturphilosophen* such as Friedrich Schelling who also see the "natural world as a dynamic, self-generative unity-in-diversity" (see Rigby's discussion in *Topographies of the Sacred* 35).[1] In this way, the romantic era anticipates some of material ecocriticism's emphases such as dynamic and agentic matter and the porosity of our subjective selves and bodies.

Ecological Posthumanism

I formulate these material and agentic emphases as "ecological posthumanism." That is, Goethe's solidly humanistic and Promethean views are imbalanced by ideas very similar to what we now term "posthumanism," as a destabilizing of our bodily and cultural boundaries. In both posthumanism and many of Goethe's works, the masterful, rational, and clearly bounded humanist subjects are reinscribed as participants enmeshed within and cocreating material and discursive flows. According to Louise Westling, posthumanism has two main directions that undermine "humanist" assumptions regarding the supreme status of human beings. The first of these two directions is the "techno," or "cyborg," posthumanism of Donna Haraway and N. Katherine Hayles, for whom we are always already intermixes of technology and the organic. The second direction, according to Westling, is that of animal studies such as the work done by Derrida, Cary Wolfe, and Haraway, who write about our companion species and place humanity on the same continuum as other animals. Human beings are a species in the biosphere, in other words. Both the animal studies and cyborg strands of posthumanism question our bodily, "subject," or categorical boundaries, reconfiguring them to include technology or other species or both with the intent of overcoming anthropocentric and binary humanist assumptions. To these two directions, Westling adds a third possibility, one she describes as an "ecological ontology" based on Maurice Merleau-Ponty's work. Human beings in this vision are immensely influential, but still only one of many "kindred species." In such a posthumanist view, "we are no longer alone as transcendent Minds locked in decaying bodies on an Earth where we don't belong, and separate from the myriad creatures around us. Now we can see ourselves as vibrant bodies pulsing in harmony with our whole environment" ("Literature" 36). Although I am more skeptical than Westling regarding the "pulsing harmony" of our "vibrant bodies" with our "whole environment" (indeed, one basic necessity of life is its requisite ability to delineate itself from its surroundings sufficiently enough to have its own rhythms, temperature, and chemical content), I nevertheless follow her proposal to add a third option for posthumanism based on ecological considerations. This I rephrase as "ecological posthumanism," and suggest that future work link not only to cyber-posthumanism and animal studies but also to the new materialisms and hopefully, in future work, to questions of environmental justice. Like Westling's "ecological ontology," ecological posthumanism contextualizes the human being within the material environment of the biosphere; unlike Westling, it is not grounded on idealized notions of harmony.

The metamorphosing biotic and abiotic exchanges are our surroundings in the ecology of color and light, and they are as often discordant as they are aesthetic and soothing. Rather than Merleau-Ponty, thus, I look to Goethe's literary and scientific works for insights: he provides a nonpastoral, nonharmonious, and, most necessarily, ironic model in his literary works that keeps us alert to oversimplified idealizations of nature. Goethe's texts are particularly helpful for ecological posthumanism because he begins with the standard "humanist" assumption that we human beings do belong in an entirely different category than the rest of life, yet his science and literature virtually always veer off from that certainty into exploded bounds and proliferating elemental forces of which we are merely one part. Goethe typically begins his works with a Faustian quest for knowing and controlling nature, yet his figures and narratives repeatedly, despite their best efforts, merge with forms of agentic matter. The final scene in his drama *Faust*, for example, depicts the physical remains of the titular hero floating upward with angels whose patterns and movements follow exactly Goethe's description of rising air currents in his meteorological writings as if they were part of the water and air cycles.[2] His works document both humanist assumptions and their recontextualization in modern materiality, even potentially posthumanist, perspectives of lateral relationality rather than hierarchical differences. I therefore use Goethe to reformulate Westling's phrase asserting that "now we can see ourselves as vibrant bodies pulsing in harmony with our whole environment" and assert instead that now we can see ourselves—when aided by the ecology of color—as vibrant bodies pulsing *without harmony* yet fully within the energetic patterns of ecological and cultural intra-actions that make up the biosphere.[3]

Reading Goethe in terms of the "material turn" invokes postmodernism's insights yet avoids the matter-neglecting aspects of the so-called linguistic and cultural turns that appear to assert that all of reality is entirely culturally constructed. Construction of our experiential realms, as material ecocriticism makes clear, is as much a cultural process as it is a physical process involving atoms, light, bacteria, colors, electricity, food, caffeine, and toxic substances. Material ecocriticism arises from the work in the new materialisms carried out by Karen Barad, Stacy Alaimo,

Jane Bennett, Diana Coole, Samantha Frost, Serenella Iovino, Serpil Oppermann, and others. This material turn highlights how our human bodies coemerge with the dynamic and agential material processes in which we are entangled and is the basis for ecological posthumanism. Alaimo's concept of trans-corporeality, for example, undermines the traditional subject boundaries, revealing how porous our bodies and subjectivities are to the flows of substances around us. She emphasizes the movement across sites and bodies, and it is specifically a lateral movement rather than a hierarchical one. Similar is Barad's notion of diffraction, which describes not only the fuzzy boundaries of the actions of light and subatomic particles, but also the problematic discernment between the (human) observer and the observed. Although bodily boundaries of things may seem clear, Barad describes how recent science and postmodernism demonstrate "it has become increasingly clear that the seemingly self-evidentiary nature of bodily boundaries, including their seeming visual self-evidence, is a result of the repetition of (culturally and historically) specific bodily performance" (*Meeting* 155). In other words, there are no ultimate boundaries, and so we must think in terms of diffraction, not simple delineations: "Diffraction marks the limits of the determinacy and permanency of boundaries. . . . *Diffraction is a matter of differential entanglements. Diffraction is not merely about differences and certainly not differences in any absolute sense, but about the entangled nature of differences that matter*" (381; emphasis in the original). In fact, "diffraction" itself is her term for the process of "*making a difference, for topologically reconfiguring connections*" (381). We do not see absolute borders and ontological difference, but rather see practices of diffraction that reconfigure our relationality. In Barad's posthumanist perspective, bodies and things and energy "intra-act," instead of "interact." That is, *relations* precede individualized things encountering each other. In straightforward terms: we human beings and bodies are always part of our material surrounding and engaging with agentic matter. As Val Plumwood declares in *Environmental Culture,* we cannot leave behind our "enabling conditions" (though we often ignore them) (see Plumwood, *Environmental Culture* 17).

Goethe's Active Colors and Acts of Perception as Ecological "Intra-actions"

Goethe's *Theory of Color,* his self-proclaimed greatest contribution to the world, offers us a provocative model for the posthumanist negotiations of bodily and subjective boundaries. After all, sensory perception is a concrete form of our "trans-corporeality" and is an embodiment of how our bodily boundaries directly incorporate parts of our material surroundings. Goethe's work seems to assume a bounded, individualized body isolated and rationally observing, but his treatise continually slips into documentations of just how enmeshed we are with our material surroundings and how our bodies are coemerging with nature rather than standing aside and observing it. With much relevance for questions of bodily boundaries, Goethe's writings on physics describe human beings as "people of the air-ocean" (*Völker des Luftmeers*), a neologism he coins for human beings in a parallel description to the idea of fish being people of the (watery) ocean.[4] Our bodies are, in other words, fully immersed in air and shaped by this seemingly invisible form of matter all around us, through which we move. Hence, we may think that we dictate the flows with our agency, but we are all too often wrong in that regard. Instead, these toxic or natural flows move through our bodies and with or against them, and they also influence our thinking in ways that we simply do not see.

In his famous essay "The Experiment as Mediator of Object and Subject," Goethe directly addresses the problem of learning to see what is right in front of us. He writes:

> Since everything in nature, especially, however, the general forces and elements exist in eternal action and counter-action, thus one can say of every single phenomenon that it exists in connection to innumerable others just as we say of a free-floating point of light that all of its rays are sent out to all sides. ("Versuch" 33)

His work on perception reveals vision to be part of this action and counteraction occurring as ongoing exchanges across bodily boundaries: most obviously, we perceive light as it enters our eyes. Furthermore, Goethe places equal weight on light's refraction, the chemically produced color of objects, and optical illusions as inevitable outgrowths of our eyes' visual apparatus. That is, he grasps color and light in terms of their interaction with our eyes and brain. If humanism draws the lines around the individual body and consciousness as if they were clear and stable, Goethe posits our agency, bodily form, and sensory perception as being drawn from and constantly reshaped by our surroundings.

This shaping goes both ways, and Goethe also states that light can be thought of only in relation to other things:

> We call darkness the circumstances of space around us, when we, with open healthy eyes, perceive no objects around us. We think of it abstractly without object as a negation; it is, like quietness, welcome for the tired, but uncomfortable for those who are energetic. Light, in contrast, we can never think of in the abstract, but rather we become aware of it as the result of a specific object that exists in space; precisely through this process [it] makes other objects visible. (*Beiträge* 23)

Raging against Newton in his second, polemical, section of *Theory of Color*, Goethe insists on explaining light not in abstract terms but rather through its interactions with objects and matter. That is, whereas Newton understands light as an abstract object of study existing independently of perception, Goethe, in contrast, sees light and color *always and only in interaction with other matter, perceiving bodies, and the scientific processes of investigation*. Part two (of three) in Goethe's thousand-page optical study *Theory of Color* quotes Newton's optics, line by line, and attempts to disprove each assertion, often word for word. One main critique dominating this "polemical section"—there is not space here to document his vast and dogmatic dissection of Newton—is Goethe's quest to prove that Newton's sense of light remains too abstract and without context. When Newton writes in his first proposition, first theorem, for example, "Lights which differ in color differ also in degrees of refrangibility," Goethe is disgraced, because he wants to know the *context:* which colors, what kind of light, where did the light come from, who is viewing it, what education and training did she have, what is she wearing, what is the room like, or is the viewer outside in the sun or shade or clouds, and what is the historical, cultural, physical nature of viewer, tools, and the reader, too? To say that Goethe may overdo the demand for "context" might seem reasonable for scientists wanting to restrict their study to mathematical observations only, but for this chapter on the ecology of colors and lights, and for material ecocriticism's broader project of rethinking bodily and discursive coemergences all the way to the level of the quantum, Goethe may have a point.

For Goethe, light is contextualized within the world of things, beings, and colors, whereas we are contextualized within light and darkness (and the natural elements). While Newton remains abstract and posits colors as being an integral part of white light, Goethe—with much relevance for material ecocriticism—studies light through its impact on the world and the emergence of colors. That is, Newton explains "light" mathematically, whereas Goethe strives for an explanation of color perception and appearance. Hence, Goethe claims that Newton overlooks the *boundaries,* the context, and all the conditions that influence the light. This is an essentially "ecological" aspect to his work:

> The theory, in contrast, of which we are convinced, and of which we in this case speak only in so far as it opposes the Newtonian theory, has to do also with white light. This theory utilizes also *external conditions* in order to bring forth colored appearances. It gives credence, in fact, to these conditions, and does not pretend to develop colors out of light; it attempts to convince us rather that color is brought forth *both from light and from that which it encounters.* Hence, thinking here only of the refraction issue with which Newton above all works in his optics, it is in no way the diffraction [of light] that lures the colors out of light, rather there remains a second essential condition, [which is] that the diffraction acts on an image that is shifted away from its position. An image arises only with the *borders;* these borders are entirely overlooked by Newton, indeed he denies their influence. We however ascribe *completely equal influence not only to the picture but also its surroundings, to the bright medium as well as to the dark border, to the activity as well as to the restrictions.* (Zur Farbenlehre 303; emphasis added)

Newton, in contrast, as cited by Goethe, claims, "The white [light] of the sunlight is composed out of all the primary colors united in a fitting relationship" (cited by Goethe in *Zur Farbenlehre,* 460). Goethe's elaborate emphasis on all the various conditions from which color emerges out of light's interactions, such as the eye's apparatus, the angles, the materials encountered, and, especially, the all-important borders that break or bend light, provides us with an ecology of color. Of course, his notion of light's "purity" is not entirely correct, since white light *does* contain the other colors. Despite his inaccuracy with regard to light unto itself, Goethe is accurate in his insistence that light on earth is present to living beings through its encounters with objects, photosynthesizing plants, and perception. This relationality provides a concrete model for material ecocriticism's engagement with the activity of matter at the level of the body's environment.

The Ecology of Colors: Goethe's Three Categories

Furthermore, Goethe's *Theory of Color* has three advantages for material ecocriticism and the formulation of an ecology of colors more specifically. First, with this kind of material-based "nature writing," we assess matter directly as light and color, which reminds us that nature is not merely a lost distant place of purity but rather is always right here as a process—wherever here is, and however humanly constructed it is. Although nature writing has often been a form of natural history documentation of our world, such portrayals can potentially perpetuate the notion that the "environment" is primarily a site of (distant) wilderness rather than something concretely and etymologically all around us. In other words, we may leave the forest or seashore, but we cannot escape from light and darkness or colors, matter, and energy. Abiotic factors are exceedingly significant aspects of our "vibrant" environments, as are the microscopic biotic contributions of such heavy hitters as bacteria, without which we would not "be" at all.[5] Second, Goethe's three-part structure in the *Theory of Color* (didactic, polemic, and historical) and his three types of colors provide a compellingly nondualistic model. His colors are, first, the physiological tones that *belong to the eye as optical illusions;* second, the physical colors that emerge from *the interactive engagements* of light, our eyes, and opaque or translucent substances; and, third, the chemical colors that actually belong to an object due to its encounter with light. Because much of ecocriticism has struggled to overcome traditionally formulated dichotomies such as nature-culture, male-female, natural-unnatural, self-other, subject-object, and so forth, it is very promising to have a nondualistic model to move us into a spectrum of intra-actions. Goethe's optical studies are, indeed, based on the multifaceted intra-actions of light, our eyes, our brain's processing, our measuring apparatus, and other objects experiencing light. There are no absolute or impermeable boundaries distinguishing among these participating elements, and hence there is also no magisterial, objective, "humanist," or nonparticipatory "eye." This relational, or "ecological," view at the core of Goethe's optics and colors thus resonates with Barad's work on "quantum physics and the entanglement of matter and meaning" (her book's subtitle). Specifically, both Goethe and Barad build on the optical notion of "diffraction" in order to explain the interactive processes of observers with the world. Third, Goethe sees colors as being representative of all of "nature," as interactive, fluidly becoming phenomena that emerge only in relation to other things. Color is, in his terms, "something that becomes, grows, moves" and so is ideal to reveal "the most delicate influences of nature" (*Zur Farbenlehre* 29). Goethe may begin with humanist assumptions, but his discussions of color and light erupt with prismatic variance into destabilizing narratives of interactivity. Light itself may be "pure" for Goethe, but it never exists without being in space, time, and a world populated with material things and perceiving beings.

For ecological posthumanism, Goethe's work on perception is the most relevant section of his optics; it is also the most accurate scientifically. This is the second advantage of using his *Theory of Color* as the basis for an ecology of color: his perception is a nondualistic, interactive study. In the "didactic" section, Goethe records his experiments and conclusions about colors and light based on his three categories of physiological, physical, and chemical colors. His "physiological" colors are those "colors that belong to the eye" (*Zur Farbenlehre* 31). This emphasis on visual perception and the process of light being absorbed by the eye as well as the actual brain processing of the impulses received from the intra-action with light is part of the reason for the resurging interest in Goethe's science.[6] In essence, Goethe's study of light and colors begins with a presentation of optical illusions such as the bright patterns and colors one sees when staring at a window and then closing one's eyes. The emphasis in Goethe's optics on the intra-actions of light, ourselves, and the surrounding world contextualizes our perceptive practices. There is a concrete element of performance in which light and perception are seen not as two preexisting phenomena but rather as processes that inflect each other so that our visual world emerges. Note how he clearly specifies the active "emergences" of our surroundings and the ongoing shaping processes:

> With a light weight and counterweight, nature weighs itself back and forth; and thus emerges a here and there, an up and down, a before and after, through which all the apparitions/emergences [*Erscheinungen*] that we encounter in space and time are conditioned. We become aware of these general movements and determinations in the most diverse ways: sometimes as a simple repulsion and attraction, other times as a blinking and disappearing light, as movement of air, as shaking of the body, as acidification and de-acidification; nevertheless always as connecting or separating, an agitating of Being [*Dasein*] and fostering of some kind of life. (*Zur Farbenlehre* 13)

This is entirely different from Newtonian concentration on light in abstract terms that, according to Goethe, are part of a chaotic abstraction that qualify as "laughable," "unspeakable," "distasteful," and even "insulting."[7] Above all, Goethe rages that Newton studies light in isolation rather than in terms of "external conditions" or influences. Goethe seeks a contextualized version of nature, one with much relevance for an ecological posthumanism.

Part 2 of Goethe's didactic section examines the "physical" colors, or those that result through intra-actions among us, light, and other materials, such as when a light passes through or reflects from opaque or translucent materials, shimmering. "These colors," he writes, "are produced in our eye through such externally determined causes, or, if they are somehow produced externally, they are reflected back to our eye" (*Zur Farbenlehre* 70). Goethe spends much of this chapter assessing how light can be influenced or shaped through its contact with other materials and how these shimmering colors are concretely the emergences or intra-actions from these processes. Again, this kind of "nature" is, above all and in Goethe's terminology, "murky." Light and colors have such complexly energetic impact that trying to abstract them from the rest of the physical world leads us away from our concrete bodily experiences. An ecology of color and light embraces the murky intra-actions fully from within the processes. In other words, it does not provide answers to problems of fracking pollution, for example, but it does seek to shift our sense of our materiality and bodily natures so that we might all the more persuasively *see* how such anthropogenic damage inevitably and directly impacts us and all of the participants and emerging forms in intra-actions. An ecology of color and light is inclusive: it includes human beings, bodies, cultures, practices, and the vast array of more-than-human biotic and abiotic factors.

Finally, Goethe's third category of colors is "chemical," or those that derive from specific bodies. These are long-term rather than the short-term fluidity of the physiological or physical colors and are the concrete colors that one may expect to be the main emphasis of an optical study. Despite the fact that these are the more solid, "fixed" colors, Goethe describes them as "processes" rather than final properties. As he writes, "Thus we name those [colors] that we activate on certain bodies, [that we] more or less fix, intensify on them, take away from them again, and that we can impart to other bodies" (*Zur Farbenlehre* 174). The starting point for "chemical colors" is hence the processes of actual bodies (by which he means "objects"). Goethe notes that every "body" is capable of having color that it either "activates, intensifies, step-by-step fixes, or at least can have imparted to it" (172). In contrast, Goethe opens his first category of colors, the physiological, with an assessment with our eyes and perception, and he begins his second category, the physical, with the reflection and diffraction of light engaging with materiality. Goethe's categories of colors therefore always consider intra-actions of our eyes, the bodies having color, the action of light, and our measuring processes. The most important determining factor for each category is simply his *starting point*, not the exclusive impact of one abstract entity. In sum, Goethe lays the ground for the material ecocritical approach of ecological posthumanism that understands human beings and bodies *in terms* of their relations, intra-actions, or coproduction and coemergence with their surroundings rather than as separable subjects or objects. One cannot, Goethe asserts, think of an eye without also thinking light.[8] By extrapolation, one cannot think light without thinking the sun and solar energy and photosynthesis—material ecocriticism brings us right into the thick of matter and its many forms.

The Ecology of Colors and Material Ecocriticism

For ecocriticism, such descriptions derived from optics and physics may seem disconcertingly distant from our concrete ecological concerns about habitat destruction, pollution, and the demise of unknowable numbers of species yearly. Yet it should not be disheartening in the sense that the new materialists like Barad—and Goethe, I argue—bring a shift in our understanding of nature as those processes that are *all around us, all the time*. The goal here is to overcome the spatial distinction between ourselves and the rest of the biosphere. Rather than locating nature elsewhere or in the wild or outdoors, nature appears—visually, sensually—all around us in its most energized form of light and colors. Nature is, to reiterate, the processes of emergence of material reality of which we are a part. For Barad, that brings as much, if not more, responsibility as the more traditional views of natural places. She notes, "We are responsible for the world in which we live, not because it is an arbitrary construction of our choosing, but because it is sedimented out of *particular practices that we have a role in shaping*" (*Meeting* 203; emphasis added). Moving from simple analyses of our devastation of landscapes into our complex shaping of cultural, physical, and environmental practices brings with it a powerful critique of our choices, but also some relief for the deep horror and mourning that many environmental thinkers face when viewing the anthropogenic manifestations of habitat destruction and toxic infusion. That is, we might have a very concrete tool for altering our currently unsustainable path if we can reshape our own human practices and awareness—our very *perception* of the world and not just our understandings of it.

As another way of manifesting the concrete environmental relevance of an ecology of colors and light—in addition to the not insignificant processes of perception, the impact of photosynthesis for life on the planet, and the daily engagement of most life forms with the resulting spectrum of colors—I mention the impact of our human practices in the industrial production of particulate matter that becomes airborne. Such waste products may well be toxic as they are, or they may contribute to unsavory-looking plumes emerging from smokestacks. Yet that is just part of their environmental exchanges, for then they, too, intra-act with light in photochemical reactions. These chemical reactions are driven by sunlight, and they can produce smog as well as all kinds of photochemical oxidants, including the acidic compounds responsible for acid rain. Light, in other words, is the essential ingredient to a great many issues relating to pollution (see Southwick for more information). This does not mean that we wish to eradicate light; instead, as the foundational assertion of an ecology of color and light, I suggest that we strive to become aware of our physical, material surroundings that are actively, vibrantly, even possibly "agentically" participating in processes of which we are a part, and that this awareness and perceptive ability might help us seek forms of "intra-actions," to borrow from Barad, with less destructive trajectories. To put it otherwise, we are in the world of photochemical intra-actions, and all the technology in the world cannot alter that fundamentally nonspatial position within manifold processes. Human hubris all too often looks at its own role or, at best, its products, but not at the entire webs of intra-actions driven by, say, photochemical processes or bacteria. In that manner, one might say that Lynn Margulis presents us with an "ecology of bacteria" that precisely contextualizes human beings within our biotic mesh.

While Goethe and Barad present models based on the challenges of perceiving the processes and substances in which we are immersed, Jane Bennett's concept of "vibrant matter" offers another relevant insight from the new materialisms for an optical view. That is, Bennett also works toward "opening our eyes" to matter's direct influences on our cultural and biological systems. We *see* human agency, she notes, but we *fail to see* all the other forms of agency all around us. In Bennett's terms, agency is distributed and exists like a "mosaic" of multiple influences and actions or actants. The issue here, too, is bringing the world's vibrancy (back) into our consciousness. Human striving (the very thing for which Goethe's Faust figure is so famous) is contextualized within the vibrancy of nonhuman agencies. Bennett writes:

> If human culture is inextricably enmeshed with vibrant, nonhuman agencies, and if human intentionality can be agentic only if accompanied by a vast entourage of nonhumans, then it seems that the appropriate unit of analysis for democratic theory is neither the individual human nor an exclusively human collective but the (ontologically heterogeneous) "public" coalescing around a problem. We need not only to invent or reinvoke concepts like conatus, actant, assemblage, small agency, operator, disruption, and the like but also to devise new procedures, technologies, and *regimes of perception* that enable us to consult nonhumans more closely, or to listen and respond more carefully. (*Vibrant* 108; emphasis added)

Much like Rigby, Bennett highlights questions of perception and learning to "hear" or see that with which we "intra-act." Additionally, Bennett's vibrant matter requires new "regimes of perception," which is what I propose with the ecology of color and light.

Timothy Morton also places human agency, bodies, and cultures among all kinds of processes in which we are "enmeshed." For Morton, the problem of falsely understood boundaries is predominant. We believe in our bounded lives and categories at our own peril. He describes our ecological interconnectedness with both material and discursive energies as a "radical openness" to the world in his latest work, *The Ecological Thought*. This radical openness is both a form of thinking and a physical situation: "The ecological thought imagines interconnectedness, which I call *the mesh*. Who or what is interconnected with what or whom? The mesh of interconnected things is vast, perhaps immeasurably so" (15). *The Ecological Thought* is dedicated to drawing our attention to the mesh and its openness even as it is webbed together. Again, the new materialists highlight the challenge of perception itself. In learning to perceive our existence within the mesh of, for example, invaluable bacterial action at every level of life, we might actually shift our actions toward acknowledging our surroundings in reference to other aspects of life in the biosphere as well.

Material ecocriticism rejects the human body as a closed "self" engaging only *by choice* with the world according to his or her whim. Instead, our bodies exist among other bodies, enmeshed, and intra-acting trans-corporeally, with all sorts of substances, including food, water, air, and a full range of industrial chemicals. One of ecological posthumanism's most significant questions is the negotiation of our bodily boundaries in relationship to other bodies and all surrounding matter in the environment. Of course, much of this negotiation occurs without our knowledge, whether as physical processes (breathing, eating, perceiving, and absorbing light or toxins) or as cultural expressions. Our bodily boundaries are constantly under negotiation even as the most fundamental requirement of life is that some stability is maintained in the form of membranes or delineation between the body and its surroundings. This is a precarious balance and one that becomes clearer when we think optically about matter. As Goethe says, one cannot think of the eye without light, and so one might also say that we cannot think of human beings and bodies without also thinking gravity, oxygen, other animal lives, plants, dirt, geological structures influencing weather and seasons, and, of course, colors emerging from sunlight, for which our eyes evolved and which provides the energy for the entire biosphere and its many ecological systems. This is a starting point for ecological posthumanism, one building on material ecocriticism broadly and supported by such perspectives as an ecology of colors.

Irony and the Ecology of Colors and Light

Despite Goethe's radical slippage out of humanism into an ecological posthumanism-like contextualization of human beings within light, colors, and the elements as trans-corporeal entanglements, I nevertheless want to conclude this chapter with an equally relevant aspect of his *Theory of Color*: its insistence on irony. Irony is essential for this process, as it is for most of postmodernism, because it helps us to avoid one-sided views and clannish mind-sets that righteously proclaim proper (and "improper") approaches to environmental problems. Irony destabilizes our thinking even as it stabilizes our ability to maintain awareness of the broad spectrum and diffraction processes, to borrow from optics yet again, of possibilities and the complexity of environmental issues. Ecological posthumanism must be ironic. Goethe's foreword to his optical treatise states that the greatest danger we face in encountering and thinking about nature is that we inevitably have preconceived notions, or "theories," before we begin to assess our perceptual process and intra-actions. Such premature theorizing is best avoided, according to Goethe, by maintaining awareness of this tendency and to remain girded *with irony:*

> Every viewing turns into a considering, every considering in a pondering, every pondering into a connecting, and so can one say that we already theorize with every sentient glance into the world. To do this and to attempt this, however, with consciousness, with self-awareness, with freedom, and to make use of a daring term for us, *with irony,* is a necessary skill [in order to avoid the abstract and to have useful results]. (*Zur Farbenlehre* 14)

Morton, too, insists on irony in terms of "dark ecology":

> [The] more honest ecological art would linger in the shadowy world of irony and difference. With dark ecology, we can explore all kinds of art forms as ecological: not just ones that are about lions and mountains, not just journal writing and sublimity. The ecological thought includes negativity and irony, ugliness and horror. Democracy is well served by irony, because irony insists that there are other points of view that we must acknowledge. (*The Ecological* 17)

The irony of multiple perspectives, optical illusions, and the diffraction of light and boundaries: these views are shared by Goethe's theory of color, Barad's entanglement of meaning and matter, Alaimo's trans-corporeality, and Morton's mesh. Ecological posthumanism materially enmeshes us within our own and nature's prismatic forms. Ironically, the negotiations of our bodily boundaries amid our material surroundings engage anew each time we blink our eyes. Viewing our enmeshment and ongoing engagements in the intra-actions of an ecology of color might inspire an awareness of our material circumstances that we impact by being alive. The ironic—or perhaps sardonic—question emerging from an ecology of colors and light is whether the human spectrum is like the eternal sequence of colors in the rainbow that never changes, or if our spectrum might be shifted toward greener intra-actions.

Notes

1. Yet as Arthur Zajonc ("Goethe and the Science" 18) points out, Goethe shared a critique of Newtonian science with the *Naturphilosophen* even as he differed significantly from many of them with his very concrete emphasis on empirical research.

2. For a detailed analysis of Faust's final ascent in terms of Goethe's meteorological studies, see Sullivan, "Ecocriticism."

3. For discussions of unbalanced nature and "discordant harmonies" in ecology, see Botkin's *Discordant Harmonies* and Kricher's *The Balance of Nature*. Both of these ecologists assert that any notion of "balance" in nature is more a cultural tradition than a biological reality.

4. All translations from Goethe's scientific writings here are my own.

5. Lynn Margulis has changed much of evolutionary biology and reshaped our understanding of life with her bacterial studies. See especially her books co-authored with her son: Margulis and Sagan, *Dazzle*; and *Microcosmos*.

6. See the applications of Goethe's views in contemporary science described by Peter Matussek, John McCarthy, and David Seamon and Arthur Zajonc.

7. Goethe adds many other curses to his list of descriptive terms for Newton's "convoluted" system of optics in his *Theory of Color*. These terms are taken just from page 199 of his long "polemical" section dissecting word-for-word Newton's entire optical treatise.

8. His *Theory of Color* cites Plotinus in the introduction: "Wär' nicht das Auge sonnenhaft, / Wie könnten wir das Licht erblicken? / Lebt' nicht in uns des Gottes eigne Kraft, / Wie könnt' uns Göttliches entzücken?" (If the eye weren't sun-like / How could we perceive the light? If God's own power did not live in us, / How else could we be enraptured by the divine?) (*Zur Farbenlehre* 24).

PART 2

Narratives of Matter

6   Bodies of Naples
Stories, Matter, and the Landscapes of Porosity

Serenella Iovino

IN THE HEART of the city of Naples there is a place with a curious name: Largo Corpo di Napoli. This little square opens up like an oyster at a point where the *decumani*, the Greek main streets, become a tangle of narrow medieval lanes and heavy gray-and-white buildings. Like an oyster, this square has a pearl: an ancient statue of the Nile, popularly known as *Corpo di Napoli,* the body of Naples. The story of this statue is peculiar. Dating back to the second or third century, when it was erected to mark the presence of an Egyptian colony in the city, the statue disappeared for a long time and was rediscovered in the twelfth century. Its head was missing, and the presence of children lying at its breasts led people to believe that it represented Parthenope, the virgin nymph to whom the foundation of the city is mythically attributed. In 1657 the statue was restored, and a more suitable male head made it clear that the reclining figure symbolized the Egyptian river and the children personifications of its tributaries. In spite of evidence and philology, however, for the people the sculpture remained the symbol of their city's body. In this body, as it sometimes happens in local rituals and legends, the boundaries of gender roles, like those of matter and spirit, present and past, are blurred and shifting.

Not far from the *Body of Naples*, concealed in a side lane, the city offers its corporeality again, this time in the overflowing baroque splendors of the San Severo Chapel. Here, other bodies appear: bodies of marble, like the *Veiled Christ* and the *Veiled Modesty,* two emphatic eighteenth-century sculptures in which the presence of a shroud makes the corporeal dimension even more naked and exposed, and, stunningly displayed in a scientific cabinet, a man and a pregnant woman, known as "anatomic machines." These bodies, whose circulatory systems and internal organs have been carefully reconstructed with wax using real skeletons as a basis, have also been for centuries the subjects of legends and popular tales about alchemical transubstantiations and mysterious practices that would preserve matter from corruption.

In a few square meters, there is an accumulation of bodies: of mythical bodies alluding to the elemental forces and intermediate divinities presiding over the birth of the city, of bodies used as "anatomical machines" for protoscientific experiments, of marble bodies covered with marble veils to give the illusion of mystic weightlessness, and, most of all, of living human bodies. With three million residents in its metropolitan area, a volcanic region in coastal Campania, Naples is indeed one of the most populated Italian cities, and, within this overpopulated city, this quarter is one of the most filled with people, their emerging dynamics, and their stories.

This chapter is about some of the many bodies of Naples and its turbulent surroundings and about how stories, memories, and meanings are materially carved onto them. These are bodies of humans and nonhumans, hybrid bodies that coalesce with the materiality of places and natural forces, intra-acting with flows of substances, imagination, and discourses. Via these reciprocal transformations, the lively matter of these bodies becomes a template for the stories of this region, a narrative agency, a "storied matter."

Interpreting bodies—the bodies of Naples—as texts conveying the signs and meanings expressed by material forces, this chapter tries to shed light on the complexity of levels, at once ecological, political, telluric, artistic, cultural, that craft the life of this place. In the examination of two examples, taken from archaeological research and from literature, respectively, I will illustrate the Neapolitan landscape as a fluid compound of agencies in mutual determination in which every part emerges as a crossroad of ongoing stories.

A Porous City

Like many German intellectuals and artists of his age, Walter Benjamin visited Naples several times during the 1920s. In a short memoir he wrote with Asja Lacis, the Brechtian actress with whom he was in love, the city is described with excited impressionism and defined with a recurrent adjective: "porous." In their Mitteleuropean eyes, Naples's porous texture involved forms and styles, gestures and behaviors, relationships and places (see Benjamin and Lacis, "Napoli" 33–39; Velardi). Most of all, though, the city looked porous to them because of its predominant building material: a pale-yellow, spongy, and sandy stone called "toof" (in Italian, *tufo*). Naples's toof, whose scientific name is *Ignimbrite campana*—literally, Campania's "fiery rock dust cloud" (from the Latin *ignis*, "fire," and *imber*, "rain")—is a sedimentary formation of pyroclastic rock, resulting from deposits of ash and lapilli explosions, and lava flows.[1] Toof exists in huge concentrations in the Campi Flegrei (literally, "Flaming Fields," from the Greek *phlégo*, "burn"), a vast volcanic area delimited at the Southeast by Mount Vesuvius. In the middle of this land, suspended between the sea and the volcano, and erected on toof, is Naples: a porous, volcanic city built up with porous, volcanic rock.

Bodies of Naples | 99

Figure 6.1. *Corpo di Napoli* (2012). Courtesy of Christian Arpaia.

Easy to work, light, resistant, and very abundant, toof is practically everywhere in Naples. Indeed, this rock is so copious that it has been used for almost every palace, church, house, fisherman cave, or storage room fabricated here prior to the advent of reinforced concrete. Permeating the very soil of Naples, toof is also an immediately available material, and this creates one of the city's fascinating paradoxes. The majority of the buildings, in fact, lie directly on the caves from where the construction materials were taken, giving the feeling of a city rising from its own womb. Thus, if Venice is erected upon an underwater forest of innumerable trees, Naples is founded on hollows, its bodies literally staying at the bottom of burning fields and living in houses and streets fabricated with volcanic rocks, whether toof or other kinds of lava formations. Developing in a vast network of subterranean tunnels, these hollows—used as storage spaces, domestic dumps, and, during World War II, as antiaircraft shelters—have filtered for centuries the matter and emotions of the city above, participating in its life with their underground mineral agency.

Although intended to be more picturesque than scientific, Benjamin and Lacis's definition of Naples as a "porous city" is very effective. Naples is porous in many ways. It is spatiotemporally porous: a city upon other cities, where traces of the Greek and Roman settlements, preserved in the underfoot layers, systematically overflow onto streets and corners, sharing transversal portions of space with medieval tribunals, Renaissance palaces, or baroque churches. Naples is porous because of its overall volcanic aura, a pervious agency that permeates the city's history. Indeed, eruptions have absorbed Naples's life for millennia. The last upsurge, in 1944, almost coincided with the entry of the Allied forces in the city. And volcanic porosity also fills the city's cultural imagination: to the many intellectuals and artists who, like Benjamin or Goethe long before him, stopped here on their Grand Tour, Mount Vesuvius's lush and sulfurous landscape provided a vibrant and swallowing experience of "volcanic sublime," a telluric variety of *Et in Arcadia ego*.

But, examined more carefully, Naples's porosity replicates the porosity of all bodies taken as sites of "interchanges and transits" (Alaimo, *Bodily* 2), crossroads of agencies, and "congregational" entities (Bennett, *Vibrant* 34): permeable and compound systems, in which the alternation of plenum and void is the very condition of every possible existing thing. As Karen Barad explains, "According to the quantum field theory, the vacuum is far from empty; indeed, it's teeming with the full set of possibilities of what may come to be" (*Meeting* 354). If, from a physical viewpoint, void is literally the site where particles of matter can move, combine, and carry on activity, from a more general perspective, all possible bodies emerge from this interplay of emptiness and density. And it is this interplay that makes all bodies, from atoms and molecules to assemblages and collectives of humans and nonhumans, permeable to the world. This porosity occurs at many levels, both material and semiotic, allowing transformations, metabolism, and flows of matter, energy, and information. It is interesting to notice that, before being proven by biologists and physicists, the permeability of matter had been a cornerstone of natural philosophy (more notably, of atomism) for millennia. The Epicurean poet Lucretius, for example, who lived and philosophized at the foothills of Mount Vesuvius, wrote in his lyrical treatise *The Nature of Things* that "however solid things appear . . . even these are porous":

> In a cave of rocks the seep of moisture trickles
> And the whole place weeps its fat blobs of tears.
> Food is dispersed all through a creature's body;
> Young trees grow tall and yield their fruit in season,
> Drawing their sustenance from the lowest roots
> Through trunks and branches; voices penetrate
> Walls and closed doors; the seep of stiffening cold
> Permeates bone. Phenomena like these
> Would be impossible but for empty spaces
> Where particles can pass. (30)

Filtering through time and visions, these ideas resonate with a passage from *The Fold*, where, commenting on Leibniz's ontology, Gilles Deleuze writes that matter "offers an infinitely porous, spongy, or cavernous texture without emptiness, caverns endlessly contained in other caverns: no matter how small, each body contains a world pierced with irregular passages" (5). This description seems to fit Naples's reality perfectly.

Many centuries after Lucretius and Leibniz, today we know that every body, every corporeal entity, is intrinsically open, intrinsically "of and in the world" (Tuana, "Viscous" 198). It is, as Levy Bryant has written, "a heterogeneous and complex network of entities that is itself an entity or unity," a singularity that, in order to be what it is, has to be microscopically vast and to contain multitudes. Bodies, in other words, "are more like sponges than marbles"—also because, considered in their inner structure, "even marbles are a sort of sponge" (Bryant n.p.). Like every transformative or metabolic process of the world, thus, corporeality is always already open and trans-corporeal.[2] This trans-corporeality expresses itself in the way material substances interfere and intermingle with each other, determining the world as a site of ongoing hybridizations, from evolutionary processes to environmentally related illness. Also food consumption, as Lucretius reminds us, is a way through which bodies are reciprocally transformed. Eating is a mutual hybridization of bodily matters, and so are sweating, the chlorophyllian synthesis of plants, the physicochemical transformation of atoms into molecules with properties of their own, and the flowing of lava from the recesses of the earth to the "open" world up above. All these are examples of the world's metabolic porosity, accurately expressed by the German word for "metabolism," *Stoffwechsel*: literally, an exchange of matter.

As bodies are what they are via their permeable boundaries (membranes that cause the flows of energy and matter), so, too, bigger entities and formations follow the same dynamics. A city, for example, is a porous body inhabited by other porous bodies, a mineral-vegetal-animal aggregate of porous bodies. Following the patterns of intra-action, cities are compounds of matter and energy in mutual transformation with human and nonhuman beings, living and nonliving matter, thus participating in the world's "geochoreographies" (Cohen, "Stories" 56). A convincing model for this porous geochoreography is provided by Manuel De Landa, who writes: "From the point of view of energetic and catalytic flows, human societies are very much like lava flows; and human-made structures (mineralized cities and institutions) are very much like mountains and rocks: accumulations of materials hardened and shaped by historical processes" (55). There is a substantial—ontological and historical—continuity in the formation of cities and volcanic rocks. The rhythms of "mineralization" and "catalysis" of cities might differ from those of geological structures, but they are part of the ongoing morphing process that involves together organisms, structures, genes, languages, or ideas: "Living creatures and their inorganic counterparts share a crucial dependence on intense flows of energy and materials. . . . Our organic bodies are, in this sense, nothing but temporary coagulations in these flows" (104). Seen in this light, porosity is not only the basis of change, growth, and decay both on a geological and a human level, but the very condition of history: a history that is not a linear succession of events, but rather a path emerging from the fluxes of matter and energy in which our organic bodies are "nothing but temporary coagulations," as De Landa says.

In the vast landscape of porosity, cognition occupies an important part, too. As Varela, Thompson, and Rosch explain, cognition "depends on the kind of experience that comes from having a body with various sensorimotor capacities"—capacities that "are themselves embedded in a more encompassing biological, psychological, and cultural context" (173). As a set of embodied practices, knowledge consists "in the interface between mind, society, and culture, rather than in one or even in all of them" (Varela, Thompson, and Rosch 179). Knowledge—human and nonhuman informational interchange with the world—is a form of porosity; it is the way the world enters and conditions habits of living, thus determining the way living beings *in-habit* the world. To say that knowledge is "embodied" means that the world acts together with bodies, becoming sedimented in and filtered through cognitive practices. This is what N. Katherine Hayles, in *How We Became Posthuman*, describes as a process of cognitive "embodiment." Every cognitive experience, whether an "incorporated practice" ("an action that is encoded into bodily memory by repeated performances until it becomes habitual" [199]) or the enactive processes of "embodied knowledge," is rooted in the mutual porosity of bodies and world. Embodied knowledge, in particular, is a process and a flux, "a mode of learning which is . . . different from that deriving from cogitation alone" (201), and therefore "contextual, enmeshed with the specifics of place, time, physiology, and culture" (196). In other words, knowledge comes from the give-and-take between bodies and the world. It materializes the porous exchange of inside and outside, the progressive becoming-together of bodies and the world, their intra-action.

This discloses another important dimension of this permeability, which is also discursive and semiotic: the flow of information and discursive practices through bodies. Phenomena such as gender, sexuality, class, social practices, *and their narratives* are filtered through this porosity as forms of an "emergent interplay" of natural-cultural factors. This is the key of Alaimo's trans-corporeality and of what Nancy Tuana calls an "interactionist ontology": an ontology in which the social is considered in its materiality, in strict combination with the agency of the natural, thus challenging essentialist visions and their normative constructions (see "Viscous" 188). "Porosity" means here the permeability not only "between our flesh and the flesh of the world we are of and in" (198), but also between bodies and the discursive worlds in which they are located: bodies "produc[e] culture at the same time that culture produces . . . bod[ies]" (Hayles 200). This "emergent interplay" or, in Barad's compelling term, intra-action of matter, discourses, and cognitions shows that there are not clear-cut boundaries separating "the natural from the human-constructed, the biological from the cultural, genes from their environments, the material from the semiotic" (Tuana, "Viscous" 198), but that every body is a crossing of flesh and meanings, a unique coagulation in the stories of matter.

The landscape of Naples and its region not only is materially and historically porous, alternating hollows and density in "a mosaic of ecological and semiotic processes" (Farina 64), but also, with its coemerging bodies, epitomizes such a vision. Being themselves players in the making of the world, all of these bodies are in fact enactive and cognitive filters for agencies, which are natural and social, human and nonhuman, visible or invisible, foreseen or unpredictable. Their narrative porosity becomes therefore both the point where the world enters bodies and the point from which bodies deliver their stories to the world. In this junction, made of material, social, and cognitive mergings, material ecocriticism concentrates its analyses.

(Absent) Bodies

An interesting chapter of this story of bodies and porosity is to be found a few miles south of Naples, displayed in the dusty showcases of Pompeii's *antiquar-*

ium. It tells us about the eruption that in AD 79 affected a vast territory at the foothills of Mount Vesuvius, modifying life and landscape of the Neapolitan area.

Forgotten for many centuries, the site of ancient Pompeii had been rediscovered (and severely plundered) by the Bourbons, Naples's Spanish sovereigns, at the beginning of the eighteenth century, and finally identified in 1763. Over time, many bodies have emerged from the excavations. These were bodies that, covered with volcanic debris, had left their imprints in the solidified lava, so that one could see "the full form of the dead, their clothing, and their hair" (Beard 6). But similarly eloquent were other kinds of bodies, the absent ones. Here, again, porosity is part of the picture. As cyberneticians know, information is not only embodied in the *presence* of the object, in its material density; absent objects can also convey a message and a meaning. In other words, the void also possesses a semiotic dimension. Similar to Naples's buildings emerging from the hollows of the city, Pompeii's bodies emerged from their own absence, from the hollows they left in the petrified ash after decomposing. These absent bodies started materializing around the 1860s, via a technique developed to obtain casts of wooden doors, shutters, furniture, and other perishable objects. Like a photonegative, this void was charged with information; combined with plaster, it made it possible to look into that historical moment, literally giving a face to the—human and nonhuman—victims of the eruption.

From an archaeological viewpoint, the combination of excavated and "photonegative" findings, of plenum and void, constitutes a site full of narratives: narratives about social roles and gender practices, about what Bruno Latour calls assemblages and collectives, about human and nonhuman agencies in ancient everyday life. It is not by chance that archaeology is one of the fields in which the dialogue with the new materialisms has emerged more significantly.[3] Reading into the stratified natural-cultural ecologies of this place, the archaeological research has indeed opened windows on more-than-human realities both in larger visions and in little but meaningful segments. From the many examples that can be quoted, one is the discovery of small breads left in an oven where they were being baked when the upsurge started. Baked twice, both by human and by volcanic heat, these breads remained suspended in the twilight zone where intentionality is overcome by material agency, thus turning into an involuntary *mise en abyme* of the town swallowed by lava. Another compelling snapshot on this world of confluent forces is offered by the cast of a guard dog, suffocated by the ash and pumice in the hopeless attempt to get rid of his chain. With his bronze studded collar and the excruciating fear still visible in his (absent) face, the dog shared the same fate of a man, probably a slave, who died while trying to unshackle his ankles from the iron bonds that tied them. Like material texts emerging from the void, these plaster casts render the agony of human and nonhuman bodies in a pitiless combination with the agency of the elements and of socially constructed bindings.

But, following the tracks of porosity, I would like to focus now on another narrative, complementary to the one collected by archaeologists. In this intra-active narrative, the alternation of plenum and void—in terms of bodies, memory, and cognition—sheds light on the "emergent interplay" of agencies at work in the event of AD 79.

The surprise inscribed in these bodies is a key element of this narrative. When the German philosopher Karl Löwith saw the plaster casts in 1924, he commented, "Death took them in the middle of life, not leaving them, so to speak, the time of dying" (63; my translation). Although this might appear normal for people facing a natural cataclysm, in Pompeii the people's surprise reveals another important element of this story of presence-absence, density and void. Considered on a cognitive level, the volcanic eruption is a breach, an epistemic rupture in the mind of this place. For a long time Mount Vesuvius was believed to be a mountain. Some Roman writers had commented on the mountain's similarity to Mount Etna, an active volcano in Sicily, or conjectured about Vesuvius's being a volcano. Strabo, for example, had written that the summit "shows pore-like cavities in masses of rock that ... [look] as though they had been eaten out by fire; and hence one might infer that in earlier times this district was on fire and had craters of fire" (453). However, Vesuvius had been dormant for eight hundred years: the memory of its agency had simply disappeared from the general narratives about this place—thus, the epistemic (and physical) shock. As Jeffrey Cohen says, nature's active powers "surprise and then confound" ("Ecology's" xxiv).

In her essay "Landscape, Memory, and Forgetting," Catriona Mortimer-Sandilands has expressed inspiring considerations on the ties between memory, body, and landscape. Drawing from the medical research about Alzheimer's disease and from David Abram's ecophenomenology, she writes:

> Remembrance—the act of embodying an act or object or place or concept in some portion of the brain or another—is not solely a question of the remembering subject. Both the written page and the storied landscape are warehouses of memory that are external to the individual body. . . . [T]he act of remembering involves a recognition of a relationship between the body/mind and the external world that is not only determined by internal forces. The experience of memory is thus always already social, technological, and physical in that the conditions of the relationship between brain and object cannot help but be located in a complex range of conditions that offer the subject to the experience, and experience to the subject. (274)

There is, in other words, a mutual porosity, an intra-action, between individuals and their landscapes, both embodying, as Abram suggests, the mind of place (see Abram, *Becoming* and *The Spell*; Iovino "Restoring"). Lacking the recognition of the way the "relationship between the body/mind and the external world" could be articulated, these bodies express the surprise in the place's mind—a mind whose memory, Sandilands maintains, is "always already social, technological, and physical" ("Landscape" 274).

But the place's mind is, here, an amnesiac mind. Ironically enough, already a couple of centuries after Pompeii had been buried by lava, there was almost no memory of its site anymore. The excavations and the emerging of these bodies from the hollows of space-time-matter represent therefore another epistemic rupture. This is a clear example of how material agency and discursive practices mingle in shaping the human and nonhuman world—bodies, landscape, and memory. The world is not simply "fabricated" by discourses and cultural memory. There is a strong, deep, and complex interrelation between the agency of natural forces and the agency of cultural practices. The landscape of discourses, words, and conceptual descriptors melts with the landscape of elements, of geology, of telluric and atmospheric agencies, of biotic and ecosystemic balances. The case of these bodies—and houses, and things, and forgotten places—emerging from the underground levels of a buried city is dialectically complementary to the surge of lava from the body of a mountain. Being rich with signs and meanings, and therefore with information, both these bodies and the lava create a material-semiotic compound. In this compound, while the bodies inform (and narrate) about an almost forgotten complexity (the site of the ancient Pompeii), the lava informs (and narrates) about the forgotten orographic structure of this site, inhabited by volcanic and seismic agencies, even though believed to be "simply" a mountain.

The forgetfulness about the fact that every mountain has its own rhythms of motion, its telluric choreography, signals the human forgetfulness of nature's agentic force. The material correlation of memory and forgetting, however, is meaningful evidence about how society and nature cooperate in shaping "a world of complex phenomena in dynamic relationality" (Tuana, "Material" 239). If these bodies left their imprints and transmitted their narratives over time, it is because of the interstice opened by a combination of biochemical elements, environmental conditions, and geophysical energies over time. This interstice is filled with apersonal agency and is pervaded by forces that, as Jeffrey Cohen says, are inhuman per definition:

> *Inhuman* means not human . . . and therefore includes a world of forces, objects, and nonhuman beings. But *in-human* also indicates the alien within (a human body is an ecosystem filled with strange organisms; a human collective is an ecosystem filled with strange objects), and requires as well a consideration of the violently *inhumane*. ("Zombie" 271)

The "violently inhumane" can have many forms: a volcanic eruption, a virus, a falling asteroid, war, and even politics. Combined with human life, all these things shape "collectives" in which strange objects express their agency in pulsating porosity. What material ecocriticism suggests is that these collectives are dynamically contextual, their agency always porously "in the making" with an outside.

Taken in their process of becoming with the world—of intra-active embodiment—bodies display "the importance of context to human cognition," also in relation to memory: "Just as disembodiment require[s] that context be erased, so remembering embodiment means that context be put back into the picture" (Hayles 203). In this porous dimension in which bodies are absorbed by the world, and the world—in the form of lava or discourses—is absorbed by bodies, landscape is the material and cognitive context of memory. And it is, therefore, a transformative site of cognitive categories. If remembrance is "a recognition of a relationship between the body/mind and the external world that is not only determined by internal forces" (Mortimer-Sandilands, "Landscape" 274), then landscape is the deciding site where the relation of inside and outside, body-mind and world, gets reinforced or progressively erased. In the shadow of Vesuvius, an intra-action of multifarious elements produced an ironic phenomenon: just like the "natural" body of a volcano was forgotten in the evolving human narratives, the "cultural" and more-than-human body of Pompeii was forgotten only a couple of centuries after it was buried by the eruption.

In the choreography of agencies moving in the hollows and plenums of space-time-matter, the erratic emergences of naturecultures always surprise, and then confound.

Flesh and Skin

In 1944, just after the arrival of the Allied Army, another eruption hit the Vesuvian area. Curzio Malaparte (1898–1957), a former Fascist journalist who subsequently became a philo-American writer, described the event in his novel *The Skin:*

> The sky to east was scarred by a huge, crimson gash, which tinged the sea blood-red.... Shaken by subterranean convulsions, the earth trembled; the houses rocked at their foundations.... Vesuvius was screaming in the night, spitting blood and fire. Never since the day that saw the final destruction of Herculaneum and Pompeii, buried alive in their tomb of ashes and lava, had so dreadful a voice been heard in the heavens. (280)

The violence of nature and the violence of the humans over Naples's bodies go hand in hand in this controversial book, written immediately after the end of the war and published in 1949. Fiercely attacked by many Italian intellectuals of the time and even censored for the crudeness of its descriptions of Naples's "moral plagues" (in the English translation, several scenes and an entire chapter on an ancient ritual of "queer maternity" are missing), *The Skin* (*La pelle*) is the story about the "liberation" of Naples, occupied by the Allied Army in 1943. More than a novel with a traditional plot, the book is a memoir-like succession of apparently autobiographic episodes taken from the author's experience as an officer of the Italian Army. Having the function of facilitating the "interchange" between the Americans and "liberated" Naples, Malaparte himself seems to act as a membrane, a filter between these two different worlds. (This is also evident from the recurring usage of English expressions in the novel.) With his dense and provocative prose, Malaparte—who had already represented the brutality of World War II in his previous novel *Kaputt* (1944)—scratches the surface of this world of liberators and victims, pointing out the penetration of the "violently inhumane" (volcanic eruptions, war, corruption) into the city's flesh. Showing Naples's destroyed urban body and its innumerable wounded bodies (both human and nonhuman), Malaparte's novel represents how, coupled with the uncontrollable agency of nature, war and liberation create an unpredicted mixture of material and discursive elements that penetrate the skin of people and the land, irremediably changing them, leaving them without protection, either from the outside or from the inside.

The quoted passage on the eruption of 1944 is exemplary in this respect. Here, as in several other similar places, the author's rhetorical artifice of humanizing natural elements is evident, even excessive: the sky is disfigured and bleeds into the sea; the earth trembles in convulsions, and houses rock; the volcano screams in the night, "spitting blood and fire"; its "dreadful voice" is "heard" in the heavens. In spite of their apparent (at times naive and grotesque) anthropomorphism, however, these lines convey a complex vision of nature and history. In this vision, the volcanic eruption and the scars on land act as a counterpoint to the discourse about the city being "liberated" by the Allied Army. Even if war—the "violently *inhumane*" per definition—is apparently over, there is no liberation from the "violently *inhuman*" agency of the elements: an agency so gruesome to assault the body of the land itself and to make the elements "scream" in terror and convulsion. But something clearly emerges in this place suffering the tremendous aftermaths of the conflict: in front of the violence of both war and nature, everything is a body, and everything is ripped and exposed. Like the bodies of people and animals, also the land, the sea, the sky, and the volcano are bodies. The eruption and the war affecting the land's body play a natural-cultural mirroring game—again, a *mise en abyme*—with the eruption and war affecting the bodies of Naples. Saturating this porous corporeal "collective," a dangerous—sometimes terrifying—intra-action of agencies scratches every skin and penetrates every flesh.

In Malaparte's novel the skin is thus both a membrane and a metaphor: it is a medium for and a sign of the permeability of substances. Once the skin has been damaged, these substances—and elements, discourses, practices, and worldviews—enter in collision with each other, leaving bodies fully exposed to the "violently inhumane." As a result, all the oddities, the contradictions, and the "moral" ruins of this place are conjured up on the surface, materializing into Naples's bodies and their stories.

Among these bodies, the most vulnerable to the violence of "History" (the capitalized "History" that figures as the magmatic and obscurely agentic background in Elsa Morante's famous novel *La storia*) are those of the "innocents":

children, virgins sold to American soldiers, animals, and even rare fishes taken from the Aquarium to be served as a meal in surreal banquets.

All of these bodies, in Malaparte's book, are transformed into narrative agencies that testify to the entanglements of politics, violence, illness, moral discourses, and survival struggles in a city whose rich and glorious past seems to be turned into damnation. Naples's damnation, Malaparte suggests, is its failed transformation of the body politic into a real, modern, citizenry.[4] In the imagination of the city, the body is therefore everything: it is language, it is money, it is food, it is a battlefield, an abyss, and a fate. It is even a convulsive proscenium for queer sexuality, as in the censored episode "Il figlio di Adamo," "Adam's son" (*La pelle* 135–56). Invited by an American officer, Malaparte attends a secretly performed ritual of "queer maternity." In a villa at the foothills of Mount Vesuvius, a young man, disguised as a woman and surrounded by several other figures (Allied officers, male members of the local aristocracy, young peasants, and an old woman acting as a midwife), "gives birth" to a "little monster" (150), a baby-like wooden puppet. After this dramatic scene, pervaded by grotesque excitement, an orgy takes place. Here the puppet, which displays a huge phallus, similar to the augural priapic statuettes found in Pompeii, is taken in triumph and then dismembered.

Interesting comments could be made here, for example, on the connection between queerness, power, and pre-Christian rituals of generation.[5] However, this episode reminds us that the bodies of Naples are intrinsically hybrid and queer: in the novel and in the city's imagination, they are in fact male and female, human and nonhuman, sacred and impure. Seen in this light, the *Corpo di Napoli* is also a queer statue: a male body apparently breast-feeding its children. Even Parthenope, the nymph or siren who, according to legends, founded the city, is a hybrid being, halfway between the human and the nonhuman. In Malaparte's novel, Naples itself emerges as city and noncity: a preurban dimension inhabited by a historically porous collective of human and nonhuman forces, in which the human part waits to "progress" toward citizenry and reason. In this world, whose history is always hybridized with mythos, and whose bodies are always interspersed with all sorts of material-discursive agencies, the human "is determined in that no-one's land between myth and reason, in the ambiguous twilight where the living accepts to be confronted with the inanimate images delivered to it by historical memory, so that it can take them back to life," as Giorgio Agamben says (*Ninfe* 34–35, my translation). In *The Skin,* this queer and posthuman dimension is the other side of the Arcadian Mediterranean dream of (philosophical and physical) light and (natural and moral) lushness. Dark, violent, and queer, Malaparte's Naples is the Mediterranean's Underworld.

An uncanny continuity unifies the bodies that populate this porous Underworld. This is the continuity of blurred ontological boundaries: here all bodies, human and nonhuman, are metamorphoses of each other, blends of material elements in their formative and performative histories. But this porous interchange of substances is even more visible in the inescapably metabolic and quasi-cannibalistic dimension of life: as Malaparte insists, commensality and mutual ingestion are basic relations among Naples's bodies.

An interesting episode to be quoted in this context is that of "General Cork's Banquet." In a starving Naples, fishing in the bay has been prohibited due to the pollution caused by bombing (an element through which the trans-corporeal dimension of the environments of war is interestingly depicted). As a result, the Americans start eating fish from the Aquarium, and, in a gala dinner at the headquarters, a "siren" is served over a bed of lettuce and corals. In an expressionist crescendo of bodily details, this rare fish—here claimed to belong to the family of Sirenoidei—is described as having the look of a boiled little girl:

> In the middle of the tray was a little girl, or something that resembled a little girl. She lay face upwards . . . encircled by a large wreath of pink coral stems. . . . She might have been not more than eight or ten years old. . . . Here and there . . . the skin had been torn out or pulpified by the process of cooking, and through the cracks and fissures a glimpse was afforded of the tender flesh, which in some places was silvery, in others golden. . . . She had short, fin-like arms, pointed at the ends and similar in shape to hands with no fingers. . . . Her flanks were long and slender, and terminated, exactly as Ovid says, *in piscem*—in a fish's tail. . . . It was the first time that I had even seen a little girl who had been cooked . . . and I was silent. . . . All the diners were pale with horror.
>
> General Cork raised his eyes and looked at his guests. "But it isn't a fish . . . It's a little girl!" he exclaimed in a trembling voice.
>
> "No," I said, "it's a fish. . . . It's the famous Siren from the Aquarium." (235–36)

Besides the trustworthiness of the episode, which is closer to surrealism than to ichthyology and certainly a literary invention of the author's, in this context the idea of eating rare fish from an aquarium has a very powerful symbolic significance. It represents the devastation of a war serving on plates of the finest porcelain a library of evolution—a natural evolution, but also a symbolic-cultural one. The siren is part of the imagination of a city stemming from a "virginal" mermaid (the mythical Parthenope), and where even the virginity of the children's bodies is disrupted by the violence of war. Eating the siren is a "naked lunch" disclosing a material-symbolic abyss: it means, indeed, eating the substance and body of the city and ritually consuming its identity through a marine and evolutionary Eucharist. In this precultural cannibalistic dimension, the body of a fish is enmeshed with that of a human being, producing an intermediate and hybrid deity, which is here much more concrete, physical, and ontologically eloquent than the disembodied Spirit of transcendental theology. In this paradoxical ritual, metaphysics is turned into metabolism. *Parousía*—the advent and presence of God—is turned into porosity.

The fact that the diners (among whom military officers, a lady, and a Catholic priest) refuse to eat this meal, and the fact that, nevertheless, this humanlike fish is killed and cooked, recalls the dialectic antithesis between conscious and unconscious, totem and taboo.[6] It is a cultural self-censorship that clashes with war as a total openness and wildness, both corporeal and moral. And in fact, the territory, like its bodies, is now wildly open. War opens the corporeal breach, which is the breach wide open in the body of land, society, and the city. Trans-corporeality becomes here inter-corporeality, in the sense that there is no frontier in the attack to the bodies of Naples, even more if these bodies are sacred. Once sirens have been slaughtered, everything that happens afterward is simple corollary.

* * *

What are the stories of Naples's bodies *today*? The discussed examples have been chosen to answer this very question, because the stories they tell are still written in today's bodies. The first is a story of forgetfulness: an amnesia that—despite the plethora of popular songs and rhetorical statements—is still visible in the fissure between the Vesuvian people and their volcanic land. In fact, regardless of physical evidence, embodied cognitions, and any precautionary principle, in the local imagination Mount Vesuvius has returned to being "simply" a mountain, and it is covered with a crust of (mainly unlawful) constructions, which nearly reach the crater. The second is a story of violence and war: a violence and war pervading in many forms the flesh and skin of this land's bodies. These bodies are often toxic, absorbing in their porosity the millions of tons of pollutants illegally dumped in this region by the so-called ecomafia and its vast network of political complicities.[7]

All of these stories are written on the living bodies of Naples. They are bodies in which, like in Pompeii's plasters, an absence is often encapsulated: it is the absence of citizenship and of collective protection, the absence of a political ecology both of things and of humans. Here material ecocriticism veers into environmental justice. Here, as Marco Armiero and Giacomo D'Alisa write about Naples's waste crisis, "the very frontier between surrounding and surrounded is blurred up . . . placing human body at the crossroad of this meeting" (56). In a material-ecocritical perspective, it is not only the frontier between surrounding and surrounded to be blurred up, but also the frontier of the text. The body is a semiotic agency in its very materiality. It is *in* the body that the formative agencies at work in a place's life materialize and express themselves. Naples's bodies are texts, the city itself is a text, and its texture is its own narrative. It is a narrative populated by substances, choices, voices, human presences, illness, scars, memory, forget-

Figure 6.2. *The Sleep of Reason* (2012). Courtesy of Christian Arpaia.

fulness, natural catastrophes, war, contamination, fear, death, and life. The narrative agency of these porous bodies conveys the matter and discourses of their formative histories. In so doing, it creates ties of awareness that, disclosing the processes at work in these bodies' becoming, restore their political imagination. Here the role of literature and creativity is essential: when human creativity "plays" together with the narrative agency of matter, intra-acting with it, it can generate stories and discourses that "diffract" the complexity of our porous collective, producing narrative emergences that amplify reality, also affecting our cognitive response to this reality. In ethical and political terms, this has a great potential for a practice of liberation.

Here this Vesuvian antipastoral, filtered by my compound body-mind, temporarily pauses. This journey across storied matter of Naples, however, is not finished. The narrative crossroads where this city, like every other place, tells its stories through all of its bodies will continue to produce creative diffractions. This will happen through all those who, intra-acting with their complexity, will be part of the landscapes of porosity. Including you, reader. Because now you, too, are part of the story.

Notes

1. The term "ignimbrite" was coined by New Zealand geologist Patrick Marshall (1869–1950). See his essay "Acid Rocks" 1.

2. A recurrent word and a foundational concept of material ecocriticism, trans-corporeality has been firstly developed by Stacy Alaimo in her essay "Trans-corporeal Feminism" and in her award-winning book *Bodily Natures*. For a discussion, see Iovino, "Steps."

3. For the role of archaeology in the material turn, see *The Oxford Handbook of Material Culture Studies* and *The Cambridge Companion to Historical Archaeology*, both edited by Dan Hicks and Mary C. Beaudry. Particularly useful are, in our perspective, the methods of documentary archaeology, for which each body is a "body of evidence," a unique lens to visualize "past lives" in variable "scalar and temporal resolution" (Wilkie 13). See also the essays on archaeology and material agency in Knappett and Malafouris, *Material Agency* (in particular, Sutton, "Material Agency, Skill, and History"; and Yarrow, "In Context").

4. On this point, see also Iovino, "Naples," in particular the discourse of "thwarted citizenship."

5. For a reading of this scene in relation to the ancient gnostic cults once widespread in the region (Mithra, Zoroaster), see Albrile 17–18. On the tie between queerness and "race" under Fascism, see Benadusi 100.

6. Malaparte's comment about his having seen a "cooked girl" for "the first time" is also noteworthy, implying that the serving up of the bodies of Naples will be repeated in future banquets. I thank Elena M. Past for drawing my attention to this element.

7. See Armiero, "Seeing"; Iovino, "Naples," "Stories," and "Keyword." See also Past, "Trash."

7 When It Rains

Lowell Duckert

> Does life only make sense as one side of a life-matter binary, or is there such a thing as ... a life of the it in "it rains"?
> —Jane Bennett, *Vibrant Matter*

Responding to his country's record rainfalls in the beginning of the twenty-first century, British journalist Brian Cathcart seems to bring more of it. *Rain* makes a dreary forecast: "It is only when things go wrong that our dim consciousness of scientific meteorology rises to the surface" (66). French sociologist of science Bruno Latour would diagnose this tendency as "blackboxing." Focusing only on the *success* of a scientific or technological apparatus paradoxically renders "the joint production of actors and artifacts entirely opaque" (*Hope* 183).[1] When a meteorology machine runs smoothly, it produces factual climates that we can reasonably predict and accurately monitor. But an error (like an overflowing levee) exposes the box's inner complexities. For Cathcart, scientific analysis provides a false sense of security. We are to make a "managed retreat from the assumptions that science has the answers, that even if the price is high we can always buy protection, that we can cope with downpours and their consequences" (95). What are our options, then? If we cannot build better shelters, we cannot put off contemporary matters of concern like drought or acid rain, either. Arguing against inevitable catastrophe, Cathcart believes that only a "new humility" can shake our egocentric delusions of domination (89). Simply put, "there is no such thing as getting above the rain" (95).

For the "humility" it promotes (89), Cathcart's pocketbook rightly deserves praise. Yet I fear that *Rain* opens one black box known as "scientific meteorology" (66) only to box up another substance: its subject matter, the rain. The agency of rain is typically hidden until it falls irregularly or causes something to fail. (The timing of *Rain* is a case in point.) I want to rephrase Cathcart's warning against climate control as a way to open this "box" of rain: what if we stayed *in* the rain rather than held our egos and our knowledge systems *below* it? I am not merely caviling here. The preposition is crucial, as Michel Serres reminds Latour during one of their *Conversations*: "Pre-positions—what better name for those relations that precede any position?" (105). Pre-positions are directions to things as well as ways of plotting our relationships with them. While Serres prefers the phrase "fluctuating picture of relations" (105), Latour calls this model of relationality an "actor-network." For Latour, reality is composed of (non)human things known as "actants" that continually form alliances with human agents. Instead of a world divided into autonomous subjects and objects, we have assemblages, collaborations, "collectives."[2]

If you have ever been "caught" in the rain, you have made an alliance. Or perhaps you gained a new position by running "out of" it. Yes, rain *catches* us. Consider political scientist Jane Bennett's meditation on nonorganic life cited above: "Is there such a thing as . . . a life of the it in 'it rains'?" (*Vibrant* 53). Here rain is not merely a metaphor *for* life; it is lively and *a* life, life defined in her own words as "a restless activeness, a destructive-creative force-presence that does not coincide fully with any specific body" (54). According to Bennett's vital materialist philosophy, rain is "vibrant" matter, since "matter itself is lively" (13). Rain participates in her thought experiment. More important, rain materially represents *it*—pure immanence, affect, (a) life. Invoking the tired metaphor for procreation is something entirely different from recognizing rain's agency and (a) life. A living rain propels (non)human things into new relationships and new material embodiments; it showers becomings. Bennett's question identifies rain as wet matter movement that "makes the difference, makes things happen, becomes the decisive force catalyzing an event" (9). Rain does more than check anthropocentricity, then. Rain *does;* and when it rains, it manifests "*Thing-Power:* the curious ability of inanimate things to animate, to act, to produce effects dramatic and strange" (6).

The influx of rain in contemporary ecocritical discourse corresponds with the alarming rise (and fall) of water levels throughout the world.[3] Rain's (un)predictability is a constant source of frustration. So are its effects: one ecosystem's flood may very well be another's source of life. Rather than blaming rain for the problems it causes, I suggest that we listen to the rain, when *it* rains, more closely. The stories we tell about rain are also the stories rain tells about us. Cathcart's study is only one example. Manuel De Landa argues that human history is shaped by flows of nonhuman matter-energy, which results in "phase transitions" in our social organization. "Inorganic matter is much more variable and creative than we ever imagined" (16). Our narratives are likewise shaped by their material interactions. Latour's recent essay on "compositionism"—a notably ecocritical work—sees textual composition as an example of the collaborations (non)humans make. The "composed" is a capacious rubric: "It is time to compose—in all meanings of the word, including to compose with, that is to compromise, to care, to move slowly, with caution and precaution" ("Attempt" 487). Although rain is known to flood in a "flash" or take part in "the perfect storm," by paying attention to rainy texts, even if it means slowing down, we can imagine an ontological approach to ecology that builds upon epistemological modes—studies, for instance, that ponder the conditions for how and why our knowledge of climate change is produced (see Middleton, for instance). What stories has rain told? What stories can it tell? What "positions" can it still create?

What follows is a rainy actor-network mode of inquiry, an "ecomaterialism" full of "effects dramatic and strange" (Bennett, *Vibrant* 6).[4] Rain resists our attempts to know its intentions, yet it also resists drawing the separations between climate and culture, life and matter, and subject and object. As we will see, rain assembles (non)human collectives and hurls them across space and time. Rain *precipitates* in the literal sense: it actively "throws" things "headlong" and "causes" things "to happen."[5] Thus, any attempt to bridge the gulf separating human from rain, though admirable, is misguided. Taking another cue from Latour, rain dissolves the (false) break entirely: it "dissolves nature's contours and redistributes its agents" (*Politics* 21). Our shared bodies—texts included—derive from these material meshworks. My hope is that rain does not merely force us to "cope" with a showering world, but actually takes us to a better ontological humility, a co-implication of climate and culture, that has potential for more *humane* kinds of (non)human relations.[6]

In the Early Modern Rain

To guide us through my ecotheoretical downpour and its implications for material ecocriticism, I will turn to early modern literature. Premodern critics have lately faced the weather for good reason: exhibiting a remarkable "thirst for mixed connections" that Latour associates with pre-Enlightenment thought ("Attempt" 481), meteorologically minded authors, travelers, and thinkers of the period explored the turbulent relationships between climate and culture, and, in doing so, experienced the strife and pleasures of intersaturation (see recent work by Markley, Mentz, and Rudd). Meteorology slowly gained scientific momentum during this time. Derived from the Greek meaning "something raised up," *meteors* included all atmospheric phenomena.[7] Most studies borrowed heavily from Aristotle's *Meteorologica,* which emphasized constant interactions between the four elements, their qualities (hot, cold, warm, and moist), and the two types of evaporations drawn up by the sun (exhalations and vapors). Writers often adapted and interpreted Aristotelian philosophy—supplementing it with the Roman encyclopedic tradition of Pliny, for example—rather than accepting or rejecting his views outright. In general, rain was considered to be an atmospheric phenomenon of "vapor" with "cold" and "moist" attributes. "New scientists," aided with modern inventions such as the thermometer and barometer, would ultimately triumph over the irrational discourses of astronomy, astrology, and sublunar influence in the late seventeenth century. But it was a hard battle until then: both the *Meteorologica* and superstitious types of "forecasting" were current throughout the century.

One author introduces us to the intellectual climate a meteorological writer would have faced. William Fulke's *A Goodly Gallerye* (1563) was the first to use the word "meteorology" in English. Referencing Aristotle, Fulke divides meteors three ways: bodies "perfectly" and "imperfectly mixed," "moist impressions and drie," and "fiery, aery, watery, and earthly" (26). Rain results from clouds thickened by cold, tempered by hot winds, and melted into drops, "to geue encrease of fruict to the earth" (90). Rain has a power in this process, a fructifying force that "doth more encrease and cherishe thinges growyng on the earth, then any other water" (90). Even more so in his section on "monstruous or prodigious rayne": clouds mold worms and toads, form flesh, and even forge iron (93). Rain clouds are weird wombs of spontaneous generation so that "vermyn may be generated in the ayr, as they are on earth, without copulation of male and female" (93). As a Protestant clergyman, Fulke assigns these anomalies to God's ordered plan, "the vniuersall chiefe and last end of all thinges" (30). Despite declaring meteors as "body compounde with out lyfe naturalle" (25), Fulke's clouds suggest living precipitation indifferent to a divine plan or creator. His attempts to straighten out climatic irregularities through theological explanation betray an anxiety of uncertainty.[8] Through these cracks in his *Gallerye*, we can steal glimpses of climatic actor-networks. These are spaces others would inherit—others such as the French travel writer François Bernier.

Bernier (ca. 1625–88) lived during the reign of Louis XIV (1661–1715), a "new stage in the evolution of the institutions of learning" (Dew 16).[9] By the start of the 1660s, "Orientalist" scholarship in Paris needed reinvigoration. Through the efforts of Jean-Baptiste Colbert, Louis's minister and cultural patron, a more thorough reorganization of the Republic of Letters took place. Situated "between the cultures of curiosity and erudition" (Dew 40), baroque Orientalism would not have its heyday until the eighteenth century. Early Enlightenment publications had a marginal presence for several reasons: not only was it difficult for those interested in Asia to get access to sources, expertise, and printing facilities, but the necessary linguistic skills were hard to learn. Plus, travel writing was in high demand: "Only in the case of travel accounts (written by Europeans) can it be said that literature on Asia occupied a significant place in the seventeenth-century market for books" (Dew 39). This insatiable appetite for travel writing coexisted with an increasing taste for climatic literature as well. There was a push to *explain* meteorological wonders, not just describe them, and these hypotheses importantly sold (Heninger 33).

Enter what came to be known as *Voyages de François Bernier*: a personal account of his stay in India from 1658 to 1659. Despite Bernier's identifiable views on materiality—he promoted the skeptical-empirical philosophy of his teacher Pierre Gassendi and was a staunch supporter of Descartes—it is crucial to place Bernier within this period of European intellectual history that had not quite reached its Enlightenment pinnacle and inside a book market that could demand a multiplicity of perspectives over scientific precision and authenticity.[10] First serving the court of Danishmand Khan, a Persian merchant and eventual governor of Delhi, Bernier later became physician to the Mughal emperor Aurangzeb. Traveling extensively throughout India with the imperial retinue, he amassed an encyclopedic amount of knowledge. Published in French in four tomes (1670–71) and quickly translated into multiple languages,[11] Bernier's text is actually a collation of multiple texts: political history, mostly a record of the recent civil war and Aurangzeb's accession; personal letters, including a famous one to Colbert on the issue of private property; and scientific responses to the French polymath and explorer Melchisédech Thévenot. Members in Thévenot's circle aimed "to advance the natural-historical cause by making use of travellers" (Dew 131). Not only are the answers to Thévenot's inquiries the most vivid descriptions of the natural environment found in all of Bernier's correspondence, but they also detail his affective bodily encounters with the Indian rainscape. These short replies will be my focus. Here Bernier fully feels *it*, soaking up the connections and desires shared between (non)human things and narrating the open-ended becomings that result.

To be clear, I am not trying to impose postmodern theories onto early modern literature (or onto ecocriticism, for that matter). The *Travels* puts ecocriticism, theory, and early modernity into conversation, establishing Bernier as a theorist of living rain with insights into our current climates. His geographic location plays a critical role in this process. India's monsoons are prodigious events, spectacular deluges considered both catastrophic and life giving. Local languages of Hindi and Urdu in fact erase the "it" of English and French entirely. *Baarish hai* ("rain is") and *barsaat hai* ("monsoon is") signals (a) life of rain in its very syntax.[12] India is thus a contact zone on multiple levels—of East and West, human and nonhuman—that challenges our onto-epistemological conventions about how we know and interact with the world. Although Bernier retreats to the drier ground of reason and scientific calculation at times—as we will see in his second and third answers devoted to the monsoons—his fourth reply shows him in direct contact with living rain as he passes through the fertile kingdom of Bengal. The rainscape soaks his skin and text to points of pleasure as well as fear. Like him, we may reexamine our shared and soaky materiality with rain. But first we must visit the galleries of another Frenchman's house, Michel Serres, who invites us to see houses differently.

This Mold House

In *The Parasite*, Serres points out that "parasite" signifies three things at once in French: a biological eater, a human (social) parasite, and noise (static). But what Serres sees (as only he can) is relationality in action. The parasite is absolutely relational, *para-*, next-to, "[having] a relation only with the relation itself" (39). Each parasite tries to outdo its predecessor, spurred into parasitism by the sudden eruption of a third, *noise:* "A parasite, physical, acoustic, informational, belonging to order and disorder, a new voice, an important one, in the contrapuntal matrix" (6). The system "is parasitic in a cascade" (5). To inhabit this cascade is to enter collectives. Subjects and objects persistently switch positions, scrambling the ontological chain of command between host and interrupter. The system incorporates rather than paints over the "chance, risk, anxiety, and even disorder" that constitute it (14). Thus, fluctuation is no longer an affront to the house of reason: it is the very foundation upon which reason is built. For Serres, there can be no system without parasites. The cascade is far from a closed system; it invents new systems because of its (dis)equilibrium. Rather than "restoring" harmony to eco*systems,* then, we are better off allowing for disputability, error, and disruptions: "One must write . . . of the interceptions of the accidents in the flow along the way between stations—of changes and metamorphoses" (11).

Serres can be a deeply ecocritical thinker, of course (see Serres, *The Natural*). But a cascading thing like rain plays a little-acknowledged role in his parasitical model. Just as rain falls in a cascading form, rain's *noise* crucially reveals how the cascade works: it brings collectives "into order and disorder." In other words, the noise of the Serresian cascade is the same as the noise of rain as it cascades upon our bodies, our architecture, our constructed houses of life and knowledge. Let us briefly visit the house into which Serres's opening characters chase one another. La Fontaine's fable is *The Parasite*'s prime scene of parasitism. The country rat is chased into the house; the rat chases the farmer, the farmer chases the city rat, and so on. What is the noise in the first position?

> But the excluded one, just while ago, was making his way through the countryside; the passer-by goes out again in the rain that, as far as we know, never stops, beating incessantly on the roof of the host and guest. That noise too interrupted a process: a trip. And from this noise comes the story. Hosts and parasites are always in the process of passing by, being sent away, touring around, walking alone. They exchange places in a space soon to be defined. (16)

Rain. Noise generates the stories like Serres's "story" he examines and the overall story of *The Parasite* he produces. Recall that the Latin *imbrex* (roof tile) comes from *imber* (shower of rain).[13] In this passage, the literal meeting of rain and roof creates a type of rainy ecopoesis. Wet writer and world overlap, they *imbricate,* like drizzly roof tiles. Rain makes a lot of *noise* in Serres's household. Rain materializes a system in cascade: the (non)human characters in constant pursuit of one another across haphazard lines of poetic invention. These ramblings and errors are part of the process: "Mistakes, wavy lines, confusion, obscurity, are part of knowledge; noise is part of communication, part of the house. But is it the house itself?" (12).

Yes—and we must not mistake Serres's concern for the house as an act of redemption. He is showing us its mold. Although he is addressing the house of reason (or science) in particular, we can extend his argument further to the house (*eco-*) of ecology. In this dank house buffeted by the rain, we hear alternate voices—be it rain, farmer, or rat. The parasite offers an erring and errant kind of ecocriticism that denounces the human's role as prime parasite.[14] Rain reminds us that there are only things in relations and *as* relations, beings in cascade with everywhere to fall: "The thing is nothing else but a center of relations, crossroads or passages" (39). We leave one house only to find new relations in another(s). We are drawn in and out by the noise of rain as it swerves us in a cascade that "as far as we know, never stops." It is our "trip."

Spaces Soon to Be Defined: Monsoons

I have argued that rain's unpredictability, its endless possibility to link and disrupt things in cascade, helps us imagine new ways of being in the world. Travel is essential to this process. Now let us return to the *Travels* with Serres's noisy imbrications in mind. Bernier's body endlessly inhabits the cascade of relationships. Not just any drizzle will do, however: his travels through "space soon to be defined" depend on some of the world's wettest phenomena (Serres, *Parasite* 16). Europeans were enthralled by extraordinary climatic events such as unusual downpours. But most had never experienced the rain of South Asian monsoons. Monsoons are seasonal prevailing winds that typically blow from the southwest during May to September and from the northeast during April to October. Known primarily for the heavy rains of summer, monsoons last long enough to constitute a season: the "rainy season" known as *barsaat* in Hindi and Urdu. For the first European explorers to India, monsoons required acclimation. Robert Markley calls these climate-culture hybrids "monsoon cultures" ("Monsoon" 527). Such collectives promote a deeper understanding of rain's role within political ecologies and other material networks. There were certainly economic reasons to understand the rain: transportation was dangerous during these tempestuous months. And the embodied effects of rain were especially noted. Edward Terry complained of the painful monsoon climate during his brief stay in the Mughal Empire as chaplain to the English ambassador, Sir Thomas Roe (Markley, "Monsoon" 535–36). In short, monsoons are turbulent networks of wind, rain, and traveler. Even their etymology bespeaks a swirling nature: "monsoon" is a composite of merchant-travelers' tongues: Portuguese (*monção*), Arabic (*mawsim*), Turkish (*mevsim*), and Dutch (*monson*).[15]

Bernier's interest in the Indian monsoons reflects his era's fascination with extraordinary weather. His second reply to Thévenot—"concerning the Periodical Rains in the Indies" (431)—shows him at his most analytical. Bernier does not just describe the weather; he tries to explain it. The subcontinent is so hot that it would be completely "sterile and uninhabitable . . . if Providence did not kindly provide a remedy" (431). The remedy comes in July, when the rains begin their three-month duration. "The temperature of the air becomes supportable, and the earth is rendered fruitful" (432). Rain is the great fertilizer, understandably, and Bernier is careful to note that it merely *brings* life. The effect of rain is something easily noted. His more difficult task here is to accurately pinpoint the monsoons' "periodical" nature. The rains are predictable to only a limited extent: "They are never the same two years together," and they do not "descend undeviantingly" (432). The rains' beginning, end, and quantity depend upon location and vary from year to year. The rains come from different directions—usually determined by the proximity to the sea—and even if they originate in one location, they may not follow a direct course. In Delhi, for example, rain clouds form in the south but first appear in the east. These clouds "burst and descend in rain" by finding "some impediment" like landmasses or types of air that offer differing degrees of "resistance" (434).

It seems that the only thing predictable about monsoons is their propensity to deviate. What is more, because monsoons can commence in different regions and at different times, they challenge European notions of temporality. Time itself is upset. If the monsoon's arrival marks the onset of summer, for example, "summer is sooner" on the rainy coast of Coromandel than on the parched coast of Malabar (433). Bernier essentially discovers the combined flux of weather and time. Serres playfully notes how the French language, in its "wisdom," uses the same word for weather and time, *le temps*. Like time, "meteorological weather, predictable and unpredictable, will no doubt some day be explainable by complicated notions of fluctuations, strange attractors" (*Conversations* 58). Bernier's rainy "day" has come. European seasons certainly fluctuated in time and experienced drastic changes.[16] Yet the idea of an (un)predictable season that encroaches on temporal borders is uniquely complicated. Monsoons are periods of rain that resist "periodical" stability. They reveal time's messiness. Thus, any knowledge of rain always arrives soon: maybe after *this* point, sometime indefinitely in the future, but not *now*. Like the rain, time is ever fluctuating, never complete, a substance always "soon to be defined" yet escaping definition.

The "strange attractor" of rain will not let up, compelling Bernier to define his subject matter—and soon. What is rain? Adding a scientific "dissertation" about its materiality (433), he conjectures:

> The heat of the earth and the rarefaction of the air are the principal causes of these rains which they attract. The atmosphere of the circumjacent seas being colder, more condensed, and thicker, is filled with clouds drawn from the water by the great heat of the summer, and which, driven and agitated by the

winds, discharge themselves naturally upon land, where the atmosphere is hotter, more rarefied, lighter, and less resisting than on the sea; and thus this discharge is more or less tardy and plentiful, according as the heat comes early or late, and is more or less intense. (433)

Bernier's description resembles our modern rain cycle. In the simplest terms possible, the sun evaporates seawater to make vapor, vapor rises and condenses into clouds, water falls upon mountains as rain, and rain makes rivers that flow back to the sea. According to him, the sun's heat draws moisture from the water into the colder air above (evaporation), thereby making clouds (condensation) that later "discharge" upon the land (precipitation). True to the times, he explains these reactions in Aristotelian terms of attraction and opposites: the "heat of the earth" and the "rarefaction of the air" are opposed to the "colder, more condensed" watery vapors. But there is little room for living rain in his estimation: being "agitated" and "driven" to "discharge" robs rain of its vibrant materiality by rendering it passive or acted *upon*. Bernier resists the possibility. Even if rain *causes* life, the question of whether the monsoon's rain has *a* life is set aside (for now). Uncertainty simply requires more analysis. Therefore, the quandary over summer commencing sooner in some regions than it does in others "may be owing to particular causes which it would not perhaps be difficult to ascertain if the country were properly examined" (433). His second inquiry ends with this hint of eventual certainty. The "periodical rains" in the Indies organize into elements to be defined later—or so he hopes—despite their ability to disrupt Eurocentric notions of time and expose the limits of scientific analysis. Bernier's imaginary survey is a piece of a climatic puzzle he believes he can complete but can never truly finish.

In his third inquiry, "concerning the Regularity of the Currents of the Sea, and the Winds in the Indies" (434), Bernier tries to attach some sort of "regularity" onto the deviating Indian climate. Point by point, he describes when and in which direction the sea courses and the wind blows, which season has "doubtful and variable winds" perilous for travelers (434), and the difference between the Europeans' and the Indians' navigational skills (although the former is "greatly superior," he admits, sea wrecks are common for both) (435). Monsoons allow him to explain the entire globe's regulative movements. Going from micro (India) to macro (world) in scale, he proposes three conditions: the earth is composed of three bodies: air, water, and earth; it is suspended in a "free and unresisting space" where it would be "easily displaced if it came in contact with any unknown body"; and as the sun moves toward the poles, it "depresses" them and creates tilt. In doing so it "conducts and draws along with it both the sea and the wind" (436). As one pole is elevated, "the sea and the air, which are two fluid and heavy bodies, run in this declension" and thus "constitut[e] the *Monsoon-wind*" (436). In this extraordinary schema lies Bernier's hope. If only the earth's surface were unanimously free of intercepting landmasses, he believes, "regularity would reign generally" (437). Bernier's hypotheses indicate a desire to order the disorders of *le temps*. He seeks a kind of cosmic smoothing. Yet trying to disentangle the monsoons' mysteries through scientific practice leads him to more entanglement. His monsoonal analyses are "mangled," to quote Andrew Pickering, "an evolving field of human and material agencies reciprocally engaged in a play of resistance and accommodation in which the former seeks to capture the latter" (23). The monsoon is material agency that resists "capture" as well as captures the observer.

Incredibly, Bernier's desire for regularity's "reign" becomes an *acceptance* of the irregularity intrinsic to systems. He makes an unprecedented confession in the middle of his third response: "I wish it were in my power to trace every effect to its true cause; but how is it possible to unravel these profound secrets of Nature!" (435). Capitalized "Nature" is not a vault of natural laws waiting to be cracked. In this case, Bernier realizes that these "secrets" truly are "profound" because they "unravel" without end. Analysis is meant to unravel the knot at hand in the hope of reaching the "true cause" or direct route into an object's nature. Serres reminds us that "analysis," which comes from the Greek *analusis*, "action of loosing or releasing, fact of dissolving," always enacts a proliferation: "Proliferation becomes a condition for analysis or the result of its practice. To untie is to create profusion" (*Senses* 301).[17] The inexplicable nature of the monsoon makes it a knot that leads to new knots in various directions. Bernier jettisons the "providential" concept that tethered weather writers such as Fulke to a totalizing, even if unknowable, center. Instead, he supplicates himself before "Nature" in order to explore those shifty spaces "soon to be defined" (Serres, *Parasite* 16). Monsoons usher in the reign of irregularity that is always coming at you, and *soon*, over and over again. And if one body may knock the earth out of place, it does so, importantly, into another body. The fourth inquiry brings all of Bernier's data under (low) pressure. Rain washes away the illusions of human centrality and analytical enclosure. In Bengal he discovers an incredible desire to be knocked loose by rain bodies and have them penetrate the all too permeable barriers of human skin and knowledge.

Rainscapes of Desire

Like the rest of Thévenot's inquiries, Bernier's description of Bengal comes at the end of the *Travels*. The significance of this little appendix for a rainier ecomateriality cannot be overestimated. Bernier's interactions with the "fertility, wealth and beauty of the Kingdom of Bengale" are his closest encounters with the Indian rainscape (437). Bernier can think only of inferior comparisons in order to describe the country: "The pre-eminence ascribed to *Egypt* is rather due to *Bengale*" (437). It is a lively place, one that attracts foreign merchants along with asylum seekers such as Christians, Portuguese, and half-castes fleeing Dutch persecution. With its free and unmolested exercise of religion, Bengal models a vibrant cosmopolitanism. Above all, Bengal offers pure "abundance": rice, sugar, animals, and fruits; drugs and butter of the best quality; beautiful and amiable native women; and an illimitable variety of precious commodities such as silk (439). "In a word, *Bengale* abounds with every necessary of life" (438–39). Noting his own attraction, he reiterates a well-known proverb: "The Kingdom of *Bengale* has a hundred gates open for entrance, but not one for departure" (439). The country absolutely swells with diverse agents in mixture and exchange, all moving across energetic networks. Bengal is a place of utterly expansive heterogeneity.

Although the weather is noticeably absent from his introductory descriptions, the general atmosphere is a force to be reckoned with. Just as the Bengali kingdom is open to foreign visitors, so, too, are its inhabitants' bodies. Bernier displays the people and its sicknesses more impartially than other travel writers: "It is fair to acknowledge . . . that strangers seldom find the air salubrious, particularly near the sea" (441). The earliest Dutch and English strangers faced annihilation. Now Europeans exercise more caution, meaning that they drink "less punch," and the masters of ships do not allow their crews "so frequently to visit the *Indian* women, or the dealers in *arac* and *tobacco*" (441). Bengal is full of biological parasites that find a way to enter the human via its air or commodities. Bernier remains reassuring: "I maintain that those who live carefully need not be sick, nor will the mortality be greater among them than with the rest of the world" (441). He diminishes the dangers of Bengal by leveling its air with the "rest of the world." By this logic, insalubrious air is not exclusively Bengali because unwholesome air (like venereal disease) is pandemic. Thus, Bernier's cultural descriptions cannot be fixed to simple dichotomies of *them* and *us*. Expanding this point demonstrates that the human body cannot be divided from its material (Indian) enmeshment, either. "It is fair" to resist placeholders such as *this* healthy air and *that* sickening air when comparing climes, but it is even "fair[er]" to challenge the ontological division between climate and corporeality, nonhuman landscape and human body, altogether.

The Bengali waterscape is one "fair[er]" way to situate Bernier in the (non) human coconstitutiveness I am implying. Bengal gets its beauty from the "endless number of channels" cut from the Ganges that transports merchandise and provides water "reputed by the *Indians* to be superior to any in the world" (442). Towns and bountiful fields dot the channels nearly a hundred leagues in length. Bernier's interest in the unending quality of these waterways shows an interest in a more circuitous method of description, one in stark contrast to his monsoonal analyses. At one point, he enters what must be the Sundarbans region in the Bay of Bengal: "But the most striking and peculiar beauty of *Bengale* is the innumerable islands filling the vast space between the two banks of the *Ganges*" (442). His experience with the infinite islands around him encourages an archipelagic imagination.[18] A new kind of analysis built upon multiplicity and fluidity emerges. Thinking like a river—in terms of identifiable sources or "causes" we saw earlier—meets the effusiveness of the delta. Because the "extremely fertile" islands have "a thousand water-channels run through them, stretching beyond the sight" (442), Bernier inhabits a true place of pre-position. The water has no perceivable terminus—only embarkations that open up new horizons. The delta houses flowing things and relations that, traveling through their "passages" and across their "channels," also pass through things. When Bernier dwells in the delta, he gains a different perspective on the "secrets" of scientific experimentation: meaning becomes a series of interconnected islands that lead to other "innumerable" islands. Linear models of travel and knowledge are useless in such an environment. And with this change in analysis importantly comes a change in embodiment. Bernier's body becomes deltaic, a channel within channels of (non)human things.

There are dangers on the delta, of course. Pirates and swimming tigers snatch victims alike. But if both sorts of kidnapping expose his fears of entanglement, the "striking . . . beauty" of Bengal significantly relates its pleasures (442). Bernier's realization in the Bengali delta sets him up for his rainiest encounter. Perhaps he finally overcomes his penchant for linear and closed systems of analysis because he does not have an ostensible destination while in Bengal. In his discourses with Thévenot, he had the explicit natural-historical charge to "communicate whatever observations" he had regarding the monsoons (428). When he recalls his nine-day journey "from *Pipli* to *Ogouli,* among these islands and channels," then, his newfound sense of fluidity is put to the test (443). Ogouli is an endpoint, arguably, but it is a point among a host of other points that distract him, intervene, and reroute his movement. And what emerges along the way? For nearly a week and a half, "no day passed without some extraordinary accident or adventure" (443). Moreover, the "extraordinary" accidents that befall him—those interceptions "one must write" about, says Serres (*Parasite* 11)—are meteorological. Bernier's narrative trip to Ogouli is actually a series of trips.

On the second night, Bernier and his men bed down in a "snug creek" beyond the main channel (444). With the boat tied to a tree and at a safe distance from tigers, he keeps watch. *What* he watches exhilarates him:

> While keeping watch, I witnessed a *Phenomenon* of *Nature* such as I had twice observed at *Dehli*. I beheld a lunar rainbow, and awoke the whole of my company, who all expressed much surprise, especially two *Portuguese* pilots, whom I had received into the boat at the request of a friend. They declared that they had neither seen nor heard of such a rainbow. (444)

Aristotle considered rainbows to be a phenomena of reflection caused by clouds opposite the sun or moon (Heninger 240). Like the descriptively ambiguous nature of rainbows (something in between water and light), Bernier is on the brink of consciousness as well. The rainbow seems like a hallucination (somewhere in between material and immaterial). According to biblical tradition, the rainbow represented God's promise to Noah (and mankind) after the Flood. Never again would rain destroy the earth. Life in postdiluvian times therefore meant a life of peace and futurity. But the rainbow is not just a sign or comprehensible wonder Bernier wants to narrate to others. Following what Latour has called the slight "surprise" of action, the rainbow surprises him, and his companions, with its agency (*Reassembling* 45).[19] The lunar rainbow is an actant that makes a *"Phenomenon of Nature"* (444). The rain infiltrates Bernier on the river and catalyzes a series of events: it moves him emotionally and holds his gaze ("I beheld"), and then it transports him physically as he scrambles to notify the others ("I . . . awoke"). His decision to awaken the company and share his experience with the rain is a powerful moment of collaboration made between rain, light, and human (to name just a few participants). Though "twice observed" at Delhi, it is when Bernier inhabits the vibrant Bengali waterscape that the rainbow's true colors—as a cascading collective—become clear. The biblical covenant had forestalled destruction. What Bernier witnesses on the bank is a (non)human contract that promotes creative connections instead.

The rain(bow) proves to be a catching thing, initiating a cascade of activity and setting actants adrift. On the third day, Bernier and his men are literally drifting, "lost . . . among the channels" (444), when Portuguese salt makers put Bernier's party back on track. That night the watch changes: "My *Portuguese,* who were full of the strange appearance on the preceding night, and kept their eyes constantly fixed toward the heavens, roused me from my sleep and pointed out another rainbow as beautiful and as well defined as the last" (445). Who is watching whom? For the Portuguese, the rainbow is that object at the center of relations, the atmospheric thing upon which their attention is "fixed." The "heavens" interact as well, "filling" the men with its "strange appearance." Being suddenly "roused" expectedly discomforts Bernier, who quickly grounds himself in his scholarship: "You are not to imagine that I mistake a *halo* for an *iris*" (445). Yet he quickly abandons his treatise to focus on his arousal: something "beautiful" and "well defined." Although "well-defined" in his estimation, the rain once again crosses temporal definitions. Rain takes you somewhere other than authoritative realms—*it* takes you to new places in space and time. "Thus you see that I am more happy than the ancients, who, according to *Aristotle,* had observed no lunar rainbows before his time" (445). Once an "ancient" before the dawn of lunar rainbows, Bernier is suddenly rushed into Aristotle's time of first light, and finally into a modernity in which these rainbows may be more than "twice observed." Ultimately, Bernier's nighttime encounters are pleasurable ways to compose with the rain. The rainbow invents collectives and the routes for them to travel. Was not Iris both the Greek goddess of the rainbow and the gods' messenger? Bernier's eye is the meeting point of iris and Iris, a lively conversation between human and sky, eye and rainbow. It is a "beautiful" thing.

Bernier's ecological equanimity abruptly discontinues. On the fourth night, the air is "so hot and suffocating that we could scarcely breathe" (445). Glowworms seemingly ignite in the air, and Bernier fears the same incendiary relationship between his body and the landscape. But the unbearable heat proves to be the least of his worries; the worst is when it rains. A torrential storm catches him unawares on the fifth night. The company attaches the boat to nearby trees for safety. When the cable breaks, Bernier is forced to hug trees for several hours: "Our situation while clinging for our lives to the trees was indeed most painful; the rain fell as if poured into the boat from buckets, and the lightning and thunder were so vivid and loud, and so near our heads, that we despaired of surviving this horrible night" (445). The elements viciously attack the men. Far from the rainbow's surprise, the rain's "painful" affect produces pure terror. Raindrops harass human skin; the noise of rain rattles their senses. One could argue that Bernier's entwinement celebrates rain's ability to connect—as in the more mediators, the better—or that it even discloses a strange love for trees. But the relationships he makes are clearly meant for human life preservation. To do anything else would be "inevitably to perish" (446). There is no way to get "above the rain" (Cathcart 95). Bernier inhabits the cascade, and his body nearly unravels in the rain's "profound secrets" he had tried to trace—rain's "*Thing-Power*" to the extreme (Bennett 6).

Once beautiful, now catastrophic, rain precipitates Bernier into near destruction on the fifth night. Rain is utter turbulence. Still, it is rain's (un)predictable nature that swerves him into uncertain collectives—and thus into sites of potential. Indeed, his trip is not yet over; it is raining again. Rain continues to create new passages and pushes his *Travels* onward. Arriving at Ogouly four days after the storm, Bernier arrives in a rainscape of desire:

> Nothing, however, could be more pleasant than the remainder of the voyage. We arrived at *Ogouly* on the ninth day, and my eyes seemed never sated with gazing on the delightful country through which we passed. My trunk, however, and all my wearing-apparel were wet, the poultry dead, the fish spoilt, and the whole of my biscuits soaked with rain. (446)

The same cruel rainscape transforms into "delightful country." And as the rain passes through his body, Bernier becomes rain-man. His eyes are washed over, and, never "sated," they are incapable of being filled. His relationship with the rainscape at Ogouly is entirely based on desire rather than lack: (non)human desires to touch and be touched, to cohabit, and to interconnect. Rain fills without a point of fulfillment. "Nothing . . . could be more pleasant" than being caught in and by the rain. His eyes, like his body, remain open-ended and ready for "more." Bernier is constantly gazing, always absorbing, and energetically on the move. He ends his inquiry (and, shortly thereafter, his *Travels*) with this Bengali rainscape of desire. In a wet way, he brings us back to where we have always been: in a cascade of (non)human things that takes us on both "painful" and "pleasant" (446) journeys.

Whenever it rained, Bernier reacted widely: exhibiting scientific control (the discourses on monsoons), composing a beautiful contract (the lunar rainbows), braving turbulent contact zones (the storm en route to Ogouli), and desiring intersaturated becomings (to be soaked without satiation). Whether it is embraced or not, whether drizzly or diluvial, living rain resists any solid position. Rain (dis) joins actants, simultaneously interrupting and inventing collectives. Drip by drip, we have seen where rain took Bernier. Rain is a trip to *both* pleasure and catastrophe. In his masterful reading of Serres's parasite, Julian Yates describes "agentic drift": "a way of representing agency as a dispersed or distributed process in which we participate rather than as a property which we are said to own" (48). "Agentive drift" characterizes the distributed agency of rainscapes—and we, like Bernier, may "drift" into newer ecological assemblages. So whither rain?

Latour's compositionist manifesto is close at hand: "We need to have a much more material, much more mundane, much more immanent, much more realistic, much more embodied definition of the material world if we wish to compose the common world" (484). Our precipitation-participation begins by hearing the rain on our rooftops, feeling it on our bodies, and listening to the stories it tells. At the same time, we need to reexamine the kinds of stories we are told and the types of embodied experience we narrate. Bernier's *Travels* might be preimperialist, yet it does not take an avowedly postcolonial ecocritical reading to connect his narrative to the eventual colonization of India and the harmful extraction of its resources. The ethics of the cascade need to be explored as well. Within Bernier's rainscape of desire, after all, "the poultry [is] dead" (446). And what might rain desire? These are important starting points for our own inquiries. A theorist of living rain like Bernier shows us to be always already (with)in rainy weather. Once we realize that a house (*oikos*) "out of" the rain is illusory, once we stop tiling our houses of reason in vain efforts to protect them, we begin to build new houses altogether. *Together.* So let *it* rain.

Notes

1. For more on black boxes, see the introduction to *Science in Action*. A smart survey is in Harman, esp. 36–47.
2. Latour's *Reassembling the Social* is an excellent introduction to actor-network theory.
3. Currently, "new ecologists . . . see constant change and instability as fundamental to natural systems" (Mentz 139).
4. Watch for *Ecomaterialism*, the special issue of *postmedieval* 4.1 (2013) I edited with Jeffrey J. Cohen.

5. See *Oxford English Dictionary*, s.v. "precipitation," both noun and verb.

6. Latour again: "*The more nonhumans share existence with humans, the more humane a collective is*" (*Hope* 18; emphasis in the original).

7. What follows is from Heninger's extensive study of Renaissance meteors.

8. Jankovic believes this dilemma was pervasive, from early modernity to Enlightenment: "The history of meteorology may . . . be conceived as an effort to resolve . . . uncertainty, or, better yet, as a series of recurring failures to do so" (16).

9. My brief survey is a condensed version of Dew 16–40.

10. In his letter to Jean Chapelian, Bernier belittles the "superstitions, strange customs, and Doctrines of the Indous or Gentiles of Hindoustan" (300). The letter is typically noted for its attack on astrology, among other spiritual traditions. See Dew 131–67. I read Bernier's scientific foundation as inherently unstable. Rain, we will see, challenges his Enlightenment logic.

11. Henry Oldenburg of the Royal Society published an English translation in 1671. I will use a different English translation, *Travels in the Mogul Empire,* translated by Archibald Constable. For consistency, I will refer to Bernier's text henceforth as the *Travels.* Page numbers are Constable's.

12. *Shukriya* to Jonathan Gil Harris for bringing this to my attention.

13. See *Oxford English Dictionary*, s.v. "imbrex," noun; and "imbricate," adjective and noun.

14. Serres does not put it mildly: "History hides the fact that man is the universal parasite, that everything and everyone around him is a hospitable space. Plants and animals are always his hosts; man is always necessarily their guest. Always taking, never giving" (*The Parasite* 24).

15. See *Oxford English Dictionary*, s.v. "monsoon," noun.

16. England's Little Ice Age (roughly 1350–1800) is a case in point. See Markley's climatic reading of Shakespeare, "Summer."

17. See *Oxford English Dictionary*, s.v. "analysis," noun.

18. See Ghosh for a gorgeous modern example. Characters reference Bernier, visit the same area, and replay key scenes from the *Travels.*

19. "Action should remain a surprise, a mediation, an event" (Latour, *Reassembling* 45).

8 Painful Material Realities, Tragedy, Ecophobia

Simon C. Estok

THE BIOLOGICAL, CHEMICAL, and material bases of human ontology constitute central sites of investigation and theoretical comment for material ecocriticisms. If we understand pain as a fundamental part of human ontology, then we must also understand that *theorizing matter* profits from understanding the importance of relationships among cultural representations of pain, matter, and environment. Building on "a field that defines itself by a neologism (*ecocriticism*), based on another neologism (*ecology*)" (7), as Middlebury Shakespearean ecocritic Dan Brayton has recently described ecocriticism, material ecocriticisms seek both to further complicate and to further define what it is that ecocriticism pursues and how. For a movement such as ecocriticism, which has sought, from its inaugural moments, to cross disciplinary boundaries, to avoid intellectual isolationism and hermeneutic sequestration, and to connect with and affect the material world, engaging with new and evolving theories about matter is fundamental and vital—indeed, it is surprising that these theories and developments came so late in ecocriticism's history. Out of the welter of books and articles that have recently appeared relating to material ecocriticisms, human bodies have reappeared as the site and source of concerns about our changing relationships with the material world. These bodies are often a site of beleaguerment from a threatening "outside." They are, in Iovino and Oppermann's terms, "material narratives" about the way human corporeality is dangerously entangled within a complex of discourses and material agents that determine its very being. Because imagining a menacing alterity of the natural environment (an otherness often represented as ecophobic life-and-death confrontations for humans) means imagining materials and their intractable grip on our lives and deaths, the utility of theorizing about ecophobia for material ecocriticisms through discussions about pain (and about threats of pain) can help not only to illuminate theoretical connections that allow us to see how we participate in the systems we critique but also to contextualize what it is about nonhuman agency that evokes such strong resistance (philosophical and material).

We take agency outside of ourselves as threats. It is precisely these nonhuman agentic forces that determine so very much of our environmental ethics: the felt or imagined material effects of these forces, the felt or imagined material threats, the felt or imagined challenges to our existence (and forget the obverse side, for a moment—the good, the sustenance, the pleasure, and so on), the felt dangers of material agencies beyond us simply do not fit into any friendly epistemological familial mesh we may design, and history speaks to this; we have a history of what Freud called "the will to mastery, or the will to power" ("The Economic" 418), a history of hostility to agentic forces outside of ourselves, variously articulated as a will to live, as a pleasure principle, as existential angst. Ecophobia is part of this history, of how we respond emotionally and cognitively to what we perceive as environmental threats and as a menacing alienness. Influencing both the human self and its more-than-human surroundings, ecophobia is itself an "embodied narrative" about how humans both materially and discursively construct such environmental alterity.

Scholars and artists have long known and worried about the agentic capacities that reside well beyond and threaten the human. Stacy Alaimo and Susan Hekman note that the materials owning these agentic capacities are imbricated in a "mix" in which each element "interacts with and changes other elements in the mix, including the human" (7). These interactions and the fears they evoke about our own transience, about the transience of our corporeal materiality (no doubt the basis of so much thinking about *immateriality*—spirituality, theology, metaphysics, and so on), are the basis of material ecocriticisms. These fears are important. In the very simplest of terms, the contempt and fear we feel for the agency of the natural environment (a cultural tendency I have elsewhere defined as "ecophobia" and discuss more below)[1] need theorizing because they allow for conceptualizing the material-discursive junctures, the ways (and, more important, the implications of how) "materiality is discursive," as Karen Barad has put it ("Posthumanist" 140).[2] Conceptualizing the natural environment must, therefore, be seen as the effect of what Hans-Georg Gadamer terms an "interactionist ontology," a coinage and position Nancy Tuana productively embraces and develops. It is, Tuana explains, "an ontology that *rematerializes the social and takes seriously the agency of the natural*" ("Viscous" 188; emphasis in the original).

As the center of each of our own universes, the human body is the expressive site upon which material agencies flow and are reworked (not as a passive element but as a coplayer), as Alaimo has aptly shown. It is this body that we seek to protect, and as "we shelter ourselves from the harrowing vulnerability of bodied existence" (Abram, *Becoming* 7), the drama we encounter is enacted by, on, and through our body: "The body, revealing the reciprocal interferences of organisms, ecosystems, and other substances, is a living text in which ecological and existential relationships are inscribed in terms of health or disease" (Iovino, "Steps" 137). Our bodies are, in other words, the narrative agents that reveal both our exposure to and our participation in this complex of relationships. The diseases, the pain, the threats, and the increasingly new material realities of existence that we try to keep at bay, to forget, and to will away are the source and guarantee of much human knowledge, and it is therefore perhaps not very surprising that humanity has such a penchant for agony, suffering, and pain, for the tragedies that take discursive enactment through the bodies of human and nonhuman animals.

Our penchant for agony and suffering takes form, among other sites, in tragedy. As a Shakespearean by training, I would surely be remiss not to remember that definitions of tragedy almost invariably elevate and ennoble the concepts of pain and suffering. Gilbert Murray argues that tragedy "attests the triumph of the human soul over suffering and disaster" (66), George Steiner that suffering "hallows" the victim as if he/she "had passed through fire" (10), and Terry Eagleton (summarizing Schiller) that "the protagonist shakes himself free from the compulsive forces of Nature and exultantly affirms his absolute freedom of will in the face of a drearily prosaic necessity" (32). The "unfathomable agencies of Nature," Eagleton goes on to argue in his summary of Percy Shelley's idiosyncratic views on the topic (33), are at least in part the antagonist that the tragic hero faces. This nexus of suffering, identity in crisis, and the "unfathomable agencies of Nature" has implications that move far beyond generic definitions, especially in light of the fear of material agencies outside of the body—agencies that often threaten to dissolve us—that we find at the very core of ecophobia. It is here that the new materialist approaches can prove a useful supplement in helping to delineate matters and narratives of ecophobia (or vice versa).

Ecophobic personifications of the natural environment as a kind of terrorist at once assert and efface material-discursive emergences and narrative, at once voice and voice-over. Observing the act of *witnessing* things such as Katrina means observing enormous narrative efforts to order and control, efforts to contain the very things that cause fear and fascination, that attract and repel. The material *and narrative* agency of Katrina is both (among a great many other things) terror and tragedy.[3] The conceptual isomorphism between Terror and Tragedy, it would seem, therefore, warrants some attention.

It is not simply that both Terror and Tragedy attract and repel, that both compel "us to approach with sympathy and recoil with alarm" (Douglas-Fairhurst 62), that both exploit our aversion toward unpredictability, that both stimulate our distaste for violence against our own agency, and that both present unequivocal notions of right and wrong: they both also assert a relatively firm ecophobic stance, a stance whose enthymematic assumption presupposes that it is ultimately the human (not the nonhuman natural) that takes ethical and ontological priority and has agency. Although it is time to be done with these enormously destructive and arrogant kinds of assumptions, mainstream media (not to mention the genre of tragedy) profit from continuing to pump them out.

There is a large and growing corpus of filmic and media material proffering an implicitly ecophobic vision of a Nature that will finally conquer humanity, will reclaim all of the world, and will remain long after humanity is gone. While the educational value of these materials is heavy, no less weighty are the assumptions they carry and reproduce, assumptions that are part of (and therefore in some ways perpetuate) the problems. It is important to respond to these, especially when they reach a global audience, as they do in reportage, filmic, or cyber media. Like food once eaten becomes a part of the body, the unacknowledged positions embedded in such media once consumed become part of a fallacious material ethics.[4] We unwittingly reproduce these unacknowledged positions. Even in the dazzlingly brilliant *The Age of Stupid*, we hear uncritiqued Alvin DuVernay III describing his experience of Katrina in terms that epitomize an "ethics" that is part of the problem, not the solution: "You stare Mother Nature in the eye. Usually, she's fairly benign. Then she comes along, methodically, ruthlessly. And then she stands toe-to-toe with you and dares you. *Dares* you: 'Go ahead and get your best equipment out. Go ahead. Do it. Let's dance.'" Sexist, anthropomorphic metaphors of a malevolent nature are not going to help. This is not the kind of agency—gendered, emotional, and calculating—that material ecocriticism is talking about.

Perhaps gendering Katrina is inevitable, given the clearly female name of the storm; perhaps this is why even Nancy Tuana uses the feminine pronoun "herself" ("Viscous" 206) to describe the storm; and perhaps it is okay to ignore the material implications (both for women and for the natural world) of using sexist, anthropomorphic metaphors of a malevolent nature. Perhaps, on the other hand, however, so doing exacerbates the problems; perhaps so doing is something we (audience, scholars, all of us) let slip by, thinking it does no harm; perhaps so doing is (and I hope this does not seem dogmatic and judgmental) as bad as using racist slurs or homophobic phrases or comments clearly offensive and outside of the boundaries of free speech. Recognizing agency in nonhuman materials only through ecophobic lenses is on the same side of history as racist fears of African American agency, sexist fears of women's agency, ableist fears of the differently ableds' agency, homophobic fears of queer sexuality, and so on. Ecophobia must be addressed. "Believing that human agency will win out over other forms of material agency" (Tuana, "Viscous" 197) is not a safe bet. When Andrew Pickering argues that the world "is continually *doing things,* things that bear upon us . . . as forces upon material beings," he is talking about agencies that humanity has tried to capture, control, and rein in to "a field of facts and observations" (6). The "business of coping with [the] material agency" (6–7) of the world is the business of maintaining boundaries and, indeed, of maintaining discursive control.[5]

Pain, Elaine Scarry long ago argued compellingly, has the capacity to rip away discursive control and to dissolve human identity. Pain is "language-destroying: as the content of one's world disintegrates, so the content of one's language disintegrates; as the self disintegrates, so that which would express and project the self is robbed of its source and its object" (35). Pain dissolves the boundaries (at least in our heads) of the body while forcing the sufferer to recognize or imagine material agency outside of that body, and it becomes difficult "to maintain one's extension out into the world" (33). For many of us, there is no fear greater than the dissolution of our bodies—that way lays death.

Fear of a loss of agency does strange things to people. Fear of the loss of agency and fear of the loss of predictability are what form the core of ecophobia, and it is a fear of a loss of agency alone that is behind our primary responses, at least, to pain, death, and even sleep. Although history shows that we seem to like pain, proximity is the key here: pain *at a safe and controlled distance* is fine. The stage of Tragedy, like the apocalyptic films that have recently been flooding the market, achieves that control of distancing us from the material realities that surround us. Perhaps all the world is a stage, but all of the stages are not the world.

The arrogance of humanism is its belief that all of the stages *are* the world. Positing the notion of agency in matter, material ecocriticisms challenge human exceptionalism and unseat humanity from its self-appointed onto-epistemological throne, its imagined singular embodiment of agency, subjectivity, and ethical entitlements.[6] Literary representations of such unseatings have tended not to be celebratory; tragedy does not celebrate the rise and preeminence of the self but rather mopes and whines about its impossibility, an impossibility rooted in isolation. The spatial and environmental dimensions of tragedy chart connections, connections that make impossible the preeminent self.

What is at stake here for the human is beliefs in its own agency, autonomy, and, of course, superiority. David Ehrenfeld's lyrical discussion of humanism, though dated, still speaks directly to these matters:

> Anyone who copes regularly with Nature has met the winds, frosts, droughts, floods, heat waves, pests, infertile soils, venoms, diseases, accidents, and general uncertainty that it offers in succession or simultaneously. The primitive way to confront this darker side is with toil, and the human faculty of invention has ever worked to lessen that toil. Small wonder that humanism, which elevates our inventiveness to divine levels and celebrates it as infallible, has been embraced by many of those who believe they have been released from toil.... What are the implications of this way of thinking about humanity and Nature? (10)

One of the implications is that there is a *lot* at stake here with this way of thinking about humanity and Nature.

As Diana Coole and Samantha Frost convincingly show in the introduction to their collection entitled *New Materialisms*:

> What is at stake here is nothing less than a challenge to some of the most basic assumptions that have underpinned the modern world, including its normative sense of the human and its belief about human agency, but also regarding its material practices such as the ways we labor on, exploit, and interact with nature. ("Introducing" 4)

This seems an echo of Rosi Braidotti's 2006 comment that "what is at stake is the very possibility of the future, of duration or continuity" and that what is required for such a future "is a regrounding of the subject in a materially embedded sense of responsibility and ethical accountability for the environments she or he inhabits" (137).

Put together in an essay in this way, the image of so many people claiming that so much is at stake appears slightly hyperbolic, an odd kind of celebration of the singularity and importance of human agency, which is unfortunate and certainly unintentional. Even so, the inescapable fact that the human is central to the humanist project is clear: redefining our relationship with the world around us means redefining our sense of who and what we are.[7] Nothing else will work. There are, moreover, limits to our redefinition of ourselves. We live finite lives. This is nonnegotiable. We eat, drink, piss, and shit. These are nonnegotiable. We feel pleasure. This is nonnegotiable. We feel pain. This too is nonnegotiable.

At the core of all of this is matter, and the matter realities of our bodies, the pain we feel, the deaths we move toward, even the sleep that we have each night, constitute the core both of our existence and of the orders we have designed and on which we have come to rely. The control of materials (and people) constitutes so very much of the self-mythologizing of humanity that a loss of both that order and control is, to put it bluntly, dangerous. This is a point that Mary Douglas made almost a half century ago now. Douglas argues:

> Granted that disorder spoils pattern, it also provides the material of pattern. Order implies restriction; from all possible materials, a limited selection has been made and from all possible relations, a limited set has been used. So disorder by implication is unlimited, no pattern has been realized in it, but its potential for patterning is indefinite. That is why, though we seek to create order, we do not simply condemn disorder. We recognize that it is destructive to existing patterns; also that it has potentiality. It symbolizes both danger and power. (95)

Imagining the power and the danger of nonhuman agency often means imagining threats to human control. Being a part of diverse narratives with potent material effects, ecophobia turns nature into a fearsome object in need of our control, the loathed and dangerous thing that can result only in pain and tragedy if left in control; as Neil Levy so aptly puts it, though, "We are not in control of the non-human world, because we are unable to predict with any accuracy the effects of our actions upon it" (210). It may very well be true that, as archaeological theorist Christopher Tilley asserts, the natural world often "structures an entire series of values and attitudes that pervades the manner in which . . . people live" (50) and that from early times, people have sought "to establish a structured series of correspondences between an ordering of nature and an ordering of culture" (20); however, whether we are talking about these correspondences or similar nature-based scientific approaches such as biomimicry,[8] the order that is being patterned is (at the moment, at any rate) resolutely human, resolutely in the service of the human, and resolutely troubled by all of the things that make us human—our biases, our fears, our illusions, our delusions, our obsessions, and so on.

We are obsessed with the pain of others. We are glued to CNN reports on flatscreens that offer us Katrina, Sendai, Banda Aceh, and other disasters. These events "have a visceral, eye-catching and page turning power," as Rob Nixon explains, a power that materializes the present and dematerializes more longue durée emergencies (3). Nixon wonders "how can we convert into image and narrative the disasters that are slow moving and long in the making, disasters that are anonymous and star nobody, disasters that are attritional and of indifferent interest to the sensation-driven technologies of our image world" (3). Nixon's concern is with bringing issues into public consciousness, a task to which narrative is eminently well suited. As I have argued elsewhere (see Estok 2010), it is a strength of narrative to take nonnarrative science (and, indeed, sometimes very technical science) and to make it compelling: "Presenting technical information in narrative form," as William Kittredge explains in an interview with Terre Satterfield and Scott Slovic, "helps readers [and listeners] to internalize values, make them their own, emotionally, as necessary to life rather than simply interesting or distracting, as platforms from which to act" (22, 25). Narrative translates.[9] Narrative translates data (sometimes to audiences that may not be at all interested in data). Narrative translates values and ideologies. Narrative translates ethics. The ethical assumptions we wittingly and unwittingly consume through disaster narratives are materially consequential. Accepting blitheness about our involvement with agencies quite beyond us is a dangerous thing. Nixon's concern has to do with the failure to see the embeddedness of the self in "a process of interacting agencies" (Iovino, "Steps" 138) that encompass a temporal space stretching backward and forward, a big space that extends beyond the space of the moment. New media enjoy the moment and represent it well. Nixon is asking about moving beyond the moment.

Wai Chee Dimock similarly asks about the possibilities for representing these big material realities, some immediate and some slow, that define disaster and tragedy: "What sort of analytic language can capture this kind of plot, featuring a large-scale, nonhuman actor, on the one hand, and large-scale human casualties, on the other? In everyday speech, of course, we never hesitate to use the word 'tragedy'" (68). In the classical definition of tragedy as the fall of a person from a high place to a low place, perhaps vulgar uses of the term to describe the human consequences of environmental events are not so very far off. Tragedy is the failure to see the self as embedded in materials with "interacting agencies," to accept the intercourse and conflict between agencies that are material and agencies that are more self-originating.

Delusions about human exceptionalism and anxieties about human puniness and mortality inhere in our obsessions with pain, in CNN, and in the genre of tragedy. Such is certainly a position with which Terry Eagleton would seem to agree. Discussing the genre of tragedy, he ponders that "perhaps the form [of tragedy] satisfies our desire for immortality, leading us to a sense of being indestructible as long as this magnificent poetry pulses on" (26). This anxiety about natural cycles (for instance, the cycle of life) and contempt for its constituent parts (death being one of them) resonates deeply in tragedy. "But," Stephen Greenblatt might respond, "nothing—from our own species to the planet on which we live to the sun that lights our days—lasts forever. Only atoms are immortal" (6).[10] It is these atoms that have recently caught the eye of the new materialists and ecocritics.

The current theorizing in quantum physics marks a radical—indeed, paradigmatic—break, in some ways, from previous notions about the material world, how we relate with it, and how it relates with our bodies.[11] One of the effects of this work is to give scientific credence to what ecocritics (and others before them) have long known: we are all interconnected; current theorizing moves us one step further and forces us to recognize the foundations and implications of this interconnectedness. Things that are not us have agencies that determine us and are themselves emergent narratives. Understanding those emergences, the narratives in which we are embedded,[12] is delusional. We cannot. They are too big, and we are—after all—only human. But one of the effects of recognizing our embeddedness in materials of interacting agencies is to compel an ethical rethinking of our behaviors. When Jane Bennett, discussing our bodily implications with the material world, asks if we would "continue to produce and consume in the same violently reckless ways" if we took these involvements seriously (*Vibrant* 113), we are forced to question with her the implications of considering pain—not only our own pain but also the environmental pain implicit through our embeddedness with the world.

Although pain is obviously the essence of our own embodiment, scant attention has been focused within ecocritical circles on theorizing of pain as constitutive of our ontological and material boundaries and realities (and the processes sustaining them). Theorizing about ecophobia through discussions about pain, as I have shown, allows material ecocriticisms to source resistances to notions of nonhuman agency. It also allows us to see that our own (perhaps sometimes hardwired) aversions are clear bases of some ecophobic drives. It allows us to see the centrality of ecophobia to tragedy. It allows us also to see the failure of mainstream filmic and news media to transcend ecophobia and rather to cook it up and serve it as a sort of hidden ingredient. Theorizing about ecophobia through discussions about pain allows us to see the thick materiality of our embeddedness, an embeddedness synonymous with *involvement* in processes of interacting agencies. The task of the ecocritic is to see these connections. Praxis—real praxis—starts with theoretical connections that allow us to see how we participate in the systems we critique. Jane Bennett maintains that "a newfound attentiveness to matter and its powers will not solve the problem of human exploitation or oppression, but it can inspire a greater sense of the extent to which all bodies are kin in the sense of [being] inextricably enmeshed in a dense network of relationships" (13). To read these connections in all their narrative materiality is surely the goal of ecocriticism.

Notes

1. Because the term is central to the discussion here, it is appropriate to spend a bit of time discussing this "cultural tendency to relate antagonistically to nature" (Brayton 226). Although there is undeniably a biophilic impulse in humanity, there is equally an undeniable impulse to imagine badness in nature and to market that imagination. This is the very stuff that tragedy is made of. Ecophobia, while often the imagining and marketing of badness in nature, is perhaps more accurately seen as the marketing of nature's perceived or imagined unpredictability. It is the unpredictable (and often inexplicable) power imagined in nature that dooms characters in tragic narratives, both vulgar and classical. When we recognize that ecophobia is located in representations of nature as an opponent that hurts, hinders, threatens, or kills us (regardless of the philosophical value or disvalue of the ecosystemic functions of the dynamics being represented), we see a play such as *King Lear* quite differently. We begin to see that nature is not some background or backdrop to the tragedy. Tragedy, after all, is the frustrated assertion of human agency in the face of those "unfathomable agencies of Nature" about which Terry Eagleton has spoken. A play such as *King Lear* is vivid in its foregrounding of environmental unpredictability, its dramatization of a king powerless before nature, of a king who is victimized by the weather, unhoused, and alienated.

The prevalence of ecophobia, in spite of the enormous investments in ecologically progressive narratives, strongly suggests that contemporary economic systems need varieties of ecophobia (fear of bugs or loathing of bodily odors or ethical disregard for animals, for instance) in order to continue functioning. It would not do for Al Gore (to take one example) to advocate for and succeed in *stopping the use* of fossil fuels—the system would grind to a halt; nor would it do for Pete Postlethwaite (to use another example) to use his voice to shut down the meat industry either. On the matter of ecophobia, capitalism and environmental ethics seem in many ways incommensurable. See also Estok "Theorizing," "Narrativizing," and *Ecocriticism*.

2. Nancy Tuana presents a similar position, articulated with a symmetry reminiscent of Louis Montrose's famous formulation of "the historicity of texts and the textuality of history" (20): Tuana speaks of the urgency of recognizing "the materiality of the social and the agency of the natural" ("Viscous" 210).

3. The concept of narrative agency has been introduced by Serenella Iovino in her essay "Toxic Epiphanies: Dioxin, Power, and Gendered Bodies in Laura Conti's Narratives on Seveso." For an extended discussion of this notion, see the introduction and Serpil Oppermann's essay in this volume.

4. Stacy Alaimo uses the term "material ethics" (*Bodily* 130) as a kind of follow-up on Karen Barad's argument that "ethics is about mattering, about taking account of the entangled materializations of which we are a part" (*Meeting* 384).

5. Although there perhaps does not yet seem to be a compelling case for Alaimo's position deeming matter "literate" ("Trans-corporeal" 244), there is certainly an urgent case for seeing the textuality of matter. Serpil Oppermann, in fact, maintains that *the fundamental problem facing ecocriticism . . . concerns representations of the material world as the realm of the extra-textual*" ("Ecocriticism's" 155; emphasis added). Whether we deem matter "literate" or not, it is possible (and necessary) to see the textuality of matter without fallacious missteps. This whole issue is reminiscent of earlier conversations within ecocriticism about the "voice" of nature. Some theorists argued that the environment speaks and that we may somehow be the voice piece for this speaking (Jim Cheney in "Postmodern Environmental Ethics"), and other theorists argued—in response—that there is no other "language source other than the human brain" (Peter Quigley in "Rethinking Resistance"). This is a worrying debate because it is pointless. Lawrence Buell sensibly maintains that to articulate the natural environment entirely on its own terms is futile: "The constraints of human perception, and of art, make zero-degree interference impossible" (*Environmental* 81), a position that Cate Sandilands addresses in claiming that "speaking nature is impossible: there cannot be an authentic voice of nature without profound revision of either the notion of speech or the notion of the speaking subject" ("From Natural" 80). At this stage, we have to *wonder* about the very possibility of abandoning anthropocentrism, yet we also have to agree with Christopher Manes that it is time to dismantle the model where "a certain kind of human subject . . . only speaks soliloquies in a world of irrational silences" (25).

6. Stacy Alaimo makes a similar point discussing what she terms trans-corporeality (examined and defined vigorously elsewhere in this volume; see, for example, Alaimo's essay "Oceanic Origin, Plastic Activism, and the New Materialism at Sea"). Citing Andrew Light and Holmes Rolston III, Alaimo maintains, "If the predominant understanding of environmental ethics has been that of a circle that has expanded in such a way as to grant 'moral consideration to animals, to plants, to [nonhuman] species, even to ecosystems and the Earth' [Light and Rolston 7], trans-corporeality denies the human subject the sovereign, central position" (*Bodily* 16).

7. This redefinition of who and what we are will have to involve, as Braidotti notes, "a shift away from anthropocentrism, in favor of a new emphasis on the mutual interdependence of material, biocultural, and symbolic forces in the making of social and political practices" ("The Politics" 203–4). This is not to say that we *can* actually salvage the term "humanism": although it *may* very well be possible to do so, such is not the goal of this chapter.

8. In the opening pages of her extraordinary *Biomimicry: Innovation Inspired by Nature*, Janine Benyus defines "biomimicry" in beautifully poetic terms (worth quoting in full) as follows: "You'll meet men and women who are exploring nature's masterpieces—photosynthesis, self-assembly, natural selection, self-sustaining ecosystems, eyes and ears and skin and shells, talking neurons, natural medicines, and more—and then copying these designs and manufacturing processes to solve our own problems. I call their quest *biomimicry*—the conscious emulation of life's genius. Innovation inspired by nature" (2).

9. I use the word "translate" in its original Latin sense, meaning "to carry across."

10. If longings for immortality are rejections of the body and the agential realities of the material processes of life, no less than anorexia nervosa is a rejection of the body and its material agencies and needs, then it is entirely fitting to see this all for what it is: ecophobia. No one would balk at calling the denial of women the right to vote sexism or the denial of LGBT people the right to teach in elementary schools homophobia, so recognizing the rejection of the body as ecophobic is hardly provocative.

11. A comparable event occurred in the early modern period with anatomies. The revolutionary break with the premodern, the ancient, and the classical—initiated by Andreas Vesalius—

is a pivotal redefining in Europe with relationships toward the body, among people, and with nature at large. It is a pivotal move toward the Enlightenment with a collapsing of certainties in the old hierarchies that organized previous ways of thinking, a collapse that heralded enormous new regimes of control over nature.

12. I prefer to use the term "embedded" than "enmeshed" because it gives a sense of what we might see more as a "thick materiality" than simply as the multiple linearities implied by mesh images.

9 Semiotization of Matter
A Hybrid Zone between Biosemiotics and Material Ecocriticism

Timo Maran

A BASIC CLAIM OF the newly developing field of material ecocriticism appears to be that matter has agency and embodied meanings and that it is possible to decipher this matter in the framework of textual criticism. As Serenella Iovino has put it in her *ISLE* introductory essay on material ecocriticism, "The 'material turn' is the search for new conceptual models apt to theorize the connections between matter and agency on the one side, and the intertwining of bodies, natures, and meanings on the other side" ("Stories" 450). Material ecocriticism, she continues, "comes from the idea that it is possible to merge our interpretive practice into ... material expressions" (451). Such an approach raises broad philosophical questions, such as the following: In which ways is the agency of matter expressed? How do we interact with material processes? What are the relations between meanings embodied in matter and our representational practices?

Quite similar issues have been addressed within biosemiotics, a discipline that studies semiotic and communicational processes in and between organisms. After all, all biological organisms live in a certain physical location and under certain physical conditions of the environment, which they need to perceive, respond to, and adapt for. Biosemiotics describes such relations as being based on signs and sign exchange by employing concepts such as *codes* and *coding*, *Umwelt* (the species-specific attachment to the environment, organized by meanings; see J. Uexküll, "The Theory"), and *semiotic niche* (Hoffmeyer, *Biosemiotics* 183), among others.[1] At the same time, there is a crucial difference between material ecocriticism and biosemiotics; whereas the former has taken a critical approach to human social and cultural processes, the latter has not. The common ground between material ecocriticism and biosemiotics, rather, appears to be foremost in their attentiveness to the connections between the physical realm and meaning processes. With this understanding, I wish to consider a biosemiotic view on what can be called the "semiotization" of matter, namely, how human actions change the semiotic properties and signification of matter. I believe this is a preliminary step that will increase the potentially fruitful interchanges between biosemiotics and material ecocriticism. This chapter includes three subsequent arguments in three sections: a demonstration that matter has the potential to initiate meanings and participate in semiotic processes, a demonstration of different ways that humans and nonhuman animals can make sense of material objects and environments through the process of modeling, and a conclusion that by applying such models back to the material environment, humans semiotize matter by altering it based on human perceptions and understandings.

A challenge for biosemiotics has been to rethink the dualistic distinction between semiotically active humans and a semiotically inactive nature, as overcoming this distinction appears to be a prerequisite for treating nonhuman biological organisms as having semiotic and communicative capacities. In doing this, biosemiotics has relied heavily on the works of Charles S. Peirce, who developed a philosophy and understanding of semiotics based on the principle of continuity as an alternative to both idealism and realism.[2] Although there is a diversity of views present within semiotics, the Peircean interpretation that I am presenting in the first section of this chapter shows that material structures are capable of influencing representations and other semiotic processes; this approach could be fruitfully used to consolidate the theoretical framework of material ecocriticism. Adopting a nondualistic philosophy is a precondition of analyzing relations and effects between matter and human-semiotic activities (including the semiotization of matter). Such analysis is carried out in the final sections of this chapter.

The second major argument focuses on the concept of modeling, which can be used to describe processes by which living organisms make sense of and relate to the environment. The theory of modeling developed by American semiotician Thomas A. Sebeok, Russian Estonian cultural semiotician Jury Lotman, and other theorists appears to be a useful tool with which to postulate a methodological distinction between "matter" and "model," as well as to demonstrate the relations between them—in other words, between structures and properties of matter, on the one hand, and our interpretations, depictions, and representations, on the other. Distinguishing types and layers of modeling makes it possible to address the issue of the anthropomorphization of the nonhuman semiotic sphere by human culture and science, a topic that has been a serious concern for biosemiotics. It also allows for further distinctions to be made between the way humans and nonhuman animals use their models to change the material environment.

In the third section of this chapter, I will focus on the semiotization of matter by asking what happens if we constantly create models of the material world and subsequently base our actions on these models and interpretations; that is, what if we transform matter according to our human perceptions and understandings? With the help of Jakob von Uexküll's concept of the "functional cycle" (a schema demonstrating the cyclical relations of the subject and the environmental object), it is possible to show that an organism's activities of perception and action lead to the semiotization of matter and the growing imprinting of semiotic patterns into matter. We see that because of such feedback loops in the contemporary human-influenced environments, the borders between the material and the semiotic realm become blurred. This could raise practical environmental problems, as matter semiotized by humans contributes to the degradation of the habitats of many endangered species, which are not able to perceive and interpret human-altered environments adequately.

Semiotic Potential of Matter

In order to make material structures and processes the object of a study, it is first necessary to demonstrate how matter relates to human textual discourses and semiotic practices. This relationship is not self-evident and needs special attention, as there are a number of scholarly traditions, from Berkeleyan idealism to French postmodernism, that diminish the role of material processes for human discourses. Opposite views are presented, for instance, in the philosophy and semiotics of Charles S. Peirce. I am proposing a particular interpretation of Peirce's theory about the relation of matter and signs that reinforces the argument that matter influences meanings and interpretations to a great extent. According to this view, not only human-made artifacts but all natural objects have the potential to direct semiotic processes.

For a theoretical explanation of this assumption, we should turn to the basic concept of semiotics—the sign—and consider the way Peirce understood it. A sign, according to Peirce, is a "triple connection of sign [*representamen*], thing signified [*object*], cognition produced in the mind [*interpretant*]" (*Collected Papers* 1:372).[3] Our interest in this definition lies predominantly in Peirce's conception of the object, which according to him can be further divided into two aspects: the "immediate object," which is the object as it is revealed within the sign itself, and the "dynamical object," which is the object that exists outside the sign. The dynamical object we know by "collateral," that is, through indirect knowledge (Peirce, *Collected Papers* 8:314). For instance, "In the example of animal tracks, the immediate object would be the knowledge of an elk as it appears to us by looking at the tracks, and the dynamic[al] object would be the elk as it is, or the elk as the sum of all other experiences of it" (Maran, "An Ecosemiotic" 83).[4] The crucially important point in Peirce's approach to the object is that it allows us to treat material objects and perceptions of them as being connected to each other.

An important property of the object is its ability to trigger or determine the sign. As Peirce notes, a "sign [is] anything which is so determined by something else, called its Object" (*Semiotic* 80–81).[5] As this definition highlights it, there is a causal aspect of the sign process in any given semiotic universe, or *Umwelt*. The sensation of burning, the temperature indicated on a thermometer, and traffic lights, among other signs, force us to make certain types of interpretations, and overcoming the limits of these interpretations, although possible, requires additional interpretive effort. Without this causal aspect, we could hardly talk about "semiotic causation," described by Jesper Hoffmeyer as the "causation of bringing about effects through interpretation . . . , as when, for example, bacterial movements are caused through a process of interpretation based on the historically defined needs of a sensitive system" ("Semiotic" 154). This causal aspect is especially important if we consider the sign's object (*sensu* Peirce) to be an environmental or physical object. There are features of the environment (for example, the physical terrain, gravity, water and weather conditions, open and sheltered areas) that trigger signs and indeed influence interpretations and subsequent behaviors. For instance, the sight of pebbles of a particular size can initiate pecking behavior among waterfowl, as the pebbles are interpreted as being suitable to be swallowed as gastroliths (small stones that help waterfowl to break up the food in their stomachs).

Peirce describes the types of relationships between what is perceived (the sign or *representamen*) and what is referred to (the object) to distinguish between three types of signs: icons, indices, and symbols. This typology is relevant for our discourse in that it positions the symbolic signs used by humans correctly among the other sign types and shows the relation between each sign type and reality. In icons, this relation is present solely because of similarity (for example, the color red signifying blood). In indices, the relation exists because of a physical relation or causation (for example, a higher value in the thermometer signifies a warmer temperature). In symbols, finally, the sign (or *representamen*) is related to its objects because of habit or convention (for example, a national anthem signifies a particular country). Peirce's typology brings out an important theoretical point in regard to the question of whether there are meanings in matter: it demonstrates that the existence and specific features of icons and indices are dependent on the specifics of their objects. Structures and properties of matter direct and constrain our interpretations of them, in cases where we rely on indices or icons for our interpretation, due to the causal relationship between sign and object—based either on qualitative similarity (in icons) or on physical relation (in indices).[6] However, the symbol, the most developed type of sign, can preserve its integrity outside of any particular relation and can thus form the content of a cognition or culture without any reference to what is "out there."

Based on the distinction originally made by Augustine (II 2, 3), icons and indices could be described as natural signs, which are opposed to conventional signs. A classic example of a natural sign (an index) is smoke as an indication of fire. In this example, the development of the sign is easy to track: from the causal link between fire and smoke to the limited scope of possible interpretations of the smoke as standing for fire. One peculiar feature of natural signs is their relative independence from the interpreter. Smoke stands for fire for humans and for numerous other species of mammals, birds, and insects, including bees—this is what makes peat smoke a valuable aid in beekeeping. When handling bees, the beekeeper uses a smoker to puff smoke into the beehive. The smoke is interpreted by the bees as a sign of an approaching forest fire. This sign process prevents the alarm behavior of the colony and keeps the bees busy consuming honey as a precaution for the possible abandonment of the hive.

Peirce's typology of signs demonstrates the important role of environmental properties and material structures for semiotic activities. This understanding may have important outcomes for ecosemiotics (a discipline within biosemiotics that explores the semiotics of environmental relations), as it highlights the interdependence of human cultural processes and the richness and diversity of the environments in which these processes take place (see Maran, "Locality"). A nondualistic view of human culture and nonhuman nature draws attention to the particular properties of an environmental or material substrata, as well as the necessity of having appropriate conceptual tools for describing them. One useful concept in this respect is that of "affordance," as proposed by American perceptual psychologist James J. Gibson. Gibson defines affordances as follows: "The *affordances* of the environment are what it *offers* the animal, what it *provides* or *furnishes,* either for good or ill" (127). He specifies:

> The composition and layout of surfaces *constitute* what they afford. . . . [T]o perceive them is to perceive what they afford. This is a radical hypothesis, for it implies that the "values" and "meanings" of things in the environment can be directly perceived. Moreover, it would explain the sense in which values and meanings are external to the perceiver. (127)

Most examples provided by Gibson are related to the physical activities of animals: a surface that affords support, terrain features such as slopes and steps that guide movement, and so on. We can also define affordances in a more specifically semiotic sense as those environmental elements that have a tendency to act as objects of signs. Such elements could be physical areas, such as hybrid zones between biological communities, animal trails in the landscape, water currents, but also temporal events, such as seasonal rains, forest fires, and the melting of the snow. Such elements and events "stand out" from the rest of the environment; they have peculiar or important structural relations with other elements of the environment that allow them to function as "anchor points" for semiotic processes.

Charles S. Peirce's continuity-based philosophy and semiotics give strong support to the view that material objects may initiate meaning. This is not the same as saying that there is a sign process taking place in matter regardless of any reference to living organisms. Rather, the result is that we cannot talk about meaning content without considering the organism in its environmental context. If material structures are often a precondition of sign processes, then these material structures and sign processes should be studied within the same framework. A common interest between biosemiotics and material ecocriticism could be identifying environmental objects with semiotic potential for living organisms and studying how these objects function in multispecies environments, as well as how they trigger semiotic processes and narrative sequences in human culture. For instance, signs of drought could initiate changes in the behavior of humans and nonhuman animals alike, as well as influence human culture by motivating the creation of mythical narratives, art, and literature; this is especially evident in arid environments (see Pálsson).

Models We Make, Models We Use

Although all living beings are capable of participating in semiotic processes and using signs, there is something uniquely specific to human's semiotic competence as compared to that of other living organisms. Humans are capable of writing and reading poetry, calculating predictions on population growth, and compiling algorithms that allow us to assemble technical equipment. No other animal species displays these kinds of abilities, although they are capable of other marvelous things. Some semioticians have proposed that the Peircean distinction between icons, indices, and symbols could also explain the difference in semiotic competences among different life forms (on this point, see T. Uexküll; Deacon, *The Symbolic*; Kull, "Vegetative, Animal"). I would rather leave Peirce's typology of signs aside, to denote the basic building blocks of the semiotic universe, and argue that the difference between humans and other animals lies in the process of modeling.[7] Such an approach would allow us to distinguish and map the semiotic competence of organisms based on the hierarchical complexity of modeling processes and to show later how the process of making sense of the material environment leads to its semiotization. One specific feature of models is that they are created in relation to the object and that they keep their analogy-based linkage and thus can later be applied back to the object.

Modeling in this context has a relatively wide meaning, as a process of making sense of some process or phenomena, with the help of (internal or external) representations that are at least partly based on analogies (Lotman, "Tezisy" 130). Thomas A. Sebeok and Marcel Danesi define modeling as the use of forms for comprehending and processing perceived information in a species-specific way (5–6). Ladislav Tondl adds that a "model is able to substitute for the original . . . [and] permits some important functions of decision-making or evaluations concerning the original" (85). Models can include analogy-based representations of different complexities: from prototype-based categorical perception and conditioned associations in nonhuman animals to the anthropomorphic descriptions and mathematical models of human discourses. For instance, we can consider a migratory bird's mental map, which incorporates inherent and experiential knowledge, the image of certain landmarks, and the position of the sun and the constellations, among other sources of environmental information; this mental map can be thought of as a model of its migratory route. The representations that are created in the course of modeling can remain internal (in the case of mental associations) or can be externalized (writing, artistic works, and other forms of human modeling). Models and modeling are thus broad concepts that allow us to treat human and nonhuman semiotic activities within the same theoretical framework and, in the context of the present arguments, to demonstrate that there are different types of analogy-based interpretations of the material world.

Humans are capable of several layers and types of modeling. According to Thomas A. Sebeok, humans share with other animals the activity of "zoosemiotic modeling," a kind of modeling where signs are distinguished by the organism's species-specific sensory apparatus and are aligned with their behavioral resources and motor events ("In What" 54). This broad description of zoosemiotic modeling is based on Jakob von Uexküll's *Umwelt* concept (understood as a species-specific attachment to an environment that is organized by meanings). The basic associations in animals' *Umwelten* (for example, between signs in the terrain and movement or between signs of food and consumption) can be considered the universal grounds for modeling in animals. We can also think of the processes of recognition and mapping that take place in our immune system and of other centers of biosemiotic competence in our body such as the peripheral nervous system or the endocrine system as forms of unconscious modeling activity. Verbal modeling is a unique capacity of the human species, and it may lead to higher, poetic, artistic, ideological, or religious forms of modeling, denoted as "secondary modeling systems" by the Tartu-Moscow semiotic school (Lotman, "Tezisy" 131). Structural characteristics of the model-object relationship allow for further distinctions between "technical modeling," which relies on strict algorithmic relations (see Rosen 85ff), and "artistic modeling," which uses a number of codes to create a poetically organized and complex image (on this point, see Lotman, "Struktura" 203ff).[8]

An important feature of modeling is that a model represents an object not in all aspects but in a certain respect, and the specifics of this relation itself have semiotic significance and meaning. "The model represents a homomorphic representation, i.e. not identical to the original. It means the representation in the sense of the Latin 'pars pro toto,' the part instead of the whole" (Tondl 83). It is in this relation between the original and the model where the specifics of the species, the *Umwelt*, the language, the cultural tradition, the discipline, and so on of the interpreter, become involved and make the difference. In this point the causality of natural signs can be overcome, as the subject can model the sign processes from a certain aspect, based on the specifics of its *Umwelt*, culture, and personal motivation.

In humans, the ground that has been used to establish the relationship between object and model can also be used to distinguish a number of metaphoric ascriptions—or so-called morphisms. Czech historian of science and philosopher Stanislav Komárek has proposed a typology of such morphisms, including biomorphism, technomorphism, and sociomorphism (108ff). In biomorphism, the bases of meaning transmission are general characteristics of living beings; in technomorphism, the world or any entity of it is described by emphasizing its machinelike properties; in sociomorphism, human society, culture, and economics are taken as a measure with which to describe the rest of nature. Among such analogy-based modeling strategies, anthropomorphism is the most studied and criticized (see, for example, R. W. Mitchell et al.; Guthrie; Daston and Mitman). By using different morphisms, humans are able to model matter as alive, humans as machines, machines as pets, nonhuman animals as humans, and so on.

Different morphisms allow us to comprehend things that are rather unknown to us, based on their analogies to things that are more common. We can, for instance, use humans or other living organisms as bases for metaphoric ascription to make better sense of material processes, or to give to these processes a human or at least an animate dimension. It is quite clear that matter itself does not model. Matter might have history, it might save traces and even produce copies of objects—as mud reproduces the image of the foot, for example—but it does not model in the sense of using forms to produce a representation of specific aspects of the object. Therefore, if we are talking about inanimate matter as having semiotic capacities or competences, we are executing biomorphism or anthropomorphism. In other words, we are describing material nature by making analogies with living organisms or humans. This process is, in fact, a widely occurring cognitive strategy that can be exemplified by the expression "sleeping volcano," used to describe volcanic mountains that have been inactive in their recent history, or "the calm that precedes the storm," used to refer to the kind of dense silence that anticipates a rapid change in the weather. Indeed, we can interpret meteorological signs almost as an expression of intentionality, as a silence standing for the unwillingness of the emitter to participate in the communication, therefore implying a secrecy, a concealed plan or revenge of the natural force. Herman Melville's words in *Moby-Dick* exemplify this human tendency: "As the profound calm which only apparently precedes and prophesies of the storm, is perhaps more awful than the storm itself; for, indeed, the calm is but the wrapper and envelope of the storm; and contains it in itself, as the seemingly harmless rifle holds the fatal powder, and the ball, and the explosion" (254).

Modeling is also a powerful tool in scientific research, as it allows for the making of generalizations and predictions. We should, however, be aware of the grounds of our models and of the fact that this ground is never neutral (as it is selected consciously or unconsciously by us). For instance, if we depict material processes based on a narrative logic, then our depiction belongs to the sphere of anthropomorphic modeling. Narrative assumes the involvement of language, since the description of a sequence of events requires syntactic elements (on this point, see Maran and Kull). Such a modeling approach could be beneficial, as it accumulates and highlights the causality of the process (for instance, human involvement in environmental degradation) and may introduce empathy in humans for understanding and appreciating environmental processes. At the same time, it should be recognized that narrative description is a part of symbolic interpretation and therefore alien to the material world. As we will observe in the next section, such interpretations, if incorporated into policies and applied back to the environment, may bring along a semiotization of the environment itself. Attentiveness to modeling in culture and in science and the importance of distinguishing this activity from the agency of matter and its semiotic potential appear to be critical issues for the researchers both of biosemiotics and of material ecocriticism.

Matter Becomes Semiotized

Though conceptually and typologically indispensable, the distinction between matter (which may afford natural signs, *sensu* Gibson) and the semiotic realm (which may have an effect on matter) has become increasingly blurred and unstable within contemporary, human-influenced environments. To gain a clearer picture of this, what is needed is a tool with which to describe the dynamic relationship between the material structures of the world and the subjects that are capable of modeling and executing models. To describe these relationships between a semiotic subject and a given environmental object, Jakob von Uexküll has provided a basic schema called the "functional cycle" (*Funktionskreis*). In simple terms, the functional cycle represents the relationship between a subject and an object by considering the processes of perception and action (or effect). Uexküll's schema distinguishes perceptual signs and organs from effectual signs and organs and also the subject's inner world (*Innenwelt*) from the objective environmental structure. Together, the activities of perception and action form a closed feedback cycle ("The Theory" 31–33). Ecosemiotic elaborations of this model demonstrate that all organisms perceive and alter their environment based on their modeling and interpretations (see Kull, "Semiotic"; Maran and Kull). Accordingly, it is in principle possible to distinguish between different types of environmental change, based on the different types of modeling and interpretations that a certain species is capable of making—from the simple recognition of a resource to the complex structuring of human culture (for example, planning and designing gardens and parks).

All living organisms alter their environment, but in some cases the environment is changed in a way that would intentionally make it more suitable for a particular organism. This process is called "niche construction," and it is common in beavers, social insects, ground-living rodents, and humans, among others (on this point, see Odling-Smee et al.). Niche construction may result in a situation that is called "extended organism." In this case, the energy and matter moving among the ecological cycles that the animal belongs to do not accumulate in the animal's body (Turner). Rather, the surrounding environmental structures are manipulated in order to store energy and matter in a way that is profitable for the animal (the digging of burrows, the storing of seeds, and so on). The basic claim of my discourse in this chapter is that processes of environmental alteration, such as *niche construction,* are based on modeling and that these processes result in the semiotization of matter through the animal's execution of mental or externalized models.[9] In this sense, *niche construction* is simultaneously a meaning creation. By manipulating the environment for its aims, an organism transfers its modeling activities back to the environment; it changes the environment in a way that makes more sense to it and corresponds to the semiotic resources (sign systems) used by the organism. When we look at the products of such modeling activities, we recognize how matter has become semiotized: for instance, a pile of willow twigs, all with the same thickness and length, gathered by a European beaver. In this case, the length of the beaver's body and the reach of its front legs become a model that the animal uses to measure and modify its environment, and the pile of identically sized sticks is the semiotized, material result of its activities. The pile retains the semiotic imprint left by the beaver, even when the beaver is gone and the pile is happened upon by another organism.

Humans' ability to reorganize the environment on a large scale based on modeling and interpretation is well known. In the previous section of this chapter we distinguished between different types of modeling. Among humans, accordingly, we can talk about the practical results of applying functional and technical models to the environment (for example, roads and transportation networks) or the products of applying artistic models, where inner rhythms, proportions, and shapes are decisive features. The material products of modeling can also far outlive the cultures that created them. The Nazca Lines in southern Peru, for instance, stand today as a symbol of a largely unknown culture. Some examples of matter semiotized by contemporary humans include modified genetic material that has escaped into nature, sunken ships at the bottoms of oceans, and the geometrical lines of the gigantic wind turbines that are spread over our landscape; many of these have a good chance of outliving our civilization.

A good example of the specifics of human modeling and its effects on the environment is mapping and map usage. A map represents an actual landscape approximately. Smooth transitions are represented by straight lines; a diversity of biological communities is reduced to a few symbols. Some affordances (*sensu* Gibson) of the landscape are represented, others ignored (most often those that have meanings to species or social groups other than those that the mapmaker belongs to). Later, when the map is used by humans as a guide for practical activities within the landscape, the map users tend to imprint the distinctions and forms used in the mapping onto the real landscape. The map-based modeling cycle is at work in various human activities, from forestry and real estate development to military strategizing and action.

In addition to the modeling that is conscious and intentional in regard to its products, there is a kind of unconscious modeling that takes place at various levels of biological organization. The complexity of human culture and society entails various cycles of remodeling and reuse, during which conscious modeling can initially result in products that alter the environment without any conscious awareness or intention. For instance, when considering the life cycle of human-made buildings, initial planning and construction are intentional activities, as are later reconstructions and renovations. The use of abandoned buildings by animals and destitute people as well as the decomposition and breakdown of the buildings, however, are mostly unintended results. In the analysis of the semiotization of matter, it is thus possible to distinguish between conscious and unconscious modeling as well as the intentional and unintentional uses of models. These differentiations may be useful for rationalizing the model-specificity and reach of environmental alterations. For instance, one could compare the use of pesticide in a farm field, which is an intentional, local, and regulated activity, with the accumulation of pharmaceuticals and other biochemical substances in sewage systems and water ecosystems, which are much more unconscious and undirected phenomena. In both cases, the modeling activity that makes use of the correspondence between biological (plants, human bodies) and chemical agencies is traceable, but in the second case the causal connections and specific effects of human activities are much more difficult to describe or regulate.

In regard to the semiotization of matter, the main issue from a biosemiotic viewpoint is that because the modeling is not neutral, neither is the semiotized matter. Through its shape, structure, patterns, and other properties, semiotized matter embodies the imprint of the organism or culture that has created it. Its inner semiotic potential remains, waiting to be launched into new semiotic and communicative relations. It can be assumed that the semiotized matter is not fully accessible or decodable without the human codes used in its creation, but nevertheless the semiotized matter has its own semiotic potential, which can creatively or distractively interact with new semiotic processes or debar them. Jury Lotman and Aleksander Pjatigorskij noticed this, describing how "fragments of phrases and texts brought from another culture, inscriptions left by a population that has already disappeared from a region, ruins of buildings of unknown purpose, or statements introduced from another closed social group" (129) can become sources of new textual meanings in a culture. The ability of semiotized matter to be included in new semiotic relations is definitely not restricted to the human species. Bowerbirds (Ptilonorhynchidae), who in their natural habitat decorate their courtship grounds with colorful blossoms, stones, nuts, and other debris, often make use of human-made artifacts, such as bottle caps, drinking straws, or small and colorful pieces of plastic waste. Using transformed matter can also bring along deadly results, such as waterfowl pecking leaden shots instead of pebbles or seabirds ingesting the plastic litter that floats on the ocean's surface. These, too, are semiotic phenomena—caused by the inability of an organism to recognize and correctly categorize the matter semiotized by other species, in this occurrence by humans. From the semiotic viewpoint, we can describe such cases as conflicts between species-specific modeling, on the one hand, and the causality of natural signs replaced by human-semiotized matter, on the other.

Given the extent to which matter is semiotized by human culture, as well as the longevity of concrete, plastic, radioactive waste, and other human-made substances, there is an apparent need to review the main typological distinction between inert matter and the semiotic realm. This necessity arises when applying ecosemiotic methods to human-altered environments, where matter is, rather, a mix of residues from different modeling activities, partly fragmented, and in different stages of disintegration. Quite probably, the semiotized matter is more standardized; it includes stricter relations; it is more self-sufficient and resistant to decomposition. For instance, the amount of measures and relations that correspond to full integer numbers is quite probably higher in human waste compared to any other biological debris. Most important, human semiotic modeling and semiotization of matter tend to bring along increased unification and a loss of diversity of semiotic codes and regulations in the environment (on this point, see Kull, "Semiotic" 356). Although semiotized matter is not capable of conducting modeling itself, it could well include imprints and traces of models, which is potential likely to be launched into new semiotic interactions. In the contemporary world, the material environment is more and more a mixture of material objects that afford natural sign relations, on the one hand, and human semiotized matter, which embodies latent human agency, on the other, as well as many intermediate and hybrid types.

In hybrid environments, a semiotic approach could be used to study the ways in which matter changed by human modeling differs from matter organized by physical or biological processes (for example, one could compare the semiotic potential of human landfills and natural sediments). One could examine how matter semiotized by humans impedes matter's own ability to initiate natural signs and to afford (*sensu* Gibson) semiotic processes (figure 9.1). Further questions would arise about the effects of such change on different animals interacting with the matter and about the way these other species relate to said matter. This perspective is based on the understanding that semiotic affordances and natural signs

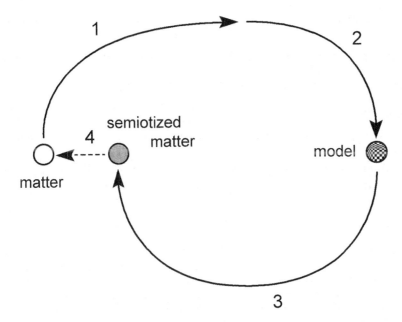

Figure 9.1. The cycle of the semiotization of matter. Courtesy of Timo Maran.

have an important role in the healthy existence of both human cultures and non-human animals (see the argumentation on affordances and natural signs in the first section). At the same time, it is important to recognize that the ways other species interact with matter semiotized by humans may be complex and require case-specific analyses. For instance, in European towns, herring gulls (*Larus argentatus*) have been successful in adopting roofs of apartment houses as nesting grounds. At the same time, they are often not able to perceive and recognize the glass walls of modern buildings, and by flying into this glass they make a mistake with often lethal consequences. Questions to be raised in future research include the following: In which ways do traces of human semiotic activities embodied in matter influence the sign activities of other animals? To what extent are organisms able to decompose this matter according to their own semiotic organization? What are the possible conflicts between the modeling activities of different species?

The Hybrid Zone

The potential of matter to trigger sign processes appears to be a common ground on which to initiate a dialogue between biosemiotics and material ecocriticism. This said, biosemiotics holds the understanding that there is a typological difference between the semiotic capacities of matter, plants, animals, and humans. In analyzing contemporary, human-altered environments, however, these distinctions have become blurred and unreliable. There appear to be two interlinked processes by which matter could become meaningful for human culture: biomorphic or anthropomorphic modeling and the semiotization of the matter. We should develop awareness of the first of these, due to the cyclical feedback loop between human culture and the environment. The semiotization of matter, however, both as a process and as a serious environmental problem, could well become a joint research topic for biosemiotics and material ecocriticism. Understanding the causes and motives for why humans semiotize matter also requires critical analysis of human cultural and social processes. Material ecocriticism appears to be well equipped for carrying out such analysis. Such a project would also likely result in a flourishing of new knowledge for biosemiotics regarding the semiotization of matter.

Notes

I would like to thank Kalevi Kull, whose work has been inspiring in writing this essay, and the editors of this volume for the invitation and constructive feedback to the manuscript of this chapter. The research has been supported by the European Union through the European Regional Development Fund (Centre of Excellence CECT, Estonia), by the Estonian Research Council Grant IUT2-4, and by the Norway Financial Mechanism 2009–2014 under project contract no. EMP151.

1. For more information on biosemiotics, see Hoffmeyer, *Biosemiotics*; Favareau, *Essential*; Emmeche and Kull.

2. An alternative approach for overcoming the dichotomy between material and the semiotic is proposed by Donna Haraway, "The Promises of Monsters." Her approach to material-semiotic structures makes use of A. J. Greimas's semiotic square and its elaborations.

3. Peirce's terms for the sign's components added in square brackets by the author.

4. For the sake of clarity, we should note that "object" in Peirce's terminology includes not just physical objects but also thoughts and ideas (*Collected Papers* 5:283–87).

5. Peirce makes it rather clear that this is a dynamical object, that is, the real object, that determines the sign: "Dynamical Object . . . is the Reality which by some means contrives to determine the Sign" (*Collected Papers* 4:536).

6. Peirce goes further on this point, specifying that without the specific relations, the signs would lose their existence: "An icon is a sign which would possess the character which renders it significant, even though its object had no existence. . . . An index is a sign which would, at once, lose the character which makes it a sign if its object were removed, but would not lose that character if there were no interpretant. . . . A symbol is a sign which would lose the character which renders it a sign if there were no interpretant" (*Collected Papers* 2:302).

7. This interpretation follows Sebeok, "Signs"; Sebeok and Danesi; Bateson, *Steps* 279–308.

8. Based on their structural characteristics, we can also distinguish between more specific types of modeling. Sebeok and Danesi, for example, differentiate between "singularized" (that is, using unitary reference), "composite" (textual), "cohesive" (code-based), and "connective" (metaphoric) modeling (3).

9. Kalevi Kull ("Semiotic") has refered to this process as the creation of "second nature."

PART 3
Politics of Matter

10 Pro/Polis

Three Forays into the Political Lives of Bees

Catriona Sandilands

> If there is someone you do not wish to recognize as a political being, you begin by not seeing him as the bearer of signs of politicity, by not understanding what he says.
> —Jacques Rancière, "Ten Theses on Politics"

> Grip on and buzz;
> emanation in the mad still air.
> I am caused quietly
> to hear.
> —Sean Borodale, *Bee Journal*

Material ecocriticism demands careful attention to the ways in which the more-than-human world writes itself into literature. In so doing, it is a politically generative practice, meaning that it opens literary texts to new possibilities for understanding the politicity of multiple agents, in this case bees. The material, literary, and political histories of bee-human relations are densely intertwined; in this complex unfolding, material ecocriticism, rather than reading bees as mostly metaphors for human politics, insists that literary experiences are crucial points from which multispecies bee-human politics might emerge. Poetry, for example, may create an aesthetic space in which bees not only enter human biopolitics (they are already there), and not only have political lives of their own (they already do), but also pierce the anthropocentric experience of human political subjectivity itself. Inspired by the poems that animate its final section, this chapter is a speculation about the multispecies possibilities of bee-human political life.

Polis

In his essay "Ten Theses on Politics," Jacques Rancière writes that politics is a specific mode of action with its own rationality: politics is neither the general exercise of power nor the specific capacity of a select group of individuals to rule, but is instead fundamentally concerned with the constitution of a particular kind of subject of ruling, one "that is at once the agent of an action and the matter upon which that action is exercised" (*Dissensus* 29). The political subject, here, is only possible on the assumption of equality. To partake in the paradox of *simultaneously* ruling and being ruled requires the disruption of any preexisting understanding according to which some actors are more entitled to govern than others—have a greater capacity for thought, for example, or are in possession of any specific qualification to rule grounded in a nonpolitical a priori. Politics, then, inheres precisely in its break with "the 'normal' distribution of positions that defines who exercises power and who is subject to it. It also requires a break with the idea that there exist dispositions 'specific' to these positions" (30).

For Rancière, then, politics is a disruption of *any* existing socioepistemic regime that assigns parts and positions based on understandings of differential capacity; in other words, it is a disturbance of what he calls the "social" world based on greater or lesser hierarchies, and even on more mutualistic interdependencies crafted from reciprocal exchange or advantage. In Rancière's model, *politics* is a sort of radical appearance of ontological equality in the midst of all of that complex difference that we might, in a more Foucauldian frame, call *biopolitics*: it is, precisely, the *event* in which a demand for the recognition of a preexisting equality erupts into the field of power and hierarchy—the demonstration of equality's ontology, if you will, that is given, fleetingly, in struggles for justice.[1] If I might put it a bit differently: It is not only that politics is a disruption of biopolitics, specifically, a disturbance of the "partitions of the sensible" through which differences and hierarchies are known, enacted, and naturalized (which Rancière calls *la police*), and through which those inequalities can be reorganized. Politics is also a momentary, experiential reminder of a *prior* ontological equality, an "all," to use Rancière's term, that is a haunting surplus to any biopolitical assemblage of bodies, lives, and relationships. Politics is a specific, disruptive experience: not of power, and certainly not of parliament, but of a "we" that precedes, yet is remembered in, claims for justice.

Of course, as Jane Bennett has also pointed out, Rancière means a *human* community, a "people." As Bennett writes:

> When asked in public whether he thought that an animal or a plant or a drug or a (nonlinguistic) sound could disrupt the police order, Rancière said no: he did not want to extend the concept of the political that far; nonhumans do not qualify as participants in the demos; the disruption effect must be accompanied by the desire to engage in reasoned discourse. (*Vibrant* 106)

As Jean-Philippe Deranty might add, Rancière makes this firm division in part because he understands that hierarchy is founded on the fact that "the masters demand to be recognised as masters by those they dominate, but for this recognition of inequality to be possible, the masters *must recognise the ability of the dominated to recognise at all*" (n.p.; emphasis added). This recognition, for Rancière, seems to require a certain *kind* of prior equality, a potential "all" that rests on the presumed ability of the subject to *respond* to ontological equality, and then perhaps also to biopolitics, in particular ways: to think, to speak, to disagree, to imagine justice, to argue.

But, even more strongly than Bennett, I am not willing to take him at his word on this issue. As she argues, the capacity to disrupt everyday biopolitical relations and to "repartition the sensible" is not limited to human speakers with their "argumentative utterances": a microbe can "overthrow the regime of the perceptible" and "an animal, plant, mineral or artefact can sometimes catalyze a public" (*Vibrant* 107). With bees in mind, I will take the matter even further: Rancière's insistence on "response-ability" as a limit to the experience of ontological equality enabled in politics is simply another worn-out gear in the anthropological machine. As Jacques Derrida argues in "And Say the Animal Responded?" many other-than-human beings can not only disrupt and catalyze, but also be seen to *respond*: including bees.[2] And in their response-ability, bees demonstrate precisely the kind of recognition of the Other that, for Rancière, lies at the basis of politics: whether this recognition crosses species boundaries or not, it may be that other-than-human creatures like bees are quite capable of experiencing their own equality and inequality *as such*, that they are capable of communicating in a way that presents a "world" to their interlocutors, and that human beings have no excuse whatsoever not to consider bees' responses through a lens that would allow us to see them as *participants* in political struggle rather than as objects to be represented.[3] As Nicole Shukin has described forcefully, animals are very much entangled in webs of biopolitical relations; indeed, it is sometimes precisely their capacities to respond that indicate their importance in particular configurations of power and inequality. But in addition, then, I will argue here that many other-than-human beings are also political animals in Rancière's sense: *part* of the dynamic of ruling and ruled, *included* in the paradox of the *demos,* and touched *as ontologically equal* in the disruptive moments by which "the underlying equality operating within social inequality is verified pragmatically in struggles and demands of equality" (Deranty n.p.). In my view, then, bees not only hold the potential to disrupt the (anthropo)sensible biopolitically, but are, in moments of political struggle, profoundly revealed as equal participants in the potentialities of governance.

Despite his resistance to the inclusion of the other-than-human world in the polis, then, Rancière gives us something very important for an imagination of a multispecies politics: the ontological condition of cross-species equality is experienced *in,* and not *prior to,* struggles *for* equality. For all our scientific, philosophical, and ethical work to trace the intricacies of ecological interdependence and the multiplicities of material cause and effect, it is in the moment of democratic paradox that the phenomenal *ontology* of that equality is revealed; where historical configurations of biopolitical relations interpellate our specific sociocorporeal capacities and desires into dense networks of structured relations, it is in the disruptive moment of politics that our foundational equality is made tangible. In my capacity to simultaneously rule and be ruled by a multiplicity of actors, I am forced to imagine a connective ontology, in the midst of yet excessive to differentiating multiplicities, in which our capacities are *comparable* more than they are *complementary*. Bees are not just interdependently *with* us in the world; they share with us a fundamental equality that, given the right conditions, we can actually experience *as equality*.

Propolis

The European honeybee (*Apis mellifera*) is, of course, very much part of complex, multispecies biopolitics. We cultivate (indeed, exploit) bees' capacities as international pollinators as we also develop intimate kinship relations with them and worry, sometimes in problematic ways, about their health in the midst of transnational migrations and industrial transformations (Tsing).[4] We consume their creations—extending to wax, royal jelly, bee venom, and propolis on an industrial scale (Burt's Bees)—as we also develop elite niche markets for local, urban honey in an attempt to nurture more sustainable bee-human relations (Lemieux).[5] We sequence their genome and manipulate their bodies and heredities to facilitate our desire for docile migrant workers, as we create intimate sanctuaries for their nonindustrial flourishing (Siegel). And we are deeply concerned about Colony Collapse Disorder (CCD), even as we are not quite sure what particular combination of parasites, neonicotinoid pesticides, industrial breeding practices, agricultural monocultures, genetically modified crops, forced migration, suburban sprawl, biological globalization, and climate change might be causing the mass bee die-offs that have even the United Nations on official alert (Benjamin and McCallum). There is, in short, no shortage of ways in which bees are biopolitical subjects; especially in the context of CCD, the welfare of *Homo sapiens* is tied to that of *A. mellifera,* and there is thus also no shortage of discourses about bee-human interactions as they contribute to a set of multispecies relationships in which humans can continue to benefit from bees, requiring their continued productivity (and, sometimes, pointing toward a more reciprocal flourishing). Indeed, it is the specific biological capacities of honeybees (their intensely social, neolocal, hive-making, honey-producing, cold-weathering tendencies) that make them such important biopolitical subjects, in that the specific abilities of *these* bees have tied their species interests so strongly to that of some humans. If European honeybees were not such capable, productive, agricultural subjects who produce such very useful things, we probably would not care as much. But then, it is also precisely these tendencies that have brought *A. mellifera* into such close contact with *H. sapiens;* our intimate species interrelations are, historically, the stuff of (sometimes mutual) domestication. And we are, in a sense, now propagating honeybee species interests on a global scale, even as our exploitation of their labor threatens their global vitality.

But bees are also politically fascinating for other reasons. As Claire Preston documents extensively, honeybees have been used to model or justify (or both) almost every kind of Western political system from monarchy to socialism, fascism to representative democracy. Bee biopolitics have a long history of entanglement with bee metaphoricity, and our intense fascination with apian sociality has derived, at least in part, from observations gleaned in the course of productive beekeeping relations.

Most recently, however, the phenomenon of bee swarming—understood in the context of a more scientific practice of bee observation—calls our attention to the specific politicality, indeed the specific democracy, of bees (as Kosek describes, the biosemiotics of swarm behavior are also of great interest to the U.S. military). In the late spring or early summer, when a colony of honeybees becomes overcrowded in its existing nesting site, a colony will divide itself: about a third of the bees stay in the old hive to rear a new queen, and the other two-thirds, about ten thousand bees, leave with the old queen in search of a new home. As biologist Thomas Seeley describes, the migrants travel about a hundred feet away from the old hive and then coalesce

> into a beardlike cluster, where they literally hang out together for several hours or a few days.... Once bivouacked, the swarm will field several hundred house hunters to explore some 70 square kilometres... of the surrounding landscape for potential home-sites, locate a dozen or more possibilities, evaluate each one with respect to the multiple criteria that define a bee's dream home, and democratically select a favourite for their new domicile. (6)

Once they have made their decision, all ten thousand bees fly to the selected location en masse, the choice a result of a hive intelligence that has fascinated observers at least since Virgil, but has been the subject of more concertedly scientific research since Karl von Frisch conducted his intimate, Nobel Prize–winning bee-communication experiments beginning in the 1940s.

Frisch gave credence to the ancient idea that honeybees communicate meaningfully to one another and also that they learn from these interactions. Specifically, as a result of years of patient experimentation and observation, he described in rich detail the "waggle dance," in which a forager bee, having found a rich source of nectar, flies back to the hive to tell all the other worker bees exactly where that nectar is to be found. In this dance, the bee, smelling of the relevant nectar,[6] reenters the hive from the forage and, in the dark and across the backs of her coworkers, tells the others with exceptional accuracy where good nectar is to be found. Adjusting for the position of the sun in the time span between her collection and her communication, the forager bee crawls, waggling her abdomen, up a straight line that points the correct direction and then arcs back to the beginning of the line to repeat the cycle, the second time arcing in the opposite direction. The duration of the waggle indicates the distance to the flowers;[7] the intensity of the dance indicates their quality.

The fact that honeybees thus seem to demonstrate use of a representational code is interesting enough in itself and has been the topic of a great deal of debate in both scientific and philosophical circles. Lacan chooses to read the bees' communications as part of a system of *reactions*: while the message of the individual bee's waggle dance "determines the action of the *socius*, it is never retransmitted by it. This means that the message remains fixed in its function as a relay of the action, from which no subject detaches it as a communication itself" (qtd. in Derrida 124); he is, here, in agreement with a large number of biologists, who take great pains to distinguish bee communication from human language—including Frisch. But ethologist James L. Gould is not so sure and has considered more carefully the ways in which bees form concepts and develop insights (his terms) and communicate these ideas to each other by way of *signs* and, to counter some of Lacan's claim, that these signs are actively *interpreted* (my terms): at the very least,

> the evidence that honey bees can perform tasks that are considered to require cognitive powers when displayed by higher vertebrates suggests . . . that cognition [may be] a capacity that has evolved as needed among animals, independent of size, number of legs, or whether the creature has an external or internal skeleton. As such, cognitive differences would be quantitative rather than qualitative. (45)

For Derrida, Lacan's insistence that the function of language is to *evoke*, to draw forth an unfixed response from the Other, is also a plausible rationale to consider bee codes *precisely* as a form of language: bees would indeed appear to be dancing in order for that dance to be *interpreted* by the community of apian interlocutors prior to action (even if, as Hugh Raffles indicates, we do not know if they display the metacognition that would have them "dance about dancing"). In other words, even on the basis of Lacan's own argument, it would appear that bees respond.[8] Clearly, as Raffles argues, "the point is not . . . to imagine that the little honeybees are somehow just like us, that their world somehow corresponds to ours, that to be a bee is somehow equivalent to being a human equipped with a different sensory apparatus" (198). But the invitation to imagine that their dance language is a *language* opens up important routes of political encounter between bees and humans.

As Martin Lindauer, Frisch's student, observed in his own experiments, bees not only communicate abstract information to each another, but in some circumstances also appear to *argue* about it, pitting abstract against abstract, in a manner that eerily (for those who consider politics to be uniquely human) resembles the practices by which male white human members of the Athenian *polis* considered the good of the collective world: *debate*. Specifically, as Lindauer and later Seeley (Lindauer's student) have observed, when bees are out in search of a new home, hundreds of individual "scout" bees go out looking and come back to the swarm to offer their individual findings as to the suitability and location of a potential new nest site.[9] To communicate this possibility, the scout dances a waggle dance much like the one she would have performed at another point directing toward nectar. In this situation, however, her point is not simply to convey information about a food source—that the other foragers may or may not follow—but rather to begin the process of having the swarm arrive at a single consensual decision. In this selection process, a scout bee reenters the hive and dances in favor of a new nest site; the better the site, the livelier the dance. Other bees respond to the scout's opinion by joining in: more dancers = more recruits = stronger collective opinion. Other scouts are doing the same thing at the same time: trying to *persuade* their coworkers of a site against the other possibilities. Sometimes in the course of debate, a new potential site can enter into the picture at quite a late stage, and if a scout can persuade enough others to agree with her estimation, the direction of the debate can change dramatically. Sometimes, an apparently ideal site can be raised by scouts and never generate interest, the hive having already been persuaded of the merits of another option. Indeed, as Seeley notes, a bee will dance in favor of a particular option without having explored that option directly herself. And sometimes—if rarely—the bees will fail to reach a consensus at all, will attempt to swarm in two directions with only one queen, and will have to return to the original overcrowded hive to start the process again in less than ideal circumstances.

Although, of course, one must consider that these ideas of "honeybee democracy" are every bit as much located in historically specific political desires as were the post-Elizabethan invocations of Charles Butler in his 1609 "The Feminine Monarchie," there still seem to be sound reasons for us to think of bees as having a public realm of their own, with varying and overlapping relations to ours.[10] Bees are, it seems, active participants in their own apiocentric public realm at the same time as they participate metaphorically in ours, and especially at the same time as the capacities of their bodies, labors, and communicative practices are enmeshed, in increasingly precarious ways, in the multispecies biopolitics of late capitalism. Indeed, these apiocentric, anthropocentric, and multispecies publics intermesh and sometimes conflict: recent research on the relationship between neonicotinoid pesticide use and CCD clearly demonstrates that the chemicals' ability to disrupt the neurotransmitter acetylcholine in insects—which is the desired effect on pests—interferes, even at sublethal doses, with worker bees' ability to navigate, and thus to bring back pollen for the hive and also to bring back information about the world to be shared and debated (Henry et al.). "Neonics," in other words, destroy not only the nutritional but also the communicative and argumentative practices that are key to honeybees' lives, and in so doing also threaten the fragile economies of bee-human interchange. Here, apiocentric publicity is revealed as not subordinate to ours, but instead as prior and constitutive, in that bee politics are a foundation on which the entire history of bee-human productive relations rests.

Pro/polis

In part because of these complex webs of multispecies (bio)political encounter, there is no shortage of recent literary work about bees that affords a strong material ecocritical reading.[11] In particular, there is a wealth of memoir, fiction, and poetry that circulates around the practice of *beekeeping*. Part of a rich bee-aesthetic tradition that dates from the earliest human attempts to draw the honeybees into agricultural production—circa 2400 BC—these works are centered, quite literally, on the ways in which bees can be "kept" and on the ways in which that keeping generates specific human practices and insights. Unlike many animals whose contributions to human food production are often absolutely exploitative—in which we keep them caged, yoked, and submissive in a corporeal story of absolute oppression and bodily expropriation—bees are not quite "domesticated," and we do not consume their bodies as much as we do their artisanal labor.[12] As a literary history of beekeeping practices from Virgil's *Georgics* onward, for example, shows, human beings are deeply concerned with creating the ongoing conditions in which bees will continue, more or less willingly, to perform their productive work in order to allow humans to reap the benefits. We attempt to understand what the bees are saying, here in order to develop a more sophisticated understanding of what they need to survive, increase, and make more of the stuff we want; we listen to them to maintain or increase the yield of honey and, especially as bee labor has been radically changed and exponentially increased in conditions of industrial agriculture, to maintain their pollination services. Although there are clearly more and less exploitative versions of this conversation—for example, the difference between planting bee-friendly gardens and developing "queen cages" to keep hives contained as they are trucked, long distance, to pollinate almonds in California and blueberries on the Eastern Seaboard—the primary thrust of these interspecies communications remains instrumental. Here, bees and humans are both in the category of *animal laborans;* our biological needs can be seduced or forced to coincide through apicultural, entomological, and even overtly imaginative attempts at conversation.

Clearly, beekeeping can be a site of a rich, storied production that ties bee with human welfare in ways that are genuinely intimate and reciprocal: shared labor is not necessarily a bad thing, and—as Marx might grudgingly admit (even if he would not call bee work *labor*)—bee and human labor could, conceivably, peacefully coincide in relatively nonexploitative ways, so that we could each, respectfully, see our desires better coalesce into tangible benefits for both.[13] Such is the sugary message of Sue Monk Kidd's *The Secret Life of Bees* (2003), for example, or the more complex flavor of Gail Anderson Dargatz's *A Recipe for Bees* (1998), or even the oddly muscular, nationalist tang of Gene Stratton-Porter's *Keeper of the Bees* (1925). Attempting to listen to the bees, here, can open up a world governed by apian space and time, for example, and propels in these novels' human narrators a heightened sensitivity to the needs of others more broadly.[14] Clearly, these multispecies exchanges are ethically interesting, but I will say, nonetheless, that these works indicate more of a *therapeutic* orientation than a political one: we cultivate bees' corporeal welfare for what are, ultimately, biopolitical reasons. Apiological research and apicultural praxis have come to coincide, at least since the mid-nineteenth century, in a multispecies biopolitical web of relations in which honeybees' welfare as a *species* is increasingly tied to our own, and it is not surprising that contemporary literary texts seek to explore and deepen these webs of corporeal and communicative interdependence according to different understandings of the social, medicinal, spiritual, ecological, or other values of bee-human relations.

Perhaps because beekeeping often involves a long-term and often difficult engagement with the question of "keeping," and thus directly with the multiple publics of bee-human interaction and not just the daily instrumentalities of bee production, it has also given rise, at times, to literary works that gesture toward the kind of struggle that, as I argued earlier, can be seen as a sort of eruption of a cross-species politics into the structured and unequal multispecies interdependencies of biopolitics: a radical experiencing of an "all" that crosses, in this case, bee-human species boundaries to expose an ontological condition of anthropo-apio equality that both precedes and founds, and is the object of, our struggles for multispecies justice. One such text is Sean Borodale's book *Bee Journal*,[15] which is a collection of dated poetic reflections on bees organized around a calendar of beekeeping activities, from bringing a box of bees home one May to capturing an early-summer swarm and taking it back to the apiary a bit more than two years later. The book is a meditation on learning the art of caring for bees, to be sure: there are poems about dusting bees for varroa mites, checking the brood frame, killing excess drones, and worrying about cold weather conditions. Borodale allows us glimpses of the cyclical caretaking labor of beekeeping, the daily march out to the hive and its attendant seasonally specific anxieties about the health of the community, the location of the queen, and the unpredictable possibility that the bees will swarm. "7th January" reads: "Four inches of snow. The hive a hut / of silence and darkness. / . . . *Are you in there?* I've brought in some light and air. / No answer" (33). "13th July" reads: "We checked. Bees have swarmed. / Nothing to say, except / we fed those left with syrup" (18). We engage with the bees through slices of his practice, and in the fine-grained details of this work, we touch the rhythms of his relations with the hives at very precise moments. In these moments, the bees are clearly *doing* things that prompt responses from Borodale: they are not answering; they have swarmed; they are demanding attention. Their actions and capacities for action are, then, clearly present as part of the constellation of bee-Borodale relations depicted in the poems; where other works might use beekeeping as a tool for the development of human self-understanding, these bees demand to be the center of attention for their own sakes, and we are constantly struck with Borodale's desire to understand *them*.

Particularly noticeable in the poems about his *failures* as a beekeeper, especially those that concern the *deaths* of bees, is the process by which Borodale comes to care *about* these bees through caring for them. He develops a strong bond with the hives, referring several times to "bee friends" and also composing several poems apostrophically, *to* the bees; these attachments are, however, felt especially acutely when they are suddenly ended. "12th March" lingers on sight of a hive full of dead and dying bees: "This is / our crematorium of hexagons, wild with crumbling debris; / crumbling / not so burnt as burnt-out, building of broken rooms" (41). "6th December" describes a hive "black with damp, / bogged in burial, mouldy bedding" (71); "18th December" details the destruction of varroa mites: "A hundred bees dead at a touch—that is not much / of thousands in a box, / but, black on the snow they go, / dropped bag of dead luck" (75). And then, "24th/25th January" is simply a blank page under the title "Bees Die" (83); its silence is the sharp intake of Borodale's breath as he lifts the hive cover to witness, yet again, a litter of bee corpses. These poems and others gently carry the imprint of Borodale's grief; along with his anxieties over queens, cold, and swarming, through his responses to bee deaths, we become deeply aware of the bees' affective presence in his life, of the ways in which he has been become part of an emotional bee-human community.

Among these details and responses, Borodale also speculates on the ways in which the bees might be considering their relations with *him*. In "27th May: Geography," for example, he reflects on how his house is part of the network of bee-human houses that is "stitched . . . in a net of flightways" (4) into bee collective memory, how the details of his home might make their way into an apiocentric conversation about their shared place, but in the context of a perceptual geography very different from his. For the bees, rigging the house's "crack, lump, recess, ridge / to the commune of memory" (4), to their meaningful landscape (hive, air, sun), is a matter of bringing *his* place into *theirs;* they connect the house, in their pollination flights, to their own systems of meaning, and thus integrate the physical manifestations of his meaning into theirs: "You are a brain in impermanence, / coding, knowing, keeping / the latitude and longitude of this, our house; each bee a synapse slowly forming an arrival" (4). Here, for Borodale, bees turn "this house to align with [theirs]" (5); in other words, he asks, "what am I to the bees?" and "what have I produced that resonates with a bee geography?" in ways that situate bees as the perceivers and humans as the *objects* of their perception. That bees perceive the same "home" but through entirely different perceptual relevancies, relations, and memorial practices is thus one of the tropes through which Borodale writes of bee-human relations as a coming together of worlds, crossing but not confined to human desires for bee dwelling: "I had to say, today, I said, / you have us locked inside your noise-truss" (4).

There are also several poems in the collection about honey, which Borodale uses to explore the idea of bee-human sensuous interrelations in an especially interesting way. Honey, in its seasonally variable flavor in the human mouth, provides for him a sort of taste map of bee geography and temporality; depending on where the bees have been and the particular flowers from which their nectar has been drawn, we experience bee-relevant places and times through *taste,* as in the "mud, tang" of winter honey, "the woods are in it" (27), as opposed to the cleaner sweetness of honey made from spring and summer flowers.[16] The poem "6th September: Wild Comb Notes" is thus about the ways honey can provide a sort of taste experience of bee *Umwelt,* a seasonal "sugar map" that requires several synaesthetic leaps for Borodale to begin to apprehend: "I taste its juice; sweet gods of the evergreen / woods' taste; / crushed music, bars and epiphanies of dripping air" (26). Here, he registers the details of bee experience through an unusual sensory apparatus that links his interpretations to bee work in ways that demand an understanding of the intricacy of cross-species sensuous *translations,* of the intense corporeality of bee-human relationality, and of the particular ways in which bee and human biopolitics are intertwined: how we organize environments for pollination registers not only in bee welfare, but also in human taste.

Finally, the poem "16th October: Super Check" does many of these things at once, showing the ways in which Borodale's daily struggles of beekeeping and understanding also give rise, in the eruptive mode discussed at the outset of this essay, to a fleeting experience of bees and humans as radically, ontologically equal. He is clearly moving in this direction throughout the book, in that his beekeeping experiences constellate such a diverse series of reflections on bees that attempt to question the world from something like an apiocentric perspective: what do the bees need (urgently), how do they know, what am I to them, and how can I imagine their lives through the translational medium of honey? But this poem goes one step further in its clear evocation of the eruption of politics *into* biopolitics.

The poem "16th October" clearly locates our understanding of the possibility of bee poetry in the labor of beekeeping and the instrumentality of the cultivated excess that is the honey super, the box that is added to the hive for the sole purpose of producing a honey store that is separate from the brood store: Borodale has taken off the honey super and is examining the potential of bee surplus value as it might mark his success as a beekeeper. There is nothing: "just a dry, papery wax-comb of empties. / No sugar syrup touched; / what is wrong with supplements?" (65). Indeed, what is *wrong* with supplements? This question is an ethical one about the relationship between facilitating the well-being of a given honeybee hive and promoting its hyperdevelopment in order to produce honey for the beekeeper's more obviously anthropocentric ends. And so, the keeper's reflection: How am I facilitating our mutual welfare? How is my labor inadequate to support yours?

But then: "Stand mesmerised / at this landing board. / It is familiar, all-relevant" (65). Out of an experience of his *inability* to create the right conditions for honey production in the midst of his ongoing attempts to listen to and to render what the bees are saying, Borodale finds himself literally caught up in the spell of the hive, and out of the sensation of *not* understanding, he finds himself considering not his apicultural *obligation* to the bees, but his potential ontological *similarity* to them: "Think what paths would be / if *we* could envisage / flights tracked to their nectaries' / pin-point co-ordinates" (65; emphasis in the original). And then, for just a moment, the "if" that marks the imaginative distance between Borodale and bee disappears: *his* "round dance tells trails in mid-air's mile or so round-trip"; "*we* bring, bee-friend, yellow pollen on our legs" (65). The struggle with bee-human sensorial experience and interrelatedness has, throughout the book, propelled Borodale's close attention to the sensuous particularities that both connect him with and differentiate him from bees. But at this one eruptive moment on October 16, before the poem comes back to rest in caretaking, he is able to imagine himself *as* bee and also as the bee's equal: "in human terms, it seems OK" (65).

Bee Journal, then, marks Borodale's attempt to "do justice" to honeybees in a variety of ways. Poetry is not politics, of course, and the struggle to do justice *to* bees in literary rendering is not the same as the struggle to do justice *with* bees.[17] However, the book is clearly marked by a tension between sensuous bee biopolitics, on the one hand, and what Rancière specifies as the more unique phenomenon of *politics* as a specific mode of relating to a community of beings, on the other. In "October 16th" in particular, Borodale describes what we might call an experience of bee dissensus: a moment in his beekeeping activity at which the bees are clearly saying something that defies his best caretaking intentions, and his best poetic attentions, to reveal a world that Borodale does not share, but that impresses on him forcefully its equal participation in the governance of the moment and, indeed, of their relationship in general. Bee politics intersect human politics in complex ways, involving their bodies and ours in a web of multispecies relations that cross at least three versions of (bio)politicality, but this moment of recognition of shared ontology is crucial: it is the place, at least in Rancière's version, where we remember the fundamental democratic paradox that lies at the heart of struggles for justice, in this case including bees as equally part of the struggle.

* * *

Again, poetic attention is not the same as political struggle: the bees are not indicating dissensus in exactly Rancière's sense because they are not directly participating in an oppositional demand for justice, and Borodale is simply leaving open the possibility of bee equality that is made apparent within his own aesthetic struggles. But material ecocriticism insists on building on the glimpses of bee politics that are uniquely enabled in literary texts. Our biopolitical entanglements with bees are pressing and powerfully revealed in many works. But sometimes poetry such as Borodale's also offers us the visceral sense of our shared ontology because it is not afraid of attempting to listen for what the bees might be saying. The attempt will fail; the failure will still remind us powerfully that there are bee poetry and politics in the same spaces as ours. And that is why we have to try.

Notes

This title clearly invokes Jakob von Uexküll's *A Foray into the Worlds of Animals and Humans*. Although I do not address this work extensively in the chapter, I certainly mean to evoke his idea that bees have an apiocentric perceptual universe (including, here, a political realm), in which humans may or may not play a part. If humans and bees share a public, it is because our shared struggles for flourishing coincide at certain points between bee and human *Umwelten*, as enabled by specific practices; our political lives are part of, and shaped by, different perceptual universes as our bodies commingle across species lines. My thanks, here, to the students in ENVS 6149/CMCT 6120 (York University, 2012) for such excellent discussions about multispecies politics, bee cultures, and anthropological machinations.

    1. Rancière draws a clear distinction between politics and biopolitics, and I follow him in this distinction here: "In Foucault's 'biopolitics,' the body in question is the body as object of power and, therefore, it is localized in the police distribution of bodies and their aggregations.... The question of politics begins when the status of the subject able and ready to concern itself with the community becomes an issue" (*Dissensus* 92).

    2. Derrida is writing to disrupt Jacques Lacan's firm distinction between response and reaction, but this division is such an old chestnut that it applies equally well to Rancière: "What [Lacan] attributes to signs that, 'in a language' understood as belonging to the human order, 'take on their value from the relation to each other' and so on, and not just from the 'fixed correlation' between signs and reality, can and must be accorded to any code, animal or human" (*The Animal* 124). In their various uses of codes, certain animals (at least) seem clearly to offer

up *signs* to their interlocutors, demanding a *response* from the other that is contingent on an interpretation of those signs, not a fixed *reaction* (Derrida's critique).

3. Rancière writes, "Political argumentation is at one and the same time the *demonstration of a possible world* in which the argument could count as an argument, one that is addressed by a subject qualified to argue, over an identified object, to an addressee who is required to see the object and to hear the argument that he 'normally' has no reason either to see or to hear" (*Dissensus* 39; emphasis added). Of course, the question of "worldliness" has also been used to distinguish between human beings and other animals and is also an issue for a multispecies political theory; for a detailed consideration of Martin Heidegger's assertion that the animal is world-poor, see Agamben, *The Open*.

4. They are also part of a specifically colonial biopolitics: the importation of honeybees (a.k.a. "white man's flies") to colonial settlements was a crucial part of the transformation of North American and Australian landscapes to particular agricultural uses (that is, many settler crops required honeybee labor in addition to that of indigenous pollinators).

5. Recent intense attention to honeybee health ignores the condition of indigenous (often solitary) bees, even as the same issues of toxicity, habitat loss, and monoculture affect them as well (see Packer).

6. The "dance-language controversy," in which California biologists Adrian Wenner and Patrick Wells discounted the dance-language hypothesis in favor of one based on solely olfactory communication ("odor plume theory"), has been resolved in favor of Frisch (who had conceded the importance of smell to the dance from the outset). Bees have a highly developed olfactory sense (163 chemical receptors for smell), and it is yet unclear how smell might be part of the communicative event of the dance as a whole.

7. For a very close patch of flowers, the bee performs what is called a "round dance" instead. Bees dance for other reasons as well, including a "tremble dance" (to involve more receiver bees in accepting nectar from the workers) and a "grooming dance" (to invite other bees to participate in social grooming).

8. Derrida is not really interested in bees here (although he has clearly read Frisch); he is interested in calling into question "the purity and indivisibility of a line between reaction and response, and especially the possibility of tracing such a line, between the human *in general* and the animal *in general*" (126; emphasis in the original). Thus, he shies away from saying that bees *do* respond. Raffles also "prefer[s] to avoid this treacherous and much-debated question of language and cognition" (199) and ends up making an argument similar to Derrida's: that the assumption that bees do not have language tells us more about the animals *assuming* than the animals *assumed*. Clearly so. But what is the harm of imagining across that species line once in a while, and why are Derrida and Raffles both so afraid to be seen to do so?

9. Scout bees are older worker bees. Worker bees, over the course of their (short) life spans, engage successively in a large number of different tasks, including hive cleaning, infant care, comb building, ventilating the hive, guarding its entrances, and foraging. They have a lot of experience of the hive's needs behind them before they go out scouting.

10. Seeley is not at all afraid to describe these behaviors as "honeybee democracy," and he ends the book by detailing the similarities between the dance debate and a faculty meeting; his is a very rationalist understanding of democracy that could be challenged for all sorts of reasons, not the least of which being its clear invocation of the U.S. "town hall" meeting as a democratic exemplar. It is *obviously* anthropomorphic, but perhaps unintentionally, it invites us to imagine both the ways in which bee politics are like ours and the ways in which ours are like bees' (for example, what is the role of pheromones in a faculty meeting, I wonder?).

11. Indeed, I might argue that bees, in their particular combination of biopolitical significance and political fascination for humans, *demand* material ecocriticism, in that their corpo-

realities and agencies tend to appear quite strongly in literary works about them, both historically and in the present, and whether we like it or not. I choose beekeeping literature, here, in part because the practice of keeping bees often cultivates an especially pronounced receptivity to the tracings of bee materialities.

12. Although that labor includes, for some products (wax, propolis), chemical transformations wrought by bee metabolisms, honey is made by bees in a process by which bee physical activity transforms an external raw material into a finished good. It is, in this respect, more akin to human labor than is a cow's production of milk. But, of course, to say that bees *labor* is to raise another specter from the anthropological machine: Karl Marx, for whom "what distinguishes the worst architect from the best of bees is this, that the architect raises his structure in imagination before he erects it in reality." If bees respond, perhaps they can also plan (and thus labor)? And how would we begin to find out?

13. This message is at the heart of the beautiful film *Queen of the Sun*, which is a very powerful moment of honeybee advocacy in that it not only fights for bees for the sake of their instrumental uses to human beings, but also demonstrates very powerfully what it might mean to struggle to create the conditions for their flowering for their own sakes. I think the film also shares a sensibility with Sean Borodale in this regard: that multispecies cherishing can allow bees to reveal to us their worlds.

14. All three of these novels instrumentalize the bees: they are involved in the unfolding of the stories much more in order to teach something to humans about humans than to teach something to humans about bees.

15. My enormous gratitude to Polly Atkin for recommending this book.

16. There is also a poem, "2nd February," in which honey simply stands as a memorial to the lives of bees, one of the only places in the book in which Borodale acknowledges that bees might be in crisis beyond his hives: "I go to the shelf where the honey lives, / and say, this is testament: bees did exist" (85).

17. Rancière does, however, explicitly consider the role of literature in the repartitioning of the sensible. See his recent book *The Politics of Literature*.

11 Excremental Ecocriticism and the Global Sanitation Crisis

Dana Phillips

> It's not leaking. It's overflowing.
> —Homer Simpson, *The Simpsons Movie*

NEW MATERIALISTS ARE fond of lists. Consider, as a first example, the beginning of Myra Hird's 2009 review essay on "material feminism": "Trans-corporeality. Entanglement. Meeting-with. Matter. Nonhuman. Causality. Intra-action. Disclosure. Agential realism." Each of the terms on this list names a concept central to the "emerging field" Hird is preparing to survey (329). Most of them have come to occupy an equally important position in the discourse of new materialist theory broadly speaking, which draws on material feminism but also taps additional sources, such as phenomenology and the philosophy of science, for ideas.

Some new materialist list makers are evidently less categorically minded than Hird seems to have been when writing her trend-spotting essay. Their lists go beyond generalities to identify the particular "matters" (that is, both things and the multifarious circumstances in which things are embroiled, are effected, and produce effects) that new materialists find striking—and illustrative of the theoretical claims they wish to make about trans-corporeality, intra-action, agential realism, and the like. For instance, political philosopher Jane Bennett writes, "Worms, or electricity, or various gadgets, or fats, or metals, or stem cells are actants, or what Darwin calls 'small agencies,' that, when in the right confederation with other physical and physiological bodies, can make big things happen" (*Vibrant* 94). Bennett devotes all or part of a chapter of her 2010 book, *Vibrant Matter,* to each of the items she identifies, in the sentence I have quoted, as a member of some "confederation" or another. Such instances of the material and such confederations, she argues, should be seen as "vibrant, vital, energetic, lively, quivering, vibratory, evanescent, and effluescent" (112). Here Bennett pays her debt to the phenomenological tradition by adding a clutch of modifiers of the kind phenomenologists like to use to the inventory of new materialist vocabulary.

Excremental Ecocriticism, Global Sanitation Crisis | 173

That ecocritics should find themselves in agreement with new materialist arguments, and that they have begun to add to new materialism's roster of concerns by formulating lists of their own, is a development less inevitable than it may seem at first glance. Thus, we find Serenella Iovino, in an essay on material ecocriticism, arguing, "Thinking materiality in environmental terms" means paying attention to "electric grids, polluting substances, chemicals, energy, assemblages, scientific apparatuses, cyborgs, waste, the things themselves" ("Material" 52). What is most striking about such an assertion being voiced in the midst of an essay on ecocriticism is the implication that ecocritics have *not* been paying attention to "things themselves," or at least not *enough* attention to things of the sort Iovino itemizes. Yet anyone who has followed the development of ecocriticism since the early 1990s will recognize that this implicit criticism of the field for neglecting some matters central to contemporary environmentalism is fair. Attending to pollution—to cite just one of the things Iovino lists—is unpleasant and disheartening and requires one to focus on the degradation of the natural world primarily in urbanized and industrialized spaces. Many ecocritics understandably have preferred to accentuate the positive by writing about wilderness and wild animals and the wild-hearted men and women who love them.

In the chapter that follows, I am going to focus on another item on Iovino's list—waste—and will try to show how such a focus affirms the central thrust of new materialism's arguments, while casting doubt on a couple of its strongest claims. The particular form of waste I will discuss here is human waste, or rather *shit*. (Most contemporary writers on the subject insist on using the four-letter word for political as well as rhetorical reasons; I will do the same here.) Shit has a long and troubled history, which ought not to come as a surprise to anyone who recalls the several mishaps of potty training or who knows that diarrhea continues to kill more people than any other disease. What *is* surprising, however, is shit's materiality. I will not strain the reader's credulity by calling shit vibrant, vital, energetic, lively, quivering, vibratory, and evanescent, as Bennett would have it, though I will acknowledge that shit is often effluescent. Yet effluescence, or a tendency to flow, is not always a good thing, and one of the bad things about shit is that it is both hard to get rid of and will not stay put. Materially, shit is perverse. This property raises the specter, one that has begun to haunt Europe along with the rest of the contemporary world, but has become especially worrisome in the Global South, of shit's future. One of the advantages of the new materialism, then, is that it allows one to understand how an everyday occurrence such as flushing a toilet—or, more likely, relieving oneself in a patch of roadside vegetation—can be a world-historic event. So I will begin with a history lesson, one in which shit plays a central and quite possibly a deterministic role. Like certain commodities (sugar, codfish, iron ore, petroleum), shit has the power to alter the course of human affairs, especially when it reminds us that the call of nature is never one we can afford to ignore.

Excrement from Colony to Postcolony and Beyond

In *Gravity's Rainbow*, a novel in which human waste makes a number of cameo appearances, Thomas Pynchon writes, "Colonies are the outhouses of the European soul, where a fellow can let his pants down and relax, enjoy the smell of his own shit" (317). Pynchon offers this observation in a chapter concerned with the aftereffects of the turn-of-the-century German adventure in what is now called Namibia, but was once known as Südwest, or Southwest, Africa.[1] The chapter details the experiences of the Schwarzkommando, a group of Herero (a tribal people indigenous to Namibia) who have been living in exile in Germany throughout the Third Reich and serving it as soldiers, though not in good faith: as World War II winds down, the Schwarzkommando pursues its own agenda, one involving scavenged V2 rockets. The novel's historical backdrop and mise-en-scène dictate that the Herero have long been familiar with Europeans dwelling both in Südwest and in the northern Heimatland of which the Third Reich and its führer made so much. The Herero understand, perhaps too well, the whims and eccentricities of their erstwhile colonial masters and military commanders.

In *Gravity's Rainbow*, Pynchon often puts the psychoanalytic notion of repression in play, though he does treat repression as integral to the European cultures (chiefly wartime England and Germany) he depicts. At the same time, he also treats repression as fundamental to the psychedelic American culture—that of the 1960s—the novel expresses, and from which it has emerged. Most of the characters in Pynchon's novel experience desires they know to be forbidden, or at best unrealistic. Given opportunities, many of them yield to their urges for, among other things, bananas in wartime London, hashish in bombed-out Berlin, and kinky sex whenever and wherever it can be found. The opportunities for self-indulgence turn out to be frequent. In Pynchon's handling, the so-called Good War seems to have been an almost ecstatic experience for many of its participants. *Gravity's Rainbow* is punctuated with the release of pent-up frustrations and with happy endings, even if the last of these—the Schwarzkommando's long-delayed firing of the ultimate V2 rocket, which begins its descent as the novel closes—carries a payload of ambiguity (the death drive is not the only drive it satisfies).

For the sort of ecocritic I am going to denominate as *excremental*, a subspecies or perhaps only a "sport" of the material ecocritic, Pynchon's reliance on the mechanics of repression poses a problem.[2] With the notion of repression in mind, shit always appears less as shit per se than as image, as metaphor and symbol. So although shit is waste, it never gets wasted; instead, it figures in the psychological and literary economy as excess and surplus. Thus, shit adds value and meaning, however deflationary its value and perverse its meaning. In literature, the history of which has shaped much of psychoanalytic theory, shit tends to be treated as the vehicle for either rollicking scatological humor or blistering social satire and therefore (merely) as a trope (see Laporte).

In *Gravity's Rainbow,* shit is indeed treated scatologically and satirically. Yet early on in the novel, Pynchon's hero, the US Army lieutenant Tyrone Slothrop, after being dosed with sodium Pentothal, recalls—or rather hallucinates—an epic journey he took some years earlier, when he was a Harvard undergraduate, down a toilet in the men's room of the Roseland Ballroom in Boston (63–71). The plumbing in this episode is accurately drawn, but the scene cannot be called realistic. Slothrop's cloacal voyage is instead a phantasmagoria of, among other things, race relations: the Roseland is located in Roxbury, which has been a predominately African American neighborhood since at least 1960, if not earlier. On his way down the Roseland's toilet, Slothrop comes across disturbing evidence of racial mixing (to learn the precise nature of this evidence, read the novel). Something roughly similar, and equally phantasmagoric, happens in another scatological scene in *Gravity's Rainbow,* when a mastermind of wartime psychological operations manipulates a general into eating the shit of the beautiful Dutch spy Katje every night. Katje's shit makes Brigadier Pudding think—he cannot help himself, given the novel's embrace of the logic of free association—of the cocks of black men (233–36).

That Pynchon is deploying the hypothesis of repression in both of these scenes, as in others, is perhaps only too obvious. After all, Tyrone Slothrop is the scion of an old New England family in the business of manufacturing toilet paper, while Katje is a dominatrix trained by an officer of the Waffen SS and the sexually confused Brigadier Pudding is an Englishman. *Quod erat demonstrandum:* the imaginary world depicted in *Gravity's Rainbow* is well organized, and it never seems more plausible than when it becomes reflexively stereotypical. Of course, this tension between the realistic warp and the fictional woof of its depictions of World War II is precisely what makes the book a *novel.* Here I would suggest that given its strategy of simultaneous representation and misrepresentation, of mixing the literal or at least the plausible with the fictional, fantastic, metaphorical, symbolic, and stereotypical, the novel may be a form with which an excremental ecocriticism is not going to be able to traffic profitably, not if it is to be as materialist as it needs to be. This is one of the reasons I turn to a work of nonfiction in the fourth section and a book-length poem (one that largely eschews the metaphorical and symbolic) in my conclusion.

Before I discuss the particularities of the task that faces a material ecocriticism focused on the excremental, however, I first need to take into account some recent scholarship that would seem to confirm Pynchon's depiction, however outlandish and stereotypical it may be, of the colonies as "the outhouses of the European soul" and of an interest in shit as the deepest, darkest, foulest secret of that soul. Historian Warwick Anderson, in a widely cited essay entitled "Excremental Colonialism," discusses what he calls the "brownwashing" (641) of the Philippines during the American occupation that followed the 1898 war with Spain. Notoriously, that war was an exercise in jingoism, so Anderson may be justified in treating "excremental colonialism" as a "discourse" in the full-blown Foucauldian sense of the term. This discourse projected the Americans' fear of shit onto the brown bodies of their Filipino subjects, simultaneously constructing them as unruly defecators and disciplining them in the hope that they might be more easily ruled in future. In American eyes, what made the Filipinos seem such unruly defecators was their habit of shitting in fields and along the byways of the archipelago's islands. The Filipinos also shat through the trapdoors in the floors of their own houses, and thus near the streams and wells from which they drew drinking and bathing water. They seemed, to the Americans, to have no desire to avail themselves of the white porcelain toilets preferred by a more civilized race.

Lest we dwell too much on the unsavory details of Filipino defecation, Anderson warns us against trying to discover "the '*true*' pattern of Filipino and American excretory practices" in the archipelago, which he identifies as an "unrewarding" topic because it is a "positivist" one. Just consider the 126,000 jars of Filipino feces collected by dogged American researchers obsessed with identifying its harmful traits (644), and thus with the "surveillance and regulation" (667) of its producers, and not only where their sanitary practices were concerned. Surely, these jars were the concrete result of one of the more extraordinary "assemblages" (the term is Latour's, but see Bennett, *Vibrant* 23–24) of *personnel* and *matériel* ever assembled. Nevertheless, Anderson insists we should not take their gross materiality into account as anything more than evidence of American discomfort with the human body. For the antipositivist Anderson, it seems, if the Filipinos violated anything, it was only the "conventional sense of disgust" (648) felt by their American masters, who were victims themselves, though not of political injustice and cultural domination, but rather of psychological "repression" (650).

If you find yourself nodding your head in agreement with Anderson, please ponder a couple of things. One is that Anderson's depiction of the American administration of Filipino lives is drawn in something of a historical vacuum. Although Anderson is fully conversant with the imperialist context of the Spanish-American War, he neglects to mention how recently Americans were fouling their own environment with shit. The great sanitary revolution of the nineteenth century had only lately concluded, or rather was still under way. Thus, many Americans continued to shit in fields and along dusty country roads, and there were plenty of poorly built outhouses yet to be found in the backwaters, and dangerously near the water sources, of the United States. So the flush toilet represented a future yet to come for many early-twentieth-century Americans. The people of the Philippines were not alone in that.

The second thing you ought to ponder is the fact that Anderson's description of turn-of-the-century Filipino defecation practices, which he derives from published reports and government archives but brackets as untrustworthy, is consonant with the description of contemporary defecation practices by those presently concerned to alleviate some of the miseries of developing nations, and in particular the miseries that characterize life in the sprawling urban slums of the postcolonies. What Anderson discounts, then, is the pungent, messy reality of shit no matter whose shit it may be. That dark night in which all shit is brown is just any old dark night whatsoever. Moreover, there is something in this world that we can think of as shit without lapsing into willful epistemological and ontological naïveté of the sort that typified the thinking of the midcentury positivists, who serve Anderson as straw men. Nor need we reflexively embrace the often vacuous notion of cultural construction as the only alternative. Like the socialism of the Eastern bloc in the 1970s, actually existing shit may be an artifact of its time and place, but that makes it no less tangible. *If you can collect it in jars, weigh it, analyze it, and catalog it, and then write up and publish the results, shit is real.*[3] Properties, and not perceptions, are the determining factors of the sort of reality I am invoking here, which is a materialist one without being a mere artifact of the outmoded positivism Anderson rejects.

Actually existing shit gets more play in a follow-up essay to Anderson's, Jed Esty's "Excremental Postcolonialism." Esty sets out to treat shit as both "naturalistic detail" and "governing trope" (23) in the fiction of two different sets of postcolonial writers, the one Irish (Joyce and Beckett) and the other African (Soyinka and Armah). Esty also recognizes that the use of shit by these writers, who depict their homelands as foul places and therefore seem to be heaping shit on their own heads, is "picaresque, grotesque, and satirical," and thus "counterdiscursive" (25). Crucially, Esty distinguishes between psychoanalytic and mythic treatments of shit as opposed to those that are historical and political (26) and tries to merge the two kinds of treatment in his essay, never losing sight of the fact that shit marks an "existential bottom line" (51–52).

Because I am trying to offer a brief on behalf of "excremental ecocriticism," I need to explain where I differ from Esty, Anderson, and Pynchon. To take these predecessors in the order in which I have just named them: Esty's insistence that shit can be both "naturalistic detail" and "governing trope" is surely right, as far as it goes. It does not go far enough, however, in recognizing the peculiarly insistent and noisome nature of shit as material object and vital substance (about which more needs to be said here). The latter—shit's stubbornly repellent nature—is something Anderson treats as if it were a figment of the bourgeois imagination, as if the bourgeois had no direct experience with the thing itself (to recall Iovino's phrase). To discount the materiality of shit, however one perceives it, is as futile, pragmatically speaking, as trying to put the proverbial toothpaste back into the tube. Where shit is concerned, there are a number of real-world difficulties that an ecocritic ought to take into account, especially one who is trying (as I am) to follow through on Timothy Morton's suggestion, in *The Ecological Thought*, that we take time to dwell on the question of where our "toilet waste" (9) goes. Much of that waste—a disturbing amount of it, in truth—does not find its way into a toilet at all, and goes nowhere. An awful lot of shit lands not in a toilet but along a woodland path, behind a garden wall or hedgerow, along the margins of a railway, or in the muck heap where the family bucket gets dumped in the predawn hours, and there it remains, at least until nature takes its course. Some of it will be carried off in morsels by houseflies, the original pooper-scoopers; the rest will dry in the sun and blow away, or will dissolve in the dew and rain, and seep into the groundwater. Such is shit's natural history, which is why it remains a major pollutant in many locations around the globe. For this reason, and a variety of others, the prospect that confronts a would-be excremental ecocritic is daunting.

The History of Shit: Fecal Matters

First one has to come to terms with the singularity of shit as a material substance. There is nothing else quite like it, and it is never quite like itself from one instance to the next. Its mutability makes shit's natural history complex, and in a manner with which we are beginning to be all too familiar in the current era of chaotic meteorology, accelerated climate change, stochastic or guesswork population dynamics, and the ecology of disturbance. In *Poop Culture*, Dave Praeger reports, "Any particular poop represents a never-to-be repeated confluence of diet, metabolism, and environment" (20). This means that poop is never an indifferent mound of homogenous stuff, but is always rich with data, which is why shit, whether human or nonhuman, can be used by biologists as an environmental indicator. Not only is it informative, but shit also has its own character and tone. "Like a snowflake," Praeger observes, "every poop is unique" (20). Unfortunately, the uniqueness of every "particular poop" frustrates the efforts of sanitary engineers to model our shit, something they badly need to do (for reasons that ought to be obvious). Shit's quantities and shit's qualities are elusive. However, that does not mean no figures or figurations are available. For instance, Praeger reports that the average human being produces a half pound, give or take, of shit a day (30), and considering the sheer number of human beings on this planet, this means that every snowflake-like poop that drops contributes to a shit storm of epoch-making proportions.

The title of Rose George's book *The Big Necessity* confirms Praeger's philosophical point ("we all answer to a lower power" [*Poop Culture* 205]). The contents of her book confirm his statistics. George says that we spend, on average, three years of our lives going to the toilet (6), which in the United States is also the amount of time it takes to earn a law degree (my observation, not hers). George also reports that we each produce 77 pounds of shit a year, at the rate of 250 grams, or roughly a half pound, a day. Yet where Praeger, who seems to have a cultural studies background, goes on to tell the usual story about the flush toilet and Victorian repression—the flush toilet, he says, is "an apparatus of ideology" (48), George, a journalist, attends more closely to the facts, or to "the things themselves," which are sufficiently alarming. According to George, whose focus is global, "2.6 billion people don't have sanitation" (2). That number was current as of 2006; by now it probably needs to be adjusted upward. One might argue, with this increase in mind, that it hardly matters if a flush toilet is "an apparatus of ideology" if so many people still do not own one. George, however, is telling us something still more dire: the 2.6 billion people whose lack of sanitation she records have nowhere at all to shit, and nothing whatsoever—"no latrine, toilet, bucket, or box" (2)—to shit in. So in places such as India, they are forced to shit in the woods and fields, or along train tracks. This alfresco approach is known in sanitation circles, according to George, as "open defecation" (174) and has been documented most infamously, among writers on the postcolonial situation, by V. S. Naipaul (notoriously "an apparatus of ideology" of a different sort). If those who practice open defecation happen to be female, and are therefore expected to be modest, they must wait until after dark to seek relief, as George observes, thereby "risking rape and snakebite" (2). Thus, the ecology of shit proves to have unlooked for social and medical dimensions. Its dilemmas are not to be resolved solely by means of utopian schemes like the recycling of human waste—just as Slavoj Žižek has argued in *Living in the End Times,* though for slightly different reasons than the ones he offers.[4]

In other parts of the world, but again in the Global South, people shit in plastic shopping bags, twist and tie the bags shut, and then fling them over a convenient wall or rooftop, to fall to earth wherever they may. In certain African slums, these bags are called "helicopter" or "flying" toilets, and perhaps because the image they conjure up is so potent, they are frequently mentioned in contemporary accounts of poor sanitation (George 210-11; Black and Fawcett 47). In *City of Slums,* Mike Davis notes that in the wake of the first Gulf War, flying toilets were also called "scud missiles" (139). It is an apt name, since an airborne plastic shopping bag filled with shit also may bring death from above.

Here is why: "A gram of feces can contain 10 million viruses, 1 million bacteria, 1,000 parasite cysts, and 100 worm eggs," Rose George writes. "One sanitation specialist has estimated that people who live in areas with inadequate sanitation ingest 10 grams of fecal matter every day" (2). This daily ingestion of shit further elevates the world's "worm burden," as George observes: "At any one time, about one billion people are carrying hookworm in their guts and expelling it in their feces," and a comparable number play host to roundworm, "which can survive in human excrement for years" (175). Our shit thus provides a home for an impressive number of creatures and is the vector for an equally impressive number of diseases and infections. So not only does it have agency, but it also hosts a myriad of agents, along with traces of our own DNA. Speaking of which, George cites a geneticist who believes that the flush toilet probably has a lot to do with the dramatic increase in human life spans since the nineteenth century (3). Yet this does not mean that the flush toilet is a technological wonder of the sort celebrated by ideologues of progress like the futurists and avant-gardes like the Dadaists and surrealists, who thought such marvels belonged in art galleries and museums. The flush toilet relies heavily on water for its operation, and most people who use one add toilet paper to the mix when they flush, so that the toilet contributes to water shortages and to deforestation. Worst of all, the shit we get rid of when we use flush toilets finds its way, sooner or later, into the water supply, either by being introduced directly into a stream (which happens in today's world more often than you might think, and not only in the Global South), or by being fed into sewers from which it flows into settlement and treatment ponds, or by being sent to unsealed septic tanks from which it slowly seeps into aquifers. Shit is ubiquitous. We are each of us likely to ingest traces of our own shit whenever we brush a housefly from our cheeks, wash our hands, or eat and drink.

The epidemiological character of shit—its service as a vector for *E. coli* and *Giardia lamblia,* its contribution to the "worm burden," and so on, almost ad infinitum—is something an excremental ecocritic cannot overlook. However, for an excremental ecocritic, the engineering perspective on shit is also indispensable.[5] After all, we reap the benefits of our toilets only if they do not malfunction. Flush toilets can be finicky, refusing to take what we offer them, and their performance even when they are in good repair is, at best, only so-so. "A flush is a chaotic event," according to George (55). That is why toilet designers and sanitary engineers have worked diligently to find substitute materials that will mimic some of the more salient properties of human shit, which include:

shit's tendency, when firm, to clump, especially when mixed with toilet paper

shit's tendency to emerge in a scattershot fashion when one is unwell, making a tidy bowl impossible to maintain

shit's tendency to float when suspended in water

shit's tendency to aerosolize each time we flush, so that minute particles of it become suspended in the stuffy air of our bathrooms

Here the reader should recall the rule of thumb announced earlier: *if you cannot flush it, and need to model it, shit must be real.* In the late nineteenth century, the jury-rigged fecal simulacra used by researchers and inventors, each one a Rube Goldberg at heart, included apples, sponges, and crumpled sheets of paper. In contemporary Japan, researchers at the TOTO toilet company rely on soybean paste as a key ingredient in a recipe that remains proprietary. An American researcher at a rival company also uses soybean paste, but like a drug mule he packs it in condoms first. Meanwhile, in England, that bastion of tradition, an instructor who leads classes of schoolchildren around the sewage treatment facility where he works uses Weetabix, a long-popular brand of breakfast cereal, to illustrate how shit *behaves*—my use of the active verb is deliberate—when immersed in water.[6] Given that soybeans and whole-grain cereals also promote regularity, their use in toilet design has a certain logic to it, which you do not need to be a sanitary engineer—or a vegan, a senior citizen, British, or Japanese—to appreciate. Toilet designers, however, are less interested in neat logic than in getting shit to pass smoothly down a drain at a single point source. What happens to it thereafter, and whether it enters a coordinated and well-maintained network featuring thousands of similar point sources, is another matter entirely, as I pointed out earlier.

It is tempting to think that sanitation is a problem we will find more manageable in the future, since so many of us have been managing our shit for quite some time now. We have done so either by letting shit compost and then spreading it on the fields where we grow our food, or more recently by treating shit in settlement ponds before reintroducing it to the open environment of our waterways, converting the residue to sludge fertilizer, a postindustrial product very different from old-fashioned night soil. Our optimism, however tempered it may be by our pragmatism, is likely to founder on the hidden reefs of shit's quantities and qualities in the contemporary world. As Homer Simpson says of the silo full of pig shit he keeps in his backyard (I will not explain why—it is a long and silly story), "It's not leaking. It's overflowing." The overflowing silo is noxious; it is also toxic. This is why pig shit, like human shit, does not make good manure. (Pig shit's epidemiological profile, moreover, is too close to that of human shit for its use as fertilizer to be wise.) Note that when I assert that pig shit and human shit are *toxic,* I speak literally: each now contains heavy metals and pharmaceuticals along with the usual vast array of pathogens (Davis, *Planet of Slums* 135). So toxic have all forms of postmodern shit become that someday soon, we may find that shit, like spent plutonium, needs to be sequestered in subterranean vaults guarded by crack teams of sanitation workers.

This nightmare scenario is less fantastic than it sounds. In *Planet of Slums,* Mike Davis details the health hazards posed by runaway urbanization in Asia, Africa, and South America, the brown triangle of the current sanitary crisis. The streets of the new "polycentric" (10) slum cities of the Global South have been created in complete defiance of the principles of urban planning and are often so choked with shit that Davis compares them to cattle feedlots (92). Slum cities also tend to be ringed by "stinking mountains of shit" and other garbage (138), where rag pickers eke out a living, exploiting one of those new economic niches of which free-market ideologues make so much, while ignoring how loathsome the enterprises these niches shelter can be for those forced to work in them. In his chapter "Slum Ecology," Davis notes that shit is so prevalent a feature of the landscape in the polycentric urban spaces of the Global South that the skies of megalopolitan

Mexico City are tainted by clouds of "fecal dust blowing off Lake Texcoco during the hot, dry season" (143). It would be a mistake, however, to see the foul weather along the shores of Lake Texcoco as exotic or exceptional, and therefore remote from the experience of anyone who does not dwell somewhere in the Global South. Thanks to a worldwide shift of human populations from country to city, an industrialized and globalized agriculture, altered climates, and redirected ocean currents, those of us who live in or near the old metropolises of the North can take no comfort from the thought that the rising tides of shit and drifting clouds of fecal dust have yet to dirty the sands of our beaches, taint our air, and besmirch our foodstuffs. Again, shit is ubiquitous. *Et in Arcadia faeces.*

"And That . . . Is All"

I will now return to the continent where I began. South African poet Antjie Krog provides some hints about how we might react when—as the saying goes—*shit happens* in our own backyards and happens in one or another of the gruesome ways I have been documenting. The final chapter of her memoir, *A Change of Tongue,* tells the story of Krog's misadventures as one of a "caravan of poets" traveling through Mali. Krog describes what it is like to pass through the streets of Bamako, a city that "stretches as far as the eye can see" (300) along the banks of the Niger. "Now they"—the poets and their Malian escorts—"are in the bus again," Krog writes. "They pass through incredible wastes of poverty and rubbish, a tumult of smell and colour, along seemingly impassable roads where 4×4s nod through gigantic potholes in low gear, past overflowing sewers, gigantic canals dug into the river, choking with garbage" (300–301). The less public spaces of Bamako are, if anything, even more squalid. Of her living quarters in the city, Krog reports the following:

> Someone takes a heartfelt dump in the toilet next door, you can hear him neighing lightly between volleys, like someone whose last drop of blood is being tapped. The stench belches into their room. They do not hear the dumper using the bucket. Later they hear another person going in and calling out in shock. He fills three buckets and flushes the toilet. Then he throws up. Then he takes a dump. Somebody starts banging urgently on the door. It sounds as if he is being allowed to pee in the bath. The smells become unbearable. She rises silently and creeps up to the roof, where people are lying peacefully asleep. As the cocks crow, the sun peels like an apricot through the haze of the river and she can hear donkeys braying and goats blaring. (309)

These scenes, the first public and the second ostensibly private (privacy in Bamako being highly relative), are less different from another scene that also transpires at the hostel where the caravan of poets is housed than they may seem at first glance.

In this third scene, nature seems to be trying to reclaim a patch of debased urban space for one of its own kind:

Around them frogs with open mouths and red eyes are leaping like part of the biblical plague. The empty, crumbling swimming pool is filled with frogs. In the corners they clamber on top of each other in silently palpitating agglomerations as they try to jump out and escape. Others dangle open-legged on the edges, about to fall in. On the way to her room they plop away from her feet in dark splashes into the night.

All night the roar of a croaking chorus fills the courtyard. (303)

Each of these passages from *A Change of Tongues* might be read according to the "excremental colonialism" and "excremental postcolonialism" outlined by Anderson and Esty, since something is clearly amiss in Mali. *Bamako is overflowing*, and you do not have to be a poet like Krog to be struck by the disarray of the imagery a flood tide of feces and frogs produces. Krog shows us vivid images of a place in which culture and nature, which in the ordinary course of events always commingle (just as any new materialist will insist), have now become so entangled and mutually degraded as to produce a dog's breakfast of an environment: shit fills the streets, while frogs fill the swimming pools. That an apricot sun illuminates the ghastly result heightens the irony and does nothing to redeem the squalor—the braying of donkeys and blaring of goats might as well be the honking of taxicabs.

Yet the magnitude of the disorder Krog describes makes Warwick Anderson's warning about "positivism" seem like a form of epistemological censorship. This magnitude also may disqualify these scenes for the purposes of the scatological satire Jed Esty finds good reasons to admire. Nor can one imagine even so fine a comic talent as Pynchon employing the excremental excesses Krog describes in one of his subversive little fantasies. In Bamako, it seems nothing is left to subvert: its landscape has become altogether cloacal, and there is no need to journey down a toilet to discover hidden truths or indulge repressed desires. Yet if one of the tenets of excremental ecocriticism is that in today's world, a situation can be considered normal *only* if it is all fouled up, then Bamako seems more important to contemplate than Walden Pond.

In *A Change of Tongues*, Krog sticks to nonfiction and worries about whether the feeling of horror she experienced in Mali does not reveal something of her guilty nature as a South African—as the only white member of the caravan of poets, and an Afrikaner to boot. So when she next returns to her hometown of Kroonstad in the Free State, she goes to see her uncle, an engineer who manages the municipal sewage works. She asks him if what she has heard—"there is a difference between the excrement of white people and the excrement of black people" (355)—is true. The question makes Krog's uncle angry: though he is an older man, he wants to belong to the new South Africa, and he has no time, or no time left, for racism. Grudgingly, he admits that there is indeed a difference between the shit of blacks and whites. Because people living in the black township on the outskirts of Kroonstad have to get up earlier to go to their jobs, their shit arrives at the sewage works sooner each day than the leisurely shit of whites, which begins to show up only around seven in the morning. Shit from the township is firmer, too, but this is because whites are able to use more water to flush their toilets and bathe, which dilutes the flow of their sewage. "And that," Krog's uncle concludes, "is all" (356). For his niece, it is an object lesson in the intertwined ecologies of race, place, and waste.

"Chunky Intermediacy"

What I have offered in the preceding pages has been less a matter of a new and different "ecological thought" of the sort Timothy Morton has urged than of an alternative environmental narrative, one that takes some surprising turns despite the familiarity of some of the details about shit that it records. I suspect this is about all excremental ecocriticism, and material ecocriticism, can hope to do: invite us to see both familiar and unfamiliar objects and materials in a different and, the world being what it is today, a less hopeful context. For the excremental ecocritic in particular, the vision that emerges is shocking: we see more brown than green. If nothing else, we need to come to terms with our discomfiture, which a reinvigorated materialism is unlikely to assuage. "Matter," as Karen Barad observes, is "always already an ongoing historicity" ("Posthumanist" 139). I think we might borrow Barad's words and add to her point by saying that the environmental crisis in which we are now fully embroiled is also—and precisely because of its materiality—"always already an ongoing historicity," which will make it that much harder to resolve. This is what shit's history and historicity—its refusal, so to speak, to behave as a good object should, and its stunning performance of its agency—have to teach us.

The lesson may be difficult for us to learn. As A. R. Ammons puts it in *Garbage*, a long philosophical poem intended to declare "the perfect / scientific and materialistic notion of the / spindle of energy" (24–25), we need to find ways to distinguish "between hallucinatory flux and pure form's rigid / thought and count: between diarrhea and constipation." To help us discover this middle ground, Ammons proposes we focus on

> chunky intermediacy, some motion with
> minor forms clear, clusters or bindings, with the
> concomitant gaps, tie-offs and recommencements
> expected. (98)

Naturally "chunky intermediacy," much of which—us included—presents itself in the shape of "trash," is going to prove "plenty wondrous" (46) and will strain our credulity, as Ammons gleefully illustrates. To borrow language folks in South Carolina used to express great surprise, epistemological quandary, and mortal uncertainty when I was a boy, we may not know "whether to shit or go blind"—not at the moment. Yet that is why we call it *environmental history*, and why shit's story needs to be told even if (especially if) we do not yet know how it will end.

Notes

1. Germany colonized Südwest in the late nineteenth century. Its repressive rule led to an uprising in the northern part of the country; this uprising was brutally put down when a policy of genocide was put into effect. The colony became part of South Africa after Germany's defeat in World War I, achieving independence only with the end of apartheid and white minority rule in the early 1990s.

2. My remarks about the mechanics of repression regarding shit parallel those Foucault makes about the "repressive hypothesis" regarding sexuality in *The History of Sexuality*, vol. 1. For a treatment of shit that seems to take the concept of repression too seriously, see Laporte.

3. I am paraphrasing Ian Hacking's often-cited argument about the reality of atoms in *Representing and Intervening*.

4. Žižek writes, "The ideal of 'recycling' involves the utopia of a self-enclosed circle in which all waste, all useless remainder, is sublated: nothing gets lost, all trash is reused," whereas "in nature itself, there is no circle of total recycling, there is un-usable waste." However, Žižek concludes that "the properly aesthetic attitude of a radical ecologist is not that of admiring or longing for a pristine nature of virgin forests and clear sky, but rather that of accepting waste as such, of discovering the aesthetic potential of waste, of decay, of the *inertia* of rotten material which serves no purpose" (35; emphasis added). The aesthetic potential of human waste would seem to be nil, but the reader should recall the discussion of the scatological in literature with which I began—and am trying to move beyond here, since shit is anything but "inert."

5. By "engineering perspective," I have in mind the philosophical interpretation of evolution promoted by Daniel Dennett in *Darwin's Dangerous Idea*: see the chapter "Biology Is Engineering" (187–228) and the mind-set promoted, and too often oversold, by civil engineering; see Pickering, "New Ontologies" 1–14.

6. For the preceding details and more, see George 55, 57–58, 151.

12 Oceanic Origins, Plastic Activism, and New Materialism at Sea

Stacy Alaimo

Trans-corporeality at Sea?

Climate change. Ocean acidification. Dead zones. Oil "spills." Industrial fishing, overfishing, trawling, long lines, shark finning. Bycatch, bykill. Ghost nets. Deep-sea mining. Habitat destruction. Dumping. Radioactive, plastic, and microplastic pollution. Ecosystem collapse. Extinction. The state of the oceans is dire. The destruction of marine environments is painful to contemplate and tempting to ignore. Having returned from a week on the Gulf of Mexico, where sea life was sparse, I could hardly bear to read Callum Roberts's *The Unnatural History of the Sea,* which describes the staggering abundance of fish and mammals that once inhabited the oceans. Roberts argues that our "collective amnesia" about the profusion of sea life in the past and our dismissal of "tales of giant fish or seas bursting with life" as "far-fetched" lead us to set our environmental baselines far too low as "we come to accept the degraded condition of the sea as normal" (xv). Oceanographer Sylvia Earle notes that since the "middle of the 20th century, hundreds of millions of tons of ocean wildlife have been removed from the sea, while hundreds of millions of tons of waste have been poured into it" (*The World* 12). Countless species have been overfished to the point of extinction, and numerous marine habitats are being destroyed. Rob Stewart's film *Sharkwater* exposes how the desire for shark-fin soup has resulted in the slaughter of sharks, taking place globally on such a colossal scale that many species of shark may soon be extinct. The destructive practice of trawling, which dates back to the fourteenth century, has now been joined by deep-sea trawling, which destroys creatures that may be endangered or as yet undiscovered or both, as well as the deep-sea coral reefs, some of which are thousands of years old, which are considered the old-growth forests of the sea. Long lines, which extend miles across the ocean, luring in birds, mammals, sea turtles, and fish with hundreds or even thousands of baited hooks, result in wide expanses of death and destruction, as the majority of the animals are killed and then discarded. Whether by long lines, trawling, or huge drift nets, industrial fisheries destroy *most* of the catch as "bycatch"—living creatures cast back as lifeless garbage.[1] Jonathan Safran Foer, in *Eating Animals,* challenges us to imagine "being served a plate of sushi. But this plate also holds all of the animals that were killed for your serving of sushi. The plate might have to be five feet across" (50). Safran Foer disrupts the radical disconnect between the aestheticized, inert food on the plate and the moment of capture, when diverse animal liveliness was quelled by industrialized fishing. But there's another animal in this scene, the reader who is being served the animals on the plate. This human, as a material being, is a pivotal node in the networks of consumption, waste, and pollution that destroy ocean ecologies.

In *Bodily Natures: Science, Environment, and the Material Self*, I argue for a conception of trans-corporeality that traces the material interchanges across human bodies, animal bodies, and the wider material world. As the material self cannot be disentangled from networks that are simultaneously economic, political, cultural, scientific, and substantial, what was once the ostensibly bounded human subject finds herself in a swirling landscape of uncertainty where practices and actions that were once not even remotely ethical or political matters suddenly become so. Trans-corporeality is a new materialist and posthumanist sense of the human as perpetually interconnected with the flows of substances and the agencies of environments. Activists, as well as everyday practitioners of environmental, environmental health, environmental justice, and climate change movements, work to reveal and reshape the flows of material agencies across regions, environments, animal bodies, and human bodies—even as global capitalism and the medical-industrial complex reassert a more convenient ideology of solidly bounded, individual consumers and benign, discrete, products. Although the recognition of trans-corporeality begins with human bodies in their environments, tracing substantial interchanges renders the human permeable, dissolving the outline of the subject. Trans-corporeality starts from a human locale but it extends into a posthumanist sense of the subject, as it is radically reconceived as a site of material agencies within global networks and systems. As a type of material feminism, trans-corporeality is indebted to Judith Butler's conception of the subject as immersed within a matrix of discursive systems,[2] but it transforms that model, insisting that the subject cannot be separated from networks of intra-active material agencies (Karen Barad) and thus cannot ignore the disturbing epistemological quandaries of risk society (Ulrich Beck). It is my hope that trans-corporeality—in theory, literature, film, activism, and daily life—is a mode of ecomaterialism that will discourage citizens, consumers, and embodied humans from taking refuge in fantasies of transcendence and imperviousness that render environmentalism a merely elective and external enterprise.

This chapter will examine to what extent the new materialisms and trans-corporeality specifically can extend through the seas. The persistent (and convenient) conception of the ocean as so vast and powerful that anything dumped into it will be dispersed into oblivion[3] makes it particularly difficult to capture, map, and publicize the flow of toxins across terrestrial, oceanic, and human habitats. Moreover, many marine habitats, such as those in the benthic and pelagic zones, are not only relatively unknown to scientists, but are often depicted as "alien" worlds, completely independent from human activities. In a related essay (see Alaimo, "States"), I examine whether evolutionary origin stories that emphasize how human bodies descend from marine ancestors can provoke an environmentalist ethos toward the oceans, discussing the work of poetry of Linda Hogan and the science writing of Rachel Carson and Neil Shubin. Here I will focus on the scholarship of Stefan Helmreich and Mark McMenamin and Dianna McMenamin and the writing and films of plastic-pollution activists, examining different ways of articulating connections between humans and the sea. Even though the long evolutionary arc that ties humans to their aquatic ancestors may evoke modes of kinship with the seas, formulations that end with the human as a finished product of that process conclude too soon. A more potent marine trans-corporeality would link humans to global networks of consumption, waste, and pollution, capturing the strange agencies of the ordinary stuff of our lives.

Saturating Terrestrial Life: Aquatic Ancestors, Hypersea, and Genetic Soup

If one of the key obstacles for ocean conservation movements is that terrestrial humans are disconnected from the vast liquid habitats that cover much of the planet, then narratives, theories, paradigms, and practices that reveal interconnections between these spheres may encourage marine environmentalisms. Indeed, several ocean scientists and conservationists, including Rachel Carson, Sylvia Earle, and Julia Whitty, evoke a sense of connection between terrestrial humans and the seas by suggesting that the sea is in our very blood (Carson), by emphasizing that every breath we take contains oxygen produced by plankton (Earle), or by contending we see the ocean through the ocean—since our eyes are surrounded by saltwater. Whitty laments that although "we carry the ocean within ourselves, in our blood and in our eyes, so that we see through seawater," we nonetheless "appear blind to its fate" (1). Sylvia Earle connects the distant evolutionary past with the immediacy of living human bodies: "Our origins are there, reflected in the briny solution coursing through our veins and in the underlying chemistry that links us to all other life" (*Sea* 15). In "Human Nature at Sea," anthropologist and science studies scholar Stefan Helmreich, quoting Earle (the same quote as above), Carl Safina, and the singer Björk, observes that such "pronouncements cast seawater as a shared substance that makes it possible to feel an embodied human kinship with the aqueous Earth. Environmentally concerned scientists hope that such kinship will lead humans to imagine themselves as linked to the planet both personally and evolutionarily" (50). I agree with Helmreich that such formulations evoke a sense of evolutionary kinship that marine environmentalists hope will translate into ethical and political commitments to sea life. But in the companion piece to this essay, which critiques Neill Shubin's book *Your Inner Fish*, I argue that even though such formulations evoke evolutionary kinship across vast temporal and oceanic expanses, they may be dismissed as ancient history if they do not open out onto the present moment, acknowledging how human bodies participate in global networks of harm.

Whereas Shubin shores up conventional ideologies of distancing and disengagement, as his formulation of our "inner fish" paradoxically shores up the boundaries of the Human, who is a positioned as a "unique," "exceptional," and discrete culmination of evolutionary processes, for Carson, Whitty, and Earle, the idea that humans originated from the seas and still carry the seas within us situates potential ethical and political recognitions as arising from a trans-corporeal tracing that traverses time and space. By dramatizing the palpable presence of our oceanic origins, they implicitly call for these evolutionary traces to catalyze contemporary commitments. Such calls occur within the terrestrial habitat of human ethics and politics even as they are informed by a blue-green environmentalist vision. The fact that they call us to realize our evolutionary origins in the seas presupposes a sense of disconnection that requires an epiphanic realization of kinship. Mark McMenamin and Dianna McMenamin, in their book *Hypersea: Life on Land*, dismiss the idea of blood as seawater, critiquing the film *Hemo the Magnificent*, which "portrayed the saltiness of blood as a legacy of the marine environment of our fishy ancestors"(23). They state that even though this idea is "lovely," and "it may have helped a lot of people bond with the planet and enjoy the idea of evolution . . . it was a fairy tale," since the blood of vertebrates is, and has been, less salty than the sea (24). Nonetheless, their book *Hypersea* "resurrect[s] albeit in a modified form, the hypothesis that the sap of plants and the blood of land animals has an evolutionary connection with seawater" (24–25). They argue not that terrestrial life has its origins in the seas but that it *is* sea life. Contending that their conception of "hypersea" is both a "physical entity" and a "new scientific theory" (6), they explain, "land organisms have, by necessity, evolved together as part of a greater interconnected mass of living cells. In moving out of marine waters, complex life has taken the sea beyond the sea and folded it back inside of itself to form Hypersea" (5). Moreover, they stress that "living fluids are not a mere remnant or analog of the sea; they are actually are a new type of sea or marine environment: Hypersea" (25). The idea that the fluids pulsing through living creatures are a kind of marine environment and that all "*plant, animal, protoctistan, and fungal life on land,*" plus their associated "*viral or bacterial symbionts or parasites*" (3; emphasis in the original), constitute the "hypersea" is, at first, an astonishing revelation. The sea seems to be everywhere, within us, around us, regardless of how arid our terrestrial habitat may be. Yet if the concept of "hypersea" blankets nearly everything in the same aqueous composition, the distinctiveness of marine habitats, ecosystems, and creatures is lost even as many new species of ocean life are only just now being found.[4] And although it may seem profoundly posthumanist to envision humans not as distinct individuals but as "reservoirs of hypersea" that are inhabited by other organisms (242), *Hypersea* concludes within a rather Humanist stance. Whereas Carson, Whitty, Earle, and others emphasize the aquatic origins of the human in order to provoke a sense of kinship, responsibility, and concern for oceanic environments, *Hypersea* concludes, not unlike *Our Inner Fish*, by shoring up the ethical confines of Humanism, claiming that the concept of hypersea will benefit human health because "many contemporary health threats have a hypermarine aspect—that is, they owe in part to the fact that body fluid is, to a certain extent, a shared resource" (255). Carl Zimmer asks:

> What difference will it make to us if Hypersea is real? For one thing, we'll have to realize that we humans are stirring it up like never before. Just as we have brought zebra mussels from Europe to the waters of the United States, we have probably brought diseases like AIDS very quickly from one reservoir of Hypersea (monkeys) to another (ourselves)—and in both cases, the invaders are wreaking havoc. We would benefit from manipulating Hypersea's currents wisely. (n.p.)

Despite Zimmer's enthusiasm for hypersea, the concept does not seem to make much of a difference, as the realization that humans are "stirring it up" merely echoes other familiar environmentalist warnings not to mess with established ecological systems, not to interfere. The precautionary principle does not require the hypersea.

Stefan Helmreich analyzes the genomic connections between terrestrial human bodies and sea life in his book *Alien Ocean: Anthropological Voyages in Microbial Seas* as well as in his article "Human Nature at Sea." In the introduction to his important study of marine microbiology, Helmreich writes, "Some readers may object that I have not written *Our Oceans, Ourselves,* a book that would highlight human intimacy with the sea, that would emphasize a sense of oceanic communion" (17). Although he admits that book is "indeed here, though submerged," he explains that *Alien Ocean* is "skeptical of any simple identification with the sea, pessimistic about whether scientific knowledge alone about the ocean is enough for making sense of it (let alone protecting it)" (17). Although there is surely not enough space within this chapter to adequately discuss this theoretically astute and poetic book, I would like to focus here on Helmreich's arguments about how the science he studies transforms our understanding of the human, especially as we are connected with the ocean. He explains that the work of marine microbiologists makes it

> possible to imagine elements of the human and the oceanic flowing into one another at a molecular scale. It allows scientists newly to describe human bodies

> as porous—to ocean-borne viruses and bacteria for example. It may become appropriate to think about the possibility that human nature, genetically understood, may be dissolving, a dissolution accomplished through the turbulent flowing together of human and oceanic biology. ("Human" 52)

This aqueous posthumanism, which is not unlike trans-corporeality in its insistence on the porousness of human bodies, challenges us to imagine how the "human," at the level of the gene, sloshes around with the rest of oceanic life. Helmreich's conclusion notes the shift from recent accounts of the human as salty like the seas to the human as composed of bacteria.

> Once upon a time, the *human*, plunged into the sea (as blood, sweat, tears, milk), was baptized into communion with the planet. But plunged into the sea as a swirl of microbial genes, something unsettling happens. Microbes are not simple echoes of a left-behind origin for humans, orphaned from all evolutionary association. Microbes are historical and contemporary partners, part of our bodies' "microbiomes." "The" human genome is full of their stories, revealing that all genomes are metagenomes. The links between the scale of human bodies and ecologies become baroque, spatially and temporally. The bacteria that inhabit our bodies do not simply mirror the bacteria that inhabit the sea—as might brine in our blood. This is not human nature reflecting ocean nature. It is an entanglement of natures, an intimacy with the alien. (*Alien* 284)

Whereas accounts of how the human evolved from the sea, such as *Your Inner Fish*, trace a trajectory that culminates in a static and separate contemporary human, Helmreich explains how the human as part of the sea's "swirl of microbial genes" makes microbes our "partners," both historically and in the present. This sense of entanglement, which traverses across realms, suggests ongoing material intra-actions as well as the inability to secure a human self as distinct from the "alien" other. This may be a potent posthumanism, which, as Helmreich concludes, saturates "human nature by other natures" (*Alien* 284) and reveals our complex and continuous entanglements with other life forms. I worry, however, along with one of the scientists Helmreich cites, that "we are losing sight of the organism" (60). Although very little is known about the ecologies of marine habitats, because they are so difficult to study and because such studies often do not attract funding, Helmreich explains that gene sequencing, which is a perfect tool for "blue-green capitalism," allows marine microbiologists "to dispense entirely with the need to zero in on individual microbes—or even populations of discrete cells. . . . This is a genomics beyond organisms, a practice that implicitly queries whether individuals are the only evolutionarily meaningful units" (53). When so many marine animals are threatened with extinction, when so many marine ecosystems are on the verge of collapse, envisioning blue and green life worlds as one vast genomic soup may dramatize "our" corporeal intimacy with "the seas" but will not enable the sorts of engaged knowledges that trace how human practices threaten particular creatures, habitats, and ecologies. In short, I share Helmreich's skepticism that this particular sort of scientific knowledge will be sufficient for understanding or protecting marine life and environments. In my critique of the film *Cracking the Ocean Code,* a film that extols Craig Venter's massive project to mine the oceans for genetic material, in order to translate "life to disk," "biochemical information" to "digital code," I argue that it would be more useful to consider marine life as always interconnected with particular environments, processes, and substances. Such considerations would be highly mediated, but they would not culminate in the discovery of isolated genes, which become mere fodder for biocapitalist ventures. Instead, they would lead from "entanglement to greater entanglement" (Latour, *On the Modern* 61), as they trace interactions between forms of sea life, their environments, and the anthropogenic threats to species survival (Alaimo, "Feminist").

Steve Mentz, in *At the Bottom of Shakespeare's Ocean,* warns that evocations of evolutionary connections to the sea may not be all that helpful:

> Look at the world through salty eyeballs, remembering that the fluid in our eyes tastes like the sea. Most of the world is water. Most of that water is salt. No matter what it looks like, what it makes us feel, how our bodies float on its swells, the ocean is no place to live. . . . Long ago we crawled out of the water. We can't go back. (96)

As Mentz suggests, nostalgia for our deep evolutionary past before tetrapods crawled up onto the land does not direct us toward solutions to current environmental predicaments. Worse, I would argue, is that such origin stories, even as they attempt to provoke concern for the sea as our original home or for sea creatures as kin, revel in a prelapsarian innocence, as they skip over a wide swath of human history in which humans slaughtered ocean creatures and destroyed ocean ecologies, eliminating an astonishing number of marine mammals, birds, and fishes, by killing them for oil, fertilizer, fur, or food, or destroying their habitats through destructive trawling, the inadvertent production of dead zones, and development.[5] Whereas Mentz argues we need "more improvisational stories of working-with an intermittently hostile world" (98), I would argue that we need trans-corporeal modes of analysis that take responsibility for human actions within, and as part of, the world. Karen Barad, drawing on Neils Bohr's theoretical physics, stresses that the world is a "dynamic process of intra-activity," in which nothing exists that precedes relations. Emphasizing the dual meaning of "mattering," Barad defines ethics as "intra-acting from within and as part of the world in its becoming" (*Meeting* 396). Trans-corporeality situates the (post)human as always already part of the world's intra-active agencies. For an oceanic sense of trans-corporeality to be an ethical mode of being, the material self must not be a finished, self-contained product of evolutionary genealogies but a site where the knowledges and practices of embodiment are undertaken as part of the world's becoming. For me, trans-corporeality emerges from the sort of risk society described by Ulrich Beck, in which the contemporary landscape of potential, or virtual, harms requires that ordinary citizens have access to scientific information. But trans-corporeality as an ethical practice requires not only that citizens seek out information, which may or may not exist in any trustworthy or usable form, about risks to their own health, but that they also seek out information about how their own bodily existence—their consumption of food, fuel, and specific consumer products—affects other people, other animals, habitats, and ecosystems. Tracing how terrestrial human bodies are intertwined with ocean ecologies is no easy matter, yet, as we will discuss below, environmental art and activism are emerging that dramatize the material agencies in the most ordinary and seemingly benign objects and practices.

Plasticizing Marine Life: New Materialism and Ocean Activism

Jane Bennett contends, in *Vibrant Matter: A Political Ecology of Things*, that one of the reasons to "advocate the vitality of matter" is that "the image of dead or thoroughly instrumentalized matter feeds human hubris and our earth-destroying fantasies of conquest and consumption" (ix). I certainly agree. Grappling with what it means to understand human corporeality and the material world as agential, rather than as passive, inert, and malleable, is at the heart of new materialist theory. Although particular strands of thing theory, object-oriented ontology, speculative realisms, new vitalisms, and material feminisms may or may not be particularly posthumanist or environmentally oriented, material ecocriticism, by definition, focuses on material agencies as part of a wider environmentalist ethos that values ecosystems, biodiversity, and nonhuman life. Serpil Oppermann, in "Ecocriticism's Theoretical Discontents," argues that we need to "advance a critical perspective in which both discursivity and materiality ... can be integrated in a relational approach" and that the "accountability of such an approach must ... lie in a correct identification of the ethical, epistemological, and ontological concerns of ecocriticism's wider interest in human and nonhuman systems" (155). I concur with Oppermann and would add that material ecocriticisms are better served by focusing on intra-active systems and entanglements rather than the contemplation of isolated objects.

Attention to material agencies is not limited to academic scholarship, but instead is emerging across different domains, as environmental activists, movements, artists, and practices emphasize the unsettling and unintended consequences of substances and things. Indeed, there is a striking sort of "new materialisms" pulsing through green subcultures, as amateur environmental practitioners think through the strange agencies of ostensibly unremarkable substances, systems, and objects.[6] Climate change, sustainability, and antitoxin movements make environmentalism a practice that entails grappling with how one's own bodily existence is ontologically entangled with the well-being of both local and quite distant places, peoples, animals, and ecosystems. Campaigns against plastic link not only coastal regions but also inland zones to the mushrooming plastic found in the oceans. Although a 1973 study on plastic pollution stated that its effect was "chiefly aesthetic," since the "inert nature of plastic means that it is unlikely to enter the food chain and threaten human welfare" (Venrick 271), plastics are now known to absorb toxins, release toxins, and enter the marine food chain. Greenpeace warns of the "sinister twist" to the plastic that has invaded the oceans: "The plastics can act as a sort of 'chemical sponge.' They can concentrate many of the most damaging of the pollutants found in the world's oceans: the persistent organic pollutants (POPs). So any animal eating these pieces of plastic debris will also be taking in highly toxic pollutants" (n.p.). Plastics affect not only the larger and more visible sea creatures but also the very small, including those in the pelagic and deep seas. "Toxin-laden microplastics may add another risk to marine life," as the many creatures such as benthic worms, sea cucumbers, and krill "will ingest tiny plastic particles" (Kaiser 1506). This is Ulrich Beck's risk society sunk to the bottom of the sea, as the benthic creatures can no longer depend on their own sensory organs to detect danger. Their ways of knowing and being have been rendered inadequate by the xenobiotic substances that surround them.

In "Plastic Materialities," Gay Hawkins, drawing on Bennett's theory of "thing power" and vital materialism, which asserts that "things have the capacity to assert themselves," directs her attention to plastic bags: "As scientists discover marine life choking on bags and environmental activists document the bags' endless afterlife in landfills, plastic bags are transformed from innocuous, disposable containers to destructive matter" (119). Hawkins asks, concerned that these formulations do not pay sufficient attention to the bag itself, "But what of the bag in all this? It appears as a passive object of reclassification" (119). Charging that "ethics slides into moralism," when humans "are not invited to be open to the affective intensities of plastic matter; rather they are urged to enact their ethical will and eliminate it," Hawkins sets out to let "plastic bags have their say" (12). After analyzing "Say no to plastic bag" campaigns, an everyday encounter with a sticky plastic bag, and the dancing plastic bag in *American Beauty*, she concludes by advocating Bill Connolly's conception of "critical responsiveness," which, in Hawkins's terms, "decenters the human as the sovereign source of agency and change; in recognizing multiple sites of agency at play in the world it invites an expanded politics attentive to how the force of matter might participate in generating new associations and ethics" (137).

As a new materialist, I agree with Hawkins that "recognizing multiple sites of agency at play in the world invites an expanded politics"; indeed, trans-corporeality contends that the recognition of intra-active material agencies expands and transforms political and ethical domains. Whereas Hawkins condemns the say-no campaigns because of the "differential agency of the bag in this process is disavowed," as it "is something to be controlled by human will, not a participant in an emergent ethical constituency" (126), I must confess that I cannot imagine how a plastic bag can be part of an "ethical constituency."[7] Although the surprising material agencies and effects of the plastic bags certainly exceed political and ethical frameworks—and that is the key problem—that does not mean that we should imagine bags as entities that contain their own voice, perspective, or rights. Although Hawkins's approach perceptively accounts for the thing power of the plastic bag, the bag is taken as a separate, discrete object rather than a phenomenon within larger economic, political, and environmental systems. By contrast, Karen Barad insists we are responsible to others because of the "various ontological entanglements that materiality entails." Thus, ethics "is therefore not about right response to a radically exterior/ized other, but about responsibility and accountability for the lively relationalities of becoming of which we are a part" (*Meeting* 393). We are always on the "hook"—on innumerable hooks—ethically speaking, always caught up in and responsible for material intra-actions. Although Barad does not offer any guidance for forging ethical paths within the limitless horizon of responsibility, her theory does not take separate, distinct, objects as a starting point, emphasizing instead that "relata do not preexist relations" (140). Even if Barad's theory does not (and could not) offer specific guidance as to how to determine what particular ethical practices would entail, it emphasizes ontological entanglements rather than encounters with discrete objects. In a related fashion, my conception of trans-corporeality does not concentrate on bodies, things, and objects as separate entities,[8] but instead traces how the (post)human is always already part of intra-active networks and systems that are simultaneously material, discursive, economic, ecological, and biopolitical.

Whereas Hawkins distinguishes her approach to plastic bags from the moralism of environmental campaigns that she claims disavow the bags' agency, I relish the parallels and affinities between new materialist theories and environmental activism. The very sense of ethics that Barad describes, that of being responsible for the "lively relationalities of becoming of which we are a part," infuses campaigns that stress the unintended consequences and surprising material agencies of everyday objects.

Activist organizations such as the Plastic Pollution Coalition, for example, devoted to "working towards a world free of plastic pollution and its toxic impacts," creatively demonstrate the surreal and uncanny effects of the banal consumer objects that populate our world, through their videos and artworks. Jonas Benarroch's brilliant two-minute video *The Ballad of the Plastic Bag* follows the plastic bag as it flies from a parking lot, across a prairie, over train tracks, above a scenic stone outcropping in the desert, over roads, fields, and forests, finally landing in a beautiful mountain lake where it sinks, just barely visible (see figure 12.1).

Figure 12.1. *The Ballad of the Plastic Bag*, video, 2012. Courtesy of Jonas Benarroch. Director of photography: Jeronimo Molero.

The ironic, romantic lyrics, sung over a plucky guitar, are reminiscent of a ballad of a drifter, a free-roaming spirit, "travelling light": "But honey, I won't be chained, This spirit can't be tamed"; "Nobody puts a hold on me / And nothing can destroy my glee." The concluding caption is less cheery, "Plastic is Not Biodegradable. Its particles enter the food chain intoxicating all organisms." Although the film doesn't portray the agencies of the bag as it releases toxins or clogs an animal's digestive track, the clever conceit of the plastic bag as a ramblin' man dramatizes the agency and "freedom" of this supposedly inanimate object, stressing that these flimsy things have gotten away from us—escaping human control. Rather than demonizing the object, the video invites the viewer to take vicarious pleasure in the bag's free-roaming, aesthetically pleasing travels. But the video is done in a playful and ironic spirit; we are not called to listen to the bag's perspective or extend our ethical concern toward it as an entity. Although the film intends to convey an environmentalist message that plastic bags, in their free-wheeling ways, cause serious harm, the pleasure provoked by the humorous song and visual narrative is not simply arrested or deflated by the concluding message that toxic plastic particles enter the food chain. Instead, the ironic pleasure we receive from the video underscores the sense that the daily practices of sustainable living proceed from environmental movements that are rich with passion, ingenuity, humor, and lively modes of critique. Notwithstanding the ominous warning that concludes the video, its billowing pleasures are akin to Rosi Braidotti's

Figure 12.2. *Plastic Seduction,* video. Courtesy of Katrin Peters, http://www.dailydifference.org.

sense of a "non-rapacious ethics of sustainable becoming: for the hell of it and for the love of the world" (*Transpositions* 278).

Another video endorsed by the Plastic Pollution Coalition, a fifty-second spoof by Katrin Peters, called *Plastic Seduction,* features a romantic seafood dinner on a secluded beach. The man lovingly feeds the woman an oyster, and as she opens her mouth rather suggestively, we notice that the oyster sports a blue plastic bottle cap—which the woman crunches in delight (see figure 12.2). They both act as if nothing is awry, as they dig into a plate of seafood mixed with colorful plastic garbage (see figure 12.3).

While the couple's passion is not dampened by their bizarre meal (they exit, stage right, presumably to indulge in other bodily pleasures), the camera pans out to reveal that the beach they had been dining upon is full of plastic garbage, and the voice-over concludes, "Not so tempting after all. Help turn the tide." The couple's dreamy, romantic state suggests, perhaps, the power of plastic to seduce us all into a collective consumerist state of blissful ignorance. Although it is unlikely anyone will be served a plate of oysters topped with colorful plastic bottle caps, there is evidence to suggest that nearly all "seafood" humans consume has been contaminated by the staggering amount of plastics that has invaded the oceanic food webs. The voice-over explains, "Every year thousands of tons of plastic ends up in our oceans. Plastic doesn't biodegrade in the sea. Over time it breaks up into tiny particles. Like sponges, these attract pollutants from the surround-

Figure 12.3. *Plastic Seduction*, video. Courtesy of Katrin Peters, http://www.dailydifference.org.

ing waters, accumulating a highly toxic chemical load before they contaminate the marine food chain." *Plastic Seduction* dramatizes a trans-corporeality in which humans ultimately consume the surprisingly dangerous objects they have produced and discarded. The crunchy, colorful plastic pieces become metonyms of—not foils for—the actual seafood on the plate, which already harbors plastics and other toxins. Whereas Ian Bogost, in *Alien Phenomenology*, wonders "what is it like to be a thing," such as the "udon noodle or the nuclear warhead" (10, 30), *Plastic Seduction* suggests something that may be equally weird but more significant: that ostensibly discrete entities such as plastic bottle caps are, in a sense, already part of who we are, as human diets ontologically entangle us with the plastic seas.[9]

Captain Charles Moore, who is known for discovering, researching, and publicizing the Great Pacific Garbage Patch, stresses the harmful agencies of seemingly benign objects. In his book *Plastic Ocean: How a Sea Captain's Chance Discovery Launched a Determined Quest to Save the Oceans,* Moore charges that the Plastic Age "has sneaked up on us almost imperceptibly," and, for a while, "we weren't as bothered as we might have been, because we still thought plastic material was inert and benign, an eyesore that couldn't do much harm" (73). He contests the assumption that plastic is inert by dramatizing the lively actions of trillions of seemingly inert objects. "Nurdles," for example, the preproduction pellets, "escape the distribution system and go feral, with billions eventually winding up in waterways and the oceans" (51). Ironically, the fact that the nurdles "go feral" invokes wildness, which has long been valuable for environmentalists because "it is not entirely dominated, monitored, transformed, and constrained or made to conform to the dictates of its efficient utilization by humans" (Smith 97). Plastic, arguably the quintessential substance for efficient domination, somehow manages to escape, mocking both the human mastery of the material world and the green ideal of wildness, as it multiplies and roams, garish and ghastly. Moore continues to animate and anthropomorphize the substance that surrounds us but ordinarily goes without notice: "Plastic is athletic. It scoots, flies, and swims. It travels without passport, crosses borders, and goes where it is, literally, an illegal alien. It has the endurance of a champ" (66). Although the comparison to an illegal alien is unfortunate, given the prejudices pulsing through the United States, the overarching theme that Moore presents is of everyday objects gone wild, contradicting the human presumption that human intentionality directs and confines material things:

> On land, it's soothing to think that all those bottles and wrappers, all that cheap plastic stuff we handle every day, winds up in a landfill, safely sequestered from polite society. But here in mid-ocean we're finding hordes of escapees. . . . Try as we may to control it, to hide it, to manage it—it mocks us and goes where it doesn't belong. (84)

Although the pathetic fallacy of the garbage as intentionally taunting us hardly seems scientific, the way Moore animates plastic stuff not only underscores how harmful—if not malevolent—plastic can be, but struggles to convey a sense of material agency that will satisfy a scientific standard demonstrating that plastic is doing harm. Moore explains that when he first attempted to enlist experts in his quest to clean up the seas, he was surprised to be told that the mere presence of a mammoth amount of garbage in the ocean was not enough to provoke concern: "It can't only be about the ugliness or wrongness of plastic garbage in the remote ocean. . . . . It's about giving credence to the sense that plastic is *doing* something out there, something very possibly unhealthy, something *harmful*" (120). So Moore sets out, as a citizen-scientist, to demonstrate what plastic is doing.

It is well known that plastic bags look like jellyfish in the water, confusing turtles and other creatures, but Moore explains that nurdles resemble fish eggs, the food of many seabirds, and, more broadly, that plastic, this spectacularly multifarious substance, mimics many sorts of "edibles in the marine environment" (176). Their resemblance to food means the plastic bits, the plastic bags, the plastic objects beckon, entice, and deceive birds, turtles, fish, and sea mammals. Vivid examples of animals occupied by plastics reveal the unfortunate results. "Many of the salps we encounter sport plastics, inside and out, little colorful chips embedded in clear tissue" (85). Moore tells of whale necropsies, one of which revealed "nearly six square yards of compressed plastics, mostly shopping bags," that were taken from the animal's gut. Another uncovered "sweatpants, a golf ball, surgical gloves, small towels, plastic fragments, and twenty plastic bags" (228–29). And another whale was full of fishing debris (ghost nets), including a piece that was forty-five square feet (230). He also includes the story of a Malibu sea lion who had thirteen plastic shopping bags in her stomach. Dr. Lauren Palmer, a veterinarian at the Marine Mammal Care Center, thinks that "the neurotoxic effects of domoic acid might have spurred the sea lion to eat bags when normally she never would have" (236). Domoic acids are produced by harmful algal blooms, which may be triggered by sewage and fertilizer run-off from land. Captain Moore urges us to consider that plastics, far from being inert, benign objects, act in the ocean as if they were "predators":

> Plastics could even be considered, in a sense, "predators," given the deadly nature of "ghost fishing" and entanglements of marine turtles, mammals, pinnipeds, and cetaceans. Though plastic is not a living organism, it acts like one and has the impact of one and should be taken into account in characterizations of the ocean biome. What is most shameful in this more realistic modern scenario is that plastic, in a sense, is man's surrogate, swimming with the fishes and doing harm. (253)

Moore's characterization of plastics as predators seeks to account for the many ways in which it kills ocean creatures and devastates marine ecosystems. Stressing that plastic is "man's surrogate" is a powerful rhetorical move, as we imagine plastic as a horrific extension of ourselves, a discarded and disavowed entity that bobs along, wreaking incalculable harm. As Serenella Iovino eloquently puts it, waste is "the other side of our presence in the world, our absence made visible" ("Naples" 6). Even where we are absent, plastic, acting as our surrogate, Moore suggests, entangles us in ghastly nets of responsibility. Perhaps it is anthropocentric to imagine plastics as our surrogates, since this figuration diminishes the "feral" agencies of plastic and its ability to exceed human control. Nonetheless, the formulation captures how individual objects have surprising agencies, yet those agencies emerge from and act within wider economic, industrial, consumerist, and ecological systems of which we are always a part.

Alison Starr's multimedia work *Baker*, made from plastic bags hand-stitched together into an accordion-like rectangle about two and a half inches thick, with black thread "tentacles" hanging menacingly below, suggests the disturbing ways in which the materials of everyday consumerism are the very stuff of destructive global networks (see figure 12.4).

This is a discomforting piece, as the tentacles, which my hand often brushes against as it searches to turn on the light, transform the stitched image of Baker, a nuclear bomb that the United States tested at the Bikini Atoll in 1946, into a jellyfish.[10] Jellyfish are horribly polyvalent here, since one of the legacies of U.S.

Figure 12.4. *Baker,* mixed media (plastic bags and thread), 2012. Courtesy of Alison Starr.

nuclear testing in the Pacific was the birth of human "jellyfish babies," children born with transparent skins and no bones. The jellyfish suggests both the violent effects of nuclear testing on Pacific peoples and the current crisis in ocean ecologies, as the explosion of jellyfish populations globally has been attributed to their ability to survive in polluted, environmentally degraded seas, and, as this chapter has discussed, plastic bags in the sea resemble jellies, confusing many animals. Thus, the very material of this artwork, a material that is always close at hand for most Western citizens, provokes us to trace trans-corporeal networks in which human bodily practices are responsible for vast networks of harm. The many thank-yous printed on the bags amplify the collision between cheery consumerism and the horrors of American imperialism, militarization, nuclear testing, and the plasticizing of the seas, provoking the viewer to grapple with these histories, forces, and substances. Although the scale and the intent of Pacific nuclear testing conducted by the United States as compared with a Western consumer blithely allowing their purchases to be placed in a plastic bag may be so incommensurate as to be unthinkable within the same sentence, it is this very unthinkability that trans-corporeality, as a mode of new materialism, material ecocriticism, and object-oriented activism, seeks to disturb.

Notes

1. See Earle, *The World*, for more on the threats to ocean ecologies.
2. See especially Butler's "Contingent": "The 'I' is the transfer point of that replay, but it is simply not a strong enough claim to say that the 'I' is situated; the 'I,' this 'I,' is *constituted* by these positions, and these 'positions' are not merely theoretical products, but fully embedded organizing principles of material practices and institutional arrangements, those matrices of power and discourse that produce me as a viable 'subject'" (9).
3. The vastness of the seas has long buoyed the cultural conception of the ocean as impervious to human harm. Kimberley C. Patton, in *The Sea Can Wash Away All Evils*, discusses how "many cultures have revered the sea, and at the same time they have made it to bear and to wash away whatever was construed as dangerous, dirty, or morally contaminating" (xi). Whether these religious beliefs have persisted or not, both the scale and the hazardous nature of what is dumped into the seas have changed, entirely, from ancient times. Nonetheless, contemporary global practices of dumping garbage, sewage, weapons, toxic chemicals, and radioactive waste assume that dispersing the substances or forces across the breadth and depth of the seas will make them disappear. For more on the problematic notion of "dispersing," see my essay "Dispersing."
4. For more on newly discovered species of marine life, see the Census of Marine Life.
5. Callum Roberts dates trawling—as well as criticism and debate about the practice—back to England in 1376. Someone complained to the king that the use of the "wondyrechaun" resulted in "great damage of the commons of the realm and the destruction of the fisheries" (131–32).

6. See my book *Bodily Natures* for more on how environmental justice and environmental health practitioners conceive of the agency of substances and objects.

7. The turn toward the nonhuman in theory provokes questions—which are not easily answered—about what should be given ethical consideration or political representation. At the end of *We Have Never Been Modern*, for example, Latour describes an example of the Parliament of things: "Let one of the representatives talk, for instance, about the ozone hole, another represent the Monsanto chemical industry, a third the workers of the same chemical industry, another the voters of New Hampshire, a fifth the meteorology of the polar regions; let still another speak in the name of the State; what does it matter, so long as they are all talking about the same thing, about a quasi-object they have all created, the object-discourse-nature-society whose new properties astound us all and whose network extends from my refrigerator to the Antarctic by way of chemistry, law, the State, the economy and satellites" (145). Note that while there is a long list of those that will be "represented," the hole in the ozone is spoken "about." There is, of course, nothing within the theory itself that would categorically differentiate the ozone hole from the other entities, and perhaps the distinction here was not even intentional, but it does suggest quandaries for environmentalism.

8. In other words, I think Barad's agential realism and my trans-corporeality diverge—in ways that are significant for environmentalism—from thing theory, thing power, object-oriented ontologies, and speculative realism.

9. Nancy Tuana, in her important essay "Viscous Porosity: Witnessing Katrina," traces another way in which plastic becomes part of human flesh. Describing herself breathing air polluted by plastic incineration, she states that "components of the bottle have an agency that transforms the naturally occurring flesh of my body into a different material structure than what occurs in nature" (202).

10. See Elizabeth DeLoughrey's superb essay "Radiation Ecologies and the Wars of Light" for an analysis of Pacific nuclear testing, radiation, planetarity, and the novel *Ocean Roads*.

13 Meditations on Natural Worlds, Disabled Bodies, and a Politics of Cure

Eli Clare

Prairie

You and I walk in the summer rain through a thirty-acre pocket of tallgrass prairie that was, not so long ago, one big cornfield. We follow the path mowed as a firebreak. You carry a big pink umbrella. Water droplets hang on the grasses. Spiderwebs glint. The bee balm hasn't blossomed yet. You point to numerous patches of birch and goldenrod; they belong here but not in this plenty. The thistle, on the other hand, simply shouldn't be here. The Canada wild rye waves, the big bluestem almost open. Sunflowers cluster, spots of yellow orange amid the gray green of a rainy day. The songbirds and butterflies have taken shelter. For the moment the prairie is quiet. Soon my jeans are sopping wet from the knees down. Not an ocean of grasses but a start, this little piece of prairie is utterly different from row upon row of corn.

With the help of the Department of Natural Resources, you mowed and burned the corn, broadcast the seed—bluestem, wild rye, bee balm, cornflower, sunflower, aster—sack upon sack of just the right mix that might replicate the tallgrass prairie that was once here. Only remnants of the original ecosystem remain in the Midwest, isolated pockets of leadplants, milkweed, burr oaks, and switchgrass growing in cemeteries, along railroad beds, on remote bluffs, somehow miraculously surviving.

You burn; you plant; you root out thistle and prickly ash. You tend, save money for more seed, burn again. Over the past decade and a half of labor, you've worked to undo the two centuries of damage wrought by plows, pesticides, monoculture farming, and fire suppression. The state of Wisconsin partners in this work precisely because the damage is so great. Without the massive web of prairie roots to anchor the earth; bison to turn, fertilize, and aerate the earth; and lightning-strike fire to burn and renew the earth, the land now known as Wisconsin is literally draining away. Rain catches the topsoil, washing it from field to creek to river to ocean. Prairie restoration reverses this process, both stabilizing and creating soil. So you work hard to restore this eight-thousand-year-old ecosystem, all the while remembering that the land isn't yours or the dairy farmer's down the road, but rather stolen a mere century and a half ago from the Dakota people. The histories of dirt, grass, genocide, bison massacre float here.

We have taken this walk a dozen times over the past fifteen years—at noon with the sun blazing, at dusk with fireflies lacing the grasses, at dawn with finches and warblers greeting the day. My feet still feel the old corn furrows. As we walk, I think about the words *natural* and *unnatural*, *normal* and *abnormal*. Does this fragment of land in transition from cornfield to tallgrass prairie define what *natural* is? If so, how do we name the overabundance of birch and goldenrod, the absence of bison? What was once *normal* here; what can we consider *normal* now?

Normal and *natural* dance together, while *unnatural* and *abnormal* bully, threaten, patrol the boundaries. Of course, it's an inscrutable dance. How does *unnatural* technology repair so-called *abnormal* bodies to their *natural* ways of being? Dismissing the distinctions between *normal* and *abnormal*, *natural* and *unnatural*, as meaningless would be lovely, except they wield extraordinary power.

Abnormal, Unnatural

It is not an exaggeration to say that the words *unnatural* and *abnormal* haunt me as a disabled person. Or maybe more accurately, they pummel me. Complete strangers ask me, "What's your defect?" Their intent is mostly benign. To them, my body simply doesn't work right, *defect* being another variation of broken, supposedly neutral. But think of the things called defective—the boom box that won't play a CD, the car that never started reliably, the calf born with three legs. They end up in the back closet, trash heap, scrap yard, slaughterhouse. Defects are disposable and *abnormal*, bodies to eradicate.

Or complete strangers yell at me down the road, across the playground, "Hey, retard!" Their intent is often malicious. Sometimes they have thrown rocks, sand, rubber erasers. Once on a camping trip with my family, I joined a whole crowd of kids playing tag in and around the picnic shelter. A slow and clumsy nine-year-old, I quickly became "it." I chased and chased but caught no one. The game turned. Kids came close, ducked away, yelling *defect, retard*. Frustrated, I yelled back for a while. *Retard* became *monkey*; became a circle around me; became a torrent, *monkey defect retard you're a monkey monkey monkey*; became huge gulping sobs of rage, frustration, humiliation, shame; became not knowing who I was. My body crumpled. It lasted two minutes or two hours until my father appeared and the circle scattered. Even as the word *monkey* connected to me the nonhuman *natural* world, I became supremely *unnatural*.

Or complete strangers pat me on the head. They whisper platitudes in my ear, clichés about courage and inspiration. They enthuse about how remarkable I am. They declare me special. Once a woman wearing dream-catcher earrings, a big turquoise necklace, and a fringed leather tunic with a medicine wheel painted on its back confided that I was, like all people who tremor, a *natural* shaman. She grabbed me in a long hug and advised that if I were trained, I could become a great healer. Before this woman, sporting a mishmash of First Nations' symbols, jewelry, and clothing, released me from her grip, she directed me never to forget my specialness. Oh, how *special* disabled people are: we have *special* education, *special* needs, *special* restrooms, *special* parking spots. That word drips condescension. It's no better than being defective. As *special* people, we are still *abnormal* and disposable.

Or complete strangers offer me Christian prayer or crystals and vitamins, always with the same intent—to touch me, fix me, mend my cerebral palsy, if only I will comply. They cry over me, wrap their arms around my shoulders, kiss my cheek. Even now, after four decades of these kinds of interactions, I still don't know how to rebuff their pity, how to tell them the simple truth that I'm not broken. Even if there were a cure for brain cells that died at birth, I'd refuse. I have no idea who I'd be without my specific tremoring, slurring, tense body. Those strangers assume my body *unnatural,* want to make me *normal,* take for granted the need and desire for cure. *Unnatural* and *abnormal* pummel me every day.

Restoration

As an ideology seeped into every corner of Western thought and culture, cure rides on the back of *normal* and *natural.* Insidious and pervasive, it impacts many, many bodies. In response, we need a politics of cure: not a simple or reactive belief system, not an anticure stance in the face of the endless assumptions about bodily difference, but rather a broad-based politics mirroring the complexity of all our bodies and minds.

The American Heritage Dictionary defines *cure* as "restoration of health." In developing a politics of cure based upon this definition, it would be all too easy to get mired in an argument about health, trying to determine who's healthy and who's not, as if there's one objective standard. As an alternative, I want to bypass the questions of who defines health and for what purposes. So many folks are working to redefine health, struggling toward a theory and practice that will contribute to the well-being of entire communities. But I won't be joining them with a redefinition of my own. Instead, I want a politics of cure that speaks from inside the intense contradictions presented by the multiple meanings of health.

Today in the white Western world dominated by allopathic medicine, the meanings of health range from individual and communal bodily comfort to profound social control. Between these two poles, a myriad of permutations exist. Health is both the well-being sustained by good food and the products sold by the multimillion-dollar diet industry. It is both effective pain management for folks who live with chronic pain and the policed refusal to prescribe narcotic-based pain relief to people perceived as drug seeking. It is both the saving of lives and the aggressive marketing of synthetic growth hormone to children whose only bodily "problem" is being short.

Rather than offer a resolution to this whole range of contradictory, overlapping, and confused meanings of *health*, I want to follow the word *restoration*. To restore an object or an ecosystem is to return it to an earlier, and often better, condition. We restore a house that's falling down, a prairie that's been decimated by generations of monoculture farming and fire suppression. In this return, we try to undo the harm, wishing the harm had never happened. Talk to anyone who does restoration work—a carpenter who rebuilds 150-year-old neglected houses, a conservation biologist who turns cornfields back to prairie—and she'll say it's a complex undertaking. A fluid, responsive process, restoration requires digging into the past, stretching toward the future, working hard in the present. And the end results rarely, if ever, match the original state.

Restoring an ecosystem means rebuilding a dynamic system that has somehow been interrupted or broken—devastated by strip mining or clear-cut logging, taken over by invasive species, unbalanced by the loss of predators, crushed by pollution. The work is not about re-creating a static landscape somehow frozen in time, but rather about encouraging and reshaping dynamic ecological interdependencies, ranging from clods of dirt to towering thunderheads, tiny microbes to herds of bison, into a self-sustaining system of constant flux. This reshaping mirrors the original or historical ecosystem as closely as possible, but inevitably some element is missing or different. The return may be close but never complete.

The process of restoration is simpler with a static object—an antique chair or old house. Still, if the carpenters aren't using ax-hewn timbers of assorted and quirky sizes, mixing the plaster with horse hair, building at least a few walls with chicken wire, and using newspaper, rags, or nothing at all for insulation, then the return will be incomplete, possibly sturdier and definitely more energy efficient, but different from the original house. Even though restoration as a process is never complete, it always requires an original or historical state in which to root itself, a belief that this state is better than what currently exists, and a desire to return to the original.

Thinking about the framework of restoration, I circle back to the folks who offer disabled and chronically ill people prayers, crystals, and vitamins, believing deeply in the necessity of cure. A simple one-to-one correspondence between ecological restoration and bodily restoration reveals cure's mandate of returning damaged bodies to some former, and nondisabled, state of being. This mandate clearly locates the problem, or damage, of disability within individual disabled or chronically ill bodies.

To resist the ableism in this framing, a disability politics has emerged in the past forty years. It asserts that disability is lodged not in paralysis but rather in the stairs without an accompanying ramp, not in blindness but rather in the lack of Braille. Disability itself does not live in depression or anxiety but rather exists in a whole host of stereotypes, not in dyslexia but in teaching methods unwilling to flex, not in lupus or multiple sclerosis but in the belief that certain bodily conditions are a fate worse than death. In short, disability politics establishes that the problem of disability is not about individual bodies but about social injustice.

But for some of us, even if we accept disability as harm to individual bodies, restoration still does not make sense, because an original nondisabled body does not exist. How would I, or the medical establishment, go about restoring my body? The vision of me without tremoring hands and slurred speech, with more balance and coordination, does not originate from my body's history. Rather, it arises from an imagination of what my body should be like, some definition of *normal* and *natural*.

Not Simple

To reflect the multilayered relationships between disabled and chronically ill bodies and restoration, a politics of cure needs to be as messy and visceral as our bodies. To reach into this messiness, I turn to story.

You and I know each other through a loose national network of queer disability activists, made possible by the internet. Online one evening, I receive a message from you containing the cyber equivalent to a long, anguished moan of physical pain. You explain that you're having a bad pain day, and it helps just to acknowledge the need to howl. Before I log off, I type a good night to you, wish you a little less pain for the morning. The next day you thank me for not wishing you a pain-free day. You say: The question isn't whether I'm in pain but rather how much. *Later as I get to know you in person, you tell me:* I read medical journals hoping for a breakthrough in pain treatment that might make a difference. *You wait, trying to get doctors to believe your pain, and once you get the appropriate scripts, working to find the right balance of narcotics. The rhetoric of many disability activists declares:* There's nothing wrong with disabled bodies and minds, even as they differ from what's considered *normal*. *I have used this line myself more than once, to which you respond:* Not assuming our bodies are wrong makes sense, but the chronic fatiguing hell pain I live with is not a healthy variation, not a *natural* bodily difference.

I pause, thinking hard about *natural*. In disability community we sometimes half-sarcastically call nondisabled people *temporarily able-bodied,* or *TABs,* precisely because of the one instant that can disable any of us. Are these moments and locations of disability and chronic illness *natural* as our fragile, resilient human bodies interact with the world? Is it *natural* when a spine snaps after being flung from a car; when a brain processes information in fragmented ways after being exposed to lead, mercury, pesticides, uranium tailings; when a body or mind assumes its own shape with withered muscles or foreshortened limbs, brittle bones or ears that do not hear sound, after genes settle into their own particular patterns soon after conception? And when are those moments and locations of disability and chronic illness *unnatural*—as *unnatural* as war, toxic landfills, and poverty? Who, pray tell, determines *natural* and *unnatural*? I'm searching for a politics of cure that grapples both with the pain, brokenness, and limitation contained within disabled bodies and with the encompassing damage of ableism.

I return to story. *You and I sit in a roomful of disabled people, slowly inching our way toward enough familiarity to start telling bone-deep truths. And when we arrive there, you say:* If I could wake up tomorrow and not have diabetes, I'd choose that day in a heartbeat. *I can almost hear the stream of memory: the daily insulin; the tracking of blood sugar level; the shame; the endless doctors judging your weight, your food, your numbers; the seizures; the long-term unknowns. You don't hate your body or equate diabetes with misery. You're not waiting desperate, half panicked. All the time and money spent on research, rather than universal health care, a genuine social safety net, an end to poverty and hunger, pisses you off. At the same time, you're weary of all the analogies: the hope that one day AIDS will become as treatable and manageable as diabetes, the equating of transsexual hormone replacement therapy with insulin. You want to stamp your feet:* pay attention to this specific experience of Type I diabetes—my daily dependence on a synthesized hormone, my life balanced on this chemical, the maintenance that marks every meal. *You'd take a cure tomorrow, and at the same time you relish sitting in this room.*

In creating a politics of cure, we need to hold both the desire to restore a pancreas to its typical functioning and the value of bodily difference, knowing all the while that we will never live in a world where disability does not exist. How do we embrace the brilliant imperfection of disability and what it has to offer the world while knowing that very few of us would actively choose it to begin with?[1]

I return again to disability community. *You and I talk, as we so often do, over food, this time pasta, bread, and olive oil. It would be cliché to start with a description of your face across from mine, a story of color and texture, which I both see and don't. Certainly, I observe the vivid outline of your birthmark, its curve of color, but that colored shape does not become your entire being. Poet Pat Parker describes this balance in the context of race in her poem "For the white person who wants to know how to be my friend." She writes, "The first thing you do is to forget that i'm Black. / Second, you must never forget that i'm Black"* (99). *I know from your stories that all too often your face precedes you into the world, that one visible distinction becoming your whole body. You say:* I don't know why I stopped wearing that thick waxy makeup; why after a childhood of medical scraping, burning, tattooing, I didn't pursue laser surgery; don't know when I stopped cupping face in hand, shielding the color of my skin from other humans. *I listen as you try to make sense, track your body's turn away from eradication toward a compli-*

cated almost-pride. *You research beauty, scrutinize the industry of birthmark removal, page through medical textbooks, see faces like yours, swallow hard against regurgitated shame. You've started meeting and talking with other people with facial distinctions; tracing all the different survival strategies, desires, kinds of love and hate, denial and matter-of-factness. Tonight you wear a bright shirt, earrings to match; insist on your whole body with all its color.*

I ask again: what becomes *natural* and *normal*? Who decides that your purple textured skin is *unnatural*, my tremoring hands *abnormal*? How do those small and life-changing decisions get made? I don't want a politics of cure that declares anyone's specific bodily experience *normal* or *abnormal*, *natural* or *unnatural*.

I turn yet again to story in disability community. *You and I meet at a disability cultural event. I've given a presentation about body shame and body love, how bodies are stolen and reclaimed. Afterward, you find me. Military pollution in the groundwater in your childhood neighborhood shaped your disabled body, toxins molding neurons and muscles as you floated in utero. Most of the time when you talk about the military dumping of trichloroethylene (TCE) and its connection to you, folks look at your body with pity* (Taylor and Taylor). *As you tell me this story, I think of all the ways disabled bodies are used as cautionary tales: the arguments against drunk driving, drug use, air pollution, lead paint, asbestos, vaccines, and on and on. So many public campaigns use the cultural fear and hatred of disability to make the case against environmental degradation. You want to know how to express your hatred of military dumping without feeding the assumption that your body is bad, wrong,* unnatural. *No easy answers exist. You and I talk intensely; both the emotions and the ideas are dense. We arrive at a slogan for you:* I hate the military and love my body.

As simplified and incomplete as it is, this slogan is also profound. How do we witness, name, and resist the injustices that reshape and damage all kinds of bodies—plant and animal, organic and inorganic, nonhuman and human? And alongside our resistance, how do we make peace with the reshaped and damaged bodies themselves, cultivate love and respect for them? Inside this work, these stories, the concepts of *unnatural* and *abnormal* stop being useful.

Loss

The desire for restoration is bound to bodily loss and yearning—the sheer loss of bodies and bodily functions, whether it be human, bison, dirt, or an entire ecosystem. For many disabled and chronically ill people, there is a time before our particular bodily impairments, differences, dysfunctions existed.

What we remember about our bodies is seductive. We yearn; we wish; we regret; we make deals. We desire to return to the days before immobilizing exhaustion or impending death; to the nights thirty years ago when we spun across the dance floor; to the years before depression descended, a thick, unrelenting fog; to the long afternoons curled up with a book before the stroke, before the ability to read vanished in a heartbeat. We feel grief, bitterness, regret. We remain tethered to the past. We compare our bodies to those of neighbors, friends, lovers, models in *Glamour* and *Men's Health,* and we come up lacking. We feel inadequate, ashamed, envious. We remain tethered to images outside ourselves, to Photoshopped versions of the human body. Tethered to the gym, the diet plan, the miracle cure. But can any of us move our bodies back in time, undo the lessons learned, the knowledge gained, the scars acquired? The desire for restoration, the return to a bodily past—whether shaped by actual history, imagination, or the vice grip of *normal* and *natural*—is complex.

Even those of us who live with disability or chronic illness as familiar and ordinary and have settled into our bodies with a measure of self-love, even those of us who have no nondisabled past, deal with yearning. Sometimes I wish I could throw my body into the powerful grace of a gymnast, rock climber, cliff diver, but that wish is distant, dissolving into echo almost as soon as I recognize it. Sometimes the frustration of not being able to do some task right in front of me roars up, and I have to turn away again from bitterness and simply ask for help. But the real yearning for me centers upon bodily change. As my wrists, elbows, and shoulders grow chronically painful, I miss kayaking, miss gliding on the rippling surface of a lake, miss the rhythm of a paddle dipping in and out of the water. Restoration can be a powerful way of dealing with loss. Cure—when desired, possible, and successful—offers the return some of us sometimes yearn for.

* * *

Of course, the connections among loss, yearning, and restoration are not only about human bodies. Many of us mourn the swamp once a childhood playground, now a parking lot. We fear the wide-reaching impacts of global warming as hurricanes grow more frequent, glaciers melt, and deserts expand. We yearn back to the days when bison roamed the Great Plains in the millions and Chinook salmon swam upstream so numerous that rivers churned frothy white. We yearn for a return, and so we broadcast just the right mix of tallgrass prairie seeds, raise and release wolves, bison, whooping cranes. We tear up drainage tiles and reroute water back into what used to be wetlands. We pick up trash, blow up dams, root out loosestrife, tansy ragwort, gorse, scotch broom, bamboo, and a multitude of other invasive species. Sometimes we can return a place to some semblance of its former self before the white colonialist, capitalist, industrial damage was done. And in doing so, we sometimes return ourselves as human animals into the *natural* world, moving from domination to collaboration. When it works, restoration can be a powerful resolution to grief, fear, despair.

Restoration's possibilities grow even more inviting as loss extends beyond individual bodies and places to entire communities and ecosystems. I remember bison herds hunted to near extinction, carcasses left to rot. White hunters sold bison tongue and skin, returned later to collect bone. Then ranchers with cattle and farmers with plows tore up the grasslands; beef animals, wheat, corn, and soybeans replaced prairie. In a photo from the 1870s, a man stands atop an immense pile of bison skulls waiting to be ground up for fertilizer (*Bison Skull Pile*). The immensity of this mountain of bone is irrevocable. I remember whole forests of towering Douglas fir, western red cedar, Sitka spruce, and redwoods leveled. Loggers left slash piles, clear-cuts, and washouts in their wake. In a photo from the late 1800s, fourteen men stand, sit, and lounge in the deep cross-cut of a single redwood tree in the process of being felled (Ericson). The breadth of this stump provides a window into the forests demolished. I remember mountaintops removed wholesale in Kentucky. Miners cleared, blasted, dug, and blasted some more in the southern Appalachian Mountains, extracting layer upon layer of coal, creating huge, open gashes. In a photo from 2003, the mountaintop has been leveled into a pit that stretches out toward the horizon, the scale large enough that I can't quite make sense of what I see (Stockman).

As evidence of ecosystems destroyed, all three of these photos measure magnitudes of loss, a sheer loss of bodies—animal, grass, tree, earth, mountain. This devastation includes, of course, human bodies. The mass slaying of bison interweaves with the genocide of First Nations peoples who depended on those big shaggy animals and open prairie for material and cultural sustenance. So many loggers broke their backs, lost their limbs, damaged their hearing as they cut down the titan trees. The bulldozers displaced and relocated working-class and poor folks from their generational homes, turning both people and mountaintops into rubble to push over the edge.

* * *

But how do we deal with bodily and ecological loss when restoration in its various manifestations is not the answer? Sometimes viable restoration is not possible. Sometimes restoration is a bandage trying to mend a gaping wound. Sometimes restoration is an ungrounded hope motivated by the shadows of *natural* and *normal*. Sometimes restoration is pure social control. I want us to tend the unrestorable places and ecosystems that are ugly, stripped down, full of toxins, rather than considering them *unnatural* and abandoning them. I want us to respect and embrace the bodies disabled through environmental destruction, age, war, genocide, abysmal working conditions, hunger, poverty, and twists of fate, rather than deeming them *abnormal* bodies to isolate, fear, hate, and dispose of. How can bodily and ecological loss become an integral conundrum of both the human and nonhuman world, accepted in a variety of ways, cure and restoration only a single response among many? When the woman whose body has been shaped by military pollution declares, "I hate the military and love my body," she is saying something brand new and deeply complex.

Monocultures and Biodiversities

In pursuing the analogy between restoration of health and restoration of ecosystems, curious questions begin to emerge. Are disabled bodies akin to cornfields? After all, both kinds of restoration—the one grounded in medical science and the other in environmental science—arise from the certainty that cornfields and disabled bodies are damaged and need to change. Restoration declares that cornfields need to return to a *natural,* self-sustaining, interdependent ecological balance and disabled or chronically ill bodies to a *normal,* independent functioning.

I remember walking a cornfield in early autumn. The leaves, stalks, husks rattle and sway overhead. Rows envelop me, the whole world a forest of corn beginning to turn brown. I step into the furrows between rows, onto the mounds upon which the stalks grow. Sound, sweat, and an orderly density of the same plant over and over fill the space. Nothing chirps or rasps, squawks or buzzes; the cicadas and grasshoppers have gone dormant for the season. I hear no warblers, finches, sparrows; I see no traces of grouse, pheasant, fox. The earth is laced with petroleum-based fertilizers and the air laden with pesticide residue. In spite of the damage they embody, cornfields are also beautiful on the surface, lushly green and quivering in the humid Midwest summer before they dry up in the fall, becoming brown and brittle. The stalks stand tall and sturdy, tassels silky and the color of honey, kernels of corn plump and hidden. Little tastes better than ears of sweet corn fresh from the field, husked, boiled, and buttered. But this beauty is deceptive; the monoculture of a cornfield has brought nothing but soil depletion and erosion; a glut of nonnutritious, corn-based processed foods; and wholesale destruction of prairie ecosystems. Restoration is not just a pleasant environmental pastime but a desperate need.

Let me return to my prompting question: are disabled human bodies akin to cornfields? The ideology of cure answers with a resounding yes. Speaking through the medical establishment and dozens of cultural assumptions and stereotypes, cure declares that the need for the restoration of health is just as urgent as the restoration of tallgrass prairies. From this point of view, disabled bodies are as damaging to culture as cornfields are to nature.

Distrustful of this answer, including the easy separation of nature and culture, I turn my question inside out and ask: are restored prairies like disabled bodies? Certainly, the tallgrass prairie that my friends caretake is a diverse ecosystem that is whole but not as whole as it once was or could be, quirky and off-kilter, almost self-sustaining and entirely interdependent, imperfect and brilliant all at the same time. These descriptors apply equally well to disability communities.

I remember departing from a large disability gathering. It is late spring in the San Francisco airport, an environment as bland as a cornfield. I walk a long corridor toward the plane that will take me home. I have been in the foggy Bay Area for a long weekend with three hundred LGBT disabled people, queer crips, as many of us like to call ourselves. I meander through the airport, people streaming around and by me. I know something is missing, but I don't know what. I let my exhaustion and images from the weekend roll over me until all of a sudden I realize everyone passing me all looks the same in spite of the myriad of cultural differences held within these walls. A gay white businessman strides past an African American woman and her grandson; a Latino man speaking quiet Spanish into his cell phone stands next to a white teen speaking twangy English with her friends; an Asian American woman pushes her cleaning cart by, stopping to empty the trash can. In spite of all these differences, everyone has two arms and two legs. They are walking rather than rolling; speaking with their lips, not their hands, speaking in even, smooth syllables, no stutters or slurs. They have no canes, no crutches, no braces; their faces do not twitch or their hands flop; they hold their backs straight, and their smiles are not lopsided. In some profound way, they all look the same.

It would be all too convenient and neat to suggest that without disability, humans re-create ourselves as a monoculture—a cornfield, wheat field, tree farm—lacking some fundamental biodiversity. Environmentalists have named biodiversity a central motivation for ecosystem restoration and a foundation for continued life on the planet. But to declare the absence of disability as synonymous with a monoculture disregards the multiplicity of cultures among humans. It glosses over the ways in which culture and nature have been set against each other in the white Western world, as if the human ferment we call culture and the wild, interdependent messiness we call biodiversity are distinct and opposing entities. It does not acknowledge how culture dictates which bodily characteristics are considered disability and which are considered *natural* variation.

At the same time, the absence of disability, even the desire for its absence, diminishes human experience and the inextricable interweaving of bio- and cultural diversity. Certainly, the desire to eradicate disability runs deep. Even the most progressive of activists and staunchest of environmentalists have for the past 150 years envisioned an end to disability as a worthy goal. But the white Western drive to eradicate *unnatural* and *abnormal* bodies and cultures has never targeted disability alone. Patriarchy, white supremacy, and capitalism have twined together in ever-changing combinations to make eradication through genocide, incarceration, institutionalization, sterilization, and wholesale assimilation a reality in many marginalized communities. It is this long-standing, broad-based desire for and practice of eradication that threaten to create human monocultures.

I return to my prompting question turned inside out: are restored prairies like disabled bodies? Ecological restoration is one powerful way to repair the damage wrought by monocultures and to resist the forces of eradication. A radical valuing of disabled and chronically ill bodies—inseparable from black and brown bodies; queer bodies; poor and working-class bodies; transgender, transsexual, and gender-nonconforming bodies; immigrant bodies; women's bodies; young and old bodies; fat bodies—is another part of the same repair and resistance. In this way, a commitment to bio- and cultural diversity coupled with a multi-issue disability politics answers my question with a resounding yes. Simply put, the bodies of both disabled and chronically ill people and restored prairies resist the impulse toward and the reality of monocultures.

Illogic

Both kinds of restoration—one of ecosystems and the other of health—appear to value and prioritize the *natural* over the *unnatural,* yet they arrive at opposing conclusions about disabled bodies. The contradiction and lack of logic could simply mark the point at which the analogy between cure and ecological restoration falls apart. Or they could point to the profound difference between a complex valuing of disability as cultural and ecological diversity and a persistent devaluing of disability entirely as damage. Or they could underline the multiple, slippery meanings of *natural* and *unnatural, normal* and *abnormal*—a fundamental illogic rooted in the white Western framework that separates human animals from nonhuman nature.

This framework has rarely valued and prioritized the *natural* world—meaning largely intact, flourishing ecosystems, some of which include humans and others of which do not. Out of these values has emerged an out-of-control greed for and consumption of coal and trees, fish and crude oil, water and land. This framework despises and destroys the *natural* when it is not human. It declares cornfields more productive than prairies, tree farms and second-growth forest more sustaining to wildlife than old-growth forest, open coal pits more necessary than intact mountaintops and watersheds. Within this system of values, the *civilized* is named and celebrated in opposition to the *savage,* the former rising above nature and the latter remaining mired in it.

The illogic grows as these values turn toward the human world, as the pairing of *savage* and *natural* collides with what is deemed un*natural* and ab*normal.* Throughout the centuries, rich white men have determined people of color, poor people, LGBT people, women, indigenous people, immigrants, and disabled people to be *savages,* nonhuman animals, close to nature. But in the same breath this long litany of peoples has also been held up as Other, *unnatural,* and *abnormal.* The illogic names certain human bodies both *natural* and *unnatural,* using each designation by turn as justification to enslave, starve, study, exhibit, and eradicate entire communities and cultures.

I return to the word *monkey.* As a taunt, a freak-show name, a scientific and anthropological designation for human animals, this word drips with the illogic of *natural* and *unnatural.* So many disabled people or people of color (or both) have lived publicly and privately, in the spotlight and not, with *monkey* and paid dearly. Let me pause and step into a river of names: Ota Benga, William Henry Johnson, Krao Farini, Barney Davis, Hiram Davis, Simon Metz, Elvira Snow, Jenny Lee Snow, Maximo, Bartola, Sarah Baartman, and on and on. In 1906 Ota Benga, a Batwa man from central Africa, was forced to live in the Bronx Zoo monkey house. The sign on the cage he shared with an orangutan read:

> The African Pigmy, "Ota Benga." Age, 23 years. Height, 4 feet 11 inches. Weight, 103 pounds. Brought from the Kasai River, Congo Free State, South Central Africa, by Dr. Samuel P. Verner. Exhibited each afternoon during September. (Bradford and Blume 181)

This sign makes Benga's situation stunningly clear: he was imprisoned in a zoo exactly because he was considered a curiosity, a specimen, a primate. His display was neither the first nor the last, but simply one in a long, long litany. P. T. Barnum exhibited William Henry Johnson as the "What-Is-It" and the "Missing Link." Freak-show posters named Krao Farini "Ape Girl." Barney and Hiram Davis worked for decades as *savages*, the "Wild Men from Borneo." Freak-show managers sold "Maximo" and "Bartola" as the "last of the ancient Aztecs," and anthropologists studied, measured, and photographed them naked as "throwbacks" to an earlier time in human evolution. White men caged, displayed, and studied Sarah Baartman as the "Hottentot Venus." These folks—all of them intellectually disabled or people of color (or both)—became monkeys or near monkeys in the white Western framework of scientific racism.

The brutality of *monkey* arises in part precisely because it removes particular bodies from humanity and places them among animals in the *natural* world. Scientific racism of the 1800s made this removal overt. Scientists declared that "the negro race . . . manifestly approaches the monkey tribe" (qtd. in Lindfors 9). They decided that "microcephalics [intellectually disabled people with an impairment medically known as microcephalia] must necessarily represent an earlier developmental state of the human being" (qtd. in Rothfels 158). They twined racism, colonialism, and ableism together until it was impossible to tell where one ended and the other began. And this thinking has not disappeared; it has just become more subtle most of the time, more subtle until a bully hurls the word *monkey* across the schoolyard, calling upon centuries of scientific racism, whether he knows it or not.

Monkey categorizes the bodies of white disabled people and people of color—both disabled and not—as *savage* and *natural*. Within this categorization, these bodies become subject to the profound disconnect, disregard, and destruction with which the white Western world treats nonhuman animals and nature. Disabled painter, writer, and animal rights activist Sunaura Taylor puts it this way:

> I find myself wondering why animals exist as such negative points of reference for us. . . . In David Lynch's 1980 classic *Elephant Man,* John Merrick yells out

to his gawkers and attackers, "I am not an animal!" . . . No one wants to be treated like an animal. But how do we treat animals? . . . [A]t the root of the insult in animal comparisons is a discrimination against nonhuman animals themselves. (194–95)

At the same time, these *savage* bodies, these *monkey* bodies, these *natural* bodies are also Other and *abnormal*, to be studied and gawked at exactly because of their abnormality. And in their Otherness and abnormality, these bodies also become *unnatural*. *Monkey* seamlessly engages with the illogic of *natural* paired with *abnormal* and *abnormal* paired with *unnatural*. But the illogic does not stop here.

Natural slides again, pairing up with what is considered *civilized*. Certain other bodies—white, nondisabled, heterosexual, male, cisgender, rich bodies—have been established as good and valuable, as the standard of both *natural* and *normal*. Corporate advertising sells *natural* beauty, *natural* strength, *natural* sexiness, *natural* skin, *natural* hair every day, as if *natural* were a product to sell. The medical establishment provides technology to ensure *normal* height, *normal* weight, *normal* pregnancy and birth, *normal* walking, *normal* breathing, as if *normal* were a goal to achieve. The pressure to conform individually and systemically to these standards of *natural* and *normal* is immense. Whether it is curing disabled bodies or straightening kinky hair or lightening brown skin or making gay, lesbian, and bi people heterosexual, the priorities are clear. In this illogic, *normal* bodies are *natural* and *natural* bodies are *normal*.

In all its arbitrary and illogical meanings, *natural* names both what is dominated and who does the dominating. *Natural* establishes some bodies as radically *abnormal* and others as hyper *normal*. The illogic holds what is *natural* and dominated as *abnormal* and *unnatural*. And it insists that those who dominate are both *normal* and *natural*. Do not try to make sense of the illogic; it is nonsensical. These four concepts—*natural, normal, unnatural,* and *abnormal*—in all their various pairings form a matrix of intense contradictions, wielding immense power in spite of, or perhaps because of, the illogic.

Prairie

I return in early fall to the thirty acres of restored tallgrass prairie in Wisconsin. I walk, thinking not of concepts but of bodies. The grasses swish against my legs. A few swallowtail butterflies still hover. Coyote scat appears next to the path. The white-throated sparrows sing. The grasses rustle, and I imagine a white-footed mouse scurrying and a red fox pouncing. Above vultures circle on the thermals. A red-tailed hawk cries not so far away. I am one body—a tremoring, slurring human body—among many different kinds of bodies. Could it all be this complexly woven yet simple? The answer comes back an inevitable yes and no.

Right now in this moment, the prairie both contains and is made up of a myriad of bodies. But just over the rise, another cornfield turns brown and brittle.

Just over the rise are a barbed-wire fence, a two-lane dirt road, and an absence of bison. Just over the rise is the human illogic of *natural* and *unnatural, normal* and *abnormal*. Just over the rise, we grapple with loss and desire, with damaged bodies and deep social and ecological injustices. Just over the rise are the bullies with their rocks and fists, the words *monkey* and *retard*. Just over the rise, we need to choose between monocultures, on one hand, and bio- and cultural diversities, on the other, between eradication and uncontainable flourishing. In so many ways, the prairie cannot be a retreat but the ground upon which we ask all these questions.

Notes

1. The idea of brilliant imperfection as a way of knowing, understanding, and living disability or chronic illness is one of hundreds of things I have learned in disability communities. In particular I want to thank Sebastian Margaret for this phrase.

PART 4
Poetics of Matter

14 Corporeal Fieldwork and Risky Art
Peter Goin and the Making of Nuclear Landscapes

Cheryll Glotfelty

It may go without saying that a landscape photographer must do fieldwork. How can you take a picture of a place without being there? But this very presumption of physical presence tends to obscure the role of fieldwork in landscape photography, a process that resonates strongly with the material turn in ecocritical theory. Photographer Peter Goin (b. 1951) has devoted more than thirty years to photographing altered landscapes in America, documenting the legacy of human actions on the land. Author of more than a dozen books and recipient of numerous awards, including two National Endowment for the Arts fellowships, Goin has done projects on Meso-American ruins in Central America, abandoned sections of the Erie Canal, engineered beaches along the U.S. Eastern Seaboard, artificial swamps in the American South, ancient petroglyphs in Nevada, postmining landscapes of North America, California agriculture, the architected wilderness of Lake Tahoe, and the U.S.-Mexico borderline. All of these projects involved rigorous fieldwork that is beyond the scope of most people. Goin is persistently and perhaps perversely drawn to abandoned, neglected, forbidden, and condemned landscapes as he bears witness to the places that our culture sweeps out of sight, out of mind.

For Goin, who begins every project by doing extensive library research, what fieldwork adds to book knowledge about a place is an intuitive perception impossible to achieve without bringing his five senses and a brain to the site and letting the place provoke a response in him. Each project and each place demands its own visual solution as Goin manipulates the variables of the photographic art to calibrate sight with insight. Each of Goin's images is thus an artifact of the process of exposing himself—like human film—to the light, matter, and history of a particular landscape.

Goin's methodology of immersive fieldwork became eerily risky when he undertook to document the landscape legacy of U.S. atomic testing. His resulting book *Nuclear Landscapes* (1991) includes images of the Trinity Site in New Mexico, the Hanford Nuclear Reservation in Washington State, the Nevada Test Site, and the Bikini and Enewetak Atolls in the Pacific Ocean. The *Nuclear Land-*

scapes project posed many challenges. Gaining access to these restricted sites entailed long and difficult negotiations with the U.S. government. Visiting the sites presented a personal health hazard due to dangerous levels of radioactivity, particularly unnerving in that the threat is imperceptible to the senses. Yet another challenge was the lack of inherent visual interest at some of these sites. Radioactivity itself is invisible, and in a postapocalyptic, depeopled landscape, where do you aim your camera, and how do you make a compelling image? Compounding the problem of subject is the conundrum of aesthetics. Sure, it is possible to shoot film at dawn or dusk to capture the beauty of pink light and long shadows. But what meaning would be communicated by a beautiful picture of a nuclear landscape? Conversely, if the picture is not beautiful, will people look at it?

When Goin shows slides from the *Nuclear Landscapes* project, invariably someone in the audience will ask, "What was it like?" and "Why did you do it?" Audiences want to understand not only the photograph but the photographer, and they rightly suspect that behind every photograph lurks an interesting story. Once told, the story of its making animates the photograph, becoming part of its meaning. In the spirit of material ecocriticism, I have chosen to pursue an ecobiographical approach to Goin's work, interviewing him extensively to explore the interconnections—or, perhaps better, "intra-actions"—between his life, the places he has experienced, and his art.[1] I seek to understand the mind behind the lens and to bring that understanding to contemplation of the work, believing that reintegrating maker, mind, and material artifact will release the photographs' potential to raise consciousness and arouse conscience more effectively than simply analyzing the photographs as objets d'art. Because fieldwork constitutes the essence of Goin's method, learning the story behind the making of an image becomes a way of studying the imprint of matter on mind and of examining the artistic and technical processes by which intuitive perception gained in the field is rendered back into matter to become the material object of the photograph. This essay describes the (double) "making" of a landscape, through both the nuclear experiments and the artistic representation of the photographer. At the same time, it describes the "making" of the photographer (in his mind and body) through the landscape itself. This relationship of reciprocal "making" opens a dimension of mutual permeability that testifies to the materiality of both ecological relationships and artistic representations.

Before considering the images themselves, I want to briefly introduce certain aspects of material ecocriticism that will come into play in this chapter. As material ecocriticism begins coalescing as a new paradigm, it incorporates concepts developed by philosophers and theorists such as Karen Barad, Jane Bennett, Stacy Alaimo, Andrew Pickering, and others reviewed in this book. The central tenets of material ecocriticism are conveyed via new terminology intended to signal the field's core insights. Taking her cue from quantum physics, Barad's "intra-action" concisely replaces the old idea that objects, observers, and observations are discrete and separate entities with the new idea that these phenomena are always already entangled, mutually constitutive, and coevolving. Matter, humans, and mind are some elements of the fabric of the universe, where a tug or shift in one part of the fabric influences and changes every other time-space-matter node in the system. Bennett's notion of "vibrant matter" similarly replaces the old idea that matter can be acted on but is not itself an actor with the new idea that matter has agency. Alaimo's model of "trans-corporeality" questions the old view that the body is separate from the environment and replaces it with the insight that the "environment"—that is, chemicals, toxins, molecules, and matter—invades, pervades, and indeed constitutes the body, such that a toxic environment produces toxic bodies (cancer is a good example) and, further, that bodies, moods, and mind are fundamentally interconnected. And Pickering's metaphor of the "mangle" complements this emerging picture of entanglement, enmeshment, and onto-epistemological-ethical unity by replacing the old view of binaries (matter and meaning) with the new "thick of things" view that society, politics, science, and technology are compressed together to form a densely layered reality.

Very often creative writers and artists anticipate theory or their work embodies theory. Their art and the way they talk about it may not employ the language of theory per se, as theoretical language is necessarily abstract, whereas many artists express their ideas and intuitions concretely or narratively. Nevertheless, art can be read as theory, and artists' statements usually ring much clearer and are more engaging to most audiences than is the discourse of theory. In this chapter I invite an artist to join the emerging theoretical conversation of material ecocriticism as an equal partner, who communicates in visual language and vivid storytelling. The photographs and the stories of their making that Peter Goin shared with me make a visual and narrative contribution to material ecocritical theory, a set of ideas that—much like exposed film immersed in a bath of developing fluid—is in the process of becoming a picture.

The Trinity Site in New Mexico is where the world's first nuclear explosion took place on July 16, 1945, on the Alamagordo bombing range in the Jornada del Muerto desert, ushering in the nuclear age. "Our culture likes origin stories, and so here you are. This is it—this is the spot." Although the site itself is a National Historic Landmark, it is fenced off and closed to the public except on one or two days per year. By special arrangement, Goin was able to gain access on a day that the area was closed. A military colonel drove Goin into the area and invited him to pick up a piece of trinitite for a souvenir. "Trinitite" is the name given to the glassy, greenish rock fused from sandy soil during the intense heat of an atomic blast. Human activities have literally produced a new geologic rock type, a material example of human-nature entanglement. Trinitite is also an example of vibrant matter. It is mildly radioactive and would likely set off airport security de-

Figure 14.1. *Trinity Site* (from *Nuclear Landscapes*, 1991). Courtesy of Peter Goin.

tectors in our post-9/11 era. But in the 1980s Goin had no problem bringing the specimen home, although he wonders whether he will suffer health problems from having carried a radioactive rock in his pocket. Goin's decision to visit nuclear landscapes despite known risks makes him wonder, "Am I crazy?" Feelings of unease were triggered by passing into restricted areas, crossing to the inside of a fenced perimeter, even if the landscape on the inside of the fence looked the same as that on the outside. But how to convey the portent of nuclear landscapes in a documentary photograph?

When we photograph it is commonplace to say that we "take" pictures, as if the photographer is a mere collector of objective scenes that, like trinkets in a curio shop, are there for the taking. Indeed, the word "photograph," Greek for "light writing," implies a passivity on the part of the photographer, who in the early years of photography was called an operator, as if he or she merely tends a machine—the camera—that mechanically records the image written by light on photosensitive paper. Goin prefers to say that he "makes" a photograph. This subtle linguistic distinction is a move toward the intra-active paradigm that material ecocriticism posits. "Making" a photograph suggests an interactive process, the photograph being the material artifact or record of the photographer's active encounter with place as mediated through the camera. In Karen Barad's model of "agential realism," one observes what one's instruments and experimental design allow one to see: not objective reality, but rather phenomena. Phenomena are always an intra-action of matter and the apparatuses that materialize what is observed (*Meeting* 85–90). When Goin did the fieldwork for *Nuclear Landscapes* in the 1980s (before digital cameras became available), professional landscape photographers favored the 4x5-view camera, which produced high-quality images with reasonable portability of equipment. But interacting with landscapes through a 4x5-view camera is physically and mentally demanding. The instrument itself is a bulky, clumsy piece of gear to carry, as it requires a tripod and four-inch-by-five-inch sheets of film in protective cases. This unwieldy contraption limits how far the photographer can venture from a vehicle and requires solid ground upon which to set up the tripod, all of which constrain what views can be documented. The camera and film must be kept clean, dry, and dust free, difficult to do in many of the places that Goin wished to document, where blowing dust (in Nevada) or high humidity (in the Marshall Islands) became uncooperative actors in the photo-making performance.

The process and action of shooting the photograph are likewise far from automatic. The photographer composes the view while crouching uncomfortably under a dark cloth that allows him or her to see the image on the ground glass of the camera. However, the image on the glass appears reversed left to right and inverted top to bottom, so the photographer must be able to imagine what the photograph will look like as a mirror image flipped right side up. Once the subject is framed, there are many variables under the photographer's control: plane tilt to control perspective, aperture and shutter speed to control exposure, aperture also controlling depth of field, while shutter speed affects whether motion is recorded as movement or frozen in space and time. The photographer must also choose when to shoot (season, time of day, weather conditions), vantage point, and camera angle, some of these dictated by local conditions and factors out of the photographer's control (such as permit dates, access, and cost). Another host of important variables and choices arises in the darkroom when the film is developed and printed. And there is yet another battery of decisions that pertain to where, when, and how the images are displayed and marketed: With text? Without text? In a book? What kind of book? In a museum? What kind of museum? How many photographs? In what sequence and arrangement? Each of the many turning points and moves in this dance among landscape, camera, photographer, photochemical industry, and publisher and curator affects the nature and meaning of the resulting image, which in turn affects how viewers will picture these places in their minds, which may in turn influence future policies that will have a bearing on the place itself or on other places.

In a controversial decision that harmed his reputation in the world of fine arts, Goin opted to create a deliberately deaestheticized effect in the *Nuclear Landscapes* project, photographing at high noon to convey oppressive heat and bright light, metaphorical allusions to radioactivity. For the first time in his career, he chose to photograph in color, because at that time, in the late 1980s, color was fugitive, meaning that the printed image decays in about twenty to twenty-five years, which seemed conceptually interesting to Goin as a process that mimicked radioactive decay. However, he avoided Kodachrome and Ektachrome color film, so popular at the time for their saturated colors that catered to consumer desires for a blue blue sky; however, it did not, in Goin's view, accurately reproduce the colors or the feel of the sites he visited. "Kodachrome developed a whole aesthetic that would take us one or two generations to delete from our expectation consciousness. I've had so many people in audiences stand up and say, 'Well, why are you using that blue?' And I said, 'Well, you're asking for this interpretive design by a corporation to create this stereotypical representation of the natural world. It's not accurate. It doesn't allow the range of interpretation.'" Goin printed in high key, pushing the whites as far as they could go without becoming the same as the border of the image on the page. He made strategic use of the horizon, sometimes using it as a teeter-totter to imply precarious balance and sometimes as the horizontal line of the subtle cross of a crucified landscape.

For the Trinity Site panorama, which was originally printed as a triptych—a visual reference to the threefold concept of the trinity—Goin chose a vantage point that shows the road swinging off to both left and right, creating the look of a concave lens, implying a depression opposite from that of the curve of the earth, a subtle reference to a bomb crater. There is something odd about the photo. Can you guess? The historical monument casts no shadow! While his military escort wondered what was taking him so long, Goin waited at this site for a couple of hours until the sun was directly overhead, arguably the exact worst time to take a photograph. Why did he make this choice? "If you think of the obelisk as a sundial, the shadow implies the passage of time. Without a shadow there is no time—time stands still. And that's the point. In terms of my conception of the work, this is about bearing witness. This is about finding what palette is available, and choosing what elements of so few available can be active. I constantly argue that 'light' is a verb, and when people look at this new light it's the antiaesthetic of contemporary landscape photography in terms of what's popularly expected, and so therein lies the key."

To make the atom bombs tested and used in and after World War II, plutonium was needed. Figure 14.2 depicts Nuclear Reactors D and DR. Nuclear Reactor D was one of the three first nuclear reactors ever built, and "DR" stands for D-Replacement. These reactors, located on the former town site of Hanford in eastern Washington, produced plutonium. Today the reactors are decommissioned, but the activity there has bequeathed a highly toxic landscape to all future generations. The whole area is contaminated and off-limits to the public, and it is all dangerous. During the fieldwork for the *Nuclear Landscapes* project, Goin carried a Geiger counter and wore film badges that registered the doses of radioactivity that he received. Far from allaying his fears, the Geiger counter exacerbated them. When he stood in one location, the counter was silent, yet if he shifted just a step to either side, the counter might erupt in a terrifying bleat of alarm. He came to regard the Geiger counter as a "scare machine." At this particular nuclear reactor site, Goin's official guide remained in the vehicle with the windows rolled up, while Peter—holding his breath to avoid inhaling radioactive dust—attempted to set a land-speed record for a 4x5 camera, worried that his shoes and tripod were pick-

Figure 14.2. *Nuclear Reactors* (from *Nuclear Landscapes*, 1991). Courtesy of Peter Goin.

ing up radioactive dirt from the ground. Even for an experienced "operator," it takes several minutes to take a picture with a 4x5 camera, and Goin's guide got increasingly agitated as the minutes ticked by, furiously tapping on the window of his vehicle and urgently gesturing for Peter to get back inside the truck. The guide was later reprimanded by his supervisor for allowing Goin out of the vehicle at this site.

The nuclear reactors at Chernobyl share a similar design to these Hanford reactors, reflecting an industrial sensibility of pure utility without aesthetics. Yet the design of this photograph is artful and symbolic. In the original color print the posts in the foreground of this picture are yellow, warning of the radioactivity buried beneath, which seeped from the two reactors. The lines in the photograph—the road track lines, the line of yellow posts, and the horizon line—open out to the right from an origin point on the left edge of the image. The left-to-right movement, in Goin's imagination, suggests a cornucopia, a sinister basket of plenty that spreads out, creating a broader sensibility of the pervasive radioactive contamination of the planet. Because the Hanford site is fenced off and out of sight, people take false comfort that toxic contamination is localized and contained. Goin is deeply upset by that complacency and intends this image to convey a more pervasive nuclear contamination—in space and time.

> The folly of human arrogance is so overwhelming, and I don't know what it will take ultimately for us as a people, as a species, to begin to reinvest in biotic diversity and communities and begin to live sustainability where our impacts don't impact generations literally twenty-four thousand years, which is the half-life of plutonium. It's beyond our comprehension. Because of its scale we're indemnified because we can't conceptualize it, so it enables us.

Any of Goin's work lends itself to material ecocritical analysis. I have chosen to focus on Goin's *Nuclear Landscapes* work not only because the March 2011 earthquake and consequent nuclear reactor catastrophe in Fukushima, Japan, reminds us of the persistent dangers of the nuclear age, but also because the project's background radiation, so to speak, sparks compelling narratives of transcorporeality. In light of the known health hazards of residual radioactivity from atomic tests and nuclear reactors, Goin's fieldwork for the *Nuclear Landscapes* project was risky. More than other substances, radioactivity (a matter-energy continuum) seems to possess its own agency, difficult to detect, hard to predict, and beyond human control. Goin began to think of the sites he visited as "landscapes of fear," as if the fear he experienced somehow inhered in the sites themselves. While documenting these sites, Goin was himself affected by them in palpable ways—elevated heart rate, nervous perspiration, anxiety, dehydration, and sunburn—and possibly in imperceptible ways. How much radiation did he absorb? Will the radiation exposure he received create cancer later in life?

After a day at Hanford, Goin, much to his surprise, was ordered to take off all his clothes except his underwear. He was then inspected with a Geiger counter by two employees in white coveralls, booties, and masks. He was told that if his levels were too high, he would have to discard his clothing and submit to a shower scrub, where the contaminated, outer, layer of skin would be abraded away. Haunting images of Karen Silkwood induced extreme anxiety, the memories of which make him shudder a decade later. "You know what's funny about this when I give public lectures about it? People ask, 'Do you worry about the effects on you?' I lift my baseball cap to reveal that I am bald, and I say, 'Well, I used to have hair.' And they crack up and they laugh and they feel guilty, 'Oh, my God.' Humor is an antidote to fear, isn't it?"

For Peter Goin, the idea for a photographic project on nuclear landscapes began taking shape not long after he moved to Nevada in 1984 to accept an assistant professor position in the Art Department at the University of Nevada, Reno. Prior to this move, Goin for several years had been manager of a large bookstore in downtown San Francisco, which afforded him scant leisure time to work on photographic and video projects on the side. The move to Nevada was an abrupt change in worlds, from the culturally diverse and cosmopolitan City by the Bay to the high desert and cowboy culture of Reno. Nevada at that time and even today is dismissed by many Americans as a wasteland. Yet Goin was intrigued by Nevada's wide-open valleys and sharply etched mountains, abundant sunshine, uplifting blue skies, and opportunities for solitude. Goin began to bond with the basin-and-range country through his camera, responding to the spiritual power of places like the Black Rock Desert and to the altered landscapes of remote bombing ranges littered with targets such as tanks, planes, and derelict school buses, perforated with bullet holes and strewn about in the desert like carcasses.

Having begun photographing the impact of the military on Nevada's desert landscapes, Goin became curious to view the Nevada Test Site, a vast tract of land 65 miles northwest of Las Vegas. Measuring 350 square miles, the Nevada Test Site was created in 1951 during the Cold War as the nation's primary site for testing nuclear weapons. Between 1951 and 1992 more than a thousand nuclear devices were tested at the Nevada Test Site above- and belowground, creating spectacular mushroom clouds and subsidence craters. When Goin was told that the test site was off-limits to the public, he became all the more determined to gain access to the area and photograph it so that American citizens could see the effects of the legacy of atomic testing on the landscape. After lengthy negotiations with the U.S. government, which involved petitioning elected representatives of the state of Nevada, Goin, who leveraged his status as a professor and "visual researcher" at the state's flagship university, was granted clearance to document the test site, becoming the first civilian photographer allowed to work there. The test site workers regarded Goin as a curiosity and told him he was crazy.

"When you go to the Nevada Test Site, it doesn't look the way you imagine it to be," Goin recalls. "You want everything to be visually dramatic and Mad Max-ish. You want it to be this postapocalyptical world of destruction and fires and concrete buildings burned out. But it's not. A crater here, a depression there. It doesn't have the same visual effect that you would imagine." Yet, if the test site was visually anticlimactic, it was physically intense. The heat, exposure, bright light, stark aridity, and risk of radiation combined to make Goin hyperaware and alert. His challenge as an artist became to make photographs that reconciled how he *felt* and what he *knew* about the site with what it looked like, which from his vantage point on the ground was not very dramatic—a nondescript desert with some miscellaneous relics and unidentified structures here and there, some roads, and scattered pockmarks in the ground, distant, difficult to make out, and not at all apocalyptic. One location on the test site, however, possessed inherent visual interest.

In the atomic testing program the military built a fake town, complete with a family of life-size mannequins in the kitchen, to see how a middle-class American house would survive an atomic blast. The town was named Doom Town, and it is now on the National Register for Historic Places. Before Goin's site visit this house had been renovated to be preserved in a state of arrested decay. "We're becoming like the French," Goin quips. "We're enveloping the theatrics of the farce." Inside the frame of Goin's photograph looms the dark, hulking shell of a two-story wooden house, whose paint has apparently burned off. Rather than being located in a neighborhood of other suburban houses and lawns, where one would expect to see a house of this design, this house sits alone in the Mojave Desert, where a sparse array of Joshua trees recedes into the distance, as if this house with its upright brick chimney is the last fragile vestige of human habitation at the end of the world. Goin's use of jet black in the windows invokes Hitchcock, while the lower right window—where you can look all the way through the house—signals abandonment.

In Goin's sensibility the image contrasts the cultural meaning of home—shelter, security, safety—with the military's twisted idea to explode it and see what happens. "On some level, it's like, 'I wonder what would happen if I put an orange in a microwave and put it on twenty minutes? Ooooh, what would happen? It's gonna explode, isn't it? That'd be cool! Let's watch that!'" Although he considered labeling the photograph *Doom Town,* he ultimately opted for a question—*How Would a House Withstand Nuclear Wind?* The interrogative mode and the phrase "nuclear wind" ask us to consider the dramatic consequences of our actions: "We are affecting the weather."

Goin thinks of his work as both visual research and art, modes that our epistemology and institutions typically relegate to different disciplines. Documentary photography, in Goin's view, is treated as the bastard stepchild of scholarship and the arts, neither parent fully embracing or understanding this mode of visual expression. His own view, which is encapsulated by Jerry L. Thompson, a critic of Depression-era photographer Walker Evans, is that the documentary style in photography is "deliberately wrought visual poetry disguised as plain prosaic fact" (12). As "poetry," the documentary photograph repays the close reading that one might devote to a painting. However, because they are constructed to look "plain" and "prosaic," documentary photographs usually achieve their effects unconsciously, with seeming artlessness. The fact that the photographer is *interpreting* the site through the palette of light and color, framing and perspective, is subtle and not noticed by most viewers. Nevertheless, the photograph has embedded within it an interpretation. "That interpretation then comes from what? It comes from the visceral experience of being there." The immediate visceral experience in the field renders each photograph a unique artifact of a particular experience, an experience-artifact "mangle," if you will, that can never be duplicated. As Goin explains in an attempt to make the process of visual composition legible to writers, "Even in your own work history you will write a paragraph, but if you

Figure 14.3. *How Would a House Withstand Nuclear Wind?* (from *Nuclear Landscapes*, 1991). Courtesy of Peter Goin.

waited three days and wrote intentionally the same paragraph, it would come out differently. So there's this constant variability in that interpretation, based on a variety of factors that can't be measured—your mood, what happened the night before, whether you were in an argument, whether you made love, whatever you just read, whatever you just saw, whatever you ate and drank. *All* of those factors influence that view."

Goin's passionate commitment to fieldwork shows his willingness to merge intra-actively with the landscape, to let his own mind be made by the landscape, while "making" the landscape's meaning and (after)life emerge in the photograph. Absent the intra-active presence of the photographer in the land, one might take a picture of a landscape, but the photograph will not be *of* the landscape.

> If you don't do [intra-active] fieldwork, what happens then is that you feel compelled to use a preexisting formula. You might say, "Well, you are a landscape photographer so of course you would want to go into the field." But that's like saying, "You eat, so therefore of course you go into the kitchen." Well, sure, but some people boil water. Some people go to Walmart and spend their whole

time in the frozen dinner aisle and just pull out all of their stuff and put them in their microwave. That's not cooking. That's not fieldwork. I think that cooking or fieldwork means making a cream sauce. Can you do it without reading a cookbook? You have to be able to know how to do that. Do you know how to stir fry meat, for example, so that it retains its internal juices and is healthy and juicy and tender and crispy on the outside? Do you know how to do a soufflé so it doesn't collapse down? That's fieldwork. It's knowing how to absorb that information and be open and available to it.

Goin recalls his accelerated heartbeat and hyperconsciousness while at the Nevada Test Site. Crossing the guarded gates into the test site, where you show ID, are searched, and get badged, feels like crossing a boundary into a foreign land and reminded Goin of an earlier project entitled *Tracing the Line* where he photographed the entire length of the U.S.-Mexico border. When you cross the border, you *feel* different. Unlike Mexico, where the sense of danger was caused by smugglers and bandits who worked the border, in the Nevada Test Site fear is provoked by subatomic particles. If you stand in one place the Geiger counter might make a steady "tick tick tick," but take one step to either side and it might explode like a rattlesnake in a fearful "TRRTTTTTTT." He recalls:

> Being there is so charged, literally, that it elevates your central awareness of place. You're aware of the sound of walking, you're aware of the heat, you're aware of the wind, you're aware of the light. It's too present for you to be distracted by daydreaming. It's too overwhelming. It's too demanding and it's too hot, literally and figuratively. *You're demanded of.* All of these experiences are channeled into how those images are ultimately constructed.

In addition to military tests, the government also spearheaded the Ploughshares program to develop peacetime uses of the atomic bomb, such as a quick way to dig a hole. Sedan Crater, pictured here, was created by that program. Conveying the *scale* of the enormous Sedan Crater (1,280 feet in diameter and 320 feet deep) in a photograph is almost impossible. Goin did not want to do a panorama that would extend beyond and thus contain the scale of the site. "I thought that creatively photographing something which is essentially nothing but horizon with a hole in front of it would emblematically represent the scale of it," he explains, "in the sense that the whole earth has fallen except for the horizon. He also waited until a shadow bisected the view to create a visual divide and sense of dimensionality."

> Shadows have their own meaning in life, don't they? You know, "in the shadows," "He was lurking in the shadows." What happens when you're looking at a clear sky and this big, huge ominous shadow starts overtaking it? The whole idea is to subtly provide a clue to the ominous nature of these sites, which when you look at them, in a way, you might just think, "It's a big pit." We've seen pits. We don't naturally respond to a pit as postapocalyptical, yet that sense is implied by this image.

Figure 14.4. *Sedan Crater* (from *Nuclear Landscapes*, 1991). Courtesy of Peter Goin.

Goin's publisher, Johns Hopkins University Press, was suitably impressed with the *Nuclear Landscapes* book manuscript and photographs and was ready to put the book into production. When Goin should have been happy at having his project accepted by a prestigious publisher, he could not rest. The project had taken on a life of its own, and Goin could not shake the nagging feeling that the Marshall Islands should be included in the narrative. The Marshall Islands was the first place where the United States tested atomic bombs after World War II, prior to relocating to Nevada. Finally, honoring the conviction that the Marshall Islands history needed to be documented, Goin called his editor to say that the project was not over. The editor replied that he could lose his contract. Goin felt compelled to take that risk. "Am I crazy?!" he wondered. Making arrangements and raising money to visit the Marshall Islands were even more of a logistical challenge than gaining access to the Nevada Test Site, but Goin is organized, persuasive, and persistent, and he ultimately was able to make the visit.

The Marshall Islands in the Pacific, halfway between Hawai'i and New Guinea, became a protectorate of the United States after World War II under the UN trusteeship system. In 1946 the 167 inhabitants of Bikini Atoll were relocated to Rongerik Island so that their home island could be used as a test site for atomic bombs. They were told that they could return after the testing; however, despite massive cleanup efforts, which included scraping off the existing soil and replacing it with soil shipped over from Nevada, Bikini Island remains uninhabitable due to high levels of radioactivity. Other islands in the Marshall Islands cluster were similarly evacuated, bombed, and rendered radioactive and uninhabitable.

> I had it particularly bad in the Marshall Islands. I mean, if you give me five minutes, I could make my palms sweat over memories. I was dropped off. It was actually an amazing life experience because they gave you a QuadRunner. I was on Bikini Atoll with a QuadRunner. The island is a half-mile wide, three miles long, and I rode around with my camera, all by myself all day, with my Geiger counter and my gear and my water and whatever and no one there. The concept of no one there is not truly understood until you're in a place like that. No one around you for literally five thousand square miles. No one there. And then to go there and look and say, "I want to photograph here," and you get out, you set up the tripod, and you walk over, and then all of a sudden "ttthhhcccchhhhttt," that high staccato sound, and you're going, "What just happened?" And it's also hotter than hell. It felt like a hundred degrees and 95 percent humidity, and you're just sweating like nobody's business. So intense. You can put on sunscreen all day long; you have to cover your face in zinc. You are radiated by the sun's rays as well as by the rays of whatever remnants of the testing. And so it is the landscape that demands of you a certain form of attention. It requires a presence, and in that presence you then interpret it. Your mind's bodily presence, taking the risk of "making" the landscape.

This bunker complex on Aomen Island in Bikini Atoll, built to withstand a nuclear bomb, was a photographic station used during Operation Redwing in 1956. The lead bricks in the foreground were used to construct radiation barriers. The shape of this bunker, and the ladder in the center right, reminded Goin of the Meso-American ruins that he photographed in the 1970s.

> When you look at these bunkers, they now become to me these ruins of our civilization. This is our legacy. Whatever we may think we're leaving behind, what we're really leaving behind are these bunkers. Because these are designed to withstand a nuclear blast; therefore, they withstand time. This is the story of who we are. In the same way that we look at those ruins from those other societies and try to imagine who they were, our descendants in the long-distant future will look at these and say, "These people were messed up." And people will go in there, and it will still be radioactive. And they'll get exposed, and they'll die and think it's a curse of the tombs.

Goin had trouble printing the negatives from the Marshall Islands. He is not sure if the film suffered radiation damage. He does not think that the alpha waves and particles that persist on the islands should affect film, but the fact is that he "had a hell of a time printing some of these. Awful." Now, more than twenty years

Figure 14.5. *Nuclear Bunker Complex* (from *Nuclear Landscapes*, 1991). Courtesy of Peter Goin.

after printing the *Nuclear Landscapes* photographs, Goin faces the fact that the prints themselves are beginning to decay. If he does not do something to preserve them, they will deteriorate, and the visual record will be lost. Therefore, Goin recently decided to reprint the photographs. However, the negatives have degraded so badly that printing from them is not a viable option. Instead, Goin and an assistant are laboriously scanning, cleaning, and digitizing the prints so that they will be available to future generations. The process of digitizing the images is itself an exercise in intra-action as there is no exact correlation between the color of the original print and the digital palette available through the computer and inkjet printing technology. "You're going from dyes based on light-sensitive silver nitrate and chemical reactions to ink on paper. It's a change. You can try to make it as accurate to the original as you possibly can, but ultimately they're different and they're not going to look the same." After he scans an image, Goin uses Photoshop to remove blemishes and adjust variables such as saturation, temperature, tint, brightness, and contrast. Hence, the new digitized print is not a copy but rather an interpretation of the original, which itself was an interpretation of Goin's immersive, trans-corporeal, intra-action with the site. "Think of it this way," Goin explains. "Ansel Adams was accurate when he said that the negative is the score and the print is the performance." Literary scholars who are accustomed to working with a definitive text might be unsettled by the high degree of plasticity in the photographic art. In the case of the nuclear landscapes project, images appear in one form in the book, another form (different paper, different size images, different ink) in a portfolio of exhibition prints with words burned onto the image, another form when the images are digitized, and still another form as small black-and-white illustrations in this chapter. Hence, critical interpretation of "the" text is a fiction, as every reading is contingent upon and in dialogue with the state and context of the material object, not to mention the state of the critic herself and of the reader.

The coconuts in Goin's "Coconut Graveyard" photograph, washed up on the shore of Eneu Island in Bikini Atoll, are too high in cesium 137 to be safely consumed. "I walked there and saw this and thought, 'Oh, my God, it's *The Killing Fields*,'" Goin recalls, referring to a graphic film about the war in Cambodia. "Being there was just overwhelming. In other ways, many of these sites are cerebrally overwhelming. But this was emotionally overwhelming. You just think about the consequences of our actions and viscerally being so impressed with the isolation of this place and knowing it's contaminated and knowing that there's this tremendous history of detonating sixty-six nuclear bombs and that these people have been completely displaced from what was their homeland." To bear witness to destruction of this magnitude is an enormous burden. When Goin talks about his photographs, stories spill forth almost unstoppably, like Coleridge's ancient mariner. He can easily talk for more than an hour about a single photograph, as each image triggers memories of the visceral experience of engaging with these landscapes of fear and the struggle to funnel multisensory impressions through the bottleneck of the visual language. Audiences likewise tirelessly ply Goin with questions, hungry to derive meaning and an ethical orientation from *their* exposure to Goin's images. One question-and-answer session lasted three hours, nearly unheard of for a guest speaker.

By interacting with audiences, Goin's own sense of the meaning of the images has evolved. He recalls a particularly low point following a talk he gave in eastern Washington.

> I had a terrible cold, but I soldiered on. I just felt terrible, so I blame my response on my illness, but someone said, "So do you think that nuclear weapons will be used again?" And I answered, "Yes. I do. I think it's inevitable." And the audience just went, "Aww." You could feel a heaviness in the room. And I realized that I let them down by that answer. That what had happened to me was I became more than an agent of bearing witness, I became in a way a kind of postmodern preacher of optimism, unintended in some way. I didn't realize it

Figure 14.6. *Coconut Graveyard* (from *Nuclear Landscapes*, 1991). Courtesy of Peter Goin.

until that moment, but I had an opportunity, which I have subsequently used, to say that there is a tremendous opportunity for us as a people to learn the importance and sacrifice and risks of inactivity and ignorance. That an informed population who functions with civil responsibility will prevent nuclear war, and it comes down to education. If we invest in education and have a critically thinking, intelligent, informed civilized population, we will be peace seekers. War comes out of ignorance and fear. And so now we are presented with the opportunity. The audience likes that much more.

"A photograph is a doorway. It's a portal. It's an entry," Goin explains, hoping that his work will spark a debate about our nuclear legacy and our future. "I believe now that what we've ultimately wrought in the nuclear era is fundamental evidence that we must exercise civil action and responsibility to protect our habitat for our children. That's the lesson. And so now we are presented with the opportunity. So here's the challenge. It's up to you."

Notes

1. I interviewed Peter Goin six times between April and July 2011, recording more than six hours of tapes. I am grateful to Goin for these illuminating conversations and for permission to use the photographs printed in this chapter.

Thanks to Scott Hinton, who prepared the images, and Amy Bartlow, who transcribed the tapes. Serenella Iovino and Serpil Oppermann shared their essays on material ecocriticism when still unpublished and recommended many illuminating theoretical texts. In addition to the works referenced in the essay, see Andrew Pickering's *Mangle of Practice*, Susan Hekman's *The Material of Knowledge*, and Karen Barad's *Meeting the Universe Halfway* on the new materialism and Roland Barthes's *Camera Lucida*, Susan Sontag's *On Photography*, and W. J. T. Mitchell's *What Do Pictures Want?* on photography. Julia Breitbach's "The Photo-as-Thing: Photography and Thing Theory" brings new materialism and photography together via Bill Brown's work on "thing theory."

15 Of Material Sympathies, Paracelsus, and Whitman

Jane Bennett

PARACELSUS (1493–1541) EXPERIENCED the natural world as a complex order of sympathies, resonances, magnetic attractions, and analogies (Pagel 52).[1] Though Paracelsus is variously categorized as physician, philosopher, alchemist, herbalist, I like to think of him as a plant physiognomist, as, that is, a practitioner of the art of discovering temperament and character from outward appearance. Each natural object bore for him a divine "signature" encoded in the thing's shape, smell, texture, color, posture. This equivocal sign served as a spur to the human perceiver to engage in the artistry—the speculative thinking and practical experimentation—that would give determinacy to the hidden "virtues" of the object.[2] Paracelsus's practice of virtue was a medico-religious one, organized around the idea that meticulous attention to plants, animal organs and fluids, and minerals would provide hints about how those bodies might contribute to the human body's desire to live a strong and long life.

It is noteworthy that Paracelsus combined an herbalist's sensitivity to the specificities of plant bodies with a Christianish belief in a harmonious, divinely designed cosmos. His mid-seventeenth-century admirer Andreas Tentzel brings to the fore how Paracelsus's naturalism is a holism underwritten by God:

> The whole Kingdom and Monarchy of Nature doth admirably abound with consentaneous and dissentaneous (*sympatheticall and antipatheticall*) *influences*, that in . . . any wise divided from it, it will be united to it in a more noble degree, the whole by a kind of divine right of community. . . . [E]very thing [is] destined and impowered by *sacred providence*, by whose excelling strength and motions all subordinate things enjoy in every part *analogicall* and true proportionall virtues. (Paracelsus, Tentzel, and Parkhurst 20–22)[3]

Is it possible to retain Paracelsus's exquisite attunement to the specificities of bodies and to affirm his intuition that "sympathy" counts as a mode of natural causality, but lose or loosen his theology of intelligent design ("sacred providence")? In what follows, I will try to theorize such a notion of sympathy, where sympathy names not only an inner psychological state but, more fundamentally, an impersonal ontological infrastructure, an undesigned system of affinities (which persist alongside antipathies) between and within bodies. I want, in short, to explore the viability of a notion of "sympathetic causality" today. In pursuing this project, I aspire to contribute to recent attempts (in ecomaterialism, object-oriented philosophy, immanent naturalism, the nonhuman turn) to highlight a distinctively *material* mode of agency, a mundane efficacy that is not the free, willed action of humans or gods, but is also more creative than the bare *repetitions* of a machine and more uncertain than an organic *unfolding*.

For help with theorizing Sympathy as a kind of agency, I turn to poet Walt Whitman. Like Paracelsus, he thought it was important to lift the presence of sympathetic attractions out from the oblivion of the ordinary. The banal fact that bodies always have some leanings—chicory leaves tilt toward the sun, stones tend toward the ground, the eucalyptus craves fire, human heads have a propensity to incline slightly to one side when listening closely—is exposed to be the operation of a pervasive network of impersonal forces. These circuits of energy or physical propensities, of uncertain strength and duration, become evidence of the presence of nonhuman vitalities that, despite their independence from human subjectivity, might be cajoled into assemblages with human endeavors. For Paracelsus, the means for this cajoling were the alchemical arts; for Whitman, it was the sound and sense of free verse. Both men sought to *proclaim* the operations of Sympathy as a pervasive material power: "*I am he attesting sympathy. I have instant conductors all over me,*" claims Whitman in "Song of Myself" (615).

> *The spotted hawk swoops by and accuses me, he complains*
> *of my gab and my loitering.*
> *I too am not a bit tamed, I too am untranslatable,*
> *I sound my barbaric YAWP over the roofs of the world.* (1331–33)

Whitman's Sympathy is, compared to Paracelsus's system of signed virtues, a less personal and less moralized figure of agency. Whitman tones down the role that divine design plays in the network of affinities. I, perhaps even more than Whitman, seek a notion of Sympathy that, in addition to revealing the tangled threads connecting us to other bodies, can also acknowledge that Nature enacts itself and us in ways that are *indifferent* to human well-being.

Heliophilia

For neither Paracelsus nor Whitman is sympathy figured in the usual modern sense, as, that is, a subjective feeling of compassion for or commiseration with the suffering of another body. A good example of this pity-centric notion is my emotional response to a photograph that appeared on the front page of the *New York Times*: "Haitians endure suffocating heat in a theater in Les Cayes to see the spectacle of police officers on trial in a prison massacre case" (Bogdanich and

Sontag). I was struck by the suffering of the families of the prisoners, as I cofeel bits and pieces of their yearning for justice embodied in their faces and postures (rarely are prison guards called to account for acts of brutality). This experience was, as nineteenth-century psychologist Theodor Lipps describes it in his *Raumaesthetik*, that of me "recognizing" in another person an "inner liveliness" that is "a natural mode of behavior of my own." This recognition of something familiar "gives me happiness," says Lipps, a happiness that coexists with the sadness and outrage that I caught from the Haitians (qtd. in Spuybroek 180–81).[4]

The figure of Sympathy I draw from Paracelsus and Whitman bespeaks of a more dispersed and generic force, more like heliophilia than an interhuman recognition initiated and enacted in psyches. Paracelsus, invoking his theory of cosmic resemblances, notes that "the chicory stands under a special influence of the sun; this is seen in its leaves, which always bend toward the sun as though they wanted to show it gratitude. Hence it is most effective while the sun is shining" (*Selected* 122–23). The chicory shares this solar propensity with many plants, including a tree that I encountered on a walk around Baltimore.

An "invasive" species, the tree thrives in the toxin-rich soil along railroad tracks. Called a "weed tree" and "ghetto palm," its botanical name is most apt: *Ailanthus altissima*. This particular specimen first took root in the shade of an elevated road, but then reached over and up, up and over and up—*altissima*—to the sunny side of the street.

What happens if we describe the complex of forces that produced this upright, yearning posture as *Sympathy*? *Ailanthus* grows itself toward sun, emitting tentacles of indeterminate longing; simultaneously, sun casts down rays upon the warming and expanding concrete and the stretching tree; roadway lends itself as a support for the tree, expressing an inner alliance, an affinity, between its smooth concrete and the surface texture of the bark. Along with *Ailanthus* and roadway on that sunny day, I too was leaning and longing, casting and connecting, radiating and being radiated. Standing under the road, I felt an involuntary surge upward, repeating imprecisely the upward thrust of the tree, my tilted head aligning with the plant's crooked yearning. This was happening as my stance—two feet firmly planted—was resonating with the cool stolidness of concrete. Given that my body is made up of vegetal, stony, mineral, and solar solids, liquids, and gases, perhaps we can understand the mimetic relays between *Ailanthus*, sun, concrete, and flesh as nonpsychological, reverberating nods.

To "nod," "emit," "radiate," "stretch," "lean and long," "cast and connect": are these the verbs appropriate to the action-style of an onto-Sympathy? How do proximate bodies sometimes become caught up in the others' threads and join the emerging hum? Note that the threads cast outward by *Ailanthus* or me are *indeterminate* in their telos, their targets not fixed in advance: such leaning is not

Figure 15.1. *Ailanthus altissima*, 2012. Courtesy of Jane Bennett.

fully intentional even if directional; the sticky filaments sent forward have uncertain trajectories that, if they hit upon an amenable target, can produce nodes of connection and avenues of transport (on this point, see Pahl). In short, this is a *mildly* teleological encounter.

The teleology is mild because it is multiple: lines of sympathy cross and interfere and compete and coming. Paracelsus too had a sense of this. When Tentzel, his English translator, described Paracelsus's theory of disease transmission, whereby to "behold the sorenesse of an eye, Their own infected are (by Sympathie)" (Paracelsus, Tenzel, and Parkhurst, 8) he notes the obvious counterfactual: not everyone who encounters a diseased body in fact catches its disease. Tentzel summarizes Paracelsus's reply to the objection as a reassertion of the omnipresence of Sympathy, but as a multiplicity—there are always in play many, overlapping, and contesting pulls (and thus also pushes), operating through and across bodies, bodies that are themselves in constantly varying states of activity and passivity. That there are always *multiple* affinities means that it can never be known in advance *which* line of transmission will win out at a moment of encounter:

> It may be objected...that then all diseases would be infectious...I answer, All are contagious, even health itself, if we consider it only according to its proper *active* faculty...for everything naturally is endued with a power of affecting another thing with its own qualities, although every operation is not equally effectual. (Paracelsus, Tentzel, and Parkhurst 8–19)

There always exist sympathetic tendencies, but because each body always leans toward many, different, bodies, it must remain an empirical question which body will act as infector and which as infected.

Paracelsus, prefiguring a move that Spinoza too will make with his figure of *Deus sive Natura,* says that all bodies, qua natural bodies, are susceptible to each other because every thing is an expression of the same self-diversifying "Prime Matter" (primordial "semen"), which Paracelsus termed "Iliaster." Iliaster, writes Walter Pagel, "is a kind of primordial matter, but not matter in the ordinary corporeal sense. It is rather the supreme pattern of matter, a principle that enables coarse visible matter and all activity of growth and life in it to develop and exist" (112).[5] "Iliaster" or not, there does seem to be a persistent attraction between the idea of Sympathy and onto-stories that are *monistic*.[6] But again: not every monism must affirm a static or homogeneous "substance"—even Iliaster is more process than product. And not every monism need affirm an intrinsically harmonious or equilibrium-maintaining cosmos. There are, in other words, protean monisms that are both processual and allow for heterogeneity within (or, to use William James's term, "litter") and for flashes of emergent novelty. Deleuze and Guattari's "vital materialism" is an example of such an onto-picture, which is formally monistic but substantively plural.

Adhesive Love and Electric Relays

Like Paracelsus, Whitman speaks of Sympathy as the default infrastructure of relations-between-bodies; Sympathy is what he describes as the "old law" of nature. Perhaps the best example of this is Whitman's discussion of "adhesive" (in contrast to "amative") love. This special kind of affection is not a romantic or psychologically deep attachment, but an anonymous, episodic leaning or reaching toward the vitality of other bodies. Adhesive love is simultaneously intense and impersonal (Frank 163). It exists in the sparks between the shoulders of strangers brushing on the street, in the current between eyes and blazing objects and vice versa (on this point, see Massumi),[7] and in the erotic relay between feet and ground: "*The press of my foot to the earth springs a hundred affections.*"

That quotation appears in section 14 of "Song of Myself":

> *The wild gander leads his flock through the cool night,*
> *Ya-honk he says, and sounds it down to me like an invitation,*
> *The pert may suppose it meaningless, but I listening close,*
> *Find its purpose and place up there toward the wintry sky.*
> *The sharp-hoof'd moose of the north, the cat on the house-sill,*
> *the chickadee, the prairie-dog,*
> *The litter of the grunting sow as they tug at her teats,*
> *The brood of the turkey-hen and she with her half-spread wings,*
> *I see in them and myself the same old law.*
> *The press of my foot to the earth springs a hundred affections,*
> *They scorn the best I can do to relate them.* (36)

Currents of affection are, for Whitman, at work everywhere, between all sorts of bodies. They are not the effect of my conceptual relating of them. This erotic force or electric charge, this "friendship" between bodies, is an expression of the macroforce of Sympathy per se; it is unwilled, and its mechanism is not fully intelligible: "*They scorn the best I can do to relate them.*" Or, as Whitman says later on in the poem:

> *I dote on myself, there is that lot of me and all so luscious . . .*
> *I cannot tell how my ankles bend, nor whence the cause of my*
> *faintest wish,*
> *Nor the cause of the friendship I emit nor the cause of the*
> *friendship I take again.* (47)

It is important to note that even though Sympathy is an *invisible* and *not fully intelligible* set of forces, it is not for Whitman thereby indiscernible or inimical to sense. To the contrary, it is quite palpable, once one "dotes" on it. Paracelsus makes a strikingly similar claim when he describes that kind of apprehension wherein

Figure 15.2. *Foot*, drawing, 2012. Courtesy of Jane Bennett.

we "grasp" that full half of nature that "is invisible": "We do see and grasp, but we do not [fully] register what it is that we seize hold of" (Von Hohenheim 723).

As self-proclaimed bard of democracy, Whitman exhorts his readers to *attest* to this invisible or occult but tangible system of leanings and longings. Because Whitman believes that this apersonal affection can bind a diverse population into a citizenry with less violence than when religion, race, or heritage is employed for this purpose, he names as a *democratic virtue* the attempt to become more aware of the sparking threads of Sympathy along which one travels. Good democrats dote on the wondrous mundanity of Sympathy; they *proclaim* its presence. "*I am he attesting sympathy.*" "*I have instant conductors all over me*" ("Song of Myself," Whitman 50).

Like Paracelsus, Whitman apprehends, invokes, and announces the tangle of sympathetic threads at work *between* bodies. But his poetry also invokes a strange *intra*body set of sympathies, an internal relay of associations and infections at work *within* each human self. A key instance of this is the sympathy between a posture and a mood, between, that is, a bodily comportment (angle of head, position of limbs) and a particular cast of mind or disposition. Postures sympathize with moods,[8] in very much like the way yoga poses stimulate spiritual states. One of Whitman's poetic techniques is to expose and intensify this natural resonance between, on the one hand, an arrangement of arms, legs, neck, hands, tongue and, on the other hand, a mood or vibe such as nonchalance, generosity, affection, brio, or the doldrums. It is to this second, intraself, system of affinities or sympathies that I now turn.

Side-Curved Head and Nonchalance

My first example is the sympathy Whitman exposes between the posture of a *"side-curved head"* and the mood of *"nonchalance."* Nonchalance, in addition to adhesive love, is, surprisingly, positioned by Whitman as a *democratic* virtue. To be nonchalant is to be calm and composed, and, indeed, a democrat needs to cultivate the ability to keep a cool and nondefensive comportment in the face of the many daily challenges to her settled identity and habits, challenges proliferating in an America divided by civil war in the nineteenth century (and into Red and Blue states in the twenty-first).

Several of Whitman's poems cite nonhuman bodies—*"the open countenances"* of animals and *"inanimate things," "the exquisite apparition of the sky"* ("A Song of Rolling Earth," Whitman 186)—as exemplars of this lighthearted unconcern. He also finds nonchalance or *"insousiance"* in *"the unimpeachableness of the sentiment of trees in the woods and grass by the roadside"* ("Preface to the 1855 Edition," Whitman 624). Men and women, themselves natural bodies, can cultivate the stance of nonchalance, in part by allowing their bodies to "correspond" to the countenances and poses of animals, plants, and natural objects. Whitman here seems to echo Paracelsus when the latter suggests that the way to "find out" why the chicory roots "assume the shape of a bird after seven years" (Pagel 122–23) is to "'overhear' ('*ablauschen*') its inner mechanism" in order to encourage one's own body to vibrate more freely with the chicory. As Pagel puts the point: "There is an element inside the naturalist—himself a microcosmic whole—which corresponds to this particular plant and must, by an act of sympathetic and magnetic attraction, unite with it. He will then acquire knowledge of the natural object in question" (51). *Leaves of Grass* too repeatedly calls the reader to imitate the countenances of natural objects in order to produce effects upon the self, though Whitman tones down the role that divine design plays as the ground of this sympathetic causality.[9]

What exactly is the pose one might assume while resonating with the insouciance of inanimate things? Whitman suggests that one such posture is that of the *"side-curved head,"* as when he describes himself as *"Looking with side-curved head curious / what will come next, / Both in and out of the game and watching / and wondering / at it. / Backward I see in my own days where I / sweated through fog / with linguists and contenders, I have no mockings or arguments, I witness and wait"* ("Song of Myself," Whitman 29). Whitman himself assumes the position of side-curved head in the frontispiece of the 1855 edition of *Leaves*. How is this pose

Of Material Sympathies, Paracelsus, and Whitman | 247

Figure 15.3. *Side Curved Head,* drawing, 2012. Courtesy of Jane Bennett.

non-chalant, not-hot? Perhaps insofar as it introduces (or registers) a pause in or cooling down of the body's normally restless darting of sensory attention. With side-curved head one lingers to wonder, is simultaneously attentive and slightly detached—nonchalant. To look with side-curved head is for Whitman to be still enough to take in other bodies but not so passive as to fail to "broadcast" one's participation in the scene, one's vital presence.[10] "*Looking with side-curved head curious what will come next, / Both in and out of the game and watching and wondering at it*" ("Song of Myself," Whitman 29). So arranged into the calm but not slack posture of side-curved head, one is more likely to receive other bodies or forces with equanimity or tolerance, to open the portals to a more expansive experience.

A second pose associated with nonchalance appears in "A Song of the Rolling Earth," where Earth, who has taken on the form of a woman, sits comfortably as she looks at her reflection in a mirror, looks, that is, at her multiple selves, insofar as she is all of creation.

The regard of Earth is nonchalant, contentedly impartial: *"glance as she sits, inviting none, denying none"* ("A Song of Rolling Earth," Whitman 186). *"The earth does not exhibit itself nor refuse to exhibit itself"* (185), but assumes a posture of one who is *"delaying not, hurrying not"* ("Out of the Cradle," Whitman 211). The poem "A Song of Rolling Earth" recommends that the reader too assume this comportment:

> *I swear there is no greatness or power that does not emulate*
> *those of the earth....*
> *No politics, song, religion, behavior, or what not, is of account,*
> *unless it compare with the amplitude of the earth,*
> *Unless it face the exactness, vitality, impartiality, rectitude of the*
> *earth.* (Whitman 187)

Nonchalance is a *stance* in both the psychological and (as I am emphasizing) the postural sense.

By including these postures in his poems Whitman seems to be expressing his intuition of a physiocultural sympathy between posture (seated, unfocused gaze) and mood (*"vitality, impartiality, rectitude"*). Whitman also seems to be intuiting a second link, that between the reader's literary encounter with a posture and her own *mimetic* inhabitation of it. Even if a case can be made for a sympathy or rhythmic resonance between posture and virtue, and even if it can be shown that Whitman tries to put this to democratic ends, there is still the question of how his readers and auditors could be affected by the postures so described. Wouldn't that require us to physically enact the posture with our bodies? Yes. And here it seems that Whitman invokes and intensifies a second natural resonance, one at work alongside that between posture and mood. This is a sympathy between an *image* of a posture (as provoked by a sketch or arrangement of words) and the *mimetic production* of the relevant muscular configuration in the reader's or hearer's body. The claim here is that Whitman's poetry makes use of that autonomous but imperfect mimesis whereby *imagining* a posture incipiently *enacts* that arrangement of arms, legs, neck, hands, tongue in the reader and auditor.[11]

I have no doubt that the poses embedded in Whitman's poems make things happen in human bodies.[12] But I do not think the postures he celebrates are as reliably democratic in effect as the poems suggest. This is because sympathetic causality is not a closed circuit, but more like an electromagnetic wave flowing across bodies, susceptible to interference, displacements, and static.

Of Material Sympathies, Paracelsus, and Whitman | 249

Figure 15.4. Image of Walt Whitman, from the frontispiece of *Leaves of Grass*. A steel engraving by Samuel Hollyer from a lost daguerreotype by Gabriel Harrison.

Whitman is famous for his lists of persons, places, things, and activities. As I have tried briefly to show in my discussion of affinities between posture and mood, he also enacts a second sense of listing: as affinity or inclination or leaning, as in "the ship lists to one side." (There is an etymological kinship between "list" and "lust" or "desire, longing, inclination.")[13] Whitman suggests that a natural physics of sympathetic bodies is the condition of possibility of the formation of any positive relationship, be it a friendship, an artistic composition, or a democratic

Figure 15.5. *Crouch*, drawing, 2012. Courtesy of Jane Bennett.

* * *

culture. Sympathy is, in Whitman's words, the "house" that supports the items therein: "*I am he attesting sympathy, / (Shall I make my list of things in the house and skip the house that supports them?)*" ("Song of Myself," Whitman 44).

* * *

Is there value in describing the relations obtaining between tree, road, and sun, or between the side-curved head and a tolerant nonchalance, as *sympathy*? My experiment has been to think sympathy as a type of causality, as, that is, one of the modes by which bodies produce effects. This Sympathy is not predicated on a presumption of perfect sameness, but involves a more indeterminate, underspecified leaning toward, an imperfect affinity between bodies. Such a notion of sympathy could acknowledge that other bodies are often indifferent to human well-being, even as it would extend affectivity (to use a Spinozist term) to nonhuman and inorganic bodies.

This rehab of the term "sympathy" may turn out to be more trouble than it is worth. But for now, I want to see how far the term can be stretched beyond its ontotheological, subject-centered roots. My barbaric (or perhaps alchemical) yawp is this: Sympathy names a material agency, a power of bodies human and nonhuman, a mode of impersonal connection, attachment, and care that proceeds from below subjectivity into subjectivity. What more can I say?

"*What is there more, that I lag and pause and crouch extended with unshut mouth?*" ("So Long!," Whitman 49).

Notes

I am grateful to Eileen Joy (convener of "Cruising in the Ruins: The Question of Disciplinary in the Post/Medieval University," second biennial meeting of the BABEL Working Group, September 20–22, 2012) and Finbarr Barry Flood, Jas Elsner, and Ittai Weinryb (conveners of the "Beyond Representation" conference at the Bard Graduate Center and New York University's Institute for Fine Arts, September 27–29, 2012) for the occasions to develop earlier versions of this essay. Thanks also to Marcus Boon, Alex Livingston, Anatoli Ignatov, Nathan Gies, Tripp Rebrovick, Katrin Pahl, Chris Gosden, and Jennifer Culbert for comments and criticisms. All quotes from Whitman in this chapter are italicized for emphasis.

1. Paracelsus's "persistent plea for homoeopathic and isopathic measures and his doctrine of 'signatures,' so closely connected with this plea, is the outcome of his quest for knowledge through union of the object with something alike in the observer and for the 'magnetic' forces and 'sympathy' in nature at large as expressions of the fundamental unity of all its objects and phenomena" (Pagel 52).

2. As Holly Crocker notes, "virtue" is clearly a word on the move in the fourteenth and fifteenth centuries.

3. In his "The Translator to the Reader," Ferdinando Parkhurst aptly summarizes Paracelsus's test as "An epitome of the most abstruse part of Philosophy, treating of many hidden Mysteries and operations, in the rare and admirable cure of diseases at distance, by transplantation into other species, through a Mumiall and Magneticall power, drawn chiefly from the Sympathy and Antipathy of natural things" (19).

4. Van Rompay says that Lipps, in his theory of *Einfühlung* (feeling-into), argued that "people show a tendency to imitate perceived movements or dynamic postures of people and objects" (340).

5. Pagel explains how for Paracelsus, it is at the "hem" (or "margin" or "border") of Iliaster, where the matrix folds over on itself, that potentiality gives way to specific, real things. He names this hem the "limbus," the ambiguous space of becoming, where "eternal principles" become concrete.

6. See Deleuze's *Difference and Repetition*, especially chapter 3, "The Moral Image of Thought," for an influential critique of ontologies of the Same. In Spinoza's naturalized monism, God becomes "God or Nature" (*Deus sive Natura*). If Spinoza had read *Leaves*, he might have said that the bodies of the poems (that is, the images they generate in the mind and the vibrations of the spoken sounds), as themselves modes of a Substance common to all that is, produce "affections" in the bodies with which they come in contact. In the case of some poems, these alterations would also qualify as "affects," which Spinoza defined as (enhancing or depleting) modifications in the *power, vitality, or agentic capacity* of a body.

7. Whitman's understanding of touch does not require hands; he seems to shares Alois Riegl and Wilhelm Worringer's aesthetic philosophy, according to which, in Brian Massumi's words, "the word 'haptic' . . . refers to touch as it appears virtually in vision" (57).

8. I use the term "mood" to name that psycho-aesthetic-physiological "atmosphere" (in Kathleen Stewart's sense) within which more explicit or conscious ideals, concepts, and intentions arise, circulate, and evolve. I also think of moods as preliminary tendencies to action and response.

9. "The inner stars of man are, in their properties, kind, and nature, by their course and position, like his outer stars. . . . For as regards their nature, it is the same in the ether and in the microcosm, man. . . . Just as the sun shines through a glass—as though divested of body and substance—so the stars penetrate one another in the body. . . . For the sun and the moon and all planets, as well as all the stars and the whole chaos, are in man" (Pagel 21). The light

of the stars, in that example, repeats in or sympathizes with the twinkle of Paracelsus's own eyes. Here the repetition is visual, but elsewhere Paracelsus describes it in sonorous terms: the knowledge possessed by herbs (enabling them to produce their medicinal effects) resonates in our own bodies once we eavesdrop on the plant's wisdom.

10. "*The Americans of all nations at any time upon the earth, have probably the fullest poetical nature. . . . Here at last is something in the doings of man that corresponds with the broadcast doings of the day and night. . . . Here is the hospitality which forever indicates heroes. . . . Here are the roughs and beards and space and ruggedness and nonchalance that the soul loves*" ("Preface to the 1855 Edition," *Leaves* 616). Here the model is the Sun, which is open to all things even as it expends itself with assured serenity upon all of them: "*Judge not as the judge judges but as the sun falling round a helpless thing*" (620).

11. I approach here the exceedingly complex matter of the dynamic relations between word, image, and physiomimesis. I found Susan Leigh Foster's "Movement Contagion: The Kinesthetic Impact of Performance" to be a very helpful entry point into these debates. In that piece, for example, she surveys various philosophical and neuroscientific explanations of how it is that "as one is looking at the armchair, one is already simulating the motions associated with seating oneself in it" (53).

12. Michael Robertson's *Worshipping Walt: The Whitman Disciples* offers good evidence of this.

13. Listing as a tending toward or leaning into—perhaps to better *listen*. And indeed the *Oxford English Dictionary* offers this (not fully) obsolete definition: "to list" is "to give ear, be attentive."

16 Source of Life
Avatar, Amazonia, *and an Ecology of Selves*

Joni Adamson

> All the trees have spirits, they look, they listen . . .
> —Juan Carlos Galeano, *The Trees Have Mothers*

> If I had an agent, I am sure he would advise me to sue James Cameron over his latest blockbuster since *Avatar* should really be called *Pandora's Hope!*
> —Bruno Latour, "An Attempt at a Compositionist Manifesto"

AT THE END of the eighteenth century, German intellectual and scientist Alexander von Humboldt traveled to the Amazon. Later, back in Europe, the publication of his five-volume *Cosmos* would influence a generation of thinkers on several continents. Today, his work still resonates strongly among scholars who are studying "the material interactions of bodies and natures" (Iovino and Oppermann, "Material" 77). According to Laura Dassow Walls, who describes the impact of his journey on both the sciences and the aesthetics of the Americas in her book *A Passage to Cosmos,* Humboldt considered "nature" as "a planetary interactive causal network operating across multiple scale levels, temporal and spatial" (11). His views were inspired by interactions with the indigenous peoples he met and later, back in Europe, by his friendships with key figures hailing from Latin America such as Simón Bolívar.[1] Humboldt's views on liberty, the immorality of slavery, and the intelligence and agency[2] of indigenous peoples acted powerfully on Bolívar's political vision.

Today, both Humboldt's and Bolívar's influence can be seen in the emergence of what has been described as an international "cosmopolitical" movement shaping the modern nation-states of the Amazonian and Andean regions. It will be the aim of this chapter to explore how this movement illuminates the claims, made in the introduction of this volume by Iovino and Oppermann, that, in some cases, anthropomorphism can work as a "dis-anthropocentric strategy," revealing similarities and symmetries between humans and nonhumans. The chapter

253

will also suggest where there may be limits to these similarities and symmetries and show how concepts related to materialist ecology may synch with indigenous understandings of the cosmos. The movement, led by indigenous and ethnic minority groups, is based largely in South America and also has ties to political, civil society, and environmental groups from around the world that have successfully driven the adoption of new legal instruments at the national and local levels (see de la Cadena; Adamson, "Indigenous"). For example, in 2008, Ecuador revised its constitution to grant rights to "Pachamama" or "Mother Earth," and, in 2010, Bolivia passed a law giving nature the right to maintain and regenerate its life cycles and evolutionary processes (see Constitution of Ecuador; Vidal). The goals of these laws were framed by delegates to the World People's Conference on Climate Change, held in Bolivia in 2010, in the Universal Declaration on the Rights of Mother Earth, which urges all the world's citizens to become more aware of multiple, divergent worlds and to engage in a politics that will support the "recovery, revalidation, and strengthening of indigenous cosmovisions based on ancient and ancestral indigenous knowledge" (see the preamble to the Universal Declaration on the Rights of Mother Earth and Climate Change).

The conditions out of which these laws have emerged have a long history that predates the World People's Conference on Climate Change. One hundred years after Humboldt's journey to the Amazon, in 1899, German anthropologist Franz Boas arrived in the Americas and took up a post at Columbia University. There, he began dispersing Humboldtian views as he trained the scholars who would shape the field of ethnography, including Edward Sapir, Ruth Benedict, and Zora Neale Hurston (Walls 213–14). Framing Humboldt's scientific theories and practices as "cosmography," Boas considered himself a "cosmographer" and declared every phenomenon "worthy of being studied for its own sake" (Walls 212). A "cosmographer," in Boas's view, is someone who values science and who "studies the history of phenomena, what they are and how they came to be just that way," but who also "cherishes the very particulars that science uses then throws away" (Walls 212). Throughout the twentieth century, and into this century, other ethnographers, influenced by Boas, and tradition keepers from diverse ethnic groups continued collecting astronomical, ceremonial, cultural, agroecological, and ethnobotanical knowledges from around the world and treating them as "archives," or sophisticated "cosmographies," worthy of study rather than mere "superstitions" that should be dismissed by "modern" peoples. Today, a new mode of research is building on the work of Humboldt and Boas, as it gathers up the sensibilities of Charles Darwin, Claude Lévi-Strauss, Gregory Bateson, Donna Haraway, and Bruno Latour and puts them into dialogue with the knowledges of diverse indigenous and minority ethnic groups. "Multispecies ethnography," write S. Eben Kirksey and Stefan Helmreich, pulls animals, plants, fungi, and microbes once appearing only on the margins of anthropology as "part of the landscape, as food for humans, as symbols" or as *zoe* or "bare life"—that which is killable—into the realm "of bios" (545).³ This work is suggesting new ways of understanding Humboldt's observation that there is not "one world" but "pluriform and multivocalic" worlds of "humans and natures" (Walls 10).

At stake in this discussion of "bios," "life," or "pluriform worlds," writes anthropologist Eduardo Kohn, whose work has been a model for emerging conceptions of multispecies ethnography, is how to think about the "nonhuman," an analytical category that Bruno Latour (*We Have; Politics of Nature*) proposed as he sought to move the ethnographic study of science-making "practices beyond social constructivist frameworks in which humans are the only actors" (Kohn 5). However, where some of Latour's early work fails to recognize that some nonhumans are not just represented but represent, and that they can do so without having to "speak," Kohn argues for an ethnography that would explode "closed self-referential" anthropological analytics focused only on the (human) language, culture, society, and history that has been used to explain the "human" (Kohn 5). Based on his study of the Runa peoples of the upper Amazonian basin and their interactions with dreaming dogs and psychotropic plants, Kohn argues for a multispecies ethnography that would reground notions of "communication" between humans and nonhumans in a representational system that gets beyond the dualism of human-nonhuman and opens the "space of the hyphen" between nature-culture to reveal a "semiosis" that is "always embodied in some way or another, and it is always entangled, to a greater or lesser degree, with material processes" (5).⁴

Other scientists, anthropologists, and humanists, working together, are beginning to write "multispecies ethnographies" that show why dreaming animals—human or nonhuman—or trees, roots, and fungi, might all be considered "selves" that "have legibly biographical and political lives" (Kirksey and Helmreich 545).⁵ Trees, for example, collect sunlight in their canopies, turn it into energy, and send it to mutually beneficial arrangements of fungus on the forest floor that employ a chemical vocabulary of nutrients to feed sprouting tree seedlings and nourish the root systems of other entangled root systems.⁶ These fungal formations depend on "a highly regulated mechanism of self recognition" that indicates that even some of the simplest organic forms are semiotic (Giovannetti et al. 1). These processes illustrate why both multispecies ethnographers and ecocritics are considering matter, in all its forms, "a *site of narrativity,* a storied matter, embodying its own narratives in the minds of human agents and in the very structure of its own self-constructive forces" (Iovino and Oppermann, "Material" 83; emphasis in the original). These processes also offer insight into collections of indigenous oral traditions and poetry and contemporary films emerging from the same Amazonian regions where Humboldt once traveled and Kohn conducts his fieldwork today.

For example, in his collection of poetry *Amazonia,* Juan Carlos Galeano, a Colombian American poet and university professor, illustrates the Amazonian belief that when a tree is felled to make a table, its own "spirit" perceives the event. In a poem title, "Mesa/Table," a tree continues to have a perspective after "she" becomes a table. She continues to "dream" of once having been "an animal" (81).[7] Galeano left Colombia at the age of eighteen and moved to the United States, but returns most summers to the Amazon basin to spend time in communities along the riverbanks, where he supervises American college students living and working with indigenous and mestizo people in a Florida State University service-learning program. There, he still hears the cosmological tales about "spirits of the forest" that he was told as a boy (*Folktales* xvi–xviii). In the foreword to Galeano's collection of these stories, *Folktales of the Amazon,* well-known anthropologist Michael Uzendoski describes Galeano's work as "neo-Boasian" and praises its presentation of nuanced understandings of Amazonian concepts of pluriform worlds and the "boundaries" between them as sites of differentiation that "do not, by themselves, exclude or contain" (xi). In these tales, transformational forest spirits, collectively referred to as "Pachamama, " "Mothers," or "owners of the forest" (terms understood in South America *not* as a female-gendered planet or place, but as "Source of Life" or "Source of Light"), may sometimes appear as trees and, at other times, as dolphins (de la Cadena 335, 350). On other occasions, "Sachamama," as s/he is also known, may transform into the shape of a giant boa constrictor upon which "all the forest life grows" (Galeano, *Folktales* xxiii, 11–12).

In *Amazonia* these philosophies take shape in Galeano's poems. In "Mesa/Table," Galeano writes that what a table "likes best" is for the woman who lives in the house with her "to tickle her / as she gathers the breadcrumbs left behind by the children" (81). Each night, the table thinks back to the time she was a tree. Now, standing in the woman's kitchen, the table muses that she might "have run away like the / Others when the chainsaws came to take the trees that would / Become tables" (81). Galeano's words imply that before this tree was felled in the forest, she lived with other trees that successfully escaped the logger's ax. In table form, she has "four legs" that she thinks of as "haunches," especially when the woman is wiping up the crumbs "left by the children" with "a warm rag" (81). The poem suggests that the table has not only a kind of agency, but an ethical relationship with humans and other sentient beings because she chooses not to leave the woman or the chairs. After all, "an animal / would not abandon her family" (81).

To illustrate more clearly how the oral tales found in Galeano's poetry are rooted in Amazonian concepts of boundary differentiation that help us rethink anthropomorphism as a "dis-anthropocentric strategy," I turn now to two films that depict naive young men entering a rain forest. One is filmed literally in the Amazon and the other on a Hollywood sound stage. The first, coproduced and codirected by Juan Carlos Galeano, is titled *The Trees Have a Mother: Amazonian*

Cosmologies, Folktales, and Mystery (2008) and explores the mysterious disappearance of a twenty-year-old indigenous Peruvian boy, James Núñez Cataschunga.[8] James joins his grandfather and cousins to go into the forest and is last seen at a forked trailhead, leaving his mother at home, grieving his loss.

The second film, James Cameron's science fiction blockbuster *Avatar* (2009), is set in the year AD 2154. It focuses on Grace Augustine, a "xenobotanist," who is studying an Amazon-like forested moon located far from Earth named Pandora and the Na'vi, ten-foot-tall blue-skinned humanoids, who live there. Grace hires a young paraplegic ex-Marine, Jake Sully, to assist her in her ethnographic and botanical fieldwork, and for a time, Jake, like James, gets lost in the forest and lives with the Na'vi in "Hometree," a massive tree two to three times the size of an Earth redwood. Closely analyzed, Grace's research (published on Earth as a best-selling book titled *Na'vi*) is doing something very much like what Eben and Kirksey describe as "multispecies ethnography" and Iovino and Oppermann discuss as ecocritical analysis of "storied matter." Cameron represents Grace's ethnography as a text detailing the interactions between the Na'vi and other species in what real-world botanists have imaginatively described as forests that "communicate" through a "wood wide web" (Wilhelm and Mathison xv).[9] Grace understands the forest is "representing" itself in ways that are invisible to human colonizers who see Hometree as a "thing" or "dead matter." In her logbooks, Grace describes a "networked energy" in the Pandoran flora that spreads "like the neural pathways in the human brain, with every tree" and every plant acting as one "vast sentience, covering the land" (Wilhelm and Mathison xv). Cameron depicts these neural pathways in the film as bioluminescence that lights up the forest. This cinematic effect connects the film to Amazonian concepts of "Sachamama," or "Source of Life, Source of Light." To conduct their fieldwork in Pandora's toxic atmosphere, Grace and Jake must link their minds to human-engineered Na'vi avatar bodies through an electronically stimulated state of dreaming. Cameron depicts this process of neural linkage between human body and avatar body as paralleling the process that connects the Na'vi to the energy coursing through "Eywa," the name of their "forest mother."

Kohn's notion of an "ecology of selves" offers deeper, richer understandings of what Humboldt may have meant by the phrases "pluriform and multivocalic worlds" of "humans and natures" (Walls 10) and examines why it is appropriate to consider nonhuman organisms as "selves" and biotic life as "cognizant" of "sign processes," albeit ones that are often "highly embodied and nonsymbolic" (Kohn 6). With Galeano's and Cameron's films as illustration, I now go on to explore how notions of cosmological "multivocalic worlds" can provide more satisfying understandings of indigenous views on human relationship to the nonhuman and material world than "clichéd" notions of "universal connectedness" that have been rightly problematized, but perhaps too easily dismissed by some ecocritics.

I will argue that Galeano's film provides evidence that Amazonian peoples have never accepted the idea that their oral traditions speak only of a "mythic" past and therefore provide no explanatory or theoretical power in the present. This discussion will allow me to explore why Amazonian peoples recognize trees as "selves" with "mothers" that represent lively biosemiotic processes at work in the "space of the hyphen" that "exceeds human speech" (Kohn 5). Drawing parallels between the dreaming process in which the hallucinogenic plant named "Ayahuasca" (*Banisteriopis caapi*) is employed to locate James and the "dream state" in which Grace and Jake travel from the human world to the Na'vi world, I will also examine why a constant tension exists "between ontological blurring and maintaining difference" when Amazonian peoples "cross boundaries" and why they insist upon the necessity of maintaining "this tension without being pulled to either extreme" (Kohn 12).

Rethinking Indigenous "Mythologies" as Seeing Instruments

As I explain in *American Indian Literature, Environmental Justice, and Ecocriticism*, whether told orally or "transformed" into novels and poetry, indigenous "cosmological" narratives about animals and plants with quasi-human qualities continue to offer explanatory power to contemporary indigenous and ethnic minority groups throughout the contemporary world. Among the people who know these stories best, the power of oral traditions is not assigned to "the mythical past," but can be seen as a kind of "theory" generated within communities over the course of hundreds of years. For example, when included in contemporary Native North American poetry and fiction, oral traditions are employed to address contemporary social and environmental injustices by suggesting that (cultural, legal, economic, and ecological) "boundaries are permeable" (Adamson, *American* 106). Contemporary indigenous writers employ these stories to call upon their readers to think about how they, like their characters, might alter "the power relations at the root of social and ecological" imbalances caused by the forces of globalization (112).

We see an example of this in *The Trees Have a Mother* as Galeano follows Ana, James's mother, as she desperately attempts to locate her son over the course of eight months. Looking into the camera, holding the boy's plastic identification card, and caressing his washed and folded pants and hooded jacket, the only remaining material evidence of his existence, Ana summarizes various explanations for her son's disappearance with reference to stories often told in the region about trees or dolphins who transform themselves into beautiful men or women in order to lead humans away to an "enchanted city" at the bottom of the Amazon River where there is no poverty and the people do not "kill themselves with work" (Galeano, *Folktales* 91). Ana describes James as a very hard worker and her only helper in an Iquitos food stand where she sells grilled fish to support her family.

Devastated by his absence, she speculates that, perhaps, like the boy in the oral tradition, James is still alive, living in luxury, and will be back soon (*Trees*). When he cannot be found, she consults a shaman who tries to locate him by first smoking and then "listening" to psychotropic plants.

Literature and film depicting shamans, "earth mothers," and indigenous peoples telling idyllic stories about transformational trees and dolphins have led some ecocritics, including Ursula Heise and Greg Garrard, to problematize the field's early "investment in local subjects" and the ways this interest has taken the form of a "pronounced interest in Native American ways of life" (Heise, "Ecocriticism" 381, 382; see also Garrard 120–21).[10] Heise (rightly) urges literary critics to move away from romanticization of supposedly ecologically responsible premodern cultures. Galeano's documentary supports Heise's point by filming an Amazonian *mercado*, or market, where it is easy to buy penises or vaginas, cut from endangered pink dolphins accidentally caught in fishing nets. Many local people believe, as Galeano writes in his poem "Pink Dolphins," that dolphins can transform themselves into humans, "grow pubic hair" at night, and "go out stealing women" (*Amazonia* 55). It is said that this sexual prowess can be transferred to humans through dried dolphin organs sold for profit as love amulets. Heise's larger point, illustrated by the market for dolphin organs, is that association with an indigenous community does not necessarily confer ethically responsible environmental behaviors or mystical knowledge of nature on humans.

However, as I explain in *American Indian Literature*, poverty—exacerbated by a history of colonization, racial and structural inequalities, and lack of opportunity in modern economies—often draws people into economically profitable but exploitative activities that may be harmful to local environments (47–50). Heise argues for an advocacy "on behalf of the nonhuman world" that would not be based on romanticized notions of premodern peoples. She urges ecocritics to move beyond "Native American ways of life, mythologies, oratures, and literatures" ("Ecocriticism" 382) toward a more sophisticated global "eco-cosmopolitanism," defined as an ecologically inflected notion of "world citizenship" that would emphasize "cross-cultural literacy" (*Sense* 10, 159). Whereas Heise expresses confidence that "eco-cosmopolitanism" will result from expanded environmental literacy that extends protections to the nonhuman, Jane Bennett, one of the leading scholars associated with the "material turn," argues that advocacy for the nonhuman cannot be accomplished through (even cross-cultural) "human language and thought," since a "vital materialism" is "intrinsically resistant to representation" (*Vibrant* xvi). Like Kohn, who observes that the processes taking place in the "space of the hyphen" exceed the symbolic, and, therefore, must exceed the "close self-referential" loops of most humanistic fields predicated on human speech (5), Bennett observes that the struggle to represent "lively matter" chastens "fantasies of human mastery" (122).

Both Heise and Bennett acknowledge that it is still unclear how either eco-cosmopolitanism or vital materialism will work in practical political terms. Bennett writes that "more needs to be said to specify the normative implications of a vital materialism in specific contexts" (122). Heise speculates that ecologically inflected cosmopolitanism, rooted in an "alternative global culture that might arise from the politics of shared risk," would likely need to "be complemented by the more acute sense of sociocultural differences that emerge in stark relief from the fieldwork of environmental justice activists" (*Sense* 159). The challenges to building "cosmopolitan forms of solidarity" would center on the fact that the "environmental justice movement has focused primarily on the urgencies of political action, mobilization, and coalition-building"; it has drawn from feminist, postcolonial, and critical race theory without "showing how the context of communities" exposed to endangerment might transform some of these "bodies of theory" (158). This, in Heise's view, has left the movement without a "sophisticated theoretical framework" for approaching "unequal political and economic playing fields created by various types of globalization" and overly reliant on "environmentalist clichés regarding universal connectedness" (159).

However, as I argue in *American Indian Literature,* contemporary indigenous storytellers, writers, and community leaders do not generally have as their priority transforming bodies of academic theory. As I explain in more recent work,[11] their cosmopolitical activities (which have been hundreds of years in the making) and the legislative reforms we are seeing in Ecuador and Bolivia, together with the creation of documents such as the Universal Declaration on the Rights of Mother Earth, illustrate that indigenous and ethnic minority groups are not approaching unequal political and economic playing fields created by various types of globalization without theoretical tools. In the Universal Declaration, delegates proclaim that "violations against our soils, air, forests, rivers, lakes, biodiversity, and the cosmos are assaults against us." "Us" is emphasized to mean all living "beings," including humans, "forests mothers," and "sentient entities" such as significant mountains. With stories from the oral tradition about these sentient entities as guide and "theoretical" foundation, they propose—as solution to climate change—a shift in the world's attention from "living better" to "living well," by which they mean "supporting a society based on social and environmental justice, which sees life as its purpose" (Universal Declaration, article 2).

As anthropologist Michael Uzendoski observes in the foreword to Galeano's folktale collection, stories about forest mothers and transformational dolphins are not about clichéd notions of "universal connectedness." To understand how they address real problems in the world such as the increasing vulnerabilities faced by those most impacted by a changing climate, listeners must understand that storytellers are "less concerned with cultural boundaries than they are with natural ones" (Uzendoski xi). The stories abide by a complex philosophy that has been termed "perspectival multinaturalism" by renowned Brazilian anthropologist Eduardo Vivieros de Castro. This notion suggests that "the world is inhabited by different sorts of subjects or persons, human and non-human, that apprehend reality from distinct points of view" ("Cosmological" 469). Humans, animals, and spirits participate in the same world, although with different sensory apparatuses constituting not just multicultural (human) worlds, implying a unity of nature and a multiplicity of cultures, but multinatural worlds, implying corporeal diversity and its attendant diversity of perspectives ("Exchanging" 467). In the Americas, story cycles embodying these philosophies, whether oral or written, are seen as "living books" or "seeing instruments" that offer "a complex navigational system" for understanding human relation to the stars, animals, soils, and planting cycles, as well as information about how to "see" spans of time and history unavailable to a human in a single lifetime (Adamson, *American* 141). As multispecies ethnographer Julie Cruikshank explains, from the glacial North to the tropical South, indigenous story archives also often frame significant glaciers or rain forests as "intensely social spaces where human behavior, especially casual hubris or arrogance, can trigger dramatic and unpleasant consequences in the physical world" (11).

Galeano's *Folktales* clearly shows that the forest and its protector spirits such as "Sachamama" inhabit a decidedly social space where humans learn to make distinctions between "living better" and "living well." They "listen" and are aware of human hubris or arrogance, sometimes transforming themselves into a desirable shape and leading the misbehavers or those who overhunt or overfish away, never to be seen again. However, the stories are told in many versions. In one story, a boy leaves his family and goes deep into the forest. He is lured to the home of the dolphins, stays too long, living in luxury, and decides to stay. In another story, a young man knows his parents will be worried, so he sends them a letter inside a small bag with a few nuggets of gold to ease their poverty. When they open the bag, the gold falls out (91–92). In Galeano's documentary, this story provides local people with a "seeing instrument" for thinking about the material disappearance of James, a boy who did not intend to leave his family, as it also catalyzes the narration of multiple versions of the story. Importantly, Galeano explains, the story about a boy, lost in the forest, sending his parents gold was the story that first lured sixteenth-century conquistadors in search of "El Dorado" farther into the forest, with horrible consequences for forest dwellers (92). Today, this story is still retold to explain the conflict and greed that can be found in a modern world "thirsty for oil, timber, gold, cocaine, and other Amazonian products" (xx). But it can also be used to explain how inexperienced people sometimes get lost in the forest.

Like Ana, many of the local people interviewed in the film theorize James's unfortunate disappearance through familiar stories that provide explanatory power for approaching the complex forces of globalization. Stories of supernatural beings luring naive young people into the rain forest reinforce an awareness that the world is predatory, permeated by insidious, unseen risk. As townspeople read James's disappearance through the story of the boy and the gold, they remark on the loggers, miners, oil companies, agribusiness enterprises, and cocaine producers that do not "ask permission from the mothers of the trees" before they destroy "the whole forest." When the people use the story to link the conquistadors with modern-day corporate logging and wildcat gold mining, they illustrate, to use ethnographer Julie Cruikshank's words, how cosmological stories provide a "set of principles for thinking about current events" (57). The people in Galeano's film are not only distressed by James's disappearance; they are angry that the big fish they depended on for food "are gone, water is poisonous, and the children are dying from contamination." As most residents of the Amazonian basin know, the main threat to freshwater fish and dolphins is the contamination of rivers by mercury used in illegal gold-mining operations. Although they are theorizing through age-old stories rather than academic theory, the people in the film are discussing the same processes killing their children and the fish as environmentalists and academics around the world concerned with these issues. Clearly knowledgeable about the connections between deforestation, illegal mining, erosion, and climate change, they simply use different terminologies. They worry that Yakumama, the ancient Anaconda "that creates rivers to keep the fish happy" (a being representing the complexity of riverine ecosystems), will succumb to the rising temperatures and the mighty Amazon itself will be turned into "a ditch." Formulations of sentient beings, like the Amazon/Anaconda in the Amazon or glaciers in the Arctic, that "listen," Cruikshank writes, are consistently employed throughout the Americas "as timeless narratives in a timely way," not as "myth" or "cultural artifact extraneous to history" (57).

When it becomes clear that James will not be coming back, his mother consults various shamans who employ Ayahausca, a psychotropic plant, as an "instrument" that allows the shaman to gaze beyond the span of a single human life and "see" across reaches of time necessary to the survival of functioning ecosystems and to multinatural worlds that, for indigenous peoples, have never ceased to exist. This helps to explain, as anthropologist Marisol de la Cadena writes in an ethnographic study of South American cosmopolitical movements, why Amazonian movements organized around storied "earth beings" with "individual physiognomies more or less known by individuals involved in interactions with them" are enlisted in politics. These "beings" might be forests, mountains, rivers, or lakes. When their material existence and that of the worlds to which they belong is threatened by the siting of a mine, clear-cutting, pollution, erosion, large-scale monocultural agriculture, overfishing, or overhunting, they are marshaled, along with the humans who may live in or beside them, into the movement (de la Cadena

341–42). These "beings" may be categorized as "natural resources" within Western politics or science, but in Ecuador, Bolivia, and Peru, for example, indigenous activists and politicians are confronting the monopoly of discourses that provincialize "the universe" as a world inhabited by humans who are distanced from "Nature" (345). They resist the exploitation of their resources or the construction of dams or mines as they continue to organize around the notion, as it is articulated in the Universal Declaration, that multiple species and "things" that have heretofore not been considered deserving of the same rights and protections as humans should be granted the "right to regenerate . . . biocapacity and continue . . . vital cycles" (n.p.).

Pandora as Circulating Reference

In a chapter he titles "Circulating Reference," included in *Pandora's Hope: Essays on the Reality of Science Studies,* Bruno Latour spends fifteen days in Brazil studying the rain forest with botanist Edileusa Setta-Silva, two soil scientists, and a geomorphologist. While Setta-Silva and her team read their instruments, generate charts, and name their materials "data," Latour composes an ethnography about how scientists construct the world through an *active* interplay between human "knowers" and matter. Like "cosmographer" Franz Boas before him, he is fascinated with the history of phenomena and the difference between "the sciences" understood as the proliferation of methods by which humans build collective understandings of multinatural worlds and "Science" as a way to create "Nature," that mononatural entity in which secondary qualities are eliminated because of the postulation of primary ones. Latour's ethnography has some wonderfully evocative parallels to James Cameron's *Avatar.* Both circulate around a female botanist and reference Pandora, a Greek oral tradition in which several malicious beings escape from a box, while one, the goddess Astraea, who is associated with hope and justice, remains trapped (Latour, *Pandora's* 23).[12] In a long poem titled *Works and Days,* Greek oral poet Hesiod set the story of Pandora into verse sometime around 700 BC, a time of great agricultural crisis in his region. The weather was bad and the soils were poor, and he was concerned about scarcity and greed and seems to be asking questions about the differences between living "better" and living "well." Greek colonizers were being sent out to search for new lands with better conditions. For Latour, Pandora becomes a "seeing instrument" that allows him to entertain the questions suggested by Hesiod: "Is it possible to build a livable political order?" "Is it possible to protect nature from greed?" (*Pandora's* 200).

Like Latour, Cameron may have attached the circulating reference "Pandora" to his film in order to associate it with Hesiod's critique of human greed.[13] In *Avatar* an Earth corporation, the Resources Development Administration, or RDA, is determined to remove the Na'vi from their homes so they can mine "unobtainium," a rare mineral considered the solution to Earth's energy crisis. Before the attack, Grace tries to convince the head of the RDA that the real wealth of Pandora is not unobtainium but the "complex root system" of Pandora. Her words fall on deaf ears, and the chief executive officer authorizes the launch of missiles from helicopter gunships that explode the great "mother tree" with no thought to the life that will be lost. Cameron characterizes Grace as something of an Astraea, someone concerned with hope and justice. Having crossed the "species" boundary intellectually, in her research, and physically, through her avatar, Grace is acutely aware that the RDA's disruption of ecosytemic relationships threatens not only Hometree but every "being" on Pandora, including those that live imperceptibly to human eyes in the soil and roots of the forest floor. Hometree allows Grace to "see," in the words of the Universal Declaration, that each "sentient being" (read: ecosystem, forest, river, and so on) is a cosmos in itself, a "pluriform and multivocal world" with which humans "have an indivisible and interdependent relationship" (article 2).

Cameron's representation of how two groups (Grace/Na'vi and the RDA, with their very distinct perspectives on "life") come into conflict illustrates, as Latour contends, that if there is ever going to be a world in which all beings, indigenous and nonindigenous, human and nonhuman, live peacefully, it will require not just increased (human) literacy or "cosmopolitanism" but a "cosmo*politics*" capable of mediating dramatically differing (intra- and interspecies) perspectives. This will be a movement that we "will have to build, tooth and nail, together" (Latour, "Whose Cosmos" 453, 455). Rather than embracing a cosmopolitan or "common world" that requires the "modern West" to scold the rest of the world and convince them that *"we all live under the same biological and physical laws and have the same fundamental biological, social, and psychological makeup,"* cosmopolitical actors refuse to become *"prisoners of [their own] superficial worldviews"* (458; emphasis in the original). Delegates to the World Conference on the Rights of Mother Earth, for example, working from multinatural perspectives, refuse to give legitimacy to the supposedly reified poles of "past" and "present" or "ancient" and "modern" and enlist storied "selves" as allies as they organize to build a more livable political world where humans acknowledge the right of "sentient beings"—forests, rivers, mountains—to maintain and continue evolutionary cycles.

I See You/An Ecology of Selves

In Galeano's documentary, a forest dweller who has participated in the exhaustive eight-month search for James observes that there are harsh consequences for those who do not understand the concept that Kohn terms an "ecology of selves." "This is not a story," says the man. "This is a reality that is lived here in the Amazon." Humans who are seduced by forest lovers and disappear never to be seen again prove that there is risk involved in not understanding the processes constantly occurring in the "space of the hyphen." This is also illustrated by the shamans in Galeano's film who "listen" to psychotropic plants in the search for James. By consuming "potions from trees and plants and by following special diets," writes Galeano, "shamans gain access to the worlds where the 'mothers' of trees and animals live" (*Folktales* xx). They are not seeking to erase the boundaries between humans and the forest, but seeking to ensure that humans do not to lose the ability to "see" the material differences between themselves and other selves inhabiting a multinatural cosmos.

Dreaming with plants, Kohn writes, is often practiced by those who wish to "know" the animals they will hunt for food. Dreams are not representations or symbols. They are events that are understood to allow a knower a kind of "privileged mode of communication" that makes dreaming an "an important site" for negotiation between species (Kohn 12). The shaman's dream "aligns different ontologically situated points of view" and "establishes a difference in perspective between beings inhabiting different ontological domains" (12). For example, "The Runa see subjectivity—human and otherwise—as constituted via contact with other sentient beings. The soul, they hold, is what makes such transspecies intersubjectivity possible" (8). Moreover, "transspecies interactions depend on the capacity to recognize subjectivity," and losing this ability can be disastrous for beings, both humans and nonhumans, who live "enmeshed in webs of predation" (9). In other words, a Runa person who does not understand a jaguar person might become the prey of the jaguar. Understanding that jaguar persons prefer to kill by making a bite to the back of the head suggests to the Runa that it is best to sleep faceup and to never turn one's back to the jaguar. An understanding of jaguar persons, which can be increased in dreams in which a human person crosses boundaries to take the shape of and learn the ways of the jaguar person, potentially reduces risk in the forest.

In a scene in which Jake Sully, after becoming lost in the Pandoran forest, encounters animals called "viperwolves," Cameron imaginatively illustrates that the ex-Marine does not clearly understand his subject position among the multiple species in the forest. Positioning himself as master but having no knowledge of the "ways of viperwolves," Jake is attacked. He is saved by Neytiri, the daughter of the Na'vi female shaman, Mo'at. Neytiri, who has participated in many "unitaron" ceremonies in which she has "dreamed" of animals in order to know them, is forced to kill several of the attacking animals to save Jake's life (Wilhelm and Mathison 188). She upbraids Jake for unnecessary deaths and for not fully understanding that killing is not just a sport and animals are not just food. She emphatically teaches him the phrase "Oel ngati kameie," or "I see you," which implies not just a gaze but also a clear recognition of "a continuum that spans the range of ways of inhabiting an ecology of selves" (Kohn 12). By not understanding this continuum, Jake has endangered himself and others.

This scene suggests some of the reasons indigenous groups who might see predatory animals as material "selves" having souls that put them into relation with other species also acknowledge the risk to life presented by bodies with very different perspectives. A "perspective" is located in the body, writes Vivieros de Castro. It is not "a representation because representations are a property of the mind or spirit. . . . The ability to adopt a point of view is undoubtedly a power of the soul, and nonhumans are subjects in so far as they have (or are) spirit; but the differences between viewpoints . . . [lies] in the specificity of bodies" ("Exchanging" 474). Kohn builds on Vivieros de Castro's description of "perspectival multinaturalism" to propose the notion of an "ecology of selves" that allows for a "representational system that regrounds semiosis in a way" that gets "beyond dualisms" without resorting to a sociobiological reduction that assumes that "the only thing we share in common with nonhumans is our bodies" (5). Attempts "to theorize links between the material and the semiotic via hyphens (although currently necessary)," Kohn writes, can be misleading because they might encourage us to "assume a relationship among equivalent poles that obscures the hierarchical and nested dynamic by which semiosis emerges from, and continues to be entangled with, material and energetic processes. This dynamic is life itself" (6).

To get beyond dualisms, Kohn suggests a broader semiotic approach that does not take human language as a starting point, but, rather, takes a more precise account of "how our ways of representing are susceptible to the qualities, events, and forms that are in the world, how other selves represent the world, and how we interact with these other selves" (18). We must be highly attentive to the "danger-fraught, provisional, and highly tenuous attempts at communication—in short, the politics—involved in the interactions among different kinds of selves that inhabit very different, and often unequal positions" (18).

After his travels in the Amazon, Alexander Humboldt was highly aware of the politics involved in the interactions among different kinds of selves. He sought to "create a zone of exchange rather than domination" that would allow diverse human groups and natures "to speak through a range of representations" (Walls 10). Today, multispecies ethnographers are suggesting researchers can and should make ontological claims, but rather "than turning to ontology as a way of sidestepping the problems with representation," it may be "more fruitful to critique [human] assumptions about representation (and, hence, epistemology)" (Kohn 17). Bruno Latour puts the case more strongly. We will never get beyond the bifurcation of nature from culture until we tackle the tricky questions of anthropomorphism, or "animism, anew" ("An Attempt" 481). Like Iovino, Oppermann, and Bennett, Latour proposes anthropomorphism as a "dis-anthropocentric strategy."

If there is one thing to wonder about in the history of Modernism, he writes, "it is not that there are still people 'mad enough to believe in animism,' but that so many hardheaded thinkers have invented what should be call *inanimism*" ("An Attempt" 482). Inanimism "is the queer invention: an agency without agency" denied by quantum physics, biosemiotics, and, now, multispecies ethnography (483).

Traditional cosmological cycles of stories, as seeing instruments, go beyond the symbolic to raise questions about representation and suggest anthropomorphism as a dis-anthropocentric strategy. In the midst of a seemingly "modern" world, these stories are at the center of a cosmopolitics that is working "tooth and nail," with and against, depending on the situation, very powerful global players, to build community based on the continued ability of all "selves" to live not better, but well.

Notes

1. Simón Bolívar, born in Venezuela, was not from the Amazonian region, thus my use of "Latin America" in this sentence. My thanks to Juan Carlos Galeano for his comments and corrections of this chapter, which is much better for his attention.

2. The word "agency" is being used here in a somewhat different context than its use in discussions of material ecocriticism. Humboldt was, of course, aware of debates surrounding whether indigenous American peoples were human, a point intensely contested both before and after Pope Paul III's papal bull *Sublimus Dei* (June 2, 1537), which declared that "Indians" had a soul. Walls argues that Humboldt's analysis of indigenous "political agency" was far more complex than scholars have acknowledged, and she traces his references to Indian and slave revolts as comments on the potential for indigenous-led revolution in the Americas and links this to his possible influence on Bolívar's thinking (see Walls 17, 97–98). Here the use of "agency" is confined to human agency, whereas in material ecocriticism, as discussed in this book, nonhuman natures (sentient beings, animals, and matter in its inorganic forms) are considered to be agentic in the sense that all have powerful effects and in a way interact with their environment in differing degrees. My thanks to Serpil Oppermann for help with clarification here.

3. On "bare life," see Agamben, *Homo*.

4. Kohn relies here on Haraway's notion of "fleshy material-semiotic presences" (*Companion* 5) and Latour's "nature-cultures" (*We Have* 106).

5. For example, see Deborah Bird Rose, *Wild Dog*; and Anna Tsing, for the Matusutake Worlds Research Group.

6. According to Giovannetti et al., a fungus (arboreal mychorrizal) colonizes the soil, connecting contiguous plants as they move nutrients through spreading pathways that exhibit an ability to "discriminate self from non-self" (2). See also Calvo Garzón and Keijzer.

7. It is worth noting that the word *mesa*, or "table," is feminine. The same for the word *madera* (wood), which is semantically related to *materia* (matter), and hence to *madre* (mother). My thanks to Serenella Iovino for calling this to my attention.

8. Galeano's documentary is available, free of charge, at Films on Demand, http://digital.films.com/play/WNHAND.

9. For more on Grace's book, see Wilhelm and Mathison xi–xvii. Botanist Jodie Holt was a consultant for James Cameron's *Avatar: An Activist Survival Guide*, a popular press book

written by Maria Wilhelm and Dirk Matheson and marketed as if it were excerpts from Grace's "multispecies ethnography." Holt suggested that communication among plants could be credibly explained through "signal transduction." See Kozlowski n.p. For more on the representation of signal transduction in *Avatar,* see Adamson, "Indigenous" 156.

10. Both Heise and Garrard cite Shepherd Krech III's *The Ecological Indian* in support of arguments for the need for ecocritical caution when analyzing indigenous literatures and oral traditions. For more on these uses of Krech, see Adamson, "Cosmovisions."

11. For a genealogy of indigenous hemispheric political organization in the Americas that confronts the inequities of globalization while capitalizing on the opportunities offered by globalization, see Adamson, "¡*Todos.*"

12. Hope does not escape Pandora's jar. My thanks to Apostolos Athanassakis, professor emeritus in Hellenic studies, University of California, Santa Barbara, for clarifying that Astraea, a Roman goddess removed from the time of Hesiod by many centuries, is associated with justice in other versions of the Pandora story (personal communication, April 19, 2013).

13. According to Athanassakis, Cameron may also have referenced Pandora because female divinities were "attached to trees" in Greek mythology and were "hardly distinguishable from them" (personal communication, April 19, 2013).

17 The Liminal Space between Things
Epiphany and the Physical

Timothy Morton

THE TITLE OF this essay comes from Marcia Carter, my administrator in my new position at Rice University. She was recommending that I go to see the opening of the James Turrell piece, called *Twilight Epiphany*, installed at Rice and opened on June 14, 2012. Marcia said that what was valuable about Turrell was his understanding of how "art happens in the liminal space between things." As we proceed, we shall see that it is a deeply appropriate way to think about poems as relationships between beings—and indeed *relationship as such*, which here is understood to encompass causality, as a kind of poetry.

This relationship has a necessary physical dimension—many dimensions, in fact—and so we can begin to use Marcia's remark, delivered to me offhandedly as if to say such things were quite humdrum, as a tool to think material ecocriticism. This is more than simply a good analogy, since ecocriticism is just the thinking of relations between things as and in figurative language. Furthermore, it will then be possible to think how nonhumans are "storied" in the way this volume at large addresses—and, still further, how this storying is not just a candy coating on things, but is the way causality is fueled and lubricated, as we shall see.

An artist in the lineage of Dan Flavin, James Turrell has worked in light media for several decades. Turrell's *Twilight Epiphany* is a large wafer-thin square of metal with a square hole in it. This metal wafer rests on thin struts on top of a pyramid covered in grass, reminiscent of Aztec and ancient British and Egyptian burial sites. The English author of this chapter was reminded forcefully of West Kennet Long Barrow and Silbury Hill near Avebury, an ancient pilgrimage site. Silbury Hill is also a grass-covered pyramid, and the Long Barrow has entrance passages like *Twilight Epiphany*: a feeling of housing the dead, old human stories mixed with the stories of bones and stone. A barrow or pyramid or mausoleum is a place where grief, the imprint of another entity in one's inner space, is housed. This is the type of place whose very form announces that it speaks the past, a story—its form is in a sense the past, a fact that in this chapter we shall see begins to be applicable to all beings whatsoever, from carved wooden book ends to pockmarked faces and geological strata.

Figure 17.1. *Twilight Epiphany,* photograph by Timothy Morton, 2012. Courtesy of James Turrell.

Viewers enter the barrow-like pyramid and sit in the cubic central space, open to the sky. Or they ascend stairs to sit on gently sloping, perfectly smooth white concrete. They look up at the sky, through the square perforation in the center of the metal square. About 120 people can sit this way. They look up at the square, with its sliver of sky at its center. The square of sky is part of the square. Or the square is part of the sky. There is a deliberate confusion of hierarchies of foreground and background here: a square of sky color on a large pale background, or a square of pale on a gigantic sky background. The work seems to be talking to Mark Rothko's chapel about a mile away in the Museum District of Houston, a space that also contains huge squares, including a square skylight obscured yet revealed by another square of material.

Pairs of beings in conversation: metal square and sky, grassy pyramid and minimalist metal, humans and metal square, Turrell and Rothko, minimalism and ancient indigenous grief ritual. In so doing, this art joins lineages of ecological installation to be found in such artists as Nancy Holt and Andy Goldsworthy. Art happens, as has been said, in the liminal space(s) between things, in conversations between metal and sky, humans and metal, era and era, heaven and Earth. Between human spines and smooth concrete.

An algorithm enters the conversation at sunset. A computer is programmed to project a sequence of light upon the underside of the metal square. Slowly, the colors change, as if the algorithm were tuning and detuning an instrument—the metal sheet—against the ground bass of the sky, which is also tuning. There is a conversation between sky and Sun, which is also a conversation between Sun and Earth. Many beings, human and nonhuman, have entered the space to converse: Sun, Earth, sky, humans, algorithm, silicon wafers, CPU, concrete seats, grass. A gathering—a thinking together of relations between things, as Heidegger remarks about the Greek *logos*, as in *I gather*, as in *I know* (*Introduction to Metaphysics* 131–37). Before it is the making of correct propositions, logic is the gathering of coexistent beings, before logic as the saying of truth, ecology as the coexisting of things, as an irreducible condition of the possibility of logic as such.

Some of the computer-generated colors are in phase with the sky—sometimes they are exactly the color of the darkening sky. At other times, the colors of the light on the metal square produce powerful dissonances: reddish purples or searing aquamarines. It is like tuning a violin up and down, or a sitar. Indian music in particular is just a kind of tuning to a drone, a fairly constant entity, that is, a being that has a longer time scale than the sitar notes or the warbling voice. Attunement is about *timbre*—the material of which a thing is made, the way that material vibrates and pulses. A flute is metallic, an oboe is ebony, a sitar is high-pitched wire and twanging phases. Metal squares have a certain timbre—imagine *Twilight Epiphany* on a wooden square, or a tessellated mosaic of ceramic tiles. *Timbre*, timber, *hyle* (Greek, "wood," "matter").

Likewise, a poem has a physical architecture, a surface or volume on which or in which it is composed. This architecture is not irrelevant: as Derrida pointed out, *il n'y a pas d'hors-texte,* one of whose meanings is that a text must exist in some kind of (physical) medium, a carrier wave for meaning, as it were. This medium could be electromagnetic waves (radio, television, light); it could be paper or metal or stone; it could be (human) breath. All kinds of nonhumans are already involved in the existence of a poem. So poems, whether they like it or not, always speak, whether consciously or deliberately or not, about their physical architecture. A poem is a material entity.

Tuning (German, *Stimmung*) is a precondition of the aesthetic experience in Kant's philosophy. An attunement takes place—why? Because there are 1+n things in the vicinity: a metal sheet, a hole, some sky, some people. The artwork acts as a gathering point, a kind of lens that focuses the attunements between beings. The artwork is a *thing*, a meeting place between beings (Old English, *þing*). What is called *present* is not a universal container or an atomic point. *Present* and *pres-*

ence are simply the uneasy, shifting relative motion between different beings, unfolding their temporalities together in a way that becomes visible because of the focusing lens of the artwork. Just as a clock is a conversation between pieces of metal and cogwheels, tuned roughly to the motion of Earth, so *Twilight Epiphany* is a conversation between entities that acts as a gorgeous, multidimensional clock of sorts: not a clock that decisively tells time, but rather a sort of unclock that explodes the idea of time, revealing how time, like color and light, emerges from things. Time is an aesthetic appearance that flows out of a thing, as Einstein argued, depending on its material properties, so that clocks run faster in a plane at high altitude than they do on Earth's surface (*Relativity*). Earth rotates, one segment of Earth facing then turning from the Sun. A house, as Heidegger argues, is a kind of clock, since it has its sunny and its shady side (*Being and Time* 66–67, 95–97). Things *time* other things, to use the verb "time" transitively. They write stories on their surfaces.

Moreover, a thing times itself. It exists in difference "between itself," if that is not too paradoxical a thing to say. A thing is a kind of liar, because it is and is not its appearance: the Sun appears just this way in the sky, but it is not its appearance "in the sky"—it is that for a bird or for a human watching *Twilight Epiphany*. Depending where we are in the Sun's gravitational field, time itself will flow more or less slowly. From a far distance, stars are red shifted because of the effects of relativity.

Kant imagines time to be a function of the sequence of thought—we humans impose time on everything else because we think this thought, then that one. But perhaps this is just how a human knows she is "in" time—perhaps only that part of a human that is her conscious mentation. Only consider the manifold hormonal and genomic clocks that spin away in a human body. A clock is just the way one thing times itself, or another thing—itself here is indeed another thing, since being is uncanny, or, as I have termed it, "strangely strange." A life-form is a *strange stranger*, since it always eludes the consuming, measuring, and categorizing devices that seek to capture it (Morton, *The Ecological* 38–50). If the Road Runner were to be caught by Wyle E. Coyote, he would quickly become the coyote, being eaten, and some feathers—there would be no actual Road Runner, only a full stomach and some memories. The difference between the Road Runner and his appearance would have collapsed. To exist is to be smeared between what one is and how one appears—taking "appear" here to mean everything from use, manipulation, and functioning to color, smell, and shape.

So *Twilight Epiphany*, the metal square with its hole that lets in the sky, gathers a host of beings to attune and detune to one another. An epiphany is an appearance-for: *epi-* is the Greek prefix for "upon" or "for," while *-phany* comes from *phainesthai*, "to appear." Before I think about it, before I know or reason, the object is there—the Kantian turn, the very turn that limits philosophy to (human) meaning, depends upon a certain givenness that ultimately is predicated on the coexistence of me and at least one other thing. This "there" is not precisely specifiable in a rational sense, since I have not yet begun to reason—it is the precondition of reasoning. This disturbing spontaneity is shown me in an epiphany. In an epiphany, agency is on the side of the thing, by which is meant the nonhuman side—the angel appears to Mary; the Sun disappears in a sky. In this sense the title *Twilight Epiphany* is almost an oxymoron, a broken phrase: twilight is a (humanly) meaningful "time of day," a space between light and dark of indeterminate length—we can prolong it roughly for as long as we wish, or specify that it only be considered as a five-minute or half-hour segment. But an epiphany comes from the beyond, from the not-me: it is precisely something I do not impose.

What would an *epiphany about twilight* be? Or an *epiphany that was twilight*, an epiphany that consisted precisely in twilight? It would be an epiphany that showed decisively that twilight was not simply a human relation to things in "the world," the *world* here considered as more or less a uniform backdrop against which humans play out events and meanings. Different places on Earth have different kinds of twilight: in the tropics for instance, twilight is terribly brief, hardly noticeable. In the Arctic circle, twilight could be all day, or almost all of it. Twilight is a conversation between the tilted rotating Earth and the Sun, a conversation that gathers together shadows of objects that lengthen until the whole of one's surroundings is swathed in darkness.

Likewise, a poem's physical architecture is given, along with the text. Part of the meaning that the text weaves together (Latin, *tego*, "I weave") involves this basic level of its existence, such that modern poems (written, that is, after 1790) begin to talk about this level insistently. Mallarmé, for instance, distributes words across the page as if the page were a rubber sheet, forcing us to notice that the poem is printed on paper. At this level, the difference between a letter and a mark, between a mark and a smudge, between a letter and a brushstroke begins to break down. Imagine if the poem had been singed into the fur of a cat. Imagine if it had been scribbled on a note. Surely, this latter possibility is what "This Is Just to Say" talks about, the aubade by William Carlos Williams about the plums and the icebox:

> I have eaten
> the plums
> that were in
> the icebox
>
> and which
> you were probably
> saving
> for breakfast

> Forgive me
> they were delicious
> so sweet
> and so cold. (372)

A poem can talk, more or less, about the physical architecture in which or on which it is inscribed, the air that vibrates when we sing it or the ink that is used to write it. This is what is meant by Roman Jakobson's concept of a *phatic* statement, a statement that draws attention to the medium in which it necessarily exists. "I have eaten / the plums / that were in / the icebox"—the words on the note (as it were) are physically proximate to the icebox, to the plums. In the same way, each phrase is placed on a separate line, like coexisting yet separate beings. The poem is a little ecology in this sense—a coexisting of several beings, including phrases, paper, icebox, plums, and (presumably) lover and beloved human.

The relationship between the poem and its physical medium is like the relationship between the clock as a regular sequence of periodic cycles and the clock as a physical object that conveys a (human) meaningful sense of those periodic cycles. As long as things coexist, there are these shifting, liminal spaces, which we could imagine as a set of interesting zones, like fields of color or sound, which emanate from them. A sound is just a relationship between a thing and another thing—wind passing over a wind harp, breath pushing through my vocal cords. These things are given in the sound, yet also withdrawn.

Givenness thus inevitably manifests as distortion, as anamorphosis. Here I use Jean Luc Marion's beautiful and skillful analysis of givenness in perception, which he calls *saturated phenomena* (*In Excess* 37–38, 40–41, 48–49, 54–81). When something appears—when it "begins" by manifesting for something else—it must appear as a distortion. Thus, for Kant, there is a distortion in the real itself: we can count, but what on Earth is number? This crack or gap is caused by the gigantic presence of a being that is nearer than our hands and feet—our reason, or what Schopenhauer later called *will*—yet this being cannot be directly accessed. It causes the field of empirical givens to shimmer and ripple with uncertainty: all we have in science, since the days of Hume, are statistical correlations. Reason is given to me in my ability to count, to do math. Yet I cannot see it directly. It is like the shadow of an immense planet that lies too close to me to make out.

The birth of something is announced as an anamorphosis, a distortion in the world, a crack in the real. How could it be otherwise? Novelty, as Alfred North Whitehead calls it, is necessarily unrecognizable, since it bursts through into the familiar. Thanks to the gap between being and appearance, there is more than enough novelty potential in reality to fuel a trillion new births. We live in a reality stuffed full with novelty, like an insane joke shop exploding with jack in the boxes and rubber snakes. The shifting colors of *Twilight Epiphany* announce themselves as distortions of the previous color—fading or intensifying, blending and mutating. The new state of affairs has happened before we become aware of it.

If one probes down to the quantum level—the level of a single photon striking the crystal lattice that is the surface of the metal screen in Turrell's piece—we will find that this is literally the case. The initial moment cannot be specified in advance, since the reflection of the photon is uncertain, simply a cloud of probability. Beginnings are just uncertainty. It is like the beginning of a poem or of a story: how can we tell that it has started? Consider a minimalist work (Turrell's piece falls into this category)—say, an empty frame. Where does the art start and the space around it stop? Frameless work or empty frames bring out this essential ambiguity between what is excluded and what is included in an artwork. A skillful novelist handles what Aristotle calls "the beginning," which is not simply page 1 or line 1, but rather the *feeling of beginning*, which is precisely a feeling of uncertainty: Who is the main character? What constitutes an event in the story? Is this the middle of the story—exactly when are we, and where are we? I like to teach the first word of *The Picture of Dorian Gray* because the word "The" encapsulates the sheer givenness that threatens us with the distortion that constitutes a beginning. "The studio was filled with the scent of attar of roses . . ." Which studio? Why, this one, the one we must have already been in before we noticed. It is the same trick as Coleridge uses: "It is an Ancient Mariner" (line 1 of *The Rime of the Ancient Mariner*) is an answer to a question that was already posed—who is that weird-looking homeless old guy over there?

Something has already happened. Someone is already there. This is the epiphany of beginning. Because there is no way to sneak up on a beginning from behind, as it were, beginning must consist of this uncanny distortion of a habitual frame of reference, a distortion caused by the always already of the fresh new being. *Twilight Epiphany* confronts us with the always already of actually existing, coexisting beings—which is just what ecological awareness, stripped to the bone, actually is. This fact implies a potentially infinite regress of what this volume calls *storied matter*. When we look at a table, we see a story about some table parts assembled in a factory by machines and humans. When we look at the parts, we see stories about wood fashioned in turn by other kinds of machine. When we look at a plank of wood, we are seeing a story about something that happened to a tree in a relationship between humans, saws, and trees. When we look at a tree, we are seeing a story about something that happened to the genome of a tree unfolding in a certain environment: soil, water, microbes, birds, squirrels. Examining the genome, we see a story about coexisting viral code, pieces of plant DNA, and so on—DNA itself is a symbiotic system. When we look at a single piece of viral code, we see a story about replicant molecules hitching a ride in media that supported their replication. A molecule is a story about atoms. Atoms are stories about clouds of subatomic particles. And so on. There is, at least in theory, no limit—unless we think that reality was bootstrapped out of nothing.

Yet to posit nothing as the beginning of things—or even a primordial chaos—is to bestow a greater reality upon the nothing or the chaos than upon anything else, that is, any other moment in the story, or rather, in the stories. This would be to practice what in Heidegger and Derrida is called *ontotheology*—granting a greater kind or intensity of existence to one (or more) things. In the scholastic theology of the Middle Ages, God was more real than what He had created, as He was the *causa sui,* the cause that causes itself, the place in the causal chain where the buck stops. In the philosophy of Kant, it is synthetic judgments a priori that bestow reality upon things—time and space are simply functions of the way (human) thinking happens. This kind of ontotheology is not dissimilar to Protagoras's "The human is the measure of all things," also popular in certain dominant interpretations of quantum theory, in which the measuring equipment bestows reality upon what is measured. This too is a kind of ontotheology that threatens constantly to slip into pure idealism, in which the subject becomes like the medieval *causa sui* and posits itself, and hence everything else.

If, in ecological fashion, we wish to preserve the manifold beings that coexist in reality, we need not to be reducing things to other things and claiming that what a thing reduces to is more real than the thing in question. For the sake of clarity, let's call "what a thing reduces to" the *reducer* and "the thing in question" the *reduced.* There is a Western habit of thinking things as *reduceds,* namely, as things that are less real than what analysis takes them to be, analysis meaning *loosening* or breaking apart. We think that reductionism enables us not to accept things as given—they are always made of (smaller or more general) components. Yet by this same logic, being smaller or being more general becomes a greater guarantee of reality than being anything at all. An installation by James Turrell does not reduce to squares of metal and algorithms that produce light. The installation is its own unique being, just as a clearing in a forest is a kind of being, though we could see it as a reduced, that is, as "nothing but" an assemblage of trees, sky, air, and grass.

Beings are like that forest clearing or like *Twilight Epiphany.* When we look directly at them, there appears to be nothing there. Yet at the same time, there is something—there is not a blank nothing. There is, in fact, a kind of *nothingness,* by which I mean what some philosophers call a *meontic* rather than an *oukontic* nothing. This nothingness is a kind of "something," yet whenever we try to specify some feature of it, we find ourselves unable to. Oukontic nothing is absolutely nothing, "not even nothing," whereas meontic nothingness is shifting and spectral, palpable yet not quite "there" in a strong metaphysical sense.

This strange, tricky withdrawal is rather like what happens in the Kantian experience of beauty—which is one thing that contemporary philosophy might want to salvage from what has been called Kant's "correlationism," which as we saw above is the tendency to reduce things to the way in which they are correlated to a (human) subject (*Critique of Judgment* 43–95). When I find the *Mona Lisa* beautiful, I am unable to isolate any particular segment of it that contains that beauty. Say that I could—say that it's the enigmatic smile of La Gioconda. Then I could copy the smile in Photoshop five thousand times and have an artwork that was objectively five thousand times more beautiful. Say the beauty was a particular sequence of neurotransmitters released in my brain. Then I could isolate the active ingredient of that chemical cocktail and serve it to you as a pill whose beauty-bestowing potential could be doubled, tripled, and so on.

Kant argues, on the contrary, that beauty contains a necessary *je ne sais quoi*—I simply can't put my finger on what in the *Mona Lisa* is beautiful when I find it so. This means that there is a certain *nothingness* in the beauty experience—it cannot be isolated to a subject or to an object, or to any element of subject or object. Yet there it is. It is meontic nothingness rather than absolutely nothing—not an oukontic nothing, a nothing that is "not even nothing." Beauty depends upon kinds of object-like being that is not possible to break down. Beauty is irreducible. The experience of beauty cannot be broken down, nor can the beautiful thing—indeed, I cannot break down which part of the moment of beauty is "in" the thing or "in" me.

Beauty provides empirical evidence that things are not exactly capable of being reduced or, indeed, pinned down in any way. Kant holds beauty to be evidence of the region of a priori synthetic judgment, that is, of a cognitive space that is always already, which we glimpse in an epiphany. Once Kant discovered this space, it was as if a gap in the real had been detected, a gap that, in a marvelous Copernican inversion, made one realize that what had been taken as reality was in fact a series of floating islands, islands made of perishable stuff afloat on a gigantic ocean, an ocean that Kant took to be what he called *pure reason*. There was at least one being in reality that could not be reduced further, namely, the giant ocean of reason. It might not even be a human ocean—the luminous yet ungraspable quality of beauty, and the vertigo of the sublime, seems to indicate that this region is not necessarily "on our side," but is rather like the cold reaches of the outer universe itself, the view of Earth we now carry in our heads as a tiny fragile ball or "pale blue dot" adrift in a gigantic sea of space—not nothing, but space, the ocean created by trillions of objects (see Sagan).

Kant discovered nothingness, in other words. Ever since his discovery, philosophers have had to accommodate themselves to the nothing. It all boils down to where you put the nothingness. You cannot forget it. Once you have opened the bottle, the genie is out. Hume had driven a wedge into theories of causality—theories that saw things as having a determined and analyzable cause. Science is Humean, insofar as it relies on statistical correlation, rather than pregiven chunks that are linked in a chain of cause and effect. It was Kant who saw the reason Humean correlation was the case—there is a gap in the real, which we can detect by thinking, for instance, about numbers. I can count, but I cannot directly show you the essence of number—yet counting presupposes this essence, as its condition of possibility. In a wonderfully suggestive phrase, Kant calls this gap in the real the "unknown = X" (*Critique of Pure Reason* 51). This unknown X is precisely the thing—the nothingness that now intrudes into Western philosophical space. Hegel and his followers tried to wish it away by palming it off on Buddhism. Other philosophers such as Nietzsche went for a full-blown nihilism.

In their related ways, Heidegger and Derrida observed that this kind of nihilism was just ontotheology in a sophisticated getup. Nihilism too was a way to domesticate the nothingness, which is just an epiphany about the nature of reality. Object-oriented ontologists who follow this Heideggerian and Derridean tradition (I am one) have decided not to put the nothingness at the beginning of time, or outside the universe altogether. Rather, we are determined to see it as the core of anything whatsoever: a straw hat resting on a table, a car driving slowly out of a parking lot, energy passing through a Higgs field, a leopard stalking a herd of antelopes in the dead of night, bleached coral wafting gently undersea. A thing is an epiphany—a givenness whose given is irreducible, like suddenly coming across a forest clearing. When we point at twilight, we cannot isolate what it is or where it is. Yet *Twilight Epiphany* is just that—it is made of twilight, that evanescent time at which things seem to change yet remain the same, a time of shadings and deceptions.

Things just are that way. That is why and how they exist. Consider artificial intelligence—it looks and quacks intelligent; it passes our Turing test. Reality is performative in this sense, all the way down. There is something queer about it. There is no essence of duckness I can find anywhere inside a duck or in relations between ducks and nonducks such as rivers, weeds, and eggs. As Darwin argued, there is no way to posit what a duck is in advance. A duck simply satisfies various conditions for looking and quacking like one. This enables evolution to be astonishingly lazy: as long as I pass on my DNA, evolution does not care what I look or quack like.

Forest clearings, ecosystems, and biomes are all similar—they are made of nothingness. This does not mean that there are no such things as environments. It means that there are, only that phenomena that now affect all life-forms on Earth quite directly—and at present fatally—are not susceptible to being easily posited as constantly present, or as reducible, in ways that the metaphysics of presence has demanded. This metaphysics of presence is what underlies ontotheology—to take one thing as more real than another thing is to say that to be real, a thing should be constantly present. Yet a forest clearing or a storm cloud or a climate system is not constantly present in an obvious way. Yet each exists.

The problem is politically acute when it comes to global warming. As with smoking and cancer, only statistical correlations between human carbon emissions and global warming are available. Global warming is so huge and so impossible to see in one single constantly present thing—we can't ever say, "Look over there! There is global warming!" Global warming denial is a trick based on our ignorance about Hume and Kant and our fear of nothingness. Political progress at this point means accepting that a nothingness lies at the heart of things, precisely insofar as they are real. Ecological materialism must thus urgently investigate and come to terms with nothingness—unless it wants to be part of the problem, the reduction of things to smaller or more general (and thus more real, because more present) things: the problem that created the conditions in which carbon emissions began to cause human history to crisscross with geological time, the crisscross we now call the Anthropocene. In turn, ecocriticism should enable a caring attunement to the irreducibility of a red wheelbarrow, a plum, a blade of grass, a field of grass, a plum tree, a cluster of gardening tools, the Earth on which they sit, the garden in which they reside. Things are a kind of liminal space made of other things. Art happens in and as this liminal space, this *between*, which is just what a thing is: a meeting place of other beings ("thing" is Old English for "meeting place"). This meeting place is not ontically given or, in other words, metaphysically (constantly) present. Rather, it is shot through and through with nothingness. It is given in the way that beauty is given: an epiphany that coexists anarchically alongside us, physically before us, and despite us.

CODA

Open Closure
A Diptych on Material Spirituality

18 Spirits That Matter
Pathways toward a Rematerialization of Religion and Spirituality

Kate Rigby

IN ENTITLING MY contribution to this postscript "Spirits That Matter" (with thanks to the editors for their inspired suggestion), my intention is not to oppose something immaterial called "spirit" to the materiality of "the body," as might be implied for those readers who hear in this phrase an allusion to Judith Butler's influential *Bodies That Matter*. On the contrary: my implied divergence from Butler moves, rather (in company with other new materialists), in the direction of a more thoroughgoing materialism than that which is entailed in Butler's discursive constructivism. As Karen Barad has observed, Butler's model of discursive performativity accords too much power to the word and does not allow sufficiently for the contribution of nonhuman agency to the world's becoming ("Posthumanist" 122–28). The kind of materialism that I wish to advance here, however, is one that diverges from the secularism of both Butler and Barad, in that it affords an opening toward questions, and practices, of ecomaterialist religion and (for want of a better term) "spirituality."

Like Greta Gaard, who finds an ancient root of materialism in Buddhism, I am excited by the possibilities for cross-cultural conversation between postmodern science, and science studies, and what might broadly be described as nonmodern forms of understanding and practices of "worlding," which are enabled by the new materialisms. In Australia, for example, dialogue between Indigenous and non-Indigenous stakeholders around what the latter refer to as "resource management" has been stymied by the prevalence of that modern Euro-Western onto-epistemology that infamously sunders nature from culture and construes the nonhuman world primarily as an object of knowledge, economic exploitation, or aesthetic appreciation, but rarely as agentic, communicative, and ethically considerable. The onto-epistemology of vibrant matter, material-discursive enmeshment, biosemiotics, and intra-active knowing and becoming, by contrast, has the potential to edge ecological thinking in a direction where a greater measure of common ground might be found with what Aboriginal people might mean when they talk about "caring for country."

"Country," as I have gleaned primarily from the work of my colleague in the Australian ecological humanities community Deborah Bird Rose, cannot be accommodated to Euro-Western notions of Nature "over yonder," or of "the environment" as that which surrounds the human. Country is a spatial unit, extending under the ground, into the sky, and, in coastal regions, out to sea, which is forever in the process of being (re)composed through the dynamic and by no means always harmonious or predictable interactions of its diverse human and nonhuman denizens. Country is sentient, agentic, and speaking matter, and its ongoing vitality is sustained through practices of care that are inextricably social and ecological, practical and ceremonial, ranging from seasonal burning to "singing up." Caring for country demands considerable skill, knowledge, effort, and attentive love on the part of its people, who are themselves understood to share kinship ties with nonhuman (frequently animal) others in their territory (Rose, *Reports* 153–54). A new materialist ecology emphasizing connectivity, nonlinear causality, trans-corporeality, material agency, and an ethics of more-than-human "mattering" is likely to make far more sense within an Indigenous horizon of understanding than either the reductive materialist discourse of "resource management" or, its counterpart, New Age (or, worse, evangelical Christian fundamentalist) notions of "spirituality." By the same token, as Greta Gaard has argued in relation to Buddhism, new materialist ecological thought, and material ecocriticism, could be considerably enriched by entering into dialogue with older forms of nonreductive materialism, such as that which is articulated through Aboriginal narratives and practices of country.

Extending the new materialist conversation in this cross-cultural direction also opens onto postsecular territory. Another of my Australian colleagues who was heading in that direction not long before her untimely death was Val Plumwood, a nonreductive materialist from way back, who, in the final chapter of *Environmental Culture,* broaches the notion of a "materialist spirituality of place." Informed by Indigenous philosophies, Plumwood's earthy version of ecospirituality, or "philosophical animism," as she came to call it, was "place-sensitive" rather than "place-centric" or "place-bound," entailing journeying no less than abiding, and entirely compatible with what Ursula Heise terms a "sense of planet." Polyamorous rather than monogamous, such a spirituality of multiple places that is attentive to the communicativity and intentionality of the more-than-human world finds its necessary counterpart in Plumwood's "politics of dwelling," entailing ethical responsibility toward those numerous far-flung "shadow places" and their inhabitants, human and otherwise, which, for affluent Westerners under the regime of global capitalism, supply so many of our material needs (or, as is more commonly the case, cater to our consumerist desires).

Encouraged by a growing involvement with ecocriticism following her invitation to give a keynote lecture at the 2002 Association for the Study of Literature and Environment–UK conference, Plumwood had also begun to write of the capacity of narrative and poetic language to produce enlivened, and enlivening, accounts of the agency and creativity of natural phenomena, and of the complex and intimate interrelationship of humans with diverse "earth others." This she describes as a "critical green ecological writing project" that could challenge "the experiential framework of dead and silent matter entrenched by the sadodispassionate rationality of scientific reductionism" ("Journey" 17–18). In her contribution to the volume that arose from that conference, *Culture, Creativity, and Environment*, Plumwood tells a series of stone-centered "onto-tales," to use Jane Bennett's felicitous coinage, involving a literal journey to the stone country of Arnhem Land as well as a "conceptual journey that moved stone from the background of consciousness to the foreground, from silent to speaking, from mindless vacancy to intentional actor, from the ordinary to the extraordinary, the wonderful, even the sacred" ("Journey" 35).

Meanwhile, Freya Mathews, another key figure in the Australian ecological humanities, has begun advocating the practice, at once experiential, philosophical, and literary, of "ontopoetics." As Mathews explains in her introduction to the 2009 special issue of *Philosophy Activism Nature* that she edited on this topic, ontopoetics refers to the occurrence of meaningful communicative exchanges between self and world and world and self, in which we are afforded a glimpse of the inner, psychoactive dimension that, she argues, is inherent in materiality, but occluded within reductive forms of materialism. The conceptual groundwork for ontopoetics was laid out in her companion volumes, *For Love of Matter* and *Reinhabiting Reality*, which propound a renovated panpsychism and explore its implications for both cultural regeneration and ecological sustainability.[1] Mathews posits the new panpsychism as "postmaterialist," not in the sociological sense of postconsumerist or postmaterialistic, but as breaking with the fundamental metaphysical premise of reductive materialism, according to which the physical world consists only of that which is in principle empirically observable, constituting a world of mere objects devoid of inherent meaning and normative significance. Nevertheless, panpsychist postmaterialism is closely aligned with the new materialism in seeking not to transcend materiality per se, but rather to reconceive and, indeed, enter more deeply into it, namely, through forms of encounter and interaction in which the material world is disclosed not merely or principally as a series of causal relations among discrete objects, but rather as possessing what Mathews terms a "subjectival" dimension that is agentic, communicative, and unfolding temporally in ways that we can neither predict nor ordain.

Mathews's panpsychism shares with the more Deleuzean variants of new materialism a distinctly Spinozan aspect. Spinoza's concept of *conatus*, the impulse that he attributed to all physical entities, animate and inanimate, individual and collective, to preserve their being and augment their capacities, to compose and recompose themselves with and through their dynamic interrelations with others, plays a key role here, as does Spinoza's distinction between *natura naturata* and *natura naturans,* referring, on the one hand, to nature or reality under its differentiated, explicated aspect (its "modes," which Mathews terms "the Many") and, on the other, to nature or reality, as a generative, undifferentiated field of impulsion or "substance" ("the One" in Mathews's terminology). Panpsychist postmaterialism presupposes the development of the natural sciences, which have disclosed in ever more fine-grained detail, and to such profound technological, socioeconomic, and ecological effect, the structure and functioning of *natura naturata.* The inner, mentalistic dimension of materiality with which the panpsychist is concerned, however, cannot be disclosed in the reductively materialist mode of objectifying scientific inquiry, but only through a situated, interactive, and carnal kind of knowing: one that entails a mutual opening of the one to the other, full of unpredictability and risk, in which neither party is ever fully revealed to the other or totally in control of the outcome of their encounter. "The way this inner dimension of reality is expressed in the world," Mathews explains, "will be *consistent* with the findings of science but will not be *exhausted* by them" ("Beyond Modernity" 94).

From this perspective, the world appears not merely or principally as a series of causal relations, but rather as a nexus of communication, in which the One perpetually reaches out and signals to the Many, as they do, to a greater or lesser extent and intensity, to one another, in and through a shared, if variously experienced, physical reality. Lest this should sound like plunging us into a nightmare world where we risk falling prey to imperious commands issued by PowerPoints or dinner plates, let me hasten to add that Mathews cautions that not all physical entities can be supposed to communicate with us intentionally: such intentionality can be reasonably attributed only to more complex individuated selves. Moreover, Mathews warns against egocentric literalism, whereby misfortune, for example, is read as punishment, potentially requiring elaborate ritual practices of appeasement, and she explicitly differentiates panpsychist praxis from the manipulative magic of the sorcerer, who seeks to induce the world to do his bidding. For the panpsychist, "communication with the world is taken as an end in itself, as the dimension of grace in our lives, rather than as a means of securing our safety and good fortune" (*For Love* 68).

While Mathews presents panpsychism as a genuinely postmodern possibility, opening up a "third way for development" beyond tradition and modernity, she has also explored points of confluence with both Aboriginal and Daoist philosophies. These share with panpsychism an ontopoetic understanding of reality as a dynamic order of mutual arising, in which particular entities and patterns emerge and unfold only in and through their changing relations with others—an understanding, as Greta Gaard shows, that is also intrinsic to Buddhism. The Daoist connection has taken center stage in Mathews's more recent discussions of panpsychism that draw upon Lau Tzu's notion of *wu wei* to advance a mode of comportment in which human agency is aligned "with rather than against the grain of existing conativities," favoring "practices of conserving and cherishing 'the given'—that which already exists—replenishing the sources of renewal in natural cycles so that 'production' is accomplished largely by the world itself, without our having to direct and design the process" ("Beyond Modernity" 99–100). To this principle of doing by "letting be," Mathews adds a more proactive mode of engagement that she terms "synergy," entailing practices of becoming-with the conativities of multiple others, which "elicits from us potentialities that have not hitherto been made manifest just as it elicits such potentialities from the world" (102). Synergistic practices engender open-ended change, as distinct from either the stasis of tradition or the violently imposed transformations of modernity.

Daoism interests Mathews not so much as a religion, but as a philosophy. She nonetheless makes it clear that the panpsychist transformation of culture that she envisages would entail a resacralization of the cosmos, based not on the supposed existence of "any spiritual entities over and above matter but from matter's own inner principles" ("Beyond Modernity" 94). This renewed sense of the sacred would itself materialize, in Mathews's view, not in a monolithic new religion, but in a diversity of situated practices of invocation and thanksgiving appropriate to the cultural imaginary and ecosocial contexts of the participating communities, such as the Sacred Kingfisher Festival held each year at the Centre for Education and Research in Environmental Strategies (CERES) in Melbourne. The Sacred Kingfisher is a seasonal visitor to Melbourne's Merri Creek, but had not been seen for many years, presumably as a result of the degradation of this small urban waterway. In recent years, however, following concerted restoration efforts, this beautiful migratory bird has begun to return on an annual basis. This double return is now celebrated at CERES with a festival that

> brings hundreds of local performers of different ethnicity and cultural provenance . . . together with thousands of local residents, environmentalists, and activists, in a cathartic, high energy re-enactment of the retreat of the kingfisher in the face of ecological holocaust and its return in response to the efforts of local people to regenerate their "country" through revegetative healing.

For Mathews, this is an instance of place-sensitive, improvisational "participatory poetics," in which the "audience" is "evolving into participant congregation. Each year too the site joins us, adding cicada choirs and rainbows, for instance, with dazzling appositeness, at strategic junctures" (*Reinhabiting Reality* 202–3). Of particular interest to a material ecocriticism, panpsychist praxis might also give rise to new modes of literature, as well as new ways of reading earlier texts, which respond to the ontopoetic experience of the material sacred in the written word. Indeed, the lyrical-philosophical "ground studies" that constitute part 2 of *Reinhabiting Reality* could themselves be seen to model ontopoetics as lyrical life-writing.

My own forays, both experiential and academic, into postsecular territory have taken me from the fertile field of (post-Christian) feminist spirituality (Rigby, "The Goddess"), not so much back into the fold as out into the wilds of deep-green (feminist) ecotheology and the interfaith ecology movement (Rigby, "Another Talk"). Here too there is considerable potential for fruitful dialogue with the new materialism. While most feminist ecospiritualities have long been characterized by a highly immanental understanding of the divine, prefiguring to a greater or lesser extent the new materialist reconceptualization of matter as a lively and communicative participant in more-than-human meaning-making processes, some ecotheologies also share, in addition to this, the new materialist ontology of relational becoming. This is true in particular of process ecotheology, which draws on the philosophy of Alfred North Whitehead (itself an important source of inspiration for some new materialists, including Donna Haraway and Nancy Tuana).[2]

For ecological thinkers who are committed to a Levinasian ethics of alterity or the object-oriented ontology currently espoused, for example, by Tim Morton, or both, relational process ontology raises the specter of the erasure of difference. This is an important concern, and not one that I can address properly here.[3] In my analysis, however, a philosophy or theology of intra-active becoming does not necessarily plunge us into a "night in which all cows are black" (to recall Hegel's unfair criticism of Schelling's early *Naturphilosophie*, itself an important precursor, I believe, of the new materialism).[4] To hold that nothing can be said to preexist its relational becoming does not imply a disregard for the singularity of the multitude of things that do thereby come into existence and that, in their singularity, are only ever partially disclosed to one another. In Christian worship, the conjunction of connectivity and singularity is affirmed in the "kenotic [self-emptying] hospitality" (Brett 196) of the Eucharist, in which the congregation affirms, "We who are many are one body, for we all share in the one bread." Although the actual bread that is shared in the communion of fellow Christians is conventionally understood as the symbol or embodiment of the Word made flesh in Jesus Christ, within the ecotheology of "deep incarnation" (Gregersen), it is understood more inclusively as a synecdoche for the wider creation, the inspirited "flesh of the world," in which we are called into fellowship, not only with other Christians, or even other humans, but, ultimately, with all creatures, for all our differences and sometimes conflictual entanglements.

For process ecotheologians, creation is understood as a dynamically unfolding process of open-ended interactivity, in which materiality is a participant rather than a product of divine manufacture: *creatio ex profundis*, as feminist process ecotheologian Catherine Keller puts it in *Face of the Deep*, rather than *creatio ex nihilo*. While process theologians acknowledge the cultural constructedness of any and all human conceptions of God (in keeping, it might be noted, with a long tradition of negative theology), they nonetheless affirm a conception of the divine not as any kind of extraterrestrial supreme being, but as the mystery that "lures" all things toward the fullest possible actualization of their interactive becoming, relative to the situation at hand: this *calling* is the divine Eros. Its counterpart is the divine Agape, which graciously "*responds* to whatever we have become; in com/passion it feels our feelings: it is the *reception*" (Keller, *On the Mystery* 99). This "omni-amorous" divine mystery, participating in the suffering of creation, beckons us toward "abundant" life, not in some immaterial beyond, but right in the thick of things, here, now. This path is the way of love, where the passion of Eros (including human sexual desire) finds its place within the (com)passion of Agape and is materialized interactively in ways such as that instantiated in Jesus's parable of the Good Samaritan. As Australian material feminist ecocritical biblical scholar Anne Elvey (*The Matter* 82–84) explains, the Samaritan's compassionate response toward the robbed and beaten stranger (whom he would generally have viewed as an enemy) differs from that of the other passersby in its thoroughgoing corporeality: he alone is touched by the other's suffering in the depths of his own flesh (he is said to have been "moved in the guts," *splanchnízomai*) and thereby feels called to extend to this stranger a healing touch. This in turn entails a collective effort, involving the participation of a diversity of human and nonhuman others, including the plants that were used to make wine, oil and bandages, the donkey who bears the wounded man to the inn, and the innkeeper who is materially recompensed for the provision of ongoing care.

Such collaborative practices of courageous and resolute love in response not only to individual suffering, but also to social structures that perpetuate violence, injustice, and the systematic destruction and degradation of (human and nonhuman) bodies and ecologies are seen by process ecotheologians to participate in the ongoing actualization of the *basileía toû theoû,* conceived not as a hierarchically ordered "kingdom" but as an egalitarian "commonwealth." In Keller's counterapocalyptic rendering of Christian messianic hope, the *éschaton* is "not a literal time-to-come, but an ideal that *resists* every realized eschatology" (*On the Mystery* 153). Seeking salvation not "from matter but within it, within our delicate, difficult interactivities" (173), process ecotheology discerns how "possibility dances like a flame along the edges of our finitude," while "the path still bends towards the unknown" (176).

In introducing care for country, philosophical animism, panpsychism, and ecotheology into this discussion of material ecocriticism, my intention is not necessarily to advocate any one of these paths. What I do want to advance, however, is a greater ecocritical engagement with emerging manifestations of new materialist spirituality, in which contemporary forms of knowledge are being brought into conversation with nonmodern (and frequently non-Western) religions and philosophies.[5] Contrary to the (possibly "old" materialist) assumptions of those who are "unsettled" by talk of "ecospirituality," as Franca Bellarsi puts it in her introduction to *Ecozon@*'s 2011 special issue on religion and the environment (1), this modality of postsecularism is in dialogue with the sciences and supportive of political engagement in the pursuit of greater social, or, more inclusively, transpecies, justice. In the long run, moreover, it might also provide a better bulwark against fundamentalist versions of postsecularism than the radical atheist rejection of religion per se.

Notes

1. On Mathews's panpsychism, see also Rigby, "On the Eros"; and Oppermann, "Review."

2. For example, Haraway references Whitehead's *Science and the Modern World* in *When Species Meet*, while Tuana ("Viscous" 191) acknowledges Whitehead's process philosophy as the inspiration for her theory of "interactionism."

3. See, for example, Morton's contribution to this volume.

4. For an introductory ecophilosophical discussion of Schelling, see Rigby, *Topographies* 38–45.

5. See also Jea Sophia Oh's *Postcolonial Theology of Life*, which intertwines process ecotheology with the Korean Donghak, itself a hybrid of Confucianism, Daoism, Buddhism, Christianity, and native Korean shamanism, in a feminist postcolonial ecotheology of "planetarity."

19 Mindful New Materialisms
Buddhist Roots for Material Ecocriticism's Flourishing

Greta Gaard

It is saturday-morning yoga class at the Minneapolis Midtown YWCA. A diverse group of practitioners assembles, varying in ages, genders, classes, races, sexualities, and nationalities, all gathered to practice an hour of mindful yoga. In Pali (the language of the Buddha), "yoga" means "to join" or "to unite," and its practice involves joining attention to movements involving the body, the breath, the mind, and the larger interconnectedness of all beings. We begin with sun salutation and end in a position familiar to those who have seen the most common depictions of the Buddha, seated in yogic meditation. Joining body ecology with spirit ecology, we bring our attention to the breath, a flow of matter that is exchanged among our many bodies in this enclosed room, and beyond this room as well. Breath is one of the many "flows" that illustrate our interbeing and invite us to embark on a journey of mindfulness wherein the illusion of a separate self is revealed.

The ancient Buddhist concepts of impermanence (*anicca*), no-self (*anatta*), and dependent origination (*paticcasamuppāda*) echo conceptual formations of the new materialisms and material ecocriticism. Certainly, these perspectives have different appeals for different audiences: Buddhism is not freighted with the heavy scholarly discourse of the new materialisms, though it offers similar conceptual tools. Those less interested in spirituality can still access the concept of no-self through Stacy Alaimo's definition of "trans-corporeality" and Karen Barad's explorations of "intra-actions" of the human and the nonhuman; Buddhism's dependent origination is also articulated through Nancy Tuana's exploration of "viscous porosity," Andrew Pickering's definition of the "mangle," and the new materialist focus on entanglements of matter and meaning. Like new materialisms, Buddhism can also be seen as simply a philosophy—it has been called a "nontheistic" religion, in fact, because its emphasis is on the practitioner watching the mind and practicing the precepts rather than praying to a deity.[1] Material ecocriticism has both philosophical and spiritual resonances as well, since many contemporary ecospiritualities see this material world as imbued with life force, even an element of the sacred (Kate Rigby, "The Goddess"; see also Serpil Oppermann's essay and David Abram's afterword in this volume). For example, by emphasizing the interconnectedness of life-forms and the so-called nonliving matter in terms of their agentic effectivity, the spiritual dimension of material ecocriticism resonates with some Native American cultural narratives; with Australian Aboriginals, as Kate Rigby observes; and with other earth-based spiritual practices, such as shamanism. As this new ecocritical perspective develops, I suggest it could be fruitful to develop in dialogue with Buddhist philosophy, which offers conceptual tools that complement aspects of new materialisms: specifically, the inescapability of suffering (*dukka*), the root causes of suffering (craving [*tanha*], aversion [*dosa*], delusion [*moha*]), and the noble eightfold path—a set of ethical and spiritual practices toward ending suffering. Together, these concepts form the Four Noble Truths, which are necessary in some form if material ecocriticism is to fulfill its promise of making ethical meanings recognizable.

Dependent Origination

The new materialist concept of the "entanglement" of living and nonliving matters, or of bodily natures, may find its precedent and complement in Buddhism's concept of dependent origination, the understanding that no one thing exists apart from another. Material entanglements can be seen in the fact that breathing air, drinking water, or consuming food tainted with dioxins, PCBs (polychlorinated biphenyls), and other synthetic chemicals damages the immune system of many animals and is a proven cause of cancer. Dependent origination can be seen in the recognition that events such as child sexual assault are an outcome of a specific set of conditions, producing the coarising of perpetrator and victim. This recognition does not relieve the perpetrator of responsibility, but rather places these actions in a context of events, decisions, and historical and material conditions, whereby each action involves a decision that in turn produces another set of conditions and another decision. Dependent origination does not blame the victim, either, as some interpretations of "karma" have tended to do—implying that AIDS is a punishment for homosexual behaviors, for example, or that people suffering from famine or warfare somehow "deserve" to suffer; there is no one-to-one correlation between a specific action and a specific outcome. Instead, the concept of dependent origination offers a lens into the interplay of events, decisions, and material conditions of ecosocial problems (that is, suffering, or *dukka*) as coarising through a nexus of actions and conditions that may involve ecologically exploitative economic and agricultural practices, energy and transportation technologies, and colonialist and heteromasculinist histories of power, warfare, and oppression.[2]

Dependent origination illuminates ecosystem relationships as well as the operations of global capitalism and the emptiness of the separate self. Because "values are integral to the nature of knowing and being" (Barad, *Meeting* 37), detrimental practices of heteropatriarchy and global capitalism alike are inseparable from the ethical platform and the way we *know* the world, and thus from deteriorating eco-cultural and ecosystem relations. Seen this way, the concept of dependent origination sheds more light on the "mutually constitutive actions of material reality" (Alaimo, *Bodily* 157).

Onto-Epistemology and No-Self

One of the key features of the new materialisms, appropriated by material ecocriticism, is "the movement from epistemology to ontology" (Hekman, *The Material* 68). Whereas epistemology was the focus of social constructionism and the discursive perspective, "epistemology is of necessity about representation, and representation is necessarily about dichotomies. Representation gives us two choices: knowledge is either objective or subjective. As long as we remain within the purview of epistemology, this dichotomy is inescapable" (69).

The emphasis on embodiment, articulated via Karen Barad's concept of agential realism, overcomes these dichotomies through the concept of "onto-epistemology," exploring the ways human identity and material reality are continually reconstituted through material-discursive intra-actions (*Meeting* 136–41). Similarly, Stacy Alaimo's concept of trans-corporeality involves "a recognition not just that everything is interconnected but that humans are the very stuff of the material, emergent world" and "makes a profound shift in subjectivity," as "the material self cannot be disentangled from networks that are simultaneously economic, political, cultural, scientific, and substantial" (*Bodily* 20).

Buddhism also shifts the focus of its field, spirituality, from "faith" or a set of doctrines (epistemology) to ontology through mindfulness and its invitation to investigate the embodied experiences of the self: "Come and see," the Buddha is recorded as saying repeatedly. In *Thoughts without a Thinker*, Buddhist psychotherapist Mark Epstein explains "the secret weapon of Buddhism," which is "the means by which one can shift the perspective from how outraged one feels to *who it is* who feels it" (211). The Buddhist concept of "no-self" (*anatta*) arises from the understanding of dependent origination as applied to human identity. Thich Nhat Hanh calls this "inter-being," the sense that there is no separate identity: we "inter-are." Each one of us emerges as a product of specific material interactions, involving sexual desires, gestation and birth, ingestion and elimination, respiration, and responsiveness to the agency of other beings (plants, insects, animals, buildings, machines). Watching the mind through the practice of Vipassana (insight, or mindfulness) meditation, we can see what we assumed was our own separate identity fall apart into a series of discrete but interconnected processes: the five aggregates of physical form (the body), feelings, perceptions, mental formations, and sense consciousness. No one of these exists apart from the other, or apart from the material conditions of existence. With an aikido-like shift, removing the self effectively removes the added layer of mental formations or narratives of suffering where the "outraged" story appears. Again, such awareness does not erase the material effects or absolve responsibility for actions, but illuminating the chain of dependent origination creates greater understanding of causes and strategies for transforming the causes and conditions that promote suffering.

The Mangle of No-Self and Disclosure's Ethical Imperative for Action

How do socially engaged Buddhists, Buddhist feminists, and new materialists envision social movements continuing, if political actors have no separate self who experiences oppression? If we have "agency without subjects" (Alaimo, "Trans-Corporeal" 244), then how can we have responsibility for social injustices, and how can we compel accountability and compensation from corporations, governments, and citizens?

Feminist scholars such as Rita Gross, Anne Klein, Sandy Boucher, and others have pinpointed several challenges for feminists who want to practice Buddhism, namely, the concept of no-self (*anatta*). Traditional Buddhism offers no analysis of the ways that self-identity may be culturally inflected to reproduce gender roles. Feminists have argued that "no-self" is regularly a part of female gender roles and might offer good practice opportunities for men, along with letting go of attachment to view; for women, however, gaining or reclaiming a sense of self and standpoint has been a central feminist accomplishment. Feminists have noted the gender bias in the Jataka tales—legends about Buddha's earlier incarnations prior to enlightenment—particularly the story about the Buddha sacrificing himself to be eaten by a hungry tiger so that she and her cubs might live. Such laudatory narratives of heroic nonattachment praise a man for self-sacrifice, but remain silent about the countless daily and lifelong forms of self-sacrifice required of many women through traditional gender roles. Developing spiritual teachings that address how women can move from that relational self-identity to an appropriate view of *anatta* coexistent with a functional selfhood, one that does not cling to identity yet recognizes the usefulness of identity in performing daily tasks, has been a project for women dharma teachers (Gross 1993; Klein 1995; Boucher 1997). In this area, Buddhist feminists would benefit from using the tools developed by material feminists.

The imperative to address all intra-actants—all the links of dependent origination that create suffering and conditions of injustice—is explicit in the new materialist ethics articulated in the writings of material feminists. For example, Karen Barad links objectivity and responsibility in her conclusion that "we need to meet the universe halfway, to take responsibility for the role that we play in the world's differential becoming" (*Meeting* 396). As she explains, "We are responsible for the world of which we are a part, not because it is an arbitrary construction of our choosing but because reality is sedimented out of particular practices that we have a role in shaping and through which we are shaped" (390). Stacy Alaimo agrees, arguing that a "disengaged philosophical platform is uninhabitable for anyone with ethical and political commitments to environmentalism and environmental justice" (*Bodily* 11). As if speaking directly to the Buddhist feminist critique of "no-self," Susan Hekman introduces the concept of "disclosure," by which she means "the relationship between the material, the discursive, the technological, and the practices they constitute" (*The Material* 127). The feminist critique of social and environmental injustices need not be articulated through an identity politics or chain of equivalences among oppressed selfhoods or identity groups, but can be articulated and mobilized in response to the "social practices [that] disclose reality for us in particular societies" (127). As Hekman explains, "Certain disclosures have material consequences that are beneficial, others that are not" (93). To complete her argument, Hekman needs define only "beneficial," a term Buddhist feminists would define as "skillful" and "leading to the cessation of suffering."

Intra-actants and Activisms

Because ecocriticism has from the start been committed to linking environmental study with environmental practice, ecocritics addressing the nexus of Buddhism and the new materialisms may rightly ask, what kinds of congruence link Buddhist philosophy with Buddhist ethico-political practice? And is there a demonstrable congruence between the analyses of new materialists or material ecocritics and their embodied ethico-political practices?

In the United States, some Buddhist practitioners have sought to interface their mindfulness practice with diverse liberatory belief systems describing the just and unjust interactions of material bodies. "Although meditation may be indispensable," writes Kenneth Kraft, "neither it nor any other discipline can stand (or sit) alone. Socially engaged practice also entails development of character, cultivation of generosity and other virtues, refinement of ethical sensitivity, and the day-to-day activation of compassion" (Jones 101). Based on the belief that a Buddhist response to suffering must occur at both the personal (mental, spiritual, behavioral) and the political (structural) levels, Robert Aitken and practitioners at the Maui zendo formed the Buddhist Peace Fellowship in 1977. Its five-point mission includes the commitment "to raise peace, environmental, feminist, and social justice concerns among North American Buddhists" and "to make a clear public witness to Buddhist practice and interdependence as a way of peace and protection for all beings" (Simmer-Brown 78). In *Dharma Rain*, Thai monk Santikaro Bhikkhu articulates an awareness of interbeing through a critique of the word "environment" that resonates with Haraway's critique of the "human": "Environment . . .

betrays its Western origins, separating human beings from the rest of nature," writes Santikaro. "In Buddhism . . . we speak of nature or ecology as inclusive of everything, especially ourselves" (211).

But this Buddhist inclusiveness has not always included other animal species, and thus Buddhism, like the new materialisms, has room for development in regard to matters of interspecies ethics. In 1982 Buddhists who recognized interbeing among animal bodies founded Buddhists Concerned for Animals (Palmers 278), a group whose more recent incarnation is Dharma Voices for Animals. According to their view, the first precept "to refrain from killing or harming all sentient beings" has clear implications for interspecies relations, as diverse Buddhist animal studies scholars have argued (Kapleau 1986; Phelps 2004). As Buddhist and ecofeminist philosopher Deane Curtin explained in developing the concept of contextual moral vegetarianism:

> The injunction to care, considered as an issue of moral and political development, should be understood to include the injunction to eliminate needless suffering wherever possible, and particularly the suffering of those whose suffering is conceptually connected to one's own. It should be understood as an injunction that includes the imperative to rethink what it means to be a person connected with the imperative to rethink the status of nonhuman animals. (70–71)

In this, Curtin's contextual moral vegetarianism seems prescient in its neat conjunction of the new materialist and Buddhist perspectives.

On environmental matters, socially engaged Buddhists have explored our material and ecosocial entanglement (or dependent origination, in Buddhist terms), producing *A Buddhist Response to the Climate Emergency* (Stanley, Loy, and Dorje), the Buddhist Climate Project of linked activisms responding to climate change, and the website EcoBuddhism.Org: A Buddhist Response to Global Warming. These practical tools bring a Buddhist perspective to clarify our understanding of the root causes of climate change, linking science and spirituality, energy and economics, and ecopsychology, from the motivation of compassion, manifesting in actions aimed at ending suffering. The new materialisms have yet to address the movement from ethical narratives to ethical *actions* that proceed from identifying the "mangle" that discloses unbeneficial material outcomes.

Whereas the new materialisms propose that we "consult nonhumans more closely," in the words of Jane Bennett's *Vibrant Matter* (108), or recognize the "mutual constitution of entangled agencies" that emerge through "intra-actions," as Karen Barad proposes in *Meeting the Universe Halfway* (33), it is still not entirely clear how these strategies will include consideration of other animal species. If the new materialists adopt an approach that takes into consideration more visibly the intra-actions among corporate food systems of cattle production, methane, and climate change—interconnections that have been addressed not just by animal studies scholars but by the United Nations Food and Agricultural Organization (2006) as well—and the effects of human forces on sea animals, wildlife, or domesticated animals, their arguments would be stronger in challenging speciesism and human exceptionalism. As Stacy Alaimo has argued, "trans-corporeality denies the human subject the sovereign, central position" (*Bodily* 16). In this regard, my argument is that consideration of other-than-human animals as not merely homogenized species but also and simultaneously as *specific beings*—neither subordinate nor less important than humans, but simply different—is crucial to avoid perpetuating the human-animal and thus culture-nature dualisms, centrisms, and hierarchies, thereby diminishing and distorting the ethics and inclusiveness of both theory (such as new materialism) and spirituality (such as Buddhism). Both new materialism and Buddhism have the capacity and the imperative to address other-than-human animals from a *deeply posthumanist* perspective.[3] As Kate Rigby suggests, a greater ecocritical engagement with new materialist spirituality holds promise for "nurturing political engagement in the pursuit of greater social, or more inclusively, trans-species justice," and this potential needs development in both Buddhism and new materialisms alike.

Language, Narrative, Suffering

Buddhism, the new materialisms, and material ecocriticism view narrative quite differently, and comparisons among these approaches will be fruitful for those interested in developing a material ecocriticism. Beginning students of insight meditation often report, "I tell myself stories!" (as if this is a novelty they alone experience), after they have spent some time watching the mind. These stories, though certainly of interest from a Buddhist psychological perspective (Brazier 1995; Linehan 1993; Martin 1999; Segal, Williams, and Teasdale 2012), on greater examination are seen as a form of *papanja,* or proliferation, whereby the mind busily does its task of generating more and more narrative that effectively distracts our attention from a deeper awareness of the present moment. With practice, the experienced meditator learns to set aside these stories, recognizing them as diverse manifestations of the many hindrances to full awareness. Certainly, spiritual teachers of many traditions, including Buddhism, use narrative as a didactic mode for illustrating ethics—a strategy material ecocritics may use as well—but Buddhism simultaneously recognizes the limitations of narrative, even seeing narration itself as a possible form of suffering and a hindrance to insight.

New materialisms have been critical of the linguistic turn of social construction, and their description of the ways matter and language intra-act can be compared to Buddhist distinctions between pain (the material) and suffering (the added layer of narrative we bring to events and experiences). The practice of mindfulness cultivates awareness of these mental narratives (which reference the past, the future, or an added, storied dimension removed from the present) and invites practitioners to "let go of the story" in order to cultivate closer awareness of the present moment, the only moment of our existence.

As Buddhism's second Noble Truth explains, the root causes of suffering are our perpetual distraction (delusion, or *moha*) by the *narratives of the mind*, which keep us continually engaged in resisting the present moment, wishing it were somehow other than what it is, and clinging to a sense of self and a set of conditions that are impermanent. The end of suffering—the third Noble Truth—can be experienced by meeting the present moment just as it is. Doing so with clear seeing, recognizing dependent origination, leads one to recognize the three qualities of existence: suffering (*dukka*), impermanence (*anicca*), and no-self (*anatta*). Freeing the mind from the perpetual suffering involved in wanting conditions and objects we do not have (craving), pushing away conditions and objects we do have (aversion), or becoming attached to things that are always in motion (delusion), interdependent, and impermanent (that is, the material conditions of existence), the fourth Noble Truth describes the eightfold path of wisdom (right view, right attitude), morality (right speech, right action, right livelihood), and concentration (right effort, right mindfulness, right concentration).

The qualifier of "right" in these practices offers the very pragmatic essence of Buddhist ethics: perceptions, thoughts, and actions are "right" when they are "skillful," leading toward ending suffering for oneself and for others (recall Hekman's "beneficial" consequences). They are "wrong" or "unskillful" when they produce, promote, lead to, or increase pain (the material conditions) and suffering (the mental formations in response to materiality), experiences that are not limited to humanity.[4] Through an understanding of dependent origination, both pain and suffering can be seen to arise through the interaction of material conditions, sensations, perceptions, thoughts, actions. The term "skillful" frees Buddhism from the weight of morality and judgment and opens up the possibility of discernment (or, as Hekman might say, disclosure). Like Rigby in Australia, I look to the "Idle No More" movement for North American Indigenous sovereignty (Ross 2013), wherein the ethics of material conditions, intra-actions, thoughts, and narratives can be discerned or disclosed by uncovering (even narrating) their pathways to suffering or the end of suffering. This discernment is the purpose and practice of material ecocriticism.

Mindful Material Ecocriticism

From the start, ecocriticism has "shared the fundamental premise that human culture is connected to the physical world, affecting it and affected by it," as Cheryll Glotfelty writes in the introduction to *The Ecocriticism Reader* (xix). Citing Barry Commoner's first law of ecology, that "everything is connected to everything else," Glotfelty argues that "most ecocritical work shares a common motivation": finding ways to respond to an "age of environmental limits" by creating and contributing to solutions, "not just in our spare time, but from within our capacity as professors of literature" (xxi). As John Muir wrote in *My First Summer in the Sierra* (1911), "When we try to pick out anything by itself, we find it hitched to everything else in the universe"(35). With Muir, environmental writers and ecocritics have described ecological interconnections, as have Buddhist scholars, and environmental feminist writers such as Susan Griffin:

> The mind is a physical place. The mind is made up of tissue and blood, of cells and atoms, and possesses all the knowledge of the cell, all the balance of the atom. Human language is shaped to the human mouth, made by and for the tongue, made up of sounds that can be heard by the ear. And there is to the earth and the structure of matter a kind of resonance. We were meant to hear one another, to feel. . . . We are connected not only by the fact of our dependency on this biosphere and our participation in one field of matter and energy, in which no boundary exists between my skin and the air and you, but also by what we know and what we feel. ("Split Culture" 17)

Speaking of the interrelationships among art, matter, and science, queer feminist author Jeanette Winterson has commented:

> I don't believe in a static objective reality that is out there. I believe in shifting, changing patterns of energy; the shifting, changing patterns of energy that we've begun to apprehend in nature and in the very molecules and atoms and DNA of our bodies. Nothing is solid; nothing is fixed. But this movement, this energy, is not chaos. Science is just beginning to unravel the patterns and shifts and connections that seemed so impossible and implausible. But art intuitively understands these patterns and shifts and connections, because that is exactly how art functions too. . . . [T]hrough art, we recognize life's intrinsic quality, that everything is connected. ("Books" n.p.)

New materialisms have brought forward the scientific foundations for the embodied ecological intuitions of trans-corporeality expressed by Muir, Griffin, and Winterson; joined with the social sciences and the humanities, these new materialisms allow ecocritics to base our analyses and arguments on even stronger interdisciplinary foundations. As feminist scholars have argued, the best theory is characterized by its inclusiveness and its explanatory capacities; a feminist approach to the new materialisms "addresses epistemological, ontological, political, scientific, and technical issues simultaneously," argues Susan Hekman, "and most importantly . . . the interaction among them" (*The Material* 67–68). By bringing forward and exploring the inheritances and interactions among insights from all these diverse disciplinary perspectives—Buddhism, environmental literatures, cultural narratives, science studies, Indigenous studies, animal studies, environmental justice and public health activisms, feminist praxis, and more—material feminist ecocriticism promises to continue and augment the original aims of ecocriticism.

Notes

1. The Buddhist Precepts are ethical principles that a practitioner affirms both as a path of moral conduct and as a foundation for spiritual practice. Lay practitioners live by the basic morality offered in the first five precepts with vows to abstain from taking life (nonharming), taking that which is not given (theft), sexual misconduct (rape and other sexual violations), wrong speech (for example, slander, lies, gossip), and intoxicants (originally defined as drugs and alcohol, later expanded to include any compulsive behaviors that encourage mindless delusion).

2. In this short space it is not possible to do justice to the concept of dependent origination. I point the interested reader toward internet sources such as http://www.buddhanet.net/, periodicals such as *Buddhadharma,* and the International Network of Engaged Buddhists at http://www.inebnetwork.org/.

3. In defining "shallow posthumanism" as perspectives that discuss human-animal intra-actions for the purposes of scholarship and "deep posthumanism" as perspectives that explore human and more-than-human intra-actions with the commitment to bring about transspecies justice, I am indebted to the distinction between "shallow" or "light-green" ecology and deep ecology as defined in the environmental ethics discourse of the 1980s.

4. Other animal species, plants, and insects may experience pain and suffering as well—we know that; to the best of their abilities, they move away from or repel predators, suggesting that they do not want to become food for other beings, but rather prefer to be subjects of their own lives. Science continues to accumulate evidence about the experiences of other life-forms, and we may not have all the evidence needed to make ethical decisions ensuring that our own actions do not produce unnecessary pain and suffering for others. What we can do is to move as far as possible in a moral *direction,* although we may not have the information, skills, or circumstances necessary to achieve a moral *destination* (see Curtin).

Afterword
The Commonwealth of Breath

David Abram

Gusting the tops of small waves, a wind carrying salt spray collides with another thick with tree pollen; edges of both merge with a breeze plucking lichen spores from the surface of rocks as it rides up the hill where I sit, high above the coast, gazing at a far-off tanker filled with tar sands crude. Behind me another breeze lingers at the forest edge, spiced by truck exhaust and the reek from two oyster shells broken open by a raven. I breathe in, and all those unseen currents converge, pollen and petrol fumes flooding up through my nostrils (tweaking dendrites and spreading twangs of sensation along my scalp) and then down into my chest, charging my blood and feeding the vigor in my limbs. I stretch, shoulder muscles cracking, and then exhale. The feelings sparked by the sight of that tanker lend their tremor to the breath pouring out through my lips: wonder and worry texture the small vortices in front of me and the eddying flows that rush past me, informing the interference patterns between my exhalations and those of the tall cedars and the mist rising from the Salish Sea.

* * *

What is climate change if not a consequence of failing to respect or even to notice the elemental medium in which we are immersed? Is not global warming, or global weirding, a simple consequence of taking the air for granted?

It is easy, you might say, to overlook something that is invisible. We do not commonly notice our breathing, although it enables all that we do notice. And we do not commonly see the air, since it is that through which we see everything else. The atmosphere cannot be grasped or grabbed hold of and is hopelessly unpredictable—an ever-shifting flux that we are generally unable to lay eyes on. The unseen quality of the air is what prompted so many traditional peoples to pay surpassing respect to this medium, acknowledging the breath and the gusting wind as aspects of an especially sacred power, a ubiquitous and meaning-filled plenum in which they found themselves immersed.

Yet in the modern era, it is that same invisibility that led us to take the air for granted; since we could not see it, perhaps there was nothing of consequence there. We ceased speaking to the unseen spirits that gathered near rivers or lingered near certain herbs. We stopped feeling for the invisible qualities that reside in particular places. We quit tasting the breeze, stopped noticing the steady gift of our breath, and generally forgot the air. Even today, we rarely acknowledge the local presence of the atmosphere as it rests or swirls between two persons. We do not speak of the air between our body and a nearby tree, but rather speak of the empty space between us. It is empty. Just an absence of stuff, without feeling or meaning. A void.

And hence, a perfect place to throw whatever we hope to a-void. The perfect dump site for the unwanted by-products of our industries, for the noxious brew of chemicals exhaled from the stacks of our factories and power plants and refineries, and the stinging exhaust belching forth from our fossil-fueled vehicles—spewing from automobiles and airplanes, cruise ships and tug boats and giant tankers lugging thick tar sands oil to be processed in foreign ports. Even the most opaque, acrid smoke billowing out of the pipes will dissipate and disperse, always and ultimately dissolving into the invisible. It is gone. Out of sight, out of mind.

* * *

Mind—or consciousness, or awareness[1]—is a strangely amorphous and mercurial phenomenon, one that is mighty tough to pin down. Gobs of scientific papers and books have been published in recent years trying to account for the emergence of awareness, or to explain how consciousness is constituted within the brain. Many of these works are dramatically at odds with one another, for there exists no clear agreement as to just what this enigma that we call "consciousness" actually *is*.

Part of the difficulty stems from the intransigence of old notions, in particular our age-old assumption that mind is a uniquely human property, an utterly intangible substance that resides somewhere "inside" each of us. A problematic assumption. Given the blithe obliviousness with which we shove other species over the brink of extinction, and our ready capacity to wreak havoc upon ecosystems utterly essential to our own flourishing, it may be that a bit of humility is in order. We may not be quite as conscious as we have thought. At this broken moment in the human story, when the continued survival not only of our kind but of much of our world is in question, it may be that a fresh conception, or image, of mind is in order. An image that has a sort of wisdom built right into it.

Curiously, our experience of awareness—this amorphous and ephemeral power—has much in common with our felt experience of earth's atmosphere. Consider the air, the light-filled and fluid element in which you are now immersed, with its agitations and its calms, its storms and its subsidences. Consider the unseen currents drifting between the soils and the scudding clouds and circulating among us wherever we find ourselves, pouring in through the door and eddying along the walls, streaming in at your nostrils and circulating within you as well. Like the quality of awareness, the fluid air constantly informs us, yet it is exceedingly difficult to catch sight of. We glimpse the air only indirectly, as it bends the branches of a birch tree, or slants the rain, or steals a page from our fingers and sends it flapping down the street. If we are approaching a large city from a distance during the summer, we may notice the tinted miasma of smog thickening around it, although as soon as we are inside that effluvium, it has vanished once again. We drink the air ceaselessly, alchemizing it within our flesh and replenishing it with every outbreath, yet seem unable to fully bring it to our attention. Itself invisible, the atmosphere is that *through which* we see everything else—much as consciousness, which we cannot see or grasp, is that *through which* we encounter all other phenomena. We are unable to step apart from awareness, in order to examine it objectively, for wherever we step, it is already there.

Mind, in this sense, is very much like a medium in which we are corporeally situated and from which we are simply unable to extricate ourselves without ceasing to exist. Everything we know or sense of ourselves is conditioned by this atmosphere. We are intimately acquainted with its character, endlessly transformed by its influence upon us. And yet we are unable to characterize this medium from outside. We are composed of this curious element, permeated by it, and hence can take no real distance from it.

To acknowledge this affinity between air and awareness is to allow this curious possibility: that the awareness that stirs within each of us is continuous with the wider awareness that moves around us, twisting the grasses and lofting the crows. Each organism partakes of this awareness from its own unique angle or situation within it, imbibing it through our nostrils or through the stomata in our leaves, altering its chemistry and quality within us before we breathe it back into the surrounding world.

Is consciousness really the special possession of our species? Or is it, rather, a property of the breathing biosphere—a quality in which we, along with the woodpeckers and the spreading weeds, all participate? Perhaps the apparent "interiority" we ascribe to the mind has less to do with a separate consciousness located somewhere *inside me* and another entirely separate and distinct consciousness that sits *inside you* and more to do with the intuition that we are both situated *within it*—a recognition that we are carnally immersed in an awareness that is not, properly speaking, ours, but is rather the earth's.[2]

* * *

Among the Inuit and Yupik peoples inhabiting the circumpolar Arctic, the enigma is named *Sila*. There are variants in local dialects: *Hila, Hla, Shla, Sla, Tla*. All voice the same mystery, most commonly called *Sila*: the wind-mind of the world, source of all breath. *Sila* is the elemental wonder of the air, and of the winds that stir and sometimes surge within it, of storm and mist and every other kind of weather, but also: *awareness, consciousness.*

Silarjuaq: that which has no creator; constant flux and change; mind at large. *Silatuniq:* wisdom. Both from *Sila:* the intelligence of the air, the mind of the cycling seasons and the weather (Jaypeetee Arnakak, in Leduc 26–31). The great indweller in the air, *Sila* is the source of all breath, of all life, of all awareness. Awairness. Wind-mind.

In the early 1920s, an old Inuit *angakoq* (or shaman) named Najagneq spoke with the Danish explorer Knud Rasmussen. His words were translated by Rasmussen into Danish and then by others into English. Najagneq spoke of

> a power that we call *Sila*, that cannot be explained in simple words. A great spirit sustaining the world and the weather and all life on earth, a spirit so mighty that its speech to humankind is not through common words, but through storms and snow and rainfall and the fury of the sea; all the forces of nature that men fear. But it has also another means of utterance, through sunlight and calm seas and through small children innocently at play, understanding nothing. Children hear a soft and gentle voice, almost like that of a woman. It comes to them in a mysterious way, but so gently that they are not afraid; they only hear that some danger threatens.... When times are good, *Sila* has nothing to say to humankind, but withdraws into its endless nothingness, where it remains as long as people do not abuse life and act with respect toward the animals that are their food. No one has ever seen *Sila;* its place is a mystery, at once intimately among us and unspeakably far away. (Merkur 46; see also Leduc 21–22)[3]

Rasmussen's written records and many more recent ethnographies make evident the importance, for the Inuit, of another, more intimate, power: the "breath-soul," or *inua,* that indwells each living being, providing life and awareness to humans, animals, and plants. A person's breath-soul, however, is simply her part of the wider mind of the wind, since *Sila,* the sensibility in the air, subsumes all individual *inua,* or breath-souls, within itself:

> *Sila* is the life-giving element, which enfolds all the world and invests all living organisms.... *Sila* is the word for air, without air there is no life; air is in all people and all creatures.... Every individual is said to have as part of his soul the life force, the life-giving spirit, which is part of the whole animating force *Silap Inua* [the Indweller in the Wind]. This is of course something which never dies, air and the life-giving force go on indefinitely, and so then does the soul of man. When the air passes out of the body at the moment of physical death, it is simply the passing of the soul back into its original matrix. (Williamson 22–23)

This old, circumpolar understanding neatly unties the modern philosophical knot conventionally known as "the mind-body problem"—the puzzle of how a purely immaterial mind, or consciousness, interacts with (or is generated by) a thoroughly material body. To the Inuit, consciousness may be invisible and ineffable, but it is hardly immaterial; it is, rather, the sentience of the unseen but nonetheless palpable element *in which we participate with the whole of our breathing bodies.* The sun-infused air is our common medium, a broad intelligence that we share with the other animals and the plants and the forested mountains, yet each of us engages it with the particularities of our own flesh. And since your body is different from mine in many ways, so your experience of awareness—your interface and exchange with the common medium—is necessarily richly different from mine. The still more contrasting experience of a praying mantis or that of a pileated woodpecker—or of a field of wild lupines, for that matter—is as curiously different from our experience as their *bodies* are different from ours. Each being's awareness is unique, to be sure, yet this is not because an autonomous mind is held inside its particular body or brain. Rather, each engages the common awareness from its own extraordinary angle, through its particular senses, according to the capacities of its flesh. And hence even as it affirms our participation in a unitary medium, this oddly immanent, elemental understanding of mind entails a radical and irreducible pluralism.

* * *

Such an elegant conception, if taken seriously, opens a range of previously unsuspected insights into the contemporary climate predicament. Yet this perspective, at once strangely new and startlingly old, is hardly unique to the indigenous traditions of the Far North. After a long season spent teaching, and learning, on the northwestern coast of North America, I have just this week returned to my home in the southwestern desert, reacquainting myself with the sunrise hues of sandstone and the scents of juniper and sage. The sunsets in this realm have been unusually lurid of late, due to the smoke from the largest wildfires in the recorded history of New Mexico, Arizona, and Texas; in the past two years, much of the terrain has been coated over and again with ash falling from the skies. Here in this broad bioregion, there flourish an array of Native cultures, speaking languages from at least five unrelated language families, each of which practices its own intensely respectful relation to the unseen (yet increasingly evident) atmosphere.

Among the Dineh (or Navajo) people, the encompassing and fluid power that grants all beings life, movement, and awareness is called *Nilch'i*, the Holy Wind. *Nilch'i* is the whole body of the air, or atmosphere, including those parts of the air in motion and those at rest; it is the medium through which all beings (mountains, coyotes, cottonwood trees, owls) communicate with one another. The sacred nature of the Holy Wind resides not merely in our thorough dependence upon it, but in its subtlety and invisibility: we witness it only by means of the visible things that it animates. There exist innumerable local winds, breezes, storms, gusts, and whiffs that stir within the broad body of the Holy Wind, including the winds that dwell and circulate within each of us. The individual "wind within one" was long misunderstood by anthropologists, who assumed that it referred to an autonomous spirit, or soul, akin to the personal soul of Christian belief. These interpreters failed to recognize that, for the Navajo, the "wind within one" was continuous with the enveloping wind at large—that the wind circulating within each person was informed by the wider wind that sweeps the desert grasses. Similarly, the two little winds, called "wind's children," that linger in the spiraling folds of a person's ears, often whispering worded insights to her as she goes about her days, these, as well, are just a part of the expansive body of Holy Wind. For the Navajo, in other words, the very thoughts that we hear churning within our heads are spoken by small whirlwinds, or eddies, within the vast transparence of *Nilch'i*, the fluid wind-mind of the world.[4]

Within this rich cosmology, the different qualities of the various gusts, gales, whirlwinds, crosscurrents, blasts, and breezes that roll across the desert are recognized in the diverse names by which they are invoked: Dawn Man, Sky Blue Woman, Twilight Man, Dark Wind, Wind's Child, Revolving Wind, Glossy Wind, Rolling Darkness Wind, and many others. The Navajo distinguish unpredictable winds and steady winds, harmful winds and helpful winds. Each person must navigate among these invisible influences with great care, striving to bring her life into *hozho*—dynamic balance and beauty—with these immersive powers.

Nor are humans purely passive with respect to the Holy Wind. Like the mountains in the four directions, like the plants and the other animals, human persons are one of the Wind's dwelling places, one of its many centers, and just as we are nourished and influenced by the air at large, so our thoughts and our actions affect the air in turn. Human will can most effectively alter the world around us through the power of spoken utterance, through oral prayer and chanted song, which resonate and transform the very texture of the surrounding wind. Hence, among the Navajo, abundant energy and artistry are given to ceremonies like the Blessingway, wherein persons invoke and project *hozho* into the enveloping atmosphere through a ritual cycle of songs. At the conclusion of any such ceremony, the participants breathe the renewed *hozho* back into their lungs, making themselves a part of the harmony, order, and beauty that they have just established in the ambient medium through the power of the chant (Witherspoon 61). The relation between the Navajo people and the animate cosmos that enfolds and includes them is participatory and reciprocal; they are not just passive recipients of Wind's influence, but instead are both passive and active, inhaling and exhaling, receiving the nourishment of the myriad beings and actively nourishing them in turn.

Meanwhile, among the diverse pueblo cultures (including the Hopi of Arizona and the many pueblo villages of northern New Mexico), another emphasis predominates: the preciousness of life-giving rain within this high-desert realm.

Whenever a person from the pueblo dies, her vapor essence is felt to journey across the land to the dwelling place of the *kachinas*—the spirit ancestors. The *kachinas* are regularly "fed" by the respectful actions of those who are alive, as well as by the seasonal ceremonies, the resplendent dances and prayer offerings undertaken throughout the yearly cycle by the villagers. The spirit ancestors, feeling thus honored, return to their respective pueblos whenever they choose: they gather and thicken within the sky's transparence, materializing as clouds carrying and bodying forth the rain essential for the corn and the other crops upon which the people depend. In the pueblo cosmologies, death brings into existence the ancestors, who return as rain-bearing clouds fertilizing the soil with water. The moisture feeds the corn that, in turn, nourishes the living. Human life and human death are here an integral part of the hydrological cycle. As the people depend upon the climate, so, reciprocally, the climate is dependent upon the people for its continued flourishing.

I shudder to speak of matters held so sacred to these oral traditions, and even more so to *write* of these understandings, which were never meant to be written down. Much as I tremble to speak aloud the most sacred name of the Holy in my own tribal, Jewish tradition, the four-letter name that—rightly spoken—is not other than the inhale and the exhale, the living breath of awareness. Such traditions emerge in the intra-action between specific cultures and the multiple material agencies that engage, inform, and surge through those communities; they are traditions of storied matter, of animate elemental materials shaping and being shaped by humankind, and storying itself *through* humankind, born of the intimacy between particular peoples and places. And so I ask the blessing of my ancestors, feeling them in the unseen *ruach* (the Hebrew term for the *divine wind,* or "rushing spirit") that surrounds me, here in the high desert, as I write. I bow to the various peoples indigenous to this region where I dwell, as well as to the animals, plants, and spirits of this parched terrain, asking their permission that I may write, here, of these things. Because these storied knowings, of which I comprehend so little, nonetheless need to be heard once again, and what is common among them needs to be felt, acknowledged, and replenished if many species are to continue . . .

* * *

Oral cultures are cultures of story. Spoken and chanted stories were the living encyclopedias of our oral ancestors, dynamic and lyrical compendiums of practical knowledge. Preserved among the many layers of these tales (tucked within the complex adventures of their characters) were precise instructions for the gathering of specific plants and how to prepare them as foods and as medicines, directions for tracking bear or hunting caribou, and for enacting the proper rituals of gratitude when a hunt was successful. The stories carried instructions about how to fend for one's family when a prolonged drought dried up the local streams or—more generally—how to live well in a specific land without destroying the land's wild vitality.

Such practical intelligence, intimately related to a particular bioregion, is the hallmark of any deeply oral culture. Continually tested in interaction with the living land, altering in tandem with subtle changes in the local earth, even today such living knowledge resists the fixity and permanence of the printed page. Nor does it come across when printed or displayed on the electronic screen, whose disembodying sheen and glide ensure that the place-based secrets hidden within each tale will be lost in the digital tide, as the story loses its analog grip on a particular soil. Because it is specific to the way things happen *here,* in this high desert—or coastal estuary, or mountain forest—this kind of intimate intelligence loses much of its meaning when abstracted from its terrain and from the particular animals, plants, and practices that are a part of its life. Such intelligence, properly speaking, is an expression of the living land itself; it thrives only in the direct, face-to-face interchange between those who dwell and work in that place.

The primacy of breath in oral traditions—the identification of awareness with the unseen air and the consequent sacredness accorded to the invisible medium in which we and the other creatures are bodily immersed—has been for most human cultures a simple and obvious intuition, though interpreted, storied, and ritualized in divergent ways by different peoples in different bioregions. The intuition is compelled by the centrality of the spoken (rather than written) word in indigenous lifeways; for traditionally oral cultures, verbal language is not, primarily, a visible set of static marks, but rather an utterance carried on the exhaled breath. *Words, here, are nothing other than shaped breath.* Hence, the fluid air is the implicit intermediary in all communication, the very medium of meaning.[5]

* * *

"The media" is the phrase we use, today, to name our various forms of widespread communication. Yet all of our many media—whether written, electronic, or digital—derive from the original *medium* of communication: the unseen air that once transmitted all our songs and spoken stories as it carried the whistling of blackbirds and the gurgled utterances of frogs, bearing lichen spores and bee swarms and the exhalations of humpback whales.

Radio personnel still use the phrase "on air" or "off air" to indicate when they are broadcasting. Yet while contemporary media tacitly depend upon the fluid atmosphere, the new media all contribute to the overlooking, or forgetting, of the original medium. In this regard, our newly invented media mimic a tendency endemic to the alphabet, the invention that made them all possible.

The earliest versions of the alphabet, which arose in the ancient Near East in the second millennium BC, took care not to violate the primacy of the unseen medium that surrounds and animates all visible things. Like other early Semitic alphabets, the early Hebrew (or paleo-Hebrew) *aleph-bait* avoided inscribing the vowels upon the parchment or papyrus; in these most ancient forms of the alphabet, only the consonants were written down. The consonants, of course, are the shapes by which we sculpt our sounded breath, forming words with the tongue, lips, and teeth as we exhale. The vowels, meanwhile, are the sounds made by the breath itself as it vibrates our vocal chords and flows out through the mouth. To the ancient Hebrews, the vowels—as sounded breath—were inseparable from the *ruach*, the divine wind, a mystery whose invisibility they dared not violate. The *ruach* was the unseen but immanent presence of GD (the divine breath that the Holy One first blew into the nostrils of Adam, bringing the first human form to life). And so the Semitic scribes wrote only the consonants, the structure or skeleton of the words. Even today, the reader of a traditional Hebrew text must herself choose which vowels to pronounce between the written consonants, lending her own breath to those bones on the page in order to make them come alive and begin to speak.[6]

Phoenician traders carried the early *aleph-bait* across the Mediterranean. When the ancient Greeks encountered and adapted this Semitic invention for their own tongue, they inserted written letters to represent the vowel sounds. For the first time, the breath sounds were rendered visible and explicit on the written page. By this simple move, making a visible representation of the invisible breath, the Greek scribes effectively *desacralized* the unseen medium. They breached the older (Hebraic) taboo on imaging the invisible, effectively desanctifying the breath and the wind, making it possible for alphabetic readers to begin to overlook, or forget, the pervasive power of the air. Indeed, the sensuous interplay between the *visible* and *invisible* aspects of surrounding nature was soon replaced, in ancient Athens, by a new dichotomy between sensuous nature as a whole and another, wholly nonsensible, world hidden entirely beyond the physical. The Greek philosopher Plato, developing his new conception of an immaterial heaven of pure ideas—a dimension not just invisible, but thoroughly intangible, and hence beyond all bodily ken—was, with this conception, sanctioning a new forgetfulness of the immanent mystery of the air itself, a forgetting first made possible by the very script in which he wrote his many dialogues.[7]

With the gradual spread of the new, vowelized alphabet, and—later—with the broad dissemination of alphabetic texts made possible by the printing press, the primacy of spoken phrases that sculpt and ride the fluid air was slowly displaced by our spreading fascination with the written word. Meaning drained out of the air and became fixed on the page. Fewer and fewer people sensed their ancestors in the winds, or in the quiet stirring of leaves in a forest, since now the ancestors seemed to speak much more clearly from the *bound* leaves of books. The surrounding air, divested of awareness or psyche, lost its felt reality; it came to be felt mostly as a kind of absence, merely the hurrying of molecules, endlessly, meaninglessly.[8] And soon it was hardly felt, or noticed, at all.

* * *

Like the air, the "new media" are ubiquitous, pervasive, and ever present. With the advent of the internet and the emergence of wireless computing, the new media permeate our workspaces and our homes, suffusing the space of our cities and towns. As cellular phones, GPS, and now smartphones proliferate, digital media inform the electromagnetic spectrum throughout more and more of the countryside, infiltrating woodlands and swamps, glancing off mountain ridges, washing through even the wild backcountry. They saturate our lives. We may power off the iPhone or shut the lid on our laptop, but the information is still churning all around and even through us, ready to display itself as soon as we open whatever new handheld gadget, whatever screen-fitted thingamajig, currently accompanies us.

Omnipresent as air, seemingly *omniscient* as well, the new media perfectly deflect the atmosphere from our attention. Unlike the bothersome subjection of our animal flesh to whatever weather is brewing, we feel we have control over *these* media, able to conjure whatever data we wish onto the screen (in whatever interface we have chosen). Humans alone are online here; no other species clutter the frequencies or muddle the field with their pheromones. There is no ambiguity, nor the bother of having to expose our pimples, or render ourselves vulnerable by meeting others in the palpable world of flesh and blood. The tangible earth is getting way too weird anyway, with its fires and famines and floods, its flaring riots and refugees: better to hang out online, adrift in the cloud.

The new media grab our focus and hold our fascination, and they keep our kids occupied, too, granting us a ready vacation from the perplexity of the real, or helping us avoid it altogether.

* * *

Sooner or later, though, the media trance leaves us gasping for air. Because the ubiquitous data are all so instantaneous, so much of it instantly accessible, answers to any question right here at our fingertips and right now in our face, though we have not had a moment to digest or even chew the last meal or morsel. There is too much of it, a superfluity of information, a glut, a flood. Info on pretty much anything and everything we can think of, and mostly what we cannot, but now here it is anyway: a paragraph that is mildly relevant to the problem that my kids and I are puzzling out this afternoon, yet halfway down that paragraph a highlighted word links to another nugget of interesting knowledge attached to a video clip; the first few seconds of the segment abruptly call to mind another video I had wanted to glance at last week but forgot, regarding the luscious mating ritual of hermaphroditic leopard slugs, so I try to find it now on YouTube or Vimeo but get snagged by someone's TEDtalk about a new app for mapping gender inequality across countries and cultures. All these images, all this text, all this digital data churning past thick as flies, dense as fog, viscous as syrup laced with cornstarch and captions, mucilaginous, and we are in the thick of it, mouths wide open, glugging.

Hence the need for air. For a bit of breathing space. For a chance to breathe.

* * *

A filter would be useful, some way of standing and taking our bearings in the midst of this tide that keeps rising. A way of remembering what is primary, and catching our breath, letting our digital encounters dissolve back into the spacious quietude, an open silence broken only now and then by the sigh of the wind through the tall grasses. There is a need for depth, for possibilities that beckon from afar, for enigmas that reside in the distance. Or rather for some things that are close by and accessible while others wait in the far-off hills and still others roam the middle space between these, foraging among the stones at the edge of the creek. There is a need for distances that we feel and sometimes commit ourselves to crossing—giving our muscles to the slow, patient craft of making our way through the palpable depths of the sensuous.

* * *

The oncoming storms of climate change, the never-before-seen winds tossing down power lines and ripping out trees by their roots, the thudding torrents of rain in some regions and the unbroken heat cracking the soil in others are all a consequence of our long forgetfulness. Of our forgetting the invisible, taking for granted what we could not see. We overlooked that element held most Holy by our oral ancestors, the unseen flux long assumed to be the very source of all awareness, wind-mind of the world: the Commonwealth of Breath.

The swelling storms are a simple consequence of treating the atmosphere as an open sewer, a magic dump site for whatever we wished to avoid. *Out of sight, out of mind . . .* Or so we thought.

But for our oral elders and ancestors, that which dissipates as smoke or dissolves into the unseen air is by that very process slipping *into the mind, binding itself back into the encompassing awareness from which our bodies steadily drink, the wild sentience of the world, moody with weather . . .* [9]

* * *

We renew our participation in the more-than-human community—in the breathing commons—by telling stories. Not, however, stories that we print in books or post on glowing screens, or send out as podcasts. Stories, rather, that we tell *aloud,* face to face, sharing the same air with those who listen and offer a tale in return. Not just tales that have been written, or recorded, and hence abstracted from the whisper and singsong and push-pull of the local earth where they once drew their relevance. Stories, rather, that hold sway in particular places, carrying in their textures and rhythms something of the relation between humans and the other animals, herbs, waters, woodlands, and weather patterns that compose the cycling life of the land we inhabit.

Scholars, philosophers, and authors attentive to material ecocriticism and the other emerging discourses in which the vibrance and eloquence of material things are reasserting themselves have much necessary work to do, disclosing the manifold ways that ostensibly human narratives arise from our ongoing corporeal interchange with various other bodies and fluid trajectories—with other material agencies that express themselves to, and often through, our own bodily materiality, speaking through our actions, our technologies, our creative endeavors. But material ecocritics should consider resisting the instinctive academic impulse to write down or record every single one of their findings; they should consider withholding a few of their crucial discoveries from the page and the glowing screen, in order to let those insights dwell in their particular places, in order to shape them on the breath between their body and breathing terrain. Writing is an astonishing magic, but one that is best used judiciously, because it tends to shut out other beings that do not speak in words.[10] As long as we humans communicate mostly via these more mediated modes of interchange, as long as face-to-face oral culture remains dormant, then the human collective will likely stay somewhat impervious to the full presence of these palpable others.

Writing matters down easily interrupts our felt rapport with other earthly beings, as it involves transcribing our ongoing exchange with the many-voiced cosmos into an almost exclusively human register. We translate our dialogues with wind and pelting rain, with petrochemicals, genetically altered insects, and melting glaciers, into a discursive space that nonetheless remains largely closed to other species, impenetrable to other shapes of sentience. We maintain the pretense that humans alone can make sense of what is happening; even as we critique it, we reinscribe our aloofness from the animate, expressive earth.

Of course, our body remains participant in countless conversations that cannot be translated into words. Such corporeal exchanges *can,* however, find their way into tales and tellings that involve our whole speaking and gesturing organism; when we engage in such oral storytelling, the other beings in the sensorial vicinity—whether humans or flapping crows, whether the termite-riddled trunk of an old oak or the collapsed ruin of an old factory—can readily register (and perhaps even *feel)* something of what is being said, since our speaking has its own material rhythm and pulse, since our creaturely body is caught up in the awkward dance of the thing we are saying. And so other expressive bodies—coyotes howling, a squeaking bicycle, streamwater gushing through culverts or rolling over the guttural stones—can enter into and alter the story in the present moment of its telling.

By listening for such tales, and beginning to tell them aloud out in the terrain, in the very place where their events might have happened (whether in a backcountry stand of tall cedars or among the toxic slurry ponds left by an abandoned mine), we begin to rejuvenate oral culture (see Abram, *Becoming* 259–92). By sharing such tales as we replant a clear-cut forest, by improvising a fresh ballad out of the struggle to block a tar sands pipeline or to halt the spread of hydraulic fracking, we bring our sounding bodies back into resonance with the other beings that surround. And as we weave such stories, aloud, into the craft of gathering herbs or raising kids in that land, we begin to bind human language back into a much wider conversation. *Only when we wakefully meet one another in the palpable flesh of our common materiality are we really challenged out of the collective stupor of our abstraction from the real.* By turning off our screens, now and then, to come together in the tangible, by camping out en masse on a city square exposed to the weather, by gathering along a river to honor the cyclical return of the salmon, or telling a tale of the migrating cranes as they flap their way north above our upturned faces, we bring our spinning minds back into alignment with the broad intelligence of the biosphere.

The feathered wings of those cranes paddle *through* the invisible, as their echoing cries stutter down through the vast silence. Our animal senses awaken; we remember the primacy of the sensuous cosmos that reigns underneath all our theories. The breathing earth articulates itself not in statistics but in seedpods and storms and spoken stories. Listening, shaping a phrase on the wind, falling silent . . . in this way, we reacquaint ourselves with our real community and orient ourselves to meet the clouds massing in the distance. The land's awareness slides easily in and out of our nostrils. We reclaim our membership in the Commonwealth of Breath.

Notes

1. I use these terms, here, in their broadest sense, including within their meaning not just focused awareness (or full *waking* consciousness), but simple sensibility or sentience.

2. Of course, from the perspective of salmon, sea lions, and kelp fronds, or the divergent angle of humpbacks trading their eerie arpeggios across the fathoms, it is not *air* but rather the fluid medium of *water* that carries the glimmering quality of awareness, altering its modes and moods with the tides, hiding uncountable feeling tones within its depths—sensations that sometimes blossom out of the thickness to surround and seep into and become one's being for

a time. Yet how uncanny, how weirdly different, must be *water* from *air* when one inhabits it as one's element and medium! "Nothing of him that doth fade, But doth suffer a sea-change, into something rich and strange" (Shakespeare, *The Tempest*).

3. The English translation of Rasmussen's notes, written in Danish, varies slightly across these and other texts.

4. See McNeley, *Holy Wind in Navajo Philosophy*. This book is the fruit of twenty years of close association with the Navajo. The author is married to a Dineh woman, Grace McNeley; both of them taught for many years at Shiprock on the Navajo Reservation in Arizona. See also Abram, *The Spell* 230–37.

5. If you doubt the ubiquity of this notion, ponder for a moment the etymology of the common English words "spirit" (from Latin *spiritus*: a breath, or a gust of wind) and "psyche" (from the ancient Greek verb *psychein*: to breathe or to blow, as a wind). Consider the Latin word for the soul, *anima* (from the older Greek *anemos*, meaning wind), from whence derive such terms as "animal" (an ensouled being) and "unanimous" (being of one mind). Or consider the term "atmosphere," from the Greek *atmos* (vapor), itself cognate with the Sanskrit word *atman*, which signifies the soul (whether of the cosmos or of a person). Analogous associations are found in many other languages. Such etymologies offer no proof, yet they suggest that the common notion of mind as an entirely immaterial and nonsensuous dimension has been derived, by a gradual process of abstraction, from our ancestrally felt sense of the invisible but nonetheless tangible medium in which we found ourselves materially immersed and participant.

6. Traditional Hebraic spirituality was both literate and oral at the same time. The Hebrew scribes and priests were literate in their relation to the visible cosmos, insisting that GD could not be found in the visible things of the world. But by avoiding writing down the vowels, they preserved an intensely oral, animistic relation to the invisible air, wind, and breath—to the unseen medium that moves between and binds all visible things.

7. For carefully documented evidence for this claim, see the chapters "Animism and the Alphabet" and "The Forgetting and Remembering of the Air" in Abram, *The Spell* 93–135 and 225–60.

8. A paraphrase of Alfred North Whitehead, who described the scientific conception of nature at the end of the seventeenth century as "merely the hurrying of material, endlessly, meaninglessly" (*Science* 69).

9. From this angle, climate change is not much different from what Sigmund Freud called "the return of the repressed"—the violent resurgence of a prominent dimension of our experience that has long been hidden, or eclipsed, from our collective consciousness.

10. See Isabelle Stengers on my work and on the difference between writing and writing down, in "Reclaiming Animism" and "Reclaiming the Pharmakon." See also Abram, *The Spell* 93–179.

Works Cited

Abram, David. *Becoming Animal: An Earthly Cosmology.* New York: Pantheon, 2010.
———. *The Spell of the Sensuous: Perception and Language in a More-than-Human World.* New York: Pantheon, 1996.
Adamson, Joni. *American Indian Literature, Environmental Justice, and Ecocriticism: The Middle Place.* Tucson: University of Arizona Press, 2001.
———. "Cosmovisions: Environmental Justice, Transnational American Studies, and Indigenous Literature." *The Oxford Handbook of Ecocriticism.* Ed. Greg Garrard. Oxford: Oxford University Press, forthcoming.
———. "Indigenous Literatures, Multinaturalism, and *Avatar*: The Emergence of Indigenous Cosmopolitics." *Sustainability in America.* Spec. issue of *American Literary History* 24.1 (Spring 2012): 143–67.
———. "'¡Todos Somos Indios!': Revolutionary Imagination, Alternative Modernity, and Transnational Organizing in the Work of Silko, Tamez, and Anzaldúa." *Journal of Transnational American Studies* 4.1 (May 2012): 1–26.
Adamson, Joni, and Scott Slovic. "The Shoulders We Stand On: An Introduction to Ethnicity and Ecocriticism; Guest Editors' Introduction." *MELUS* 34.2 (Spring 2009): 5–24.
Agamben, Giorgio. *Homo Sacer: Sovereign Power and Bare Life.* 1995. Trans. Daniel Heller-Roazen. Stanford: Stanford University Press, 1998.
———. *Ninfe.* Turin: Bollati Boringhieri, 2007.
———. *The Open: Man and Animal.* Trans. Kevin Attell. Stanford: Stanford University Press, 2004.
The Age of Stupid. Dir. Franny Armstrong. Spanner Films, 2009. Dogwoof Pictures.
Alaimo, Stacy. *Bodily Natures: Science, Environment, and the Material Self.* Bloomington: Indiana University Press, 2010.
———. "Dispersing Disaster: The *Deepwater Horizon*, Ocean Conservation, and the Immateriality of Aliens." *Disasters, Environmentalism, and Knowledge.* Ed. Sylvia Mayer and Christof Mauch. Heidelberg: Bavarian American Academy, Universitätsverlag, 2012. 175–92.
———. "Feminist Science Studies: Aesthetics and Entanglement in the Deep Sea." *The Oxford Handbook of Ecocriticism.* Ed. Greg Garrard. Oxford: Oxford University Press, forthcoming.
———. "States of Suspension: Trans-corporeality at Sea." *Material Ecocriticism.* Ed. Heather Sullivan and Dana Phillips. Spec. issue of *ISLE* 19.3 (Summer 2012): 476–93.
———. "Trans-corporeal Feminisms and the Ethical Space of Nature." *Material Feminisms.* Ed. Stacy Alaimo and Susan Hekman. Bloomington: Indiana University Press, 2008. 237–64.
Alaimo, Stacy, and Susan Hekman, eds. "Introduction: Emerging Models of Materiality in Feminist Theory." *Material Feminisms.* Ed. Stacy Alaimo and Susan Hekman. Bloomington: Indiana University Press, 2008. 1–19.

———. *Material Feminisms*. Bloomington: Indiana University Press, 2008.
Albrile, Ezio. "Hermetica Italica." *Archaeus: Studies in the History of Religions* 14 (2010): 245–64.
Ammons, A. R. *Garbage*. New York: W. W. Norton, 1993.
Anderson, Myrdene, John Deely, Martin Krampen, Joseph Ransdell, and Thomas A. Sebeok. "A Semiotic Perspective on the Sciences: Steps toward a New Paradigm." *Semiotica* 44 (1984): 7–47.
Anderson, Warwick. "Excremental Colonialism: Public Health and the Poetics of Pollution." *Critical Inquiry* 21.3 (Spring 1995): 640–69.
Armiero, Marco. "Seeing Like a Protester: Nature, Power, and Environmental Struggles." *Left History* 13.1 (2008): 59–76.
Armiero, Marco, and Giacomo D'Alisa. "Rights of Resistance: Struggling for Ecological Democracy in the 21st Century." *Capitalism Nature Socialism* 23.4 (2012): 52–68.
Atkin, Albert. "Peirce's Final Account of Signs and Contemporary Philosophy of Language." *Transactions of the Charles S. Peirce Society* 44.1 (2008): 63–85.
Augustine. *De Doctrina Christiana*. Ed. R. P. H. Green. Oxford: Oxford University Press, 1996.
Avatar. Screenplay by James Cameron. Dir. James Cameron. Perf. Sam Worthington, Zoe Saldana, Sigourney Weaver. Twentieth Century Fox Film Corporation, 2009.
Barad, Karen. "Interview with Karen Barad." *New Materialism: Interviews and Cartographies*. By Rick Dolphijn and Iris van der Tuin. Ann Arbor, Mich.: Open Humanities Press, 2012. 48–70.
———. *Meeting the Universe Halfway: Quantum Physics and the Entanglement of Matter and Meaning*. Durham, N.C.: Duke University Press, 2007.
———. "Posthumanist Performativity: Toward an Understanding of How Matter Comes to Matter." *Material Feminisms*. Ed. Stacy Alaimo and Susan Hekman. Bloomington: Indiana University Press, 2008. 120–54.
———. "Re(con)figuring Space, Time, and Matter." *Feminist Locations: Global and Local, Theory and Practice*. Ed. Marianne DeKoven. New Brunswick, N.J.: Rutgers University Press, 2001. 75–109.
Barkow, Jerome H., Leda Cosmides, and John Tooby. *The Adapted Mind: Evolutionary Psychology and the Generation of Culture*. New York: Oxford University Press, 1992.
Barthes, Roland. *Camera Lucida: Reflections on Photography*. Trans. Richard Howard. New York: Hill & Wang, 1981.
Bateson, Gregory. *Mind and Nature: A Necessary Unity*. New York: E. P. Dutton, 1979.
———. *Steps to an Ecology of Mind*. Chicago: University of Chicago Press, 2000.
Bateson, Gregory, and Mary Catherine Bateson. *Angels Fear: Towards an Epistemology of the Sacred*. Toronto: Bantam Books, 1988.
Beard, Mary. *Pompeii: The Life of a Roman Town*. London: Profile Books, 2008.
Beck, Ulrich. *Risk Society: Towards a New Modernity*. Trans. Mark Ritter. London: Sage, 1992.
Beckett, Samuel. "Dante... Bruno. Vico.. Joyce." *The Samuel Beckett Reader: I Can't Go on, I'll Go On*. Ed. Richard W. Seaver. New York: Grove, 1976.
Bellarsi, Franca. "Ecospirit: Religion and the Environment." *Ecozon@* 2.2 (2011): 1–16. Web. 3 Mar. 2012.

Benadusi, Lorenzo. *Il nemico dell'uomo nuovo: L'omosessualità nell'esperimento totalitario fascista*. Milan: Feltrinelli, 2005.
Benjamin, Alison, and Brian McCallum. *A World without Bees*. New York: Pegasus Books, 2009.
Benjamin, Walter, and Asia Lacis. "Napoli." T. W. Adorno, W. Benjamin, S. Kracauer, K. Löwith, A. Sohn-Rethel. *Napoli*. Ed. and trans. Enrico Donaggio. Naples: L'Ancora del Mediterraneo, 2000. 31–41.
Bennaroch, Jonas. "The Ballad of the Plastic Bag." Video. Music composed and performed by Nick Haughton. Plastic Pollution Coalition Channel, YouTube. Web. 2 Sept. 2012.
Bennett, Jane. *The Enchantment of Modern Life: Attachments, Crossings, and Ethics*. Princeton, N.J.: Princeton University Press, 2001.
———. *Vibrant Matter: A Political Ecology of Things*. Durham, N.C.: Duke University Press, 2010.
Benyus, Janine M. *Biomimicry: Innovation Inspired by Nature*. New York: Harper Perennial, 1997.
Bernier, François. *Travels in the Mogul Empire, AD 1656–1668*. Trans. Archibald Constable. 2nd ed. Delhi: S. Chand, 1968.
Bhikkhu, Santikaro. "Dhamma Walk around Songkhla Lake." *Dharma Rain: Sources of Buddhist Environmentalism*. Ed. Stephanie Kaza and Kenneth Kraft. Boston: Shambhala, 2000. 206–15.
Birch, Charles. "The Postmodern Challenge to Biology." *The Reenchantment of Science: Postmodern Proposals*. Ed. David Ray Griffin. Albany: State University of New York Press, 1988. 69–78.
Bishop, Elizabeth. "The Fish." *The Heath Anthology of American Literature*. Ed. Paul Lauter. Lexington, Ky.: D. C. Heath, 1994. 2:2258–60.
Bison Skull Pile (1870). Detroit Public Library. Wikimedia Commons. Web. 13 Aug. 2012.
Black, Maggie, and Ben Fawcett. *The Last Taboo: Opening the Door on the Global Sanitation Crisis*. London: Earthscan, 2008.
Blake, Tim. "Fission in Gabon." Web. 15 Dec. 2011.
Bogdanich, Walt, and Deborah Sontag. "Raucous Test Is a Trial of Haiti's Legal System." *New York Times* 31 Oct. 2010.
Bogost, Ian. *Alien Phenomenology; or, What Is It Like to Be a Thing?* Minneapolis: University of Minnesota Press, 2012.
Bohm, David. *On Creativity*. Ed. Lee Nichol. London: Routledge, 1998.
———. "Postmodern Science and a Postmodern World." *The Reenchantment of Science: Postmodern Proposals*. Ed. David. Ray Griffin. Albany: State University of New York Press, 1988. 57–68.
———. *Wholeness and the Implicate Order*. New York: Routledge, 1980.
Böhme, Gernot. *Für eine ökologische Naturästhetik*. Frankfurt: Suhrkamp, 1989.
Bonabeau, Eric, Marco Dorigo, and Guy Théraulaz. *Swarm Intelligence: From Natural to Artificial Systems*. Oxford: Oxford University Press, 1999.
Books on the Radio. Web. 17 Jan. 2013.
Borodale, Sean. *Bee Journal*. London: Cape Poetry, 2012.
Botkin, Daniel. *Discordant Harmonies: A New Ecology for the Twenty-First Century*. New York: Oxford University Press, 1990.

Boucher, Sandy. *Opening the Lotus: A Woman's Guide to Buddhism*. Boston: Beacon Press, 1997.
Bourgine, Paul, and John Stewart. "Autopoiesis and Cognition." *Artificial Life* 10 (2004): 327–45.
Bradford, Phillips Verner, and Harvey Blume. *Ota Benga: The Pygmy in the Zoo*. New York: St. Martin's Press, 1992.
Braidotti, Rosi. "The Politics of 'Life Itself' and New Ways of Dying." *New Materialisms: Ontology, Agency, and Politics*. Ed. Diana Coole and Samantha Frost. Durham, N.C.: Duke University Press, 2010. 201–18.
———. *Transpositions: On Nomadic Ethics*. Malden, Mass.: Polity Press, 2006.
Brayton, Dan. *Shakespeare's Ocean: An Ecocritical Examination*. Charlottesville: University Press of Virginia, 2012.
Brazier, David. *Zen Therapy: Transcending the Sorrows of the Human Mind*. New York: John Wiley & Sons, 1995.
Breitbach, Julia. "The Photo-as-Thing: Photography and Thing Theory." *European Journal of English Studies* 15.1 (Apr. 2011): 31–43.
Brett, Mark G. *Decolonizing God: The Bible in the Tides of Empire*. Sheffield: Sheffield Phoenix Press, 2008.
Brown, Bill. "Thing Theory." *Critical Inquiry* 28.1 (Autumn 2001): 1–22.
Bryant, Levi R. *The Democracy of Objects*. Ann Arbor, Mich.: Open Humanities Press, 2011.
———. "Stacy Alaimo: Porous Bodies and Transcorporeality." Blogpost. Web. 30 Oct. 2012.
Buell, Lawrence. *The Environmental Imagination: Thoreau, Nature Writing, and the Formation of American Culture*. Cambridge, Mass.: Harvard University Press, 1995.
———. *The Future of Environmental Criticism: Environmental Crisis and Literary Imagination*. Malden, Mass.: Blackwell, 2005.
Burt's Bees. "About Us." Web. 1 Nov. 2012.
Butler, Judith. *Bodies That Matter: On the Discursive Limits of "Sex."* New York: Routledge, 1993.
———. "Contingent Foundations: Feminism and the Question of 'Postmodernism.'" *Feminists Theorize the Political*. Ed. Judith Butler and Joan W. Scott. New York: Routledge, 1992.
Calbi, Maurizio, and Marilena Parlati. "Introduction." *Things*. Spec. issue of *European Journal of English Studies* 15.1 (2011): 1–5.
Cameron, James. "Hometree." *Avatar* Wiki. Web. 23 May 2012.
Capra, Fritjof. *The Hidden Connections: Integrating the Biological, Cognitive, and Social Dimensions of Life into a Science of Sustainability*. New York: Doubleday, 2002.
Carson, Rachel. *The Sea around Us*. Oxford: Oxford University Press, 1950.
Cathcart, Brian. *Rain*. London: Granta Books, 2002.
Chen, Mel Y. *Animacies: Biopolitics, Racial Mattering, and Queer Affect*. Durham, N.C.: Duke University Press, 2102.
Cheney, Jim. "Postmodern Environmental Ethics: Ethics as Bioregional Narrative." *Environmental Ethics* 11 (Summer 1989): 117–34.
Chow, Rey. "The Elusive Material, What the Dog Doesn't Understand." *New Materialisms: Ontology, Agency, and Politics*. Ed. Diana Coole and Samantha Frost. Durham, N.C.: Duke University Press 2010. 221–33.

Christiansen, Peder Voetmann. *Downward Causation: Minds, Bodies, and Matter.* Ed. Peter Bøgh Andersen, Claus Emmeche, and Niels Ole Finnemann. Aarhus, Denmark: Aarhus University Press, 2000.
Clarke, Bruce. "Autopoiesis and the Planet." *Impasses of the Post-global: Theory in the Age of Climate Change.* Ed. Henry Sussmann. Ann Arbor, Mich.: Open Humanities Press, 2012. 58–75.
Cohen, Jeffrey Jerome, ed. *Animal, Vegetable, Mineral: Ethics and Objects.* Washington, D.C.: Oliphaunt Books, 2012.
———. "Ecology's Rainbow." *Prismatic Ecology: Ecotheory beyond Green.* Ed. Jeffrey Jerome Cohen. Minneapolis: Minnesota University Press, 2014. xv–xxxv.
———, ed. *Prismatic Ecology: Ecotheory beyond Green.* Minneapolis: Minnesota University Press, 2014.
———. "Stories of Stone." *Postmedieval: A Journal of Medieval Cultural Studies* 1.1–2 (2010): 56–63.
———. "Grey." *Prismatic Ecology: Ecotheory beyond Green.* Ed. Jeffrey Jerome Cohen. Minneapolis: Minnesota University Press, 2014. 270–89.
Cohen, Jeffrey, and Lowell Duckert, eds. *Ecomaterialism.* Spec. issue of *Postmedieval: A Journal of Medieval Cultural Studies* 4.1 (2013).
———, eds. *Elemental Ecocriticism.* Forthcoming.
Coleridge, Samuel Taylor. *Coleridge's Poetry and Prose.* Ed. Nicholas Halmi, Paul Magnuson, and Raimona Modiano. New York: W. W. Norton, 2004.
———. "Kubla Khan." *Norton Anthology of English Literature.* Ed. M. H. Abrams et al. 4th ed. New York: W. W. Norton, 1979. 2:354–55.
Connolly, William E. "Materialities of Experience." *New Materialisms: Ontology, Agency, and Politics.* Ed. Diana Coole and Samantha Frost. Durham, N.C.: Duke University Press, 2010. 178–200.
Constitution of Ecuador. *Asamblea Nacional Constituyente.* Chap. 7. 19 July 2008. Web. 20 Apr. 2011.
Coole, Diana, and Samatha Frost. "Introducing the New Materialisms." *New Materialisms: Ontology, Agency, and Politics.* Ed. Diana Coole and Samantha Frost. Durham, N.C.: Duke University Press, 2010. 1–43.
———, eds. *New Materialisms: Ontology, Agency, and Politics.* Durham, N.C.: Duke University Press, 2010.
Cracking the Ocean Code. Discovery Channel, 2007. DVD.
Crocker, Holly. "'As False as Cressid': Virtue Trouble from Chaucer to Shakespeare." *Journal of Medieval and Early Modern Studies* 43.2 (2013). Forthcoming.
Cruikshank, Julie. *Do Glaciers Listen? Local Knowledge, Colonial Encounters, and Social Imagination.* Seattle: University of Washington Press, 2005.
"Cure." *The American Heritage Dictionary of the English Language.* 1981.
Curtin, Deane. "Toward an Ecological Ethic of Care." *Hypatia* 6.1 (1991): 60–74.
Dargatz, Gail Anderson. *A Recipe for Bees.* Toronto: Knopf, 1998.
Daston, Lorraine, and Gregg Mitman, eds. *Thinking with Animals: New Perspectives on Anthropomorphism.* New York: Columbia University Press, 2005.
Davies, Paul C. W. "From It to Bit." *Information and the Nature of Reality: From Physics to Metaphysics.* Ed. Niels Henrik Gregersen and Paul C. Davies. Cambridge: Cambridge University Press, 2010.
Davis, Mike. *Planet of Slums.* London: Verso, 2006.

Deacon, Terrence W. "How I Gave Up the Ghost and Learned to Love Evolution." *When Worlds Converge: What Science and Religion Tell Us about the Story of the Universe and Our Place in It.* Ed. Clifford N. Matthews, Mary Evelyn Tucker, and Philip J. Hefner. Chicago: Open Court, 2002.

———. *The Symbolic Species: The Co-evolution of Language and the Brain.* New York: W. W. Norton, 1997.

Deely, John N. *Four Ages of Understanding: The First Postmodern Survey of Philosophy from Ancient Times to the Turn of the Twenty-First Century.* Toronto: University of Toronto Press, 2001.

———. *Purely Objective Reality.* Berlin: Mouton de Gruyter, 2009.

De la Cadena, Marisol. "Indigenous Cosmopolitics in the Andes: Conceptual Reflections beyond 'Politics.'" *Cultural Anthropology* 25.2 (2010): 334–70.

De Landa, Manuel. *A Thousand Years of Nonlinear History.* New York: Zone Books, 1997.

Deleuze, Gilles. *Difference and Repetition.* Trans. Paul Patton. New York: Columbia University Press, 1995.

De Lillo, Don. *Underworld.* New York: Scribner, 1998.

DeLoughrey, Elizabeth. "Radiation Ecologies and the Wars of Light." *Modern Fiction Studies* 55.3 (Fall 2009): 468–95.

Dennett, Daniel C. *Darwin's Dangerous Idea: Evolution and the Meanings of Life.* New York: Touchstone, 1996.

Deranty, Jean-Philippe. "Rancière and Contemporary Political Ontology." *Theory and Event* 6.4 (2003). Web. 20 Nov. 2012.

Derrida, Jacques. *The Animal That Therefore I Am.* Trans. David Wills. New York: Fordham University Press, 2008.

Dew, Nicholas. *Orientalism in Louis XIV's France.* Oxford: Oxford University Press, 2009.

Dharma Voices for Animals. Web. 15 Mar. 2012.

Dimock, Wai Chee. "After Troy: Homer, Euripides, Total War." *Rethinking Tragedy.* Ed. Rita Felski. Baltimore: Johns Hopkins University Press, 2008. 66–81.

Dolphijn, Rick, and Iris van der Tuin. *New Materialism: Interviews and Cartographies.* Ann Arbor, Mich.: Open Humanities Press, 2012.

Douglas, Mary. *Purity and Danger: An Analysis of Concepts of Pollution and Taboo.* London: Routledge and Kegan Paul, 1966.

Douglas-Fairhurst, Robert. "Tragedy and Disgust." *Tragedy in Transition.* Ed. Sarah Annes Brown and Catherine Silverstone. Malden, Mass.: Blackwell, 2007. 58–77.

Duckert, Lowell. "Speaking Stones, John Muir, and a Slower (Non)Humanities." *Animal, Vegetable, Mineral: Ethics and Objects.* Ed. Jeffrey J. Cohen. Washington, D.C.: Oliphaunt Books, 2012. 273–79.

Dupré, John. "The Polygenomic Organism." *Nature after the Genome.* Ed. Sarah Parry and John Dupré. Malden, Mass.: Wiley-Blackwell, 2010. 19–31.

Eagleton, Terry. *Sweet Violence: The Idea of the Tragic.* Oxford: Blackwell, 2003.

Earle, Sylvia. *Sea Change: A Message of the Oceans.* New York: Fawcett Columbine, 1995.

———. *The World Is Blue: How Our Fate and the Oceans Are One.* Washington, D.C.: National Geographic Society, 2009.

"Ecological Buddhism: A Buddhist Response to Global Warming." Web. 10 Dec. 2012.

Edelman, Gerald. *Neural Darwinism: The Theory of Neuronal Group Selection.* New York: Basic Books, 1987.
Ehrenfeld, David. *The Arrogance of Humanism.* New York: Oxford University Press, 1978.
Einstein, Albert. *Relativity: The Special and the General Theory.* London: Penguin, 2006.
Elder, John. *Pilgrimage to Vallombrosa: From Vermont to Italy in the Footsteps of George Perkins Marsh.* Charlottesville: University Press of Virginia, 2006.
Eliot, George. "The Natural History of German Life." *Selected Essays, Poems, and Other Writings.* Ed. Antonia S. Byatt and Nicholas Warren. London: Penguin, 1990.
Elvey, Anne. "The Matter of Texts: A Material Intertextuality and Ecocritical Engagements with the Bible." *Ecocritical Theory: New European Approaches.* Ed. Axel Goodbody and Kate Rigby. Charlottesville: University Press of Virginia, 2011. 181–93.
———. *The Matter of the Text: Material Engagements between Luke and the Five Senses.* Sheffield: Sheffield Phoenix Press, 2011.
Emmeche, Claus, and Kalevi Kull, eds. *Towards a Semiotic Biology: Life Is the Action of Signs.* Singapore: World Scientific, 2011.
Epstein, Mark. *Thoughts without a Thinker: Psychotherapy from a Buddhist Perspective.* New York: Basic Books, 1995.
Ericson, Augustus William. *Among the Redwoods, 1890.* Humboldt State University Library, Arcata. Cathedral Grove. Web. 14 Aug. 2012.
Estok, Simon C. *Ecocriticism and Shakespeare: Reading Ecophobia.* New York: Palgrave Macmillan, 2011.
———. "Narrativizing Science: The Ecocritical Imagination and Ecophobia." *Configurations* 18 (Dec. 2010): 141–59.
———. "Theorizing in a Space of Ambivalent Openness: Ecocriticism and Ecophobia." *ISLE* 16.2 (Spring 2009): 203–25.
Esty, Joshua D. "Excremental Colonialism." *Contemporary Literature* 40.1 (Spring 1999): 22–59.
Farina, Almo. *Principles and Methods in Landscape Ecology: Toward a Science of Landscape.* Dordrecht: Springer, 2006.
Favareau, Donald, ed. *Essential Readings in Biosemiotics: Anthology and Commentary.* Dordrecht: Springer, 2010.
———. "Introduction: An Evolutionary History of Biosemiotics." *Essential Readings in Biosemiotics: Anthology and Commentary.* Dordrecht: Springer, 2010. 1–77.
Finke, Peter. "Die Evolutionäre Kulturökologie: Hintergründe, Prinzipien und Perspektiven einer neuen Theorie der Kultur." *Literature and Ecology.* Spec. issue of *Anglia* 124.1 (2006): 175–217.
———. "Kulturökologie."*Konzepte der Kulturwissenschaften: Theoretische Grundlagen—Ansätze—Perspektiven.* Ed. Ansgar Nünning and Vera Nünning. Stuttgart and Weimar: Metzler, 2003. 248–79.
Foer, Jonathan Safran. *Eating Animals.* New York: Little, Brown, 2009.
Foerster, Heinz von. "Cybernetics of Cybernetics." *Communication and Control in Society.* Ed. Klaus Krippendorff. New York: Gordon and Breach, 1979. 5–8.
Foester, Susan Leigh. "Movement Contagion: The Kinesthetic Impact of Performance." Online publication of University of California, International Performance and Culture Multicampus Research Group, June 2001. Web. 10 Dec. 2012.

Food and Agriculture Organization of the United Nations. *Livestock's Long Shadow: Environmental Issues and Options*. Rome: FAO, 2006.

Foucault, Michel. *The History of Sexuality*. Vol. 1. Trans. Robert Hurley. New York: Random House, 1978.

Frank, Jason. "Promiscuous Citizenship." *A Political Companion to Walt Whitman*. Ed. John Seery. Lexington: University Press of Kentucky, 2011. 155–84.

Freud, Sigmund. "The Economic Problem of Masochism." *On Metapsychology: The Theory of Psychoanalysis*. The Pelican Freud Library. London: Penguin, 1920. 11:409–26.

Fuchs, Peter. "Adressabilität als Grundbegriff der soziologischen Systemtheorie." *Soziale Systeme* 3.1 (1997): 57–79.

Fulke, William. *A Goodly Gallerye*. Ed. Theodore Hornberger. Philadelphia: American Philosophical Society, 1979.

Gablic, Suzy. "The Reenchantment of Art: Reflections on the Two Postmodernisms." *Sacred Interconnections: Postmodern Spirituality, Political Economy, and Art*. Ed. David Ray Griffin. Albany: State University of New York Press, 1990. 177–92.

Galeano, Juan Carlos. *Amazonia*. Trans. James Kimbrell and Rebecca Morgan. 2nd Spanish/English ed. Inquitos, Peru: Centro de Estudios Teológicos de la Amazonía (CETA), 2012.

———. *Folktales of the Amazon*. Trans. Rebecca Morgan and Kenneth Watson. Westport, Conn.: Libraries Unlimited, 2009.

Garrard, Greg. *Ecocriticism*. Oxford: Routledge, 2004.

———. "Nature's Cures? or, How to Police Analogies of Personal and Ecological Health." *Material Ecocriticsm*. Ed. Heather Sullivan and Dana Phillips. Spec. issue of *ISLE* 19.3 (Summer 2012): 494–514.

Garzón, Paco Calvo, and Fred Keijzer. "Adaptive Behavior, Root-Brains, and Minimal Cognition." *Adaptive Behavior* 19.3 (June 2011): 155–71.

George, Rose. *The Big Necessity: The Unmentionable World of Human Waste and Why It Matters*. New York: Henry Holt, 2008.

Ghosh, Amitav. *The Hungry Tide*. Boston: Houghton Mifflin, 2005.

Gibson, James J. *The Ecological Approach to Visual Perception*. Hillsdale, N.J.: Lawrence Erlbaum, 1986.

Giddens, Anthony. "Risk and Responsibility." *Modern Law Review* 62.1 (1999): 1–10.

Ginsberg, Alan. "Sunflower Sutra." *Norton Anthology of American Literature*. Ed. Ronald Gottesman et al. New York: W. W. Norton, 1979. 2:2405–6.

Giovannetti, Manuela, et al. "At the Root of the Wood Wide Web: Self Recognition and Non-Self Incompatibility in Mycorrhizal Networks." *Plant Signaling and Behavior* 1.1 (2006): 1–5.

Glotfelty, Cheryll. "Introduction." *The Ecocriticism Reader: Landmarks in Literary Ecology*. Ed. Glotfelty and Fromm. Athens: University of Georgia Press, 1996. xv–xxxvii.

Goethe, Johann Wolfgang. *Beiträge zur Optik: Schriften zur Farbenlehre, 1790–1807*. 2nd ed. Vol. 23. Ed. Manfred Wenzel. Frankfurt: Klassiker, 1991.

———. "Der Versuch als Vermittler von Objekt und Subjekt." *Schriften zur allgemeinen Naturlehre, Geologie und Mineralogie*. Ed. Wolf von Engelhardt and Manfred Wenzel. Frankfurt: Klassiker, 1989. 25:26–36.

———. *Zur Farbenlehre*. 1st ed. Vol. 23. Ed. Manfred Wenzel. Frankfurt: Klassiker, 1991.

Goin, Peter. *Nuclear Landscapes.* Baltimore: Johns Hopkins University Press, 1991.
———. Personal interviews with Cheryll Glotfelty. 3 Apr.–27 July 2011. Transcription of digital recording.
Goodbody, Axel, and Kate Rigby, eds. *Ecocritical Theory: New European Approaches.* Charlottesville: University Press of Virginia, 2011.
Goodman, Nelson. *Ways of Worldmaking.* Indianapolis: Hackett, 1978.
Gould, James L. "Can Honey Bees Create Cognitive Maps?" *The Cognitive Animal: Empirical and Theoretical Perspectives on Animal Cognition.* Ed. Marc Bekoff, Colin Allen, and Gordon M. Burghardt. Cambridge, MA: MIT Press, 2002. 41–46.
Greenblatt, Stephen. *The Swerve: How the World Became Modern.* New York: W. W. Norton, 2011.
Greenpeace International. "The Trash Vortex." Web. 22 Dec. 2011.
Gregersen, Niels. "The Cross of Christ in an Evolutionary World." *Dialog: A Journal of Theology* 40 (2001): 192–207.
Griffin, David Ray. "Introduction: The Reenchantment of Science." *The Reenchantment of Science: Postmodern Proposals.* Ed. David Ray Griffin. Albany: State University of New York Press, 1988. 1–46.
———. "Introduction to SUNY Series in Constructive Postmodern Thought." *Sacred Interconnections: Postmodern Spirituality, Political Economy, and Art.* Ed. David Ray Griffin. New York: State University of New York Press, 1990. ix–xii.
———. "Of Minds and Molecules: Postmodern Medicine in Psychosomatic Universe." *The Reenchantment of Science: Postmodern Proposals.* Ed. David Ray Griffin. Albany: State University of New York Press, 1988. 141–63.
———. *Whitehead's Radically Different Postmodern Philosophy: An Argument for Its Contemporary Relevance.* Albany: State University of New York Press, 2007.
Griffin, Susan. "Split Culture." *Healing the Wounds: The Promise of Ecofeminism.* Ed. Judith Plant. Philadelphia: New Society, 1989. 7–17.
Gross, Rita M. *Buddhism after Patriarchy: A Feminist History, Analysis, and Reconstruction of Buddhism.* Albany: State University of New York Press, 1993.
Guthrie, Stewart Elliott. *Faces in the Clouds: A New Theory of Religion.* Oxford: Oxford University Press, 1993.
Hacking, Ian. *Representing and Intervening: Introductory Topics in the Philosophy of Natural Science.* Cambridge: Cambridge University Press, 1983.
Hanson, Norwood Russell. *Patterns of Discovery: An Inquiry into the Conceptual Foundations of Science.* Cambridge: Cambridge University Press, 1958.
Haraway, Donna J. *The Haraway Reader.* New York: Routledge, 2004.
———. "The Promises of Monsters: A Regenerative Politics for Inappropriate/d Others." *Cultural Studies.* Ed. Lawrence Grossberg, Cary Nelson, and Paula A. Treichler. New York: Routledge, 1992. 295–337.
———. *When Species Meet.* Minneapolis: University of Minnesota Press, 2008.
Harman, Graham. *Prince of Networks: Bruno Latour and Metaphysics.* Melbourne: re.press, 2009.
Harrington, David M. "The Ecology of Human Creativity: A Psychological Perspective." *Theories of Creativity.* Ed. Mark A. Runco and Robert S. Albert. Newbury Park, Calif.: Sage, 1990. 143–96.
Harrison, Peter. *The Bible, Protestantism, and the Rise of Natural Science.* Cambridge: Cambridge University Press, 1998.

———. *The Fall of Man and the Foundations of Science*. Cambridge: Cambridge University Press, 2007.

Hart, David Bentley. "The Offering of Names: Metaphysics, Nihilism, and Analogy." *Reason and the Reasons of Faith*. By Reinhard Hütter. Ed. Paul J. Griffiths. New York: T&T Clark International, 2005.

Hartshorne, Charles. *Creative Synthesis and Philosophic Method*. La Salle, Ill.: Open Court Press, 1970.

Hawkins, Gay. "Plastic Materialities." *Political Matters: Technoscience, Democracy, and Public Life*. Ed. Bruce Braun and Sarah J. Whatmore. Minneapolis: University of Minnesota Press, 2010. 119–38.

Hayles, Katherine N. *How We Became Posthuman: Virtual Bodies in Cybernetics, Literature, and Informatics*. Chicago: University of Chicago Press, 1999.

———. *My Mother Was a Computer: Digital Subjects and Literary Texts*. Chicago: University of Chicago Press, 2005.

Heidegger, Martin. *Being and Time*. Trans. Joan Stambaugh. Albany: State University of New York Press, 1996.

———. *Introduction to Metaphysics*. Trans. Gregory Fried and Richard Polt. New Haven, Conn.: Yale University Press, 2000.

Heise, Ursula K. "Ecocriticism and the Transnational Turn in American Studies." *American Literary History* 20.1–2 (Spring–Summer 2008): 381–404.

———. *Sense of Place and Sense of Planet: The Environmental Imagination of the Global*. New York: Oxford University Press, 2008.

Hekman, Susan. "Constructing the Ballast: An Ontology for Feminism." *Material Feminisms*. Ed. Stacy Alaimo and Susan Hekman. Bloomington: Indiana University Press, 2008. 85–119.

———. *The Material of Knowledge: Feminist Disclosures*. Bloomington: Indiana University Press, 2010.

Helmreich, Stefan. *Alien Ocean: Anthropological Voyages in Microbial Seas*. Berkeley: University of California Press, 2009.

———. "Human Nature at Sea." *AnthroNow* 2.3 (Dec. 2010): 49–60.

Heninger, S. K., Jr. *A Handbook of Renaissance Meteorology: With Particular Reference to Elizabethan and Jacobean Literature*. Durham, N.C.: Duke University Press, 1960.

Henry, Mickaël, Maxine Béguin, Fabrice Requier, Orianne Rolin, Jean-François Odoux, Pierrick Aupinel, Jean Aptel, Sylvie Tchamitchian, and Axel Decourtye. "A Common Pesticide Decreased Foraging Success and Survival in Honey Bees." *Science* 336.20 (Apr. 2012): 348–50.

Hicks, Dan, and Mary C. Beaudry, eds. *The Cambridge Companion to Historical Archaeology*. New York: Cambridge University Press, 2006.

———, eds. *The Oxford Handbook of Material Culture Studies*. Oxford: Oxford University Press, 2010.

Hird, Myra J. "Feminist Engagements with Matter." *Feminist Studies* 35.2 (Summer 2009): 329–46.

Hoffmeyer, Jesper. *Biosemiotics: An Examination into the Signs of Life and the Life of Signs*. Scranton, Pa.: Scranton University Press, 2008.

———. *A Legacy for Living Systems: Gregory Bateson as Precursor to Biosemiotics*. New York: Springer, 2008.

———. "The Natural History of Intentionality." *The Symbolic Species Evolved*. Ed. The-

resa Schilhab, Frederik Stjernfelt, and Terrence William Deacon. Dordrecht: Springer, 2012. Web. 18 Nov. 2012.
———. "Semiotic Scaffolding of Living Systems." *Introduction to Biosemiotics: The New Biological Synthesis*. Ed. Marcello Barbieri. Dordrecht: Springer, 2007. 149–66.
———. *Signs of Meaning in the Universe*. Bloomington: Indiana University Press, 1996.
Hoffmeyer, Jesper, and Claus Emmeche. "Code Duality and the Semiotics of Nature." *On Semiotic Modeling*. Ed. Myrdene Anderson and Floyd Merrell. Berlin: Mouton de Gruyter, 1991.
Hofstadter, Douglas, and Emmanuel Sander. *Surfaces and Essences: Analogy as the Fuel and Fire of Thinking*. New York: Basic Books, 2013.
Holm-Hadulla, Rainer M., ed. *Kreativität*. Berlin: Springer, 2000.
Hunter, Lawrence E. *The Processes of Life: An Introduction to Molecular Biology*. Cambridge, Mass.: MIT Press, 2009.
Iovino, Serenella. "Keyword: Pollution." *Keywords in the Study of Environment and Culture*. Ed. Joni Adamson, Bill Gleason, and David Pellow. New York: New York University Press, forthcoming.
———. "Material Ecocriticism: Matter, Text, and Posthuman Ethics." *Literature, Ecology, Ethics: Recent Trends in European Ecocriticism*. Ed. Timo Müller and Michael Sauter. Heidelberg: Winter Verlag, 2012. 51–68.
———. "Naples 2008; or, The Waste Land: Trash, Citizenship, and an Ethic of Narration." *Neohelicon* 36.2 (2009): 335–46.
———. "Narrative Agency and Storied Matter." Paper presented at "*Natura Loquens*: Eruptive Dialogues, Disruptive Discourses," the 5th EASLCE International Conference, 27–30 June 2012. Unpublished manuscript.
———. "Restoring the Imagination of Place: Narrative Reinhabitation and the Po Valley." *The Bioregional Imagination: Literature, Ecology, and Place*. Ed. Tom Lynch, Cheryll Glotfelty, and Karla Armbruster. Athens: University of Georgia Press, 2012. 100–17.
———. "Steps to a Material Ecocriticism: The Recent Literature about the 'New Materialisms' and Its Implications for Ecocritical Theory." *Ecozon@* 3.1 (2012): 134–45. Web. 10 Dec. 2012.
———. "Stories from the Thick of Things: Introducing Material Ecocriticism." Pt. 1 of Serenella Iovino and Serpil Oppermann, "Theorizing Material Ecocriticism: A Dipthych." *Material Ecocriticism*. Ed. Heather Sullivan and Dana Phillips. Spec. issue of *ISLE* 19.3 (Summer 2012): 448–60.
———. "Toxic Epiphanies: Dioxin, Power, and Gendered Bodies in Laura Conti's Narratives on Seveso." *International Perspectives in Feminist Ecocriticism*. Ed. Greta Gaard, Simon C. Estok, and Serpil Oppermann. New York: Routledge, 2013. 37–55.
Iovino, Serenella, and Serpil Oppermann. "Material Ecocriticism: Materiality, Agency, and Models of Narrativity." *Ecozon@* 3.1 (2012): 75–91. Web. 10 Dec. 2012.
———. "Onword. After Green Ecologies: Prismatic Visions." *Prismatic Ecology: Ecotheory beyond Green*. Ed. Jeffrey J. Cohen. Minneapolis: University of Minnesota Press, 2014. 328–36.
———. "Theorizing Material Ecocriticism: A Diptych." *Material Ecocritcsm*. Ed. Heather Sullivan and Dana Phillips. Spec. issue of *ISLE* 19.3 (Summer 2012): 448–75.
Iser, Wolfgang. *The Fictive and the Imaginary: Charting Literary Anthropology*. Baltimore: Johns Hopkins University Press, 1993.

Jacques, Vincent, E. Wu, Frédéric Grosshans, François Treussart, Philippe Grangier, Alain Aspect, and Jean-François Roch. "Experimental Realization of Wheeler's Delayed-Choice Gedanken Experiment." *Science* 315.5814 (Feb. 2007): 966–68.
Jakobson, Roman. "Closing Statement: Linguistics and Poetics." *Style in Language*. Ed. Thomas A. Sebeok. Cambridge, Mass.: MIT Press, 1960.
Jankovic, Vladimir. *Reading the Skies: A Cultural History of English Weather, 1650–1820*. Chicago: University of Chicago Press, 2000.
Jonas, Hans. *Gnostic Religion: Message of the Alien God and the Beginnings of Christianity*. London: Routledge, 1992.
Jones, Ken. *The New Social Face of Buddhism: A Call to Action*. Somerville, Mass.: Wisdom, 2003.
Kaiser, Jocelyn. "The Dirt on Ocean Garbage Patches." *Science* 328.18 (June 2010): 1506.
Kant, Immanuel. *Critique of Judgment*. Trans. Werner Pluhar. Indianapolis: Hackett, 1987.
———. *Critique of Pure Reason*. Trans. Norman Kemp Smith. Boston: Bedford/St. Martin's Press, 1965.
Kapleau, Philip. *To Cherish All Life: A Buddhist Case for Becoming Vegetarian*. San Francisco: Harper & Row, 1986.
Kauffman, Stuart A. "Beyond Reductionism: Reinventing the Sacred." *Edge: The Third Culture* 197 (20 Nov. 2006). Web. 10 Sept. 2012.
———. *Investigations*. Oxford: Oxford University Press, 2000.
———. *Reinventing the Sacred: The Science of Complexity and the Emergence of a Natural Divinity*. New York: Basic Books, 2008.
Kauffmann, Louis H. "Laws of Form and Form Dynamics." *Cybernetics & Human Knowing* 9.2 (2001): 49–66.
Keller, Catherine. *Face of the Deep: A Theology of Becoming*. London: Routledge, 2003.
———. *On the Mystery: Discerning Divinity in Process*. Minneapolis: Fortress Press, 2008.
Keller, Evelyn Fox. *The Mirage of a Space between Nature and Nurture*. Durham, N.C.: Duke University Press, 2010.
Kidd, Sue Monk. *The Secret Life of Bees*. New York: Penguin, 2003.
Kirby, Vicki. *Quantum Anthropologies: Life at Large*. Durham, N.C.: Duke University Press, 2011.
———. *Telling Flesh: The Substance of the Corporeal*. New York: Routledge, 1997.
Kirksey, S. Eben, and Stefen Helmreich. "The Emergence of Multispecies Ethnography." *Cultural Anthropology* 25.4 (2010): 545–76.
Klein, Anne Carolyn. *Meeting the Great Bliss Queen: Buddhists, Feminists, and the Art of the Self*. Boston: Beacon Press, 1995.
Knappett, Carl, and Lambros Malafouris, eds. *Material Agency: Towards a Nonanthropocentric Approach*. New York: Springer, 2008.
Koestler, Arthur. *The Act of Creation*. New York: Macmillan, 1964.
Kohn, Eduardo. "How Dogs Dream: Amazonian Natures and the Politics of Transspecies Engagement." *American Ethnologist* 34.1 (2007): 3–24.
Komárek, Stanislav. *Nature and Culture: The World of Phenomena and the World of Interpretation*. Munich: Lincom Europa, 2009.
Kosek, Jake. "Ecologies of Empire: On the New Uses of the Honeybee." *Cultural Anthropology* 25.4 (2010): 650–78.

Kozlowski, Lori. "*Avatar* Team Brings in UC Riverside Professor to Dig in the Dirt of Pandora." *Los Angeles Times* 2 Jan. 2010. Web. 25 Jan. 2010.
Kricher, John. *The Balance of Nature: Ecology's Enduring Myth*. Princeton, N.J.: Princeton University Press, 2009.
Krog, Antjie. *A Change of Tongue*. Johannesburg: Random House, 2003.
Kull, Kalevi. "Organism as a Self-Reading Text: Anticipation and Semiosis." *International Journal of Computing Anticipatory Systems* 1 (1998): 93–104.
———. "Semiotic Ecology: Different Natures in the Semiosphere." *Sign Systems Studies* 26 (1998): 344–71.
———. "Vegetative, Animal, and Cultural Semiosis: The Semiotic Threshold Zones." *Cognitive Semiotics* 4 (2009): 8–27.
Laporte, Dominique. *History of Shit*. Trans. Nadia Benabid and Rodolphe el-Khoury. Cambridge, Mass.: MIT Press, 2002.
Latour, Bruno. "An Attempt at a 'Compositionist Manifesto.'" *New Literary History* 41 (2010): 471–90.
———. *On the Modern Cult of the Factish Gods*. Durham, N.C.: Duke University Press, 2010.
———. *Pandora's Hope: Essays on the Reality of Science Studies*. Cambridge, Mass.: Harvard University Press, 1999.
———. *Politics of Nature: How to Bring the Sciences into Democracy*. Trans. Catherine Porter. Cambridge, Mass.: Harvard University Press, 2004.
———. *Reassembling the Social: An Introduction to Actor-Network-Theory*. Oxford: Oxford University Press, 2005.
———. *Science in Action: How to Follow Scientists and Engineers through Society*. Cambridge, Mass.: Harvard University Press, 1987.
———. *We Have Never Been Modern*. Trans. Catherine Porter. Cambridge, Mass.: Harvard University Press, 1993.
———. "Whose Cosmos, Which Cosmopolitics? Comments on the Peace Terms of Ulrich Beck." *Common Knowledge* 10.3 (Fall 2004): 450–62.
Lawrence, Elizabeth Atwood. "The Sacred Bee, the Filthy Pig, and the Bat Out of Hell: Animal Symbolism as Cognitive Biophilia." *The Biophilia Hypothesis*. Ed. Stephen Kellert and Edward O. Wilson. Washington, D.C.: Island Press, 1993. 301–41.
Leduc, Timothy. *Climate Culture Change: Inuit and Western Dialogues with a Warming North*. Ottawa: University of Ottawa Press, 2010.
Lee, Bernard J. "The Only Survivable World: A Postmodern Systems Approach to a Religious Intuition." *Sacred Interconnections: Postmodern Spirituality, Political Economy, and Art*. Ed. David Ray Griffin. New York: State University of New York Press, 1990. 49–62.
Lemieux, Jessica. "Toronto Urban Bees." *Spacing Toronto: Understanding the Urban Landscape*. 1 Nov. 2012. Web. 10 Jan. 2013.
Lewontin, Richard C. "Billions and Billions of Demons." Rev. of *The Demon-Haunted World: Science as a Candle in the Dark*, by Carl Sagan. *New York Review of Books* 9 Jan. 1997. n.p.
Lindfors, Bernth. "Circus Africans." *Journal of American Culture* 6.2 (1983): 9–14.
Linehan, Marsha W. *Skills Training Manual for Treating Borderline Personality Disorder*. New York: Guilford Press, 1993.

Lipps, Theodor. *Raumaesthetik* as cited by Lars Spuybroek in *The Sympathy of Things*. Netherlands: NAi, 2011.
Lotman, Juri M. "Struktura khudozhestvennogo teksta." *Ob iskusstve*. Saint Petersburg: Iskusstvo, 1998. 14–285.
———. "Tezisy k probleme 'Iskusstvo v ryadu modeliruyuschikh sistem': Trudy po znakovym sistemam." *Sign Systems Studies* 3 (1967): 130–45.
Lotman, Juri M., and Alexander M. Pjatigorskij. "Text and Function." *Soviet Semiotics: An Anthology*. Ed. and trans. Daniel P. Lucid. Baltimore: Johns Hopkins University Press, 1977. 125–35.
Löwith, Karl. "Pompei e il Vesuvio." T. W. Adorno, W. Benjamin, S. Kracauer, K. Löwith, A. Sohn-Rethel. *Napoli*. Ed. and trans. Enrico Donaggio. Naples: L'Ancora del Mediterraneo, 2000. 63–66.
Lucretius. *The Way Things Are: The "De Rerum Natura" of Titus Lucretius Carus*. Trans. Rolfe Humphreys. Bloomington: Indiana University Press, 1969.
Luhmann, Niklas. "The Cognitive Program of Constructivism and a Reality That Remains Unknown." *Self-Organization: Portrait of a Scientific Revolution*. Ed. Wolfgang Krohn, Günter Küpper, and Helga Nowotny. Boston: Kluwer, 1990. 64–85.
———. *Die Gesellschaft der Gesellschaft*. Frankfurt: Suhrkamp, 1997.
Luisi, Pier Luigi. "Autopoiesis: A Review and a Reappraisal." *Naturwissenschaften* 90 (2003): 49–59.
Malaparte, Curzio. *La pelle*. Ed. Caterina Guagni and Giorgio Pinatti. 1949. Reprint, Milan: Adelphi, 2010.
———. *The Skin*. Trans. David Moore. London: Alvin Redman, 1952.
Manes, Christopher. "Nature and Silence." *The Ecocriticism Reader: Landmarks in Literary Ecology*. Ed. Cheryll Glotfelty and Harold Fromm. Athens: University of Georgia Press, 1996. 15–29.
Manghi, Sergio. "Foreword in Wider Perspective." *Mind and Nature: A Necessary Unity*. By Gregory Bateson. Cresskill, N.J.: Hampton Press, 2002.
Maran, Timo. "An Ecosemiotic Approach to Nature Writing." *PAN: Philosophy Activism Nature* 7 (2010): 79–87.
———. "Locality as a Foundational Concept for Ecosemiotics." *Re-imagining Nature: Environmental Humanities and Ecosemiotics*. Ed. Alfred K. Siewers. Lanham, Md.: Bucknell University Press, 2014. 79–90.
———. "Where Do Your Borders Lie? Reflections on the Semiotical Ethics of Nature." *Nature in Literary and Cultural Studies: Transatlantic Conversations on Ecocriticism*. Ed. Catrin Gersdorf and Sylvia Mayer. Amsterdam: Rodopi, 2006. 455–76.
Maran, Timo, and Kalevi Kull. "Ecosemiotics: Main Principles and Current Developments." *Geografiska Annaler, Series B*. 96(1): 41–50..
Margulis, Lynn. *Symbiotic Planet: A New Look at Evolution*. New York: Basic Books, 1998.
Margulis, Lynn, and Dorion Sagan. *Dazzle Gradually: Reflections on the Nature of Nature*. White River Junction, Vt.: Sciencewriters Books, 2007.
———. *Microcosmos: Four Billion Years of Evolution from Our Microbial Ancestors*. Berkeley: University of California Press, 1986.
Marion, Jean Luc. *In Excess: Studies of Saturated Phenomena*. Trans. Robyn Horner and Vincent Berraud. New York: Fordham University Press, 2002.

Markley, Robert. "Monsoon Cultures: Climate and Acculturation in Alexander Hamilton's *A New Account of the East Indies*." *New Literary History* 38 (2007): 527–50.
———. "Summer's Lease: Shakespeare in the Little Ice Age." *Early Modern Ecostudies: From the Florentine Codex to Shakespeare*. Ed. Thomas Hallock, Ivo Kamps, and Karen L. Raber. New York: Palgrave Macmillan, 2008. 131–42.
Marshall, Patrick. "Acid Rocks of Taupo-Rotura Volcanic District." *Royal Society of New Zealand Transactions* 64.3 (1935): 323–66. (Off pagination: 1–44.)
Martin, Philip. *The Zen Path through Depression*. San Francisco: HarperCollins, 1999.
Massumi, Brian. *Semblance and Event: Activist Philosophy and the Occurrent Arts*. Cambridge, Mass.: MIT Press, 2011.
Mathews, Freya. "Beyond Modernity and Tradition: A Third Way for Development?" *Ethics and the Environment* 11.2 (2006): 85–113.
———. *For Love of Matter: A Contemporary Panpsychism*. Albany: State University of New York Press, 2003.
———. "Introduction: Invitation to Ontopoetics." *Philosophy Activism Nature* 6 (2009): 1–6. Web. 10 Nov. 2011.
———. *Reinhabiting Reality: Towards a Recovery of Culture*. Albany: State University of New York Press, 2005.
Maturana, Humberto, and Francisco J. Varela. *Autopoiesis and Cognition: The Realization of the Living*. Dordrecht: D. Reidel, 1980.
———. *The Tree of Knowledge: The Biological Roots of Human Understanding*. Boston: Shambhala, 1992.
Matussek, Peter, ed. *Goethe und die Verzeitlichung der Natur*. Munich: Beck, 1998.
Mazur, Suzan. "Princeton Powwow: RNA World's Last Hurrah?" *Scoop*. Scoop Media. 16 Jan. 2013. Web. 21 Jan. 2013.
McCarthy, John. *Remapping Reality: Chaos and Creativity in Science and Literature (Goethe-Nietzsche-Grass)*. Amsterdam: Rodopi, 2006.
McKinney, Dan. *Do Trees Communicate?* YouTube. Web. 10 Oct. 2012.
McMenamin, Mark, and Dianna McMenamin. *Hypersea: Life on Land*. New York: Columbia University Press, 1994.
McNeley, James Kale. *Holy Wind in Navajo Philosophy*. Tucson: University of Arizona Press, 1981.
Melville, Herman. *Moby-Dick*. New York: Oxford University Press, 2008.
Mentz, Steve. *At the Bottom of Shakespeare's Ocean*. London: Continuum, 2009.
———. "Strange Weather in King Lear." *Shakespeare* 6.2 (2010): 139–52.
Merkur, Daniel. *Powers Which We Do Not Know: The Gods and Spirits of the Inuit*. Moscow: University of Idaho Press, 1991.
Michaels, Walter Benn. *The Shape of the Signifier: 1967 to the End of History*. Princeton, N.J.: Princeton University Press, 2006.
Middleton, W. E. Knowles. *A History of the Theories of Rain and Other Forms of Precipitation*. New York: Franklin Watts, 1965.
Mitchell, Robert W., Nicholas S. Thompson, and H. Lyn Miles, eds. *Anthropomorphism, Anecdotes, and Animals*. Albany: State University of New York Press, 1997.
Mitchell, W. J. T. *What Do Pictures Want? The Lives and Loves of Images*. Chicago: University of Chicago Press, 2005.
Moeller, Hans-Georg. *The Radical Luhmann*. New York: Columbia University Press, 2012.

Montrose, Louis A. "Professing the Renaissance: The Poetics and Politics of Culture." *The New Historicism*. Ed. H. Aram Veeser. New York and London: Routledge, 1989. 15–36.

Moore, Charles, with Cassandra Phillips. *Plastic Ocean: How a Sea Captain's Chance Discovery Launched a Determined Quest to Save the Oceans*. New York: Penguin, 2011.

Morrison, Toni. *Beloved*. 1987. New York: Penguin, 1991.

Mortimer-Sandilands, Catriona. "Landscape, Memory, and Forgetting: Thinking through (My Mother's) Body and Place." *Material Feminisms*. Ed. Stacy Alaimo and Susan Hekman. Bloomington: Indiana University Press, 2008. 265–87.

Morton, Timothy. *The Ecological Thought*. Cambridge, Mass.: Harvard University Press, 2010.

———. "Ecology and Text, Text as Ecology." *Oxford Literary Review* 32.1 (2010): 1–17.

———. "The Mesh." *Environmental Criticism for the Twenty-First Century*. Ed. Stephanie LeMenager, Teresa Shewry, and Ken Hiltner. New York: Routledge, 2011. 19–30.

Muir, John. *My First Summer in the Sierra*. Boston: Houghton Mifflin, 1911.

Murray, Gilbert. *The Classical Tradition in Poetry*. Cambridge, Mass.: Harvard University Press, 1930.

Nagel, Thomas. *Mind and Cosmos: Why the Materialist Neo-Darwinian Conception of Nature Is Almost Certainly False*. New York: Oxford University Press, 2012.

Nixon, Rob. *Slow Violence and the Environmentalism of the Poor*. Cambridge, Mass.: Harvard University Press, 2011.

Noble, Denis. *The Music of Life: Biology beyond the Genome*. Oxford: Oxford University Press, 2006.

Odling-Smee, F. John., Kevin N. Laland, and Marcus W. Feldman. *Niche Construction: The Neglected Process in Evolution*. Princeton, N.J.: Princeton University Press, 2003.

Oh, Jea Sohia. *A Postcolonial Theology of Life: Planetarity East and West*. Upland, Calif.: Sopher Press, 2011.

Oppermann, Serpil. "Ecocriticism's Theoretical Discontents." *Mosaic* 44.2 (June 2011): 153–69.

———. "A Lateral Continuum: Ecocriticism and Postmodern Materialism." Pt. 2 of Serenella Iovino and Serpil Oppermann, "Theorizing Material Ecocriticism: A Dipthych." *Material Ecocriticism*. Ed. Heather Sullivan and Dana Phillips. Spec. issue of *ISLE* 19.3 (Summer 2012): 460–75.

———. "Rethinking Ecocriticism in an Ecological Postmodern Framework." *Literature, Ecology, Ethics: Recent Trends in European Ecocriticism*. Ed. Timo Müller and Michael Sauter. Heidelberg: Winter Verlag, 2012. 35–50.

———. Rev. of *Reinhabiting Reality*, by F. Mathews. *Trumpeter* 24.3 (2008): 167–74. Web. 5 Oct. 2011.

———. "The Rhizomatic Trajectory of Ecocriticism." *Ecozon@* 1.1 (2010): 17–21. Web. 20 June 2013.

———. "Theorizing Ecocriticism: Toward a Postmodern Ecocritical Practice." *ISLE* 13.12 (Summer 2006): 103–28.

Packer, Laurence. *Keeping the Bees: Why All Bees Are at Risk and What We Can Do to Save Them*. Toronto: HarperCollins, 2010.

Pagel, Walter. *Paracelsus: An Introduction to Philosophical Medicine in the Era of the Renaissance*. Basil: S. Karger, 1982.

Pahl, Katrin. *Tropes of Transport: Hegel and Emotion*. Evanston, Ill.: Northwestern University Press, 2012.
Palmers, Vanya. "What Can I Do?" *Dharma Rain: Sources of Buddhist Environmentalism*. Ed. Stephanie Kaza and Kenneth Kraft. Boston: Shambhala, 2000. 278–82.
Pálsson, Gísli, ed. *From Water to World-Making: African Models and Arid Lands*. Uppsala: Nordiska Afrikainstitutet, 1990.
Paracelsus. *De Causis Morborum Invisibilium. Essential Theoretical Writings*. Ed. and trans. Andrew Weeks. Leiden: Brill, 2008. 720–937.
———. *Selected Writings*. Ed. Joland Jacobi. Princeton, N.J.: Princeton University Press, 1995.
Paracelsus, Andreas Tentzel, and Ferdinando Parkhurst. *Medicina Diastatica; or, Sympatheticall Mumie: Containing Many Mysterious and Hidden Secrets in Philosophy and Physick, by the Construction, Extraction, Transplantation, and Application of Microcosmical & Spiritual Mumie: Teaching the Magneticall Cure of Diseases at Distance, &c*. London: T. Newcomb for T. Heath, 1653. Open Library. Web. 12 Jan. 2013.
Parker, Pat. *Movement in Black*. Ann Arbor, Mich.: Firebrand Books, 1999.
Parkhurst, Ferdinando. "The Translator to the Reader." *Medicina Diastatica; or, Sympatheticall Mumie: Containing Many Mysterious and Hidden Secrets in Philosophy and Physick, by the Construction, Extraction, Transplantation, and Application of Microcosmical & Spiritual Mumie: Teaching the Magneticall Cure of Diseases at Distance, &c*. London: T. Newcomb for T. Heath, 1653. Open Library. Web. 12 Jan. 2013.
Past, Elena Margarita. "'Trash Is Gold': Documenting the Ecomafia and Campania's Waste Crisis." *ISLE* 20.3 (2013): 597–621.
Patton, Kimberly C. *The Sea Can Wash Away All Evils: Modern Marine Pollution and the Ancient Cathartic Ocean*. New York: Columbia University Press, 2006.
Peirce, Charles S. "The Basis of Pragmaticism in the Normative Sciences." *The Essential Peirce: Selected Philosophical Writings, 1893–1913*. Vol. 2. Bloomington: Indiana University Press, 1998.
———. *Collected Papers of Charles Sanders Peirce*. 8 vols. Cambridge, Mass.: Harvard University Press, 1931–58. Vols. 1–6. Ed. Charles Hartshorne and Paul Weiss. 1931–35. Vols. 7–8. Ed. A. W. Burks. 1958. CD Folio Bound Views.
———. *Semiotic and Significs: The Correspondence between Charles S. Peirce and Victoria Lady Welby*. Ed. Charles S. Hardwick and J. Cook. Bloomington: Indiana University Press, 1977.
Peters, Katrin. *Plastic Seduction*. Video. Plastic Pollution Coalition Channel. YouTube. Web. 15 Dec. 2012.
Phelps, Norm. *The Great Compassion: Buddhism and Animal Rights*. Herndon, Va.: Lantern Books, 2004.
Phillips, Dana. *The Truth of Ecology: Nature, Culture, and Literature in America*. Oxford: Oxford University Press, 2003.
Phillips, Dana, and Heather I. Sullivan, eds. "Material Ecocriticism: Dirt, Waste, Bodies, Food, and Other Matter." *Material Ecocriticism*. Ed. Heather Sullivan and Dana Phillips. Spec. issue of *ISLE* 19.3 (Summer 2012): 445–47.
Pickering, Andrew. *The Mangle of Practice: Time, Agency, and Science*. Chicago: University of Chicago Press, 1995.

———. "New Ontologies." *The Mangle in Practice: Science, Society, and Becoming.* Ed. Andrew Pickering and Keith Guzik. Durham, N.C.: Duke University Press, 2009. 1–14.

Plastic Pollution Coalition. Web. 23 Dec. 2011.

Plumwood, Val. *Environmental Culture: The Ecological Crisis of Reason.* London: Routledge, 2002.

———. "Journey to the Heart of Stone." *Culture, Creativity, and Environment: New Environmentalist Criticism.* Ed. Fiona Becket and Terry Gifford. Amsterdam: Rodopi, 2007. 17–36.

———. "Nature as Agency and the Prospects for a Progressive Naturalism." *Capitalism Nature Socialism* 12.4 (Dec. 2001): 3–32.

———. "Shadow Places and the Politics of Dwelling." *Australian Humanities Review* (Eco-Humanities Corner) 44 (2008). Web. 10 Dec. 2008.

Polanyi, Michael. *Personal Knowledge: Towards a Post-critical Philosophy.* Chicago: University of Chicago Press, 1962.

Poole, William. *Milton and the Idea of the Fall.* Cambridge: Cambridge University Press, 2005.

Popper, Karl R., and John C. Eccles. *The Self and Its Brain.* New York: Springer, 1977.

Praeger, Dave. *Poop Culture: How America Is Shaped by Its Grossest National Product.* Los Angeles: Feral House, 2007.

Preston, Claire. *Bee.* London: Reaktion Books, 2006.

Prigogine, Ilya. *Is the Future Given?* London: World Scientific Press, 2003.

Pynchon, Thomas. *Gravity's Rainbow.* New York: Penguin, 1995.

Queiroz, João, Claus Emmeche, and Charbel Niño El-Hania. "Information and Semiosis in Living Systems: A Semiotic Approach." *S.E.E.D. Journal (Semiotics, Evolution, Energy, and Development)* 5.2 (2005): 60–90. Web. 25 Nov. 2012.

Quigley, Peter. "Rethinking Resistance: Environmentalism, Literature, and Poststructural Theory." *Environmental Ethics* 14.2 (Winter 1992): 291–306.

Rancière, Jacques. *Dissensus: On Politics and Aesthetics.* London: Continuum, 2010.

———. *The Politics of Literature.* Malden, Mass.: Polity Press, 2011.

Ricoeur, Paul. *The Rule of Metaphor: The Creation of Meaning in Language.* Trans. Robert Czerny, Kathleen McLaughlin, and John Costello, S.J. London: Routledge, 2003.

Rigby, Kate. "Another Talk on Religion to Its Cultured Despisers." *Ecophenomenology and Practices of the Sacred.* Ed. Patrick Curry and Wendy Wheeler. Spec. issue of *Green Letters: A Journal of Ecocriticism* 13 (2010): 55–73.

———. "Ecocriticism." *Introducing Criticism at the 21st Century.* Ed. Julian Wolfreys. Edinburgh: Edinburgh University Press, 2002. 151–78.

———. "The Goddess Returns: Ecofeminist Reconfigurations of Gender, Nature, and the Sacred." *Feminist Poetics of the Sacred: Creative Suspicions.* Ed. Frances Devlin-Glass and Lyn McCredden. New York: Oxford University Press, 2001. 23–54.

———. "(K)ein Klang der aufgeregten Zeit: Romanticism, Ecology, and Modernity in Theodor Storm's 'Abseits.'" *Moderne begreifen: Zur Paradoxie eines sozio-ästhetischen Deutungsmusters.* Ed. Christine Magerski, Robert Savage, and Christiane Weller. Wiesbaden: Deutscher Universitäts-Verlag, 2007. 145–56.

———. "Minding (about) Matter: On the Eros and Anguish of Earthly Encounter" (review essay of Mathews 2003 and 2005). *Australian Humanities Review* (Eco-Humanities Corner) 38 (2006). Web. 8 Dec. 2006.

———. *Topographies of the Sacred: The Poetics of Place in European Romanticism*. Charlottesville: University Press of Virginia, 2004.

Roberts, Callum. *The Unnatural History of the Sea*. Washington, D.C.: Island Press, 2007.

Robertson, Michael. *Worshipping Walt: The Whitman Disciples*. Princeton, N.J.: Princeton University Press, 2010.

Rose, Deborah Bird. *Reports from a Wild Country: Ethics for Decolonisation*. Sydney: University of New South Wales Press, 2004.

———. *Wild Dog Dreaming: Love and Extinction*. Charlottesville: University Press of Virginia, 2011.

Rosen, Robert. *Anticipatory Systems: Philosophical, Mathematical, and Methodological Foundations*. 2nd ed. New York: Springer, 2012.

Ross, Gyasi. "The Idle No More Movement for Dummies." *Indian Country Today*, Media Network.Com. 16 Jan. 2013. Web. 18 Jan. 2013.

Rothfels, Nigel. "Aztecs, Aborigines, and Ape-People: Science and Freaks in Germany, 1840–1900." *Freakery: Cultural Spectacles of the Extraordinary Body*. Ed. Rosemarie Garland Thomson. New York: Columbia University Press, 1997. 158–72.

Rudd, Gillian. "'Why Does It Always Rain on Me?': Rain and Self-Centredness and Medieval Poetry." *Green Letters: Studies in Ecocriticism* 11 (2009): 70–82.

Sagan, Carl. *Pale Blue Dot: A Vision of the Human Future in Space*. New York: Random House, 1994.

Sandilands, Catriona. "From Natural Identity to Radical Democracy." *Environmental Ethics* 17.1 (Spring 1995): 75–91.

Sapp, Jan. *Genesis: The Evolution of Biology*. New York: Oxford University Press, 2003.

Satterfield, Terre, and Scott Slovic, eds. *What's Nature Worth? Narrative Expressions of Environmental Values*. Salt Lake City: University of Utah Press, 2004.

Scarry, Elaine. *The Body in Pain: The Making and Unmaking of the World*. New York and Oxford: Oxford University Press, 1985.

Schauder, Stephen, and Bonnie L. Bassler. "The Languages of Bacteria." *Genes and Development* 15 (2001): 1468–80. Web. 10 Dec. 2012.

Seamon, David, and Arthur Zajonc, eds. *Goethe's Way of Science: A Phenomenology of Nature*. Albany: State University of New York Press, 1998.

Sebeok, Thomas A. "In What Sense Is Language a 'Primary Modeling System'?" *A Sign Is Just a Sign*. Bloomington: Indiana University Press, 1991. 49–58.

———. "Signs, Bridges, Origins." *Global Semiotics*. Bloomington: Indiana University Press, 2001. 59–73.

Sebeok, Thomas A., and Marcel Danesi. *The Forms of Meaning: Modeling Systems Theory and Semiotic Analysis*. Berlin: Mouton de Gruyter, 2000.

Sebeok, Thomas A., and Jean Umiker-Sebeok, eds. *Biosemiotics: The Semiotic Web, 1991*. Berlin: Mouton de Gruyter, 1992.

Seeley, Thomas D. *Honeybee Democracy*. Princeton, N.J.: Princeton University Press, 2010.

Segal, Zindel V., J. Mark, G. Williams, and John D. Teasdale. *Mindfulness-Based Cognitive Therapy for Depression: A New Approach to Preventing Relapse*. 2nd ed. New York: Guilford Press, 2012.

Serres, Michel. *The Five Senses: A Philosophy of Mingled Bodies.* Trans. Margaret Sankey and Peter Cowley. New York: Continuum, 2009.
———. *The Natural Contract.* Trans. Elizabeth MacArthur and William Paulson. Ann Arbor: University of Michigan Press, 1995.
———. *The Parasite.* Trans. Lawrence R. Schehr. Minneapolis: University of Minnesota Press, 2007.
Serres, Michel, and Bruno Latour. *Conversations on Science, Culture, and Time.* Trans. Roxanne Lapidus. Ann Arbor: University of Michigan Press, 1995.
Shakespeare, William. *The Tempest.* New Haven, Conn.: Yale University Press, 2006.
Shapiro, James A. "DNA as Poetry: Multiple Messages in a Single Sequence." *Huffington Post* 24 Jan. 2012. Web. 21 Jan. 2013.
———. *Evolution: A View from the 21st Century.* Upper Saddle River, N.J.: FT Science, 2011.
Sharkwater. Rob Stewart. Sharkwater Productions and Diatribe Pictures, 2007. DVD.
Sheets-Johnstone, Maxine. *The Corporeal Turn: An Interdisciplinary Reader.* Exeter: Im Academic, 2009.
Shintani, Laura. "Roman Jakobson and Biology: 'A System of Systems.'" *Semiotica* 127.1–4 (1999): 103–14.
Shubin, Neil. *Your Inner Fish: A Journey into the 3.5 Billion-Year History of the Human Body.* New York: Vintage, 2008.
Shukin, Nicole. *Animal Capital: Rendering Life in Biopolitical Times.* Minneapolis: University of Minnesota Press, 2009.
Siegel, Taggart, dir. *Queen of the Sun: What Are the Bees Telling Us?* Collective Eye, 2011. Video.
Simmer-Brown, Judith. "Speaking Truth to Power: The Buddhist Peace Fellowship." *Engaged Buddhism in the West.* Ed. Christopher S. Quinn. Boston: Wisdom, 2000. 67–94.
Simpson, James. *Burning to Read: English Fundamentalism and Its Reformation Opponents.* Cambridge, Mass.: Belknap Press, Harvard University Press, 2007.
Slovic, Scott. "Editor's Note." *ISLE* 19.4 (Autumn 2012): 619–21.
———. *Going Away to Think: Engagement, Retreat, and Ecocritical Responsibility.* Reno: University of Nevada Press, 2008.
Smith, Mick. *Against Ecological Sovereignty: Ethics, Biopolitics, and Saving the Natural World.* Minneapolis: University of Minnesota Press, 2011.
Sontag, Susan. *On Photography.* New York: Farrar, Straus, and Giroux, 1977.
Southwick, Charles E. *Global Ecology in Human Perspective.* New York: Oxford University Press, 1996.
Spretnak, Charlene. *Relational Reality: New Discoveries of Interrelatedness That Are Transforming the Modern World.* Topsham, Maine: Green Horizon Books, 2011.
———. *The Resurgence of the Real: Body, Nature, and Place in a Hypermodern World.* New York: Routledge, 1999.
Stanley, John, David R. Loy, and Gyurme Dorje, eds. *A Buddhist Response to the Climate Emergency.* Boston: Wisdom, 2009.
Starr, Alison. "Baker." Mixed media artwork. 2012. Author's personal collection.
Steiner, George. *The Death of Tragedy.* London: Hill and Wang, 1961.
Stengers, Isabelle. "Reclaiming Animism." *E-Flux Journal* 36 (2012). Web. 10 Dec. 2012.
———. "Reclaiming the Pharmakon." Conference presentation. 8 Sept. 2011.

Sternberg, Robert J., ed. *Handbook of Creativity*. Cambridge: Cambridge University Press, 1999.
Stewart, Kathleen. "Atmospheric Attunements." *Environment and Planning D: Society and Space* 29.3 (2010): 445–53.
Stockman, Vivian. *Massive Dragline*. Photograph. Mountaintop Removal Mining. Ohio Valley Environmental Coalition, 19 Oct. 2003. Web. 14 Aug. 2012.
Strabo. *The Geography*. Greek texts with facing English translation, by H. L. Jones. Loeb Classical Library. 8 vols. Cambridge, Mass.: Harvard University Press, 1917–32. Also available at http://penelope.uchicago.edu/Thayer/E/Roman/Texts/Strabo/home.html.
Stratton-Porter, Gene. *Keeper of the Bees*. 1925. Reprint, Bloomington: Indiana University Press, 1991.
Sullivan, Heather. "Affinity Studies and Open Systems: A Nonequilibrium, Ecocritical Reading of Goethe's *Faust*." *Ecocritical Theory: New European Approaches*. Ed. Axel Goodbody and Kate Rigby. Charlottesville: University Press of Virginia, 2011. 243–55.
———. "Ecocriticism, the Elements, and the Ascent/Descent into Weather in Goethe's *Faust*." *Goethe Yearbook* 17 (2010): 55–72.
Sutton, John. "Material Agency, Skills, and History: Distributed Cognition and the Archaeology of Memory." *Material Agency: Towards a Non-anthropocentric Approach*. Ed. Carl Knappett and Lambros Malafouris. New York: Springer, 2008. 37–56.
Swimme, Brian Thomas. "The Cosmic Creation Story." *The Reenchantment of Science: Postmodern Proposals*. Ed. David Ray Griffin. Albany: State University of New York Press, 1988. 47–56.
Swimme, Brian Thomas, and May Evelyn Tucker. *Journey of the Universe*. New Haven, Conn.: Yale University Press, 2011.
Taubes, Susan Anima. "The Gnostic Foundations of Heidegger's Nihilism." *Journal of Religion* 34.3 (1954): 155–72.
Taylor, Astra, and Sunaura Taylor. "Military Waste in Our Drinking Water." *AlterNet* 3 Aug. 2006. Web. 13 Aug. 2012.
Taylor, Sunaura. "Beasts of Burden: Disability Studies and Animal Rights." *Qui Parle: Critical Humanities and Social Sciences* 19.2 (2011): 191–222.
Thompson, Evan. "Life and Mind: From Autopoiesis to Neurophenomenology: A Tribute to Francisco Varela." *Phenomenology and the Cognitive Sciences* 3 (2004): 381–98.
Thompson, Jerry L. *Walker Evans at Work*. By Walker Evans. New York: Harper & Row, 1982.
Tilley, Christopher. *Metaphor and Material Culture*. Oxford: Blackwell, 1999.
Tondl, Ladislav. "Semiotic Foundation of Models and Modelling." *Modellierungen von Geschichte und Kultur: Modelling History and Culture*. Ed. Jeff Bernard, Peter Grzybek, and Gloria Withalm. Vienna: OGS, 2000. 1:81–89.
The Trees Have a Mother: Amazonian Cosmologies, Folktales, and Mystery. Dir. Valliere Richard Auzenne and Juan Carlos Galeano. New York: Films Media Group, 2008.
Tsing, Anna. "Beyond Economic and Ecological Standardization." *Australian Journal of Anthropology* 20.3 (2009): 347–68.

———. "Empowering Nature; or, Some Gleanings in Bee Culture." *Naturalizing Power: Essays in Feminist Cultural Analysis.* Ed. Sylvia Yanagisako and Carol Delaney. New York: Routledge, 1995. 113–43.
Tuana, Nancy. "Material Locations: An Interactionist Alternative to Realism/Social Constructivism." *Engendering Rationalities.* Ed. Nancy Tuana and Sandi Morgen. Bloomington: Indiana University Press, 2001. 221–44.
———. "Viscous Porosity: Witnessing Katrina." *Material Feminisms.* Ed. Stacy Alaimo and Susan Hekman. Bloomington: Indiana University Press, 2008. 188–213.
Turner, J. Scott. *The Extended Organism: The Physiology of Animal-Built Structures.* Cambridge, Mass.: Harvard University Press, 2000.
Turner, Terence S. "Narrative Structure and Mythopoesis: A Critique and Reformulation of Structuralist Concepts of Myth, Narrative, and Poetics." *Arethusa* 10.1 (1977).
Turrell, James. *Twilight Epiphany.* Artwork. Rice University, May 2012.
Uexküll, Jakob von. *A Foray into the Worlds of Animals and Humans with the Theory of Meaning.* 1934. Reprint, Minneapolis: University of Minnesota Press, 2010.
———. "The Theory of Meaning." *Semiotica* 42.1 (1982): 25–82.
Uexküll, Thure von. "Medicine and Semiotics." *Semiotica* 61.3–4 (1986): 201–18.
Ulanowicz, Robert E. "A Call for Metaphysical Reform." *Ludus Vitalis* 17.32 (2009): 459–63.
"Unearthing the Wood-Wide Web-Investigating Fungi: The Wood-Wide Web." Open University Press. Web. 15 Dec. 2011.
Universal Declaration on the Rights of Mother Earth and Climate Change. World People's Conference on Climate Change and the Rights of Mother Earth. 22 Apr. 2010. Web. 17 Sept. 2010.
Uzendoski, Michael. Foreword to *Folktales of the Amazon,* by Juan Carlos Galeano. Trans. Rebecca Morgan and Kenneth Watson. Westport, Conn.: Libraries Unlimited, 2009.
Van Dover, Cindy Lee. "Tighten Regulations on Deep Sea Mining." *Nature* 470 (3 Feb. 2011): 1–8.
Van Rompay, Thomas J. L. "Product Expression: Bridging the Gap between the Symbolic and the Concrete." *Product Experience.* Ed. Hendrik Schifferstein and Paul Hekkert. New York: Elsevier, 2007. 333–52.
Varela, Francisco J., Evan Thompson, and Eleanor Rosch. 1991. *The Embodied Mind: Cognitive Science and Human Experience.* Cambridge, Mass.: MIT Press, 1993.
Vecsey, Christopher. *Imagine Ourselves Richly: Mythic Narratives of North American Indians.* San Francisco: HarperCollins, 1991.
Velardi, Claudio, ed. *La città porosa: Conversazioni su Napoli.* Naples: Cronopio, 1992.
Venrick, E. L., et al. "Man-Made Objects on the Surface of the Central North Pacific Ocean." *Nature* 241 (26 Jan. 1973): 271.
Vidal, John. "Bolivia Enshrines Natural World's Rights with Equal Status for Mother Earth." *Guardian News* 10 Apr. 2011. Web. 15 Apr. 2012.
Viveiros de Castro, Eduardo Batalha. "Cosmological Deixis and Amerindian Perspectivism." *Journal of the Royal Anthropological Institute* 4.3 (1998): 469–88.
———. "Exchanging Perspectives: The Transformation of Objects into Subjects in Amerindian Ontologies." *Common Knowledge* 10.3 (Fall 2004): 463–84.
Walls, Laura Dassow. "From the Modern to the Ecological: Latour on Walden Pond."

Ecocritical Theory: New European Approaches. Ed. Axel Goodbody and Kate Rigby. Charlottesville: University Press of Virginia, 2011. 98–110.

———. *The Passage to Cosmos: Alexander von Humboldt and the Shaping of America.* Chicago: University of Chicago Press, 2009.

Walters, C. M., and B. L. Bassler. "Quorum Sensing: Cell-to-Cell Communication in Bacteria." *Annual Review of Cell and Developmental Biology* 21 (2005): 319–46. Also available at http://www.ncbi.nlm.nih.gov/pubmed/16212498. Web. 10 Dec. 2012.

Westling, Louise. "Darwin in Arcadia: Brute Being and the Human Animal Dance from Gilgamesh to Virginia Woolf." *Anglia* 124.1 (2006): 11–43.

———. "Literature, the Environment, and the Question of the Posthuman." *Nature in Literary and Cultural Studies: Transatlantic Conversations on Ecocriticism.* Ed. Catrin Gersdorf and Sylvia Mayer. Amsterdam: Rodopi, 2006.

———. "Merleau-Ponty's Ecophenomenology." *Ecocritical Theory: New European Approaches.* Ed. Axel Goodbody and Kate Rigby. Charlottesville: University Press of Virginia, 2011. 126–38.

Wheeler, Wendy. "The Biosemiotic Turn: Abduction; or, The Nature of Creative Reason in Nature and Culture." *Ecocritical Theory: New European Approaches.* Ed. Axel Goodbody and Kate Rigby. Charlottesville: University Press of Virginia, 2011. 270–82.

———. *The Whole Creature: Complexity, Biosemiotics, and the Evolution of Culture.* London: Lawrence & Wishart, 2006.

Whitehead, Alfred North. *Science in the Modern World.* Cambridge: Cambridge University Press, 1953.

Whitman, Walt. *Leaves of Grass, and Other Writings.* Ed. Michael Moon. Norton Critical Edition. New York: W. W. Norton, 2002.

Whitty, Julia. "The Fate of the Ocean." *Mother Jones* Mar.–Apr. 2006. Web. 4 July 2012.

Wiener, Norbert. *Cybernetics; or, Control and Communication in the Animal and the Machine.* Cambridge, Mass.: MIT Press, 1965.

Wilhelm, Maria, and Dirk Mathison. *James Cameron's "Avatar": An Activist Survival Guide.* New York: itbooks/HarperCollins, 2009.

Wilkie, Laurie A. "Documentary Archaeology." *The Cambridge Companion to Historical Archaeology.* Ed. Dan Hicks and Mary C. Beaudry. New York: Cambridge University Press, 2006. 13–33.

William of Newburgh. *The History of English Affairs.* Bk. 1. Ed. and trans. P. G. Walsh and M. J. Kennedy. Wilthsire: Aris and Phillips, 1988.

Williams, William Carlos. *The Collected Poems of William Carlos Williams.* Ed. A. Walton Litz and Christopher MacGowan. Vol. 1, *1909–1939.* New York: New Directions, 1991.

Williamson, Robert G. *Eskimo Underground: Socio-cultural Change in the Central Canadian Arctic.* Uppsala: Almqvist and Wiksell, 1974.

Wilson, Edward O. *Sociobiology: The New Synthesis.* Cambridge, Mass.: Belknap Press, Harvard University Press, 1975.

Witherspoon, Gary. *Language and Art in the Navajo Universe.* Ann Arbor: University of Michigan Press, 1977.

Wood, Michael. *Literature and the Taste of Knowledge.* Cambridge: Cambridge University Press, 2005.

Yaeger, Patricia. "The Death of Nature and the Apotheosis of Trash." *PMLA* 123.2 (Mar. 2008): 321–39.

———. "Literature in the Ages of Wood, Tallow, Coal, Whale Oil, Gasoline, Atomic Power, and Other Energy Sources." *PMLA* 126.2 (Mar. 2011): 305–26.

———. "Sea Trash, Dark Pools, and the Tragedy of Commons." *PMLA* 125.3 (May 2010): 523–45.

Yarrow, Thomas. "In Context: Meaning, Materiality, and Agency in the Process of Archaeological Recording." *Material Agency: Towards a Non-anthropocentric Approach*. Ed. Carl Knappett and Lambros Malafouris. New York: Springer, 2008. 121–38.

Yates, Julian. "Towards a Theory of Agentive Drift; or, A Particular Fondness for Oranges circa 1597." *Parallax* 8.1 (2002): 47–58.

Zajonc, Arthur. "Goethe and the Science of His Time: An Historical Introduction." *Goethe's Way of Science: A Phenomenology of Nature*. Ed. David Seamon and Arthur Zajonc. Albany: State University of New York Press, 1998. 15–32.

Zapf, Hubert. "Literary Ecology and the Ethics of Texts." *New Literary History* 39.4 (2008): 847–68.

———. *Literatur als kulturelle Ökologie: Zur kulturellen Funktion imaginativer Texte an Beispielen des amerikanischen Romans*. Tübingen: Niemeyer, 2002.

———. "New Directions in American Literary Studies: Ecocriticism and the Function of Literature as Cultural Ecology." *English Studies Today: Recent Developments and New Directions*. Ed. Ansgar Nünning and Jürgen Schlaeger. Trier: WVT, 2007. 139–64.

Zimmer, Carl. "Hypersea Invasion." *Discover Magazine* 1 Oct. 1995. Web. 22 Aug. 2012.

Žižek, Slavoj. *Living in the End Times*. London: Verso, 2010.

Contributors

David Abram, cultural ecologist and geophilosopher, is Director of the Alliance for Wild Ethics. He is the author of *The Spell of the Sensuous: Perception and Language in a More-than-Human World* (1997) and *Becoming Animal: An Earthly Cosmology* (2010). His work has helped catalyze the emergence of several new disciplines, including the burgeoning field of ecopsychology. He has numerous essays on the cultural causes and consequences of environmental disarray. In 2014 he held the Arne Naess Chair in Global Justice and the Environment at the University of Oslo.

Joni Adamson is Professor of English and Environmental Humanities at Arizona State University, where she is a Senior Sustainability Scholar at the Global Institute of Sustainability. She is the author of *American Indian Literature, Environmental Justice, and Ecocriticism* (2001) and co-editor of *American Studies, Ecocriticism, and Citizenship: Thinking and Acting in the Local and Global Commons* (2013). She served as the 2012 president of the Association for the Study of Literature and Environment (ASLE) and is co-PI on an international Consortium for Humanities Centers and Institutes Mellon-funded grant titled "Humanities for the Environment."

Stacy Alaimo is Professor of English and Distinguished Teaching Professor at the University of Texas at Arlington. She has published widely in the environmental humanities, green cultural studies, science studies, and gender theory. Her publications include *Undomesticated Ground: Recasting Nature as Feminist Space* (2000), the co-edited *Material Feminisms* (2008), and *Bodily Natures: Science, Environment, and the Material Self* (2010), which received the ASLE Award for Ecocriticism in 2011.

Jane Bennett is Professor of Political Science at Johns Hopkins University, where she teaches political theory and American political thought. Her recent work includes *The Enchantment of Modern Life* (2001) and *Vibrant Matter: A Political Ecology of Things* (2010). She is currently the editor of the journal *Political Theory*.

Hannes Bergthaller teaches at the Department of Foreign Languages and Literatures at National Chung-Hsing University, Taichung, Taiwan. He is the author of *Populäre Ökologie: Zu Literatur und Geschichte der modernen Umweltbewegung* *in den USA* (2007) and co-editor of the volume *Addressing Modernity: Social Systems Theory and U.S. Cultures* (2011). He also edited a special issue of *Komparatistik* on ecocriticism and comparative literature (2014) and authored numerous essays on ecocriticism, ecocritical theory, and American literature. He is a founding member of the European Association for the Study of Literature, Culture, and the Environment and served as president from 2012 to 2014.

White, disabled, and gender queer, **Eli Clare** happily lives in the Green Mountains of Vermont, where he writes and proudly claims a penchant for rabble-rousing. He has written a book of essays, *Exile and Pride: Disability, Queerness, and Liberation* (1999), and a collection of poetry, *The Marrow's Telling: Words in Motion* (2007), and has been published in many periodicals and anthologies. Eli speaks, teaches, and facilitates all over the United States and Canada at conferences, community events, and colleges about disability, queer and trans identities, and social justice. Among other pursuits, he has walked across the United States for peace, coordinated a rape prevention program, and helped organize the first-ever Queerness and Disability Conference.

Jeffrey Jerome Cohen is Professor of English and Director of the Medieval and Early Modern Studies Institute at the George Washington University. He has published widely on medieval studies, posthumanism, materiality, ecotheory, and the monstrous. Books include *Of Giants* (1999), *Medieval Identity Machines* (2003), *Hybridity, Identity, and Monstrosity* (2006), and *Stories of Stone: An Ecology of the Inhuman* (2015), as well as the edited collections *Monster Theory* (1996), *Animal, Vegetable, Mineral: Ethics and Objects* (2012), and *Prismatic Ecology: Ecotheory beyond Green* (2014). He has co-edited a special issue of the journal *postmedieval*, titled *Ecomaterialism,* and the collection *Elemental Ecocriticism* (2015).

Lowell Duckert is Assistant Professor of English at West Virginia University. He is co-editor of *Ecomaterialism,* a special issue of *postmedieval* (2013), and of a collection of essays titled *Elemental Ecocriticism*. He has published articles on glaciers, polar bears, and the color maroon, among others. He is currently molding a book project on early modern waterscapes and actor-network theory.

Simon C. Estok is a Distinguished Visiting Fellow in the Research Center for Comparative Literature and World Literatures at Shanghai Normal University (2013–14) and Professor of English and Literary Theory at Sungkyunkwan University in Seoul, Korea. He has published extensively on ecocriticism and Shakespeare in such journals as *PMLA, Mosaic, Configurations, English Studies in Canada, ISLE,* and others. He is the author of *Ecocriticism and Shakespeare: Reading Ecophobia* (2011). He co-edited *International Perspectives in Feminist Ecocriticism* (2013) and *East Asian Ecocriticisms: A Critical Reader* (2013).

Greta Gaard is Professor of English at the University of Wisconsin–River Falls. She is the author of *Ecological Politics: Ecofeminists and the Greens* (1998) and *The Nature of Home* (2007), editor of *Ecofeminism: Women, Animals, Nature* (1993), and co-editor of *Ecofeminist Literary Criticism* (1998). Her essays have appeared in *Hypatia, Signs, Environmental Ethics, The Ecologist, Ethics & the Environment, ISLE*, and other volumes of feminist, environmental, sexuality, and cultural studies collections. She recently co-edited *International Perspectives in Feminist Ecocriticism* (2013).

Cheryll Glotfelty is Professor of Literature and Environment and Director of Graduate Studies in English at the University of Nevada, Reno. She co-edited *The Ecocriticism Reader: Landmarks in Literary Ecology* (1996), a seminal text in the field. She is co-founder and past president of the Association for the Study of Literature and Environment and co-founder of the Literature & Environment graduate program at UNR. Glotfelty is the editor of *Literary Nevada: Writings from the Silver State* (2008) and co-editor of *The Bioregional Imagination: Literature, Ecology, and Place* (2012).

A philosopher by training, **Serenella Iovino** is Professor of Comparative Literature at the University of Turin. President of the European Association for the Study of Literature, Culture, and Environment from 2008 to 2010, she is Research Fellow of the Alexander-von-Humboldt Foundation and serves on the editorial boards of several international journals, including *ISLE, Green Letters*, and *Ecozon@*. Author of four books and numerous essays, she has guest-edited *Ecozon@*'s Special Focus Issue on *Mediterranean Ecocriticism* (Autumn 2013). In 2014 she held the James K. Binder Lectureship in Literature at the University of California, San Diego. For more information, please visit https://unito.academia.edu/serenellaiovino.

Timo Maran is a Senior Research Fellow in the Department of Semiotics at the University of Tartu, Estonia. His research interests include the theory and history of zoosemiotics, ecosemiotics and semiotic relations of nature and culture, Estonian nature writing and ecocriticism, and theory and semiotics of biological mimicry. He is the author of *Mimikri semiootika* (Semiotics of mimicry) (2008) and co-editor of *Readings in Zoosemiotics* (2011) and *Semiotics in the Wild: Essays in Honour of Kalevi Kull on the Occasion of His 60th Birthday* (2012).

Timothy Morton is Rita Shea Guffey Chair of English at Rice University. He is the author of *Ecology without Nature* (2007), *The Ecological Thought* (2010), *Hyperobjects: Philosophy and Ecology after the End of the World* (2013), *Realist Magic: Objects, Ontology, Causality* (2013), and seven other books and eighty essays on philosophy, ecology, literature, food, and music. He blogs regularly at http://www.ecologywithoutnature.blogspot.com.

Serpil Oppermann is Professor of English at Hacettepe University, Ankara, Turkey. She is the author of *Postmodern Tarih Kuramı: Tarihyazımı, Yeni Tarihselcilik ve Roman* (2006), editor of *Ekoeleştiri: Çevre ve Edebiyat* (2012), and co-editor of *The Future of Ecocriticism: New Horizons* (2011) and *International Perspectives in Feminist Ecocriticism* (2013). Her publications on ecocriticism have appeared in such journals as the *Trumpeter, ISLE, Critique, Ecozon@, Mosaic,* and *Anglia*, among others. She serves on the editorial boards of *ISLE, Ecozon@,* and *PAN*. For more information, please visit https://hacettepe.academia.edu/SerpilOppermann.

Dana Phillips is Associate Professor of English at Towson University in Maryland. He has published articles on literature and the environment and on Whitman, Cormac McCarthy, DeLillo, and Thoreau. His award-winning monograph *The Truth of Ecology: Nature, Culture, and Literature in America* was published in 2003. His current research focuses on concepts of the natural and the artificial in relation to the sense of place; on the cognitive skills, communicative abilities, and cultural traditions of animals, especially elephants and horses; and on the material turn in ecocriticism.

Kate Rigby is Professor of Environmental Humanities at Monash University. Her research ranges across German studies, European philosophy, literature and religion, and culture and ecology. She is the author of *Topographies of the Sacred* (2004) and co-editor of *Ecocritical Theory: New European Approaches* (2011). She is a founding co-editor of the ecological humanities journal *Philosophy Activism Nature* and was the founding president of the Australia–New Zealand Association for the Study of Literature, Environment, and Culture.

Catriona Sandilands is a Professor in the Faculty of Environmental Studies at York University, Toronto. Her research and teaching bring the environmental humanities to particular spaces (mostly parks) and species (mostly plants) and also to important questions of ecological politics, including feminist and queer perspectives. She is the co-editor of *Queer Ecologies: Sex, Nature, Politics, Desire* (2010) and the forthcoming *Green Words / Green Worlds: Environmental Literatures and Politics in Canada*. She has served on the Executive of ASLE in several capacities, including as president in 2015–16.

Heather I. Sullivan is Professor of German and Chair of the Interdisciplinary Minor in Comparative Literature at Trinity University in San Antonio, Texas. She is the author of *The Intercontextuality of Self and Nature in Ludwig Tieck's Early*

Works (1997). She is the guest co-editor of a recent collection of essays, *Material Ecocriticism*, in *ISLE* (2012). Her essays have appeared in *Ecozon@; Goethe Yearbook; Monatshefte; ISLE; 1650–1850: Ideas, Aesthetics, and Inquiries in the Early Modern Era; Bulletin of Science, Technology, and Society; Studies in Eighteenth-Century Culture;* and the *European Romantic Review.*

Wendy Wheeler is Professor Emeritus of English Literature and Cultural Inquiry at London Metropolitan University. She has been a visiting professor in the Environmental Studies Program at the University of Oregon and is a visiting professor in the School of Art at RMIT. She is the author of *A New Modernity? Change in Science, Literature, and Politics* (1999), *The Whole Creature: Complexity, Biosemiotics, and the Evolution of Culture* (2006), *Biosemiotics: Nature/Culture/Science/Semiosis* (2011), and many articles and essays on biological systems theory, biosemiotics, and ecocriticism. She has been an editor of *New Formations: A Journal of Culture/Theory/Politics,* where she remains on the editorial board. She also sits on the editorial board of *Green Letters* and is an editorial consultant for *Cybernetics and Human Knowing.*

Hubert Zapf is Professor and Chair of American Literature at the University of Augsburg, Germany. In the past decade, he has contributed to the growth of cultural ecology, to which he has dedicated many essays, mostly on English and American authors. He is the author, among other publications, of *Kurze Geschichte der anglo-amerikanischen Literaturtheorie* (1996) and *Literatur als kulturelle Ökologie* (2002). He has edited *Literature and Ecology,* a special issue of *Anglia* (2006), *Kulturökologie und Literatur* (2008), and *Amerikanische Literaturgeschichte* (2010) and co-edited *Redefining Modernism and Postmodernism* (2010).

Index

Page numbers in italics refer to illustrations.

abduction, 53, 70, 74, 77, 337
ableism, 207, 209, 216
Aboriginal Australian (people), 283
Abram, David, 1, 6, 11, 15, 52, 105, 292, 315
actant, 39, 42, 46, 91,115; intra-actants, 294, 295; rainbow as, 126, 128; stem cells as, 172. *See also* actor-network-theory; Latour, Bruno
actor-network-theory, 128n2. *See also* actant; Latour, Bruno
Adam, 73, 109, 309
Adams, Ansel, 236
Adamson, Joni, 15, 16n5, 36n5
aesthetics, 222, 227, 253
affect, affective, ix, 15, 24, 82, 115, 118, 127, 166, 194; affection, 244, 245, 246, 251n6; affectivity, 250; civic affection, 15
Agamben, Giorgio, 10, 109, 170n3, 267n3
agency, x–xii, 12, 13, 14, 21–22, 25–27, 32–34, 37, 39–42, 44, 52–53, 58–59, 75, 100, 103, 105–106, 133–134, 195–196, 203n6, 203n9, 228, 253, 256, 267, 267n2, 285, 293; as communication; 30; distributive, 3, 5, 26, 38, 40, 91, 128; expressive, 28; human, 2–3, 5–6, 9, 28, 34, 39, 85, 91, 132, 134–135, 138n1, 152, 194, 276n2, 287; inhuman, 108; as intrinsic property, 6, 24; limits of, 37–50; material, 8, 9–10, 24, 25, 28, 34, 48, 104, 106, 113n3, 123, 133–134, 141, 149, 199, 223, 240, 250, 284; meaning-bearing field of, 70; narrative, 2, 8, 12, 28–35, 98, 112, 132, 138n3; of nature, 108, 131, 138n2; nonhuman, 15, 35, 130, 133, 135, 137, 273, 283; of rain, 114–115, 126; as responseability, 34; semiotic, 111; of shit, 180, 184; of stone, ix–xi, 32, 34–35, 45, 240; without subjects, 294. *See also* agent
agent, 116, 124, 157, 180, 253; autonomous, 32–33; human, 3, 35, 115, 236, 255; impersonal, 3; low-level, 76; material, 48, 130; narrative, 131; nonhuman, 3, 8. *See also* actant; agency
agential realism, 4, 139n10, 172, 203n8, 224, 293. *See also* Barad, Karen; intra-action
AIDS, 209

Ailanthus altissima, 241–242
air, 16, 41, 60, 64, 65, 88, 92, 121, 122, 124, 127, 157, 166–167, 180, 182, 203n9, 213, 260, 264, 276, 293, 299, 301–306, 308–312, 313n2, 314nn6–7; air-ocean, 85; currents and cycles, 83; pollution of, 210. *See also* atmosphere; *Sila* (Inuit, intelligence of the air)
Aitken, Robert, 295
Alaimo, Stacy, 5, 10, 11, 14, 27, 83, 113n2, 131, 138n4, 139n6, 187, 203n6, 222, 295. *See also* trans-corporeal, trans-corporeality
Albrile, Ezio, 113n5
Alighieri, Dante. *See* Dante, Alighieri
Allied Army, 107–108
alterity, 130–131, 288. *See also* other, otherness
Ammons, A. R., 184
anatta (Buddhism). *See* no-self (Buddhism, *anatta*)
Anderson, Myrdene, 71
Anderson, Warwick, 176–177, 183
anicca (Buddhism). *See* impermanence (Buddhism, *anicca*)
animal, animals, x, xi, 1, 3, 6, 15, 24, 30, 36n3, 40, 49, 57, 61, 92, 108, 109, 123, 129n14, 132, 138n1, 139n6, 142, 143, 145–148, 152–153, 158, 159, 162, 164, 169n2, 170n3, 170n8, 173, 186–187, 189, 191, 193, 194, 196, 199–200, 202, 210, 211–212, 215–217, 239, 246, 254–256, 261, 265–266, 267n2, 284, 292, 296–297, 300n3, 300n4, 304–308, 314n5; agency of, 293; animality, 64; animal-vegetable-mineral, 40, 102; our animal flesh, 310, 312; our animal senses, 312; modeling, 150–151; narratives of, 258; studies, 82–83, 299
animism, 7, 266–267, 284, 289, 314n7, 314n10. *See also* religion; spirituality
Anthropocene, 7, 279
anthropocentrism, 69, 139n5, 139n7; dis-anthropocentrism, 11, 253
anthropology, 2, 254
anthropomorphism, 8, 29, 69, 108, 148, 253, 256, 266, 267

345

Apis mellifera. See bee, honeybee (*Apis mellifera*)
Aquinas, Thomas. *See* Thomas Aquinas
archaeology, 2, 104, 113n3; archaeological research, 98, 104
Aristotle, 59, 116–117, 125–126, 275
Armah, Ayi Kwei, 177
Armiero, Marco, 111, 113n7
Arnakak, Jaypeetee, 304
Arpaia, Christian, xiii, 99, *112*
art, xi, xii, 15, 32, 53–54, 56–58, 59, 60, 67, 70, 78, 139n5, 146, 165, 222–223, 225, 230, 239, 269–270, 275, 279, 299; alchemical, 240; ecological, 93; environmental, 193; as force, 65; land, 64; photographic, 221, 236
assemblage, 26, 28, 39, 40–42, 91, 100, 104, 115, 173, 176, 240, 276; biopolitical, 158; ecological, 128; material, 45
Association for the Study of Literature and Environment (ASLE), xiii, xiv, 339, 342
Astraea, 263–264, 268n12
Athanassakis, Apostolos, 268nn12–13
Athena, 41
Atkin, Albert, 79n4
Atkin, Polly, 171n15
atmosphere, 1, 11, 23, 121–122, 124, 251n8, 257; as mind, 301–303, 305–306, 308, 310–311, 314n5. *See also* air
atom, xiin2, 12, 21, 24, 32, 36n7, 48, 52, 61, 83, 100, 101, 137, 185n2, 275, 299; atomic testing, 221, 229; photon, 32, 33, 35, 275; subatomic particle, xiin2, 33, 84, 232, 276. *See also* quantum physics
Augustine, Grace, 257
Augustine of Hippo, 73
Aurangzeb, the Mughal emperor, 118
autopoiesis, 12, 40, 43–45, 46, 49, 49n1, 50n3, 56; autopoietic system, 43, 45, 48; social, 50n5
aversion (Buddhism), 292, 298. *See also Dosa* (Buddhism)
Ayahuasca (*Banisteriopis caapi*), 258
Aztec (people), 216

Baartman, Sarah (a.k.a. "Hottentot Venus"), 216
Bacon, Francis, 73
bacterium, bacteria, 4, 26, 32, 33–34, 35, 36n6, 41, 83, 87, 91–92, 94, 144, 179, 189, 191. *See also* microbiome
Banisteriopis caapi. See Ayahuasca (*Banisteriopis caapi*)
Barad, Karen, xiii, 4, 26–27, 31, 45, 47, 83, 100, 131, 138n4, 184, 187, 192, 195, 222, 224, 283, 291, 293, 294; *Meeting the Universe Halfway*, 1, 11, 26–27, 30, 31, 35, 84, 90, 100, 138n4, 192, 195, 224, 238, 293, 294, 296. *See also* agential realism; intra-action
Barkow, Jerome, 71
Barnum, P. T., 216
Barthes, Roland, 238
Bartlow, Amy, 238
Bartola. *See* Maximo and Bartola (a.k.a "Last of the ancient Aztecs")
Bassler, Bonnie L., 32–33
Bateson, Gregory, xiii, 10, 31, 54, 70, 74–75, 254
Bateson, Mary Catherine, 70
Beard, Mary, 6
Beaudry, Mary C., 16n1, 113n3
Beck, Ulrich, 187, 193, 194
Beckett, Samuel, 76, 177
bee, honeybee (*Apis mellifera*), xiv, 14, 145, 157–171. *See also* biopolitics; community; democracy; health; indigenous; justice; politics; relation, relationship
Benarroch, Jonas, 195–196
Benedict, Ruth, 254
Benga, Ota, 216
Benjamin, Alison, 160
Benjamin, Walter, 13, 98, 100
Bennett, Jane, 8, 11, 15, 22, 25, 26, 27, 36n2, 38, 52, 84, 91, 114, 115, 137, 138, 158, 172, 193, 222, 239–252, 259, 285, 296
Benyus, Janine, 139n8
Bergthaller, Hannes, 12
Bernier, François, 117–118, 120–128, 129n10, 129n18
Bhikkhu, Santikaro, 295
biodiversity, 193, 213, 214, 260. *See also* biology; biosphere; ecology
biology, 2, 6, 12, 38, 77, 79n2, 94n5, 185n5; evolutionary, 56, 67; materialism in, 68; microbiology, 190; molecular, 77; oceanic, 191; sociobiology, 71; theoretical, 69. *See also* biodiversity; biosphere; ecology
bioluminescence, 257. *See also* "Sachamama" (Source of Life, Source of Light)
biopolitics, 14, 157–160, 165, 169n1, 170n4; in bees, 160–169; multispecies, 163, 165
bioregion, 17, 305, 308
biosemiotics, 10, 12, 53–54, 68–69, 71, 73–75, 77–78, 79n1, 141–142, 145–146, 149, 153–154, 154n1, 161, 267, 283. *See also* ecosemiotics; semiosis; semiosphere; semiotic niche; sign
biosphere, 5, 13, 36n6, 45, 49, 65, 80, 82, 83, 90, 92, 299, 303; creative, 51–52; intelligence of, 313. *See also* biodiversity; biology; ecology

Birch, Charles, 23
birds, 62, 145, 150, 186, 192, 246, 272, 275; blackbirds, 308; bowerbird, 152; firebird, 60; hummingbird, ix; kingfisher, 287; migratory, 147; oven bird, 61; seabirds, 152, 199; songbird, 204; songs, 41–42; spotted hawk, 62, 240
Bishop, Elizabeth, 61
bison, 204–205, 207, 210–212, 218
Björk, 188
Black, Maggie, 179
Blake, Tim, 32
Blessingway, 306
Blume, Harvey, 216
Boas, Franz, 254, 263
body, bodies, 5, 7, 12, 31, 62, 65, 84, 87, 89, 97–113, 115, 117, 123, 132, 133, 134, 139n10, 169n1, 223, 240, 251n6, 251n9, 266, 283, 288, 293; of animal, 150; as avatar, 257; bodymind, 29, 36n4, 105, 107, 112; disabled, 204–218; ecology of, 291; of Holy Wind, 305–306; human, 2, 15, 24, 63, 85, 92, 106, 111, 120, 124, 125, 127, 131, 147, 176, 203n9, 205–206, 209–210, 211, 217, 239, 241, 243, 246–247, 257, 272, 302, 305, 312; intrabody, 245; mindbody, 50n6, 55, 58, 69, 222, 304. *See also* corporeal, corporeality; nature(s); trans-corporeal, trans-corporeality
Bogdanich, Walt, 240
Bogost, Ian, 198
Bohm, David, 10, 23, 52
Bohr, Neils, 192
Bolívar, Simón, 253, 267n1
Bolla, Peter de, 78
Bonabeau, Eric, 40
Boon, Marcus, 251
Borodale, Sean, 157, 165–169, 171n13, 171n16
Botkin, David, 94n3
Boucher, Sandy, 294
Bourbons, sovereigns of Naples, 104
Bourgine, Paul, 49n1
Bradford, Phillips, 216
Braidotti, Rosi, 10, 34, 135, 139n7, 196
Brayton, Dan, 130, 138n1
Brazier, David, 297
Breitbach, Julia, 238
Brown, Bill, 10, 238. *See also* thing, theory
Brueghel, Pieter, 64
Bruno, Giordano, 76
Bryant, Levi, R., 50n3, 101
Buddhism, 16, 278, 283, 284, 286, 290n5, 291–298, 299
Buell, Lawrence, 16n5, 139n5

Butler, Charles, 163
Butler, Judith, 187, 202n2, 283

Calbi, Maurizio, 17n10
Callicott, Baird J., 25
Calvo Garzón, Paco, 267n6
Cameron, James, 15, 253, 257, 263, 267n9
cancer, 223, 228, 279, 292
capitalism, 138n1, 163, 187, 191, 214, 284, 292, 293
Capra, Fritjof, 49n2
Carson, Rachel, 188, 189, 190
Carter, Marcia, 269
Cartesian dualism, 22, 50n6, 73, 74. *See also* Descartes, René
Cathcart, Brian, 114–115, 127
causality, x, 15, 149, 152, 172, 250, 269; circular, 47, 147; natural, 239; nonlinear, 284; sympathetic, 240
Chapelian, Jean, 129n10
chemicals, 7, 21, 32–33, 34, 36n7, 40, 52, 68, 71, 80, 83, 87–90, 92, 97, 130, 164, 170n6, 171n12, 173, 198, 202n3, 203n7, 209, 223, 235, 255, 277, 292, 302; biochemical substances, 27, 44, 106, 151, 192; code, 42, 46. *See also* contamination; dioxin; pollution, pollutants; trans-corporeal, trans-corporeality
Chen, Mel Y., ix–x, xiin4
Cheney, Jim, 25, 139n5
citizen, citizenry, citizenship, 58, 109, 111, 113n4, 181, 187, 193, 199, 202, 229, 245, 254, 259, 294. *See also* democracy
Clarke, Bruce, 49
climate, 3, 4, 13, 16, 23, 114, 118, 120, 122, 124, 278, 305, 307; Buddhist Climate Project, 296; change, 116, 160, 178, 182, 186, 187, 193, 254, 260, 262, 296, 301, 311, 314n9; intellectual, 117; justice, 16; narratives, 32
coevolution. *See* evolution, evolutionism
Cohen, Jeffrey Jerome, xiii, 7, 8, 10, 11, 32, 34, 102, 105, 106, 128n4
Colbert, Jean-Baptiste, 117–118
Coleridge, Samuel Taylor, 60, 236, 275
collective(s), 4, 6, 8, 10, 14, 16n4, 26, 30, 34, 40, 56, 104, 108, 109, 111, 112, 115, 119–120, 126–128, 163, 166, 186, 197, 263, 285, 313, 314n9; human, 41, 47, 91, 100, 106, 116, 129n6, 312. *See also* Latour, Bruno
colonial, colonialism, 14, 170, 174, 176, 177, 183, 211; excremental, 176, 183. *See also* postcolonial, postcolonialism
Colony Collapse Disorder (CCD), 160

348 | Index

color(s) colors, 13, 63, 65, 83, 126, 225, 271, 274, 313; ecology of, 80–81, 87, 90–93; Goethe's theory of, 84–89
Commoner, Barry, 298
community, 3, 32–33, 158, 168, 169n1, 239, 267; of bees, 162, 166; disability, 208–210; indigenous, 259; more-than-human, 311
complexity, 3, 8, 26, 36n6, 38, 41–43, 46, 98, 106, 112, 146, 151, 206; environmental, 47–48, 93, 262
Confucianism, 290n5
Connolly, William E., 39, 47, 81, 194
consciousness, 14, 24, 37, 56, 58, 64, 69, 79n1, 82, 85, 91, 93, 114, 125, 222, 225, 232, 285, 293, 313n1; collective, 314n9; ecological, 63; environment of, 50n6; human, 31; as mind, 302–304; planetary, 55; public, 136. *See also* mind
Constable, Archibald, 129n11
constructivism, 22, 25, 45, 283
contamination, 112, 227–228, 262. *See also* chemicals; dioxin; pollution, pollutants; trans-corporeal, trans-corporeality; waste
Conti, Laura, 138n3
Coole, Diana, 2, 27, 36n7, 84, 134
corporeal, corporeality, x, 15, 25, 97, 101, 108, 111, 124, 130, 131, 160, 164, 165, 167, 191, 193, 221, 243, 261, 289, 303, 312. *See also* body, bodies; trans-corporeal, trans-corporeality
Cosmides, Leda, 71
cosmopolitanism, 123, 260, 264; eco-cosmopolitanism, 259–260
cosmopolitics, 264, 267
craving (Buddhism). See *Tanha* (Buddhism, craving)
creativity, 6, 10, 12, 27, 36n6, 70, 112; human, 8; human and nonhuman, 8, 12; literary, 51–66; of matter, 21, 24, 29, 32–33; nonhuman, 26, 30, 285
Crocker, Holly, 251n2
Cruikshank, Julie, 261, 262
Culbert, Jennifer, 251n1
cultural ecology. *See* ecology
Curtin, Deane, 296, 300n4
cyborg, 82, 173. *See also* hybrid, hybridity, hybridization; posthumanism, posthuman

D'Alisa, Giacomo, 111
Damasio, Antonio, 10
Danesi, Marcel, 146, 154n, 154nn7–8
Danishmand Kahn, 118
Dante, Alighieri, 76
Daoism, Daoist philosophies, 286, 287, 290n5
Dargatz, Gail Anderson, 165

Darwin, Charles Robert, 57, 172, 185n5, 254, 278. *See also* evolution, evolutionism
Daston, Lorraine, 148
Davies, Paul C. W., 70
Davis, Barney and Hiram (a.k.a. "Wild Men from Borneo"), 216
Davis, Mike, 179, 181
De la Cadena, Marisol, 254, 256, 262
De Landa, Manuel, 10, 52, 102, 115
Deacon, Terrence, 75
Deely, John N., 69, 74, 78
deep ecology. *See* ecology
deep incarnation (ecotheology), 288
Deleuze, Gilles, 10, 101, 243, 251n6, 285
De Lillo, Don, 63, 64–65
DeLoughrey, Elizabeth, 203n10
delusion (Buddhism). See *moha* (Buddhism, delusion)
democracy, 93, 245; of bees, 161, 163, 170n10
Dennett, Daniel, 185n5
dependent origination (Buddhism, *paticcasamuppāda*), 16, 291, 292–294, 296, 298, 300n2
Deranty, Jean-Philippe, 158, 159
Derrida, Jacques, 28, 82, 159, 162, 169n2, 170n8, 271, 276, 278
Descartes, René, 117. *See also* Cartesian dualism; *res extensa, res cogitans*
determinism, 72
deus sive natura, 243, 251n6. *See also* God, goddess, gods; immanence, immanent; nature(s); ontotheology; Spinoza, Baruch
Dew, Nicholas, 117, 118, 128nn9–10
diabetes, 209
diffraction, diffractive methodology, 9, 10, 11, 13, 14, 84, 86, 88, 89, 93, 112. *See also* interpretation
Dimock, Wai Chee, 136
Dineh or Navajo (people), 305, 314n4
dioxin, 1, 138n3, 292. *See also* chemicals; contamination; pollution, pollutants
disability, 14, 204, 205, 207–211, 213–215, 218n1
disclosure, 172, 294, 295, 298
discourse, discursive, 4, 7, 12, 16n3, 21, 23, 25, 29, 30, 33, 34, 39, 45, 52, 53, 54, 56, 57–58, 61, 66, 76, 98, 103, 106–108, 109, 112, 113n4, 115, 116, 125, 128, 130, 143, 144, 146, 150, 158, 160, 172, 176, 202n2, 203n7, 223, 263, 284, 291, 300n3, 312. *See also* material-discursive
disease. *See* illness (disease)
disenchantment, 23, 35n1. *See also* reenchantment; postmodernism, postmodern
DNA, 1, 32, 34, 53, 68, 180, 275, 278, 299

Dolphijn, Rick, 3, 16n1, 31
Donghak, 290n5
Dorje, Gyurme, 296
Dosa (Buddhism), 292. *See* aversion (Buddhism)
Douglas, Mary, 135
Douglas-Fairhurst, Robert, 132
dualism. *See* Cartesian dualism; subject
Duckert, Lowell, xiin3, 11, 13
Dukka (Buddhism, suffering), 292, 298
Duns Scotus, John, 73
Dupré, John, 68
DuVernay, Alvin, III, 133
Dynamic balance and beauty (Navajo). *See* Hozho (Navajo, dynamic balance and beauty)

E. coli, 180
Eagleton, Terry, 132, 137, 138n1
Earle, Sylvia, 186, 188, 189, 190, 202n1
ecocentrism, ecocentric paradigm, 22, 55
eco-cosmopolitanism. *See* cosmopolitanism
ecocriticism: excremental, 14, 172, 175, 177, 178, 180, 183–184; feminist, 17n5, 289, 300; material, x, xii, xiinn1–2, 1, 2, 5–7, 9–16, 16n3, 17n5, 17n8, 17n10, 21–22, 25, 27, 28–29, 31, 34, 35, 40, 45, 47, 49, 51, 54, 78, 80, 82, 83, 86, 87, 90, 92, 103, 106, 111, 113n2, 116, 130, 131, 133, 134, 137, 141–142, 146, 149, 153–154, 157, 169, 170n11, 173, 175, 184, 193, 202, 222–223, 224, 238, 267n2, 269, 284, 287, 289, 291–293, 297, 298, 312
ecofeminism. *See* feminism
ecology, 38, 54, 64, 94n3, 105, 116, 120, 130, 271, 274, 288, 291, 296, 298, 300n3; of colors, 13, 80–81, 83, 86–93; of creativity, 59; cultural, 12, 51, 54–57, 60; dark, 93; deep, 38, 52, 300n3; of disturbance, 178; interfaith ecology movement, 288; materialist, 254, 284; of mind, 10, 54, 78; political, 111, 193; of selves, 15, 257, 264, 266; of shit, 179. *See also* cultural ecology
ecomafia, 111
ecomaterialism. *See* materialism(s)
ecophobia, 13, 130–135, 137, 138n1, 139n10; biophobia, 63
ecopsychology, 296
ecosemiotics, 145. *See also* biosemiotics; semiosis; semiosphere; semiotic niche; sign; zoosemiotics
ecotheology. *See* theology
Edelman, Gerald, 40
Ehrenfeld, David, 134
Eichendorff, Joseph von, 81
Elder, John, 17n6

electricity, 3, 83, 172
elements (natural), 7, 29, 36n7, 60, 85–86, 92, 104, 106–108, 116, 127, 145, 190, 223. *See also* air; earth; fire; water
Eliot, George, 67
Elsner, Jas, 251
Elvey, Anne, xiii, 11, 17n9, 289
embodiment, 3, 5, 29, 81, 84, 102, 107, 115, 125, 134, 137, 193, 288, 293; disembodiment, 12, 107. *See also* body, bodies; corporeal, corporeality; transcorporeal, trans-corporeality
emergence, emergent, 5, 26, 28, 32, 37, 42, 45, 48, 66, 68, 72, 77, 79n1, 103, 105, 137, 195, 243, 293; coemergence, coemergent, 30, 44
Emmeche, Claus, 71
energy, 7, 13, 17n10, 39, 41, 52, 53, 56, 62, 65, 69, 79n5, 80, 84, 87, 92, 101, 102, 173, 184, 207, 240, 255, 257, 278, 287, 292, 296, 299, 306; creative, 29, 58–60, 64; crisis, 264; matter-energy, 115, 150, 228; solar, 81, 90
entanglement, 3, 10, 13, 14, 191, 193, 195, 288, 291, 292; of human and nonhuman, 27, 35, 200; of politics, and biopolitical, 109, 169; transcorporeal, 92
environment, ix, 4, 8, 13, 30, 23–24, 27, 42–48, 56, 64, 65, 82, 135, 137, 139n15, 141–145, 149–154, 176, 178, 181, 183, 223, 259, 267n2, 275, 278, 284, 290, 296; environmental crisis, 14, 16n5, 41, 184; environmental degradation, destruction, 210, 212; marine, 186, 188, 189, 190, 192, 199; material, 52, 80, 81, 83; as material-discursive flows, 28; of multispecies, 147; natural, 103, 118, 130–132; as part of us, 36n4; physical, 32–34; semiotic, 53; vibrant, 87. *See also* ethics; justice; landscape
epistemology, 9, 35, 45, 266, 293. *See also* onto-epistemology
Epstein, Mark, 212, 293
Ericson, Augustus William, 212
Estok, Simon C., 13, 136, 138n1
Esty, Jed (Joshua, D.), 177, 183
ethics, x, 3, 12, 16, 17n8, 35, 128, 130, 133, 136, 192, 194, 195, 197, 297; Buddhist, 298; environmental, 130, 138n1, 139nn5–6, 300n3; human, 189; interspecies, 296; Levinasian, 288; material, new materialist, 138n4, 294, 298; more than-human, 284. *See also* responsibility; value
ethnicity, ethnic, 165n, 254, 258, 260, 287. *See also* indigenous
Evans, Walker, 230
evolution, evolutionism, 7, 14, 29, 31, 32, 39, 40,

51, 56–57, 67, 69, 71, 73, 75, 76–77, 79n4, 94n5, 101, 110, 117, 185n5, 188–189, 191, 192, 216, 254, 264, 278; coevolution, coevolving entities, 1, 56, 57, 223; of mind, 68; natural, 65, 75, 110; social, cultural, 49, 51, 53–55, 70, 71. *See also* Darwin, Charles Robert
excrement, 174; shit, 14, 135, 173–185, 185n2, 185n4
extinction, 3, 6, 7, 80, 186, 191, 212, 302

Farina, Almo, 103
Farini, Krao (a.k.a "Ape Girl"), 216
Favareau Donald, 71, 72, 154n1
Fawcett, Ben, 179
feminism, 2, 10, 260; Buddhist, 294, 295; ecofeminism, 16, 296; material feminism(s), 10, 172, 187, 193; ecospirituality, 288; postcolonial, 290n5; queer, 299; of science, 21. *See also* ecocriticism; gender, gendering
Finke, Peter, 56
fire, 60, 98, 105, 107, 108, 132, 144–145, 204, 207, 229, 240, 305, 310
First Nation, 206, 212
fish, 62–63, 85, 109–111, 127, 186–187, 192, 199–200, 215, 258, 262; codfish, 173; "inner fish," 189–191; jellyfish, 199–200, 202; starfish, 31
Fitzgerald, John Scott, 64
Flavin, Dan, 269
Flood, Finbarr Barry, 251
Foerster, Heinz von, 45
food, 1, 11, 33, 40, 46, 83, 92, 101, 109, 133, 144, 147, 163, 164, 181, 182, 187, 192–194, 196, 199, 206, 209, 213, 254, 258, 262, 265, 292, 296, 297, 300n4, 304, 307; seafood, 197, 198
Foster, Susan Leigh, 252
Foucault, Michel, 37, 39, 169n1, 185n2
Four Noble Truths (Buddhism), 292
Frank, Jason, 244
freedom (liberty), 24, 76, 78, 93, 132, 196. *See also* intentional, intentionality
Freud, Sigmund, 77, 131, 314n9
Frisch, Karl von, 161, 162, 163, 170n6, 170n8
Frost, Samantha, 2, 11, 16n1, 24, 27, 33, 36n7, 38, 39, 84, 134
Fulke, William, 117, 123
fungus, fungi, ix, x, 3, 7, 36n5, 254–255, 267n6. *See also* microbiome
Funktionskreis (functional cycle in semiotics), 149

Gablic, Suzy, 22
Gadamer, Hans-Georg, 131

Galeano, Juan Carlos, 15, 253, 256–262, 265, 267n1, 267n8
Gare, Arran E., 25
Garrard, Greg, 16n3, 259, 268n10
Gassendi, Pierre, 117
gender, gendering, 10, 97, 103, 104, 133, 138n3, 215, 217, 256, 291, 294, 311; transgender, 214. *See also* sexuality
genome, 160, 191, 275; Human Genome Project, 68
George, Rose, 178–180, 185n6
Ghosh, Amitav, 229n18
Giardia lamblia, 180
Gibson, James J., 145, 149, 150, 152
Gies, Nathan, 251
Ginsberg, Allen, 61
Giovannetti, Manuela, 255, 267n6
globalization, 160, 258, 260, 262, 268n11
Glotfelty, Cheryll, 6, 15, 298
God, goddess, gods, 51, 58, 73, 94n8, 111, 117, 126, 167, 228, 236, 239, 240, 251n6, 263, 268n12, 276, 288, 289, 292. See also *deus sive natura*
Goethe, Johann Wolfgang, 11, 13, 17n9, 80–93, 93n1, 93n2, 94n4, 94nn6–7, 100
Goin, Peter, 15, 221–237, 237n1
Goldberg, Rube, 180
Goldsworthy, Andy, 270
Goodbody, Axel, 11
Goodman, Nelson, 14
Gore, Al, 138n1
Gosden, Chris, 251
Gould, James L., 162
Great Pacific Garbage Patch, 198
Greenblatt, Stephen, 137
Greimas, A. J., 154n2
Griffin, David Ray, 22, 23–24, 26, 30, 31, 32, 36n1
Griffin, Susan, 299
Gross, Rita, 294
Guattari, Félix, 10, 243
Guthrie, Stewart Elliott, 148

Hacking, Ian, 185n3
Haraway, Donna J., 2, 5, 7, 10, 27, 28, 36n3, 82, 154n2, 254, 267n4, 288, 290n2, 295
Harjo, Joy, 61
Harman, Graham, 128n1
Harrington, David M., 59
Harris, Jonathan Gil, 129n12
Harrison, Gabriel, 249
Harrison, Peter, 73, 74

Index | 351

Hart, David Bentley, 79n6
Hartshorne, Charles, 22, 24, 29
Hawkins, Gay, 194–195
Hawthorne, Nathaniel, 54
Hayles, N. Katherine, 10, 28, 82, 102, 103, 107
health, 3, 4, 5, 22, 131, 181, 206–207, 209, 211, 213, 215, 222, 224, 228, 243, 300; of bees, 160, 166, 170n5; ecological, environmental, 16n3, 187, 203n6; human, 14, 190, 193. *See also* illness (disease)
Hegel, Georg Friedrich Wilhelm, 278, 288
Heidegger, Martin, 170, 271–272, 276, 278
Heise, Ursula K., 259, 260, 268n10, 284
Hekman, Susan, 2, 10, 28, 47, 131, 238, 293, 295, 298, 299
Helmreich, Stefan, 188, 190–192, 254, 255
Heninger, S. K. Jr., 117, 125, 129n7
Henry, Mickaël, 164
Herero, 174
Hesiod, 263, 268n12
Hicks, Dan, 16n1, 113n3
Higgs, Peter, 278
Hinton, Scott, 238
Hird, Myra, 172
Hitchcock, Alfred, 230
Hoffmeyer, Jesper, 68–69, 70, 71, 75, 77–78, 141, 144, 154n1
Hofstadter, Douglas, 70
Hogan, Linda, 188
holism, 239
Hollyer, Samuel, 249
Holm-Hadulla, Rainer M., 59
Holt, Nancy, 270
Holy Wind. See *Nilch'i* (Navajo, Holy Wind)
honeybee (*Apis mellifera*). *See* bee, honeybee (*Apis mellifera*)
Hopi (people), 306
Horace, 59
hormone, 207, 209
Hozho (Navajo, dynamic balance and beauty), 306
humanism, 37, 29, 92, 134, 139n7, 190. *See also* posthumanism, posthuman
Humboldt, Alexander von, 253, 254, 255, 257, 266, 267n2
Hume, David, 274, 277, 278–279
Hunter, Lawrence E., 34
Hurston, Zora Neale, 254
hybrid, hybridity, hybridization, ix, 3, 5, 7, 10, 11, 13, 30, 31, 55, 110, 120, 141, 145, 153; bodies, 98, 101, 109; environments, 152, 290n5; siren (mermaid) as, 109–111. *See also* cyborg
Hypersea, 188, 189–190

idealism, 38, 58, 69, 71, 142, 276; Berkleyan, 143
identity, 5, 26, 53, 55, 79n2, 110, 132, 246, 293, 294, 295; human, 133, 293; self, 294
Ignatov, Anatoli, 251
"Iliaster" ("Prime Matter," "primordial semen"), 243, 251n5
illness (disease), 42, 101, 109, 111, 131, 134, 173, 180, 190, 236, 243, 251; Alzheimer's disease, 105; chronic, 208–209, 211, 218n1; venereal, 124. *See also* health
imagination, 5, 29, 57, 60, 73, 98, 100, 109, 110, 111, 124, 100, 138n1, 159, 171n12, 177, 208, 211, 227; cultural, literary, 56, 58, 61; as embodied, 78; political, 112
immanence, immanent, 3, 5, 24, 29, 33, 40, 54, 115, 128, 240, 288, 305, 309. See also *deus sive natura*; nature(s)
immaterial, immateriality, 79n1, 125, 131, 283, 289, 304, 305, 309, 314n5
impermanence (Buddhism, *anicca*), 291, 298
indigenous, 16, 253–268, 270, 283, 284, 298, 299; of bees, 170nn4–5; people and groups, 174, 215, 307–308. *See also* ethnicity, ethnic
individual, 3, 21, 24, 33, 40, 41, 48, 56, 59, 61, 62, 65, 76, 79n2, 85, 91, 105, 157, 162, 163, 187, 190, 191, 200, 206, 207, 262, 285, 304, 306; bodies, 208, 211; compound individuals, 12, 24; individualism, individuality, 51, 55, 56, 62, 64, 84, 217; minds, 54, 58, 59
Innenwelt (semiotic inner world), 53, 54, 149
insight (Buddhism). See *Vipassana* (Buddhism, insight or mindfulness)
intentional, intentionality, 69, 91, 104, 135, 148, 149, 151, 199, 203n7, 231, 243, 248, 285, 286. *See also* freedom (liberty)
interpretation, 8, 11, 12, 13, 22, 45, 154n7, 185n5, 226, 230, 231, 235–236, 292; in biosemiotics, 4, 53, 68, 73–74, 76, 142–144, 147, 149–150, 167, 170n2; in material ecocriticism, 9–10
intra-action, 4, 6, 8, 9, 13, 15, 26, 36n5, 83, 84, 87, 88–91, 93, 102, 103, 105, 107, 108, 172, 191, 195, 222, 224, 235, 236, 291, 293, 296, 298, 300n3, 307; intra-active, 35, 105, 107, 187, 192, 195, 224, 231, 283, 288; intra-activity, 9, 26, 192. *See also* agential realism; Barad, Karen
Inuit (people), 303–304

Iovino, Serenella, x, xii, xiinn1–2, 8, 13, 17n8, 29, 31, 52, 78, 84, 105, 113n2, 113n4, 113n7, 130, 131, 136, 138n3, 141, 173, 177, 200, 238, 253, 255, 257, 266, 267n7
Iris, 126
Iser, Wolfgang, 56

Jakobson, Roman, 75–77
James, William, 243
Jankovic, Vladimir, 129n8
Jeffers, Robinson, 61
Jesus, 288, 289
Jewett, Sarah Orne, 61
Johnson, William Henry, 216
Jonas, Hans, 73
Jones, Ken, 295
Joy, Eileen, 251
Joyce, James, 76, 177
justice, 16, 158–159, 169, 241, 263–264, 268n12; of bees, 168–169; ecological, 218, 258, 295; environmental, 11, 83, 111, 187, 203n6, 258, 260, 295, 300; injustice, 210, 289; interspecies, multispecies, trans-species, 16, 165, 290, 297, 300n3; social, political, 176, 208, 218, 258, 289, 290, 294, 295. *See also* oppression

Kachinas (Navajo, spirit ancestors), 307
Kant, Immanuel, 271, 272–274, 276–279
Karma (Buddhism), 292
Katrina, hurricane, 132, 133, 136, 203n9
Kauffman, Stuart, 32, 33, 36n6
Kauffmann, Louis H., 58
Keats, John, 61
Keijzer, Fred, 267n6
Keller, Catherine, 288, 289
Keller, Evelyn Fox, 69
Kidd, Sue Monk, 165
Kirby, Vicki, 10, 26, 27, 30, 31
Kirksey, S. Eben, 254, 255, 257
Kittredge, William, 136
Klein, Anne, 294
Knappett, Carl, 113n3
Kohn Eduardo, 255, 257–258, 259, 264–266, 267n4
Komárek, Stanislav, 148
Kosek, Jake, 161
Kozlowski, Lori, 268n9
Kraft, Kenneth, 295
Krech, Shepherd, III, 268n10
Kricher, John, 94n3
Krog, Antjie, 182–184
Kull, Kalevi, 75, 146, 149, 152, 154, 154n1, 154n9

La Fontaine, Jean de, 119
Lacan, Jacques, 162, 169n2
Lacis, Asja, 98
landscape, 1, 3, 5, 7, 13, 15, 56, 61, 81, 90, 98, 100, 102–107, 112, 124, 127, 145, 150–151, 161, 167, 170n4, 181, 183, 187, 193, 207, 221–231, 233–234, 236, 254; altered, 221, 229; nuclear, 15, 222, 224, 227, 231, 233, 235, 236, 237; photography, 221, 226; toxic, 226
Latour, Bruno, 4, 10, 41, 114, 116, 126, 129, 176, 192, 253, 254, 255, 263, 264, 266; on actants, actors, 26; on Actor-Network-Theory, 115; on collectives, 104; on compositionism, 115; *Pandora's Hope*, 4, 17n7, 129n6, 263; *Politics of Nature*, 4, 255; *Reassembling the Social*, 126, 128n2, 129n19; *We Have Never Been Modern*, 203n7, 255, 267n4
Lau Tzu, 287. *See also wu wei*
Lawrence, Elisabeth A., 61
Leduc, Timothy, 304
Lemieux, Jessica, 160
Lévi-Strauss, Claude, 254
Levy, Neil, 135
Lewontin, Richard C., 67, 69
Light, Andrew, 139n6
Lindauer, Martin, 163
Linehan, Marsha W., 297
Lipps, Theodor, 241, 251n4
Livingston, Alex, 251
Lotman, Jury, 142, 146, 147, 151
Louis XIV (King of France), 117
Löwith, Karl, 105
Loy, David R., 296
Lucretius, 101
Luhmann, Niklas, 12, 40, 42, 47–48, 50n4, 50n6, 50n7, 57
Luisi, Pier Luigi, 43–44
Luther, Martin, 73
Lynch, David, 216

Magna Mater, 61
Malafouris, Lambros, 113n3
Malaparte, Curzio (pseud. of Kurt Erich Suckert), 13, 107–110, 113n6
mammals, 145, 186, 192, 199, 200
Manes, Christopher, 139n5
Manghi, Sergio, 54
mangle, 28, 123, 223, 230, 238, 291, 294, 296. *See also* Pickering, Andrew
Maran, Timo, 13, 16n2, 143, 145, 149, 153
Marchesini, Roberto, 10

Margaret, Sebastian, 218n1
Margulis, Lynn, 77, 91, 94n5
Marine Mammal Care Center, 200
Marion, Jean Luc, 274
Markley, Robert, 116, 120, 129n16
Marsh, George Perkins, 17n6
Marshall, Patrick, 113n1
Martin, Philip, 297
Marx, Karl, 165, 171n12
Massumi, Brian, 244, 251n7
material ecocriticism. *See* ecocriticism
material turn, 2, 12, 37–38, 83–84, 113n3, 141, 221, 259
material-discursive, xiii, 8–9, 12, 13–15, 109, 131, 132, 283, 293; material-semiotic, 2, 3, 4, 6, 14, 17n5, 30, 55, 78, 106, 154n2, 267n4. *See also* discourse, discursive; materiality
materialism(s), 12, 67–69, 72, 184, 283, 285; ecological, 279; ecomaterialism, 11, 116, 128n4, 187, 240; new, 2, 4–5, 10, 11–13, 14, 16, 16n1, 22, 25, 27, 37, 40–41, 44, 45, 49, 81, 83, 91, 104, 134, 139n6, 173, 186, 187, 193, 202, 238, 283, 285, 288, 291–293, 295–297, 299; nonreductive, 16, 284; old-style, 37; postmaterialism, 285–286; reductive, 72, 285; vital, 194, 243, 259–260
Matheson, Dirk, 268n9
Mathews, Freya, 285
Mathison, Dirk, 268
materiality, x–xi, 1–2, 4, 6, 8, 9, 10, 11, 25, 27–29, 31, 35, 36n2, 38, 43, 45, 80, 83, 89, 98, 103, 111, 117, 118, 121–123, 138n2, 173, 176, 177, 184, 193, 195, 222, 283, 285, 286, 288, 298, 312, 313; corporeal, 131; creative, 12, 21, 28, 34; narrative, 138; semiotic, 7; thick, 13, 137, 140n12; vibrant, 5, 122; vital, 13. *See also* matter
matter: agentic, agentic properties of, 4, 6–7, 12, 21, 83–84, 267n2, 284, 292; matter-energy, 115, 228; storied, ix, x, 1, 7, 13, 21, 28–29, 33–34, 98, 112, 255, 257, 275, 307; vibrant, 11, 22, 25, 36n2, 38, 41, 91, 114–115, 172, 193, 223, 283, 296. *See also* agency; materiality
Maturana, Humberto, 12, 40, 43–45, 54
Matussek, Peter, 94n6
Maximo and Bartola (a.k.a "Last of the ancient Aztecs"), 216
Mazur, Suzan, 68
McCallum, Brian, 160
McCarthy, John, 94n6
McKinney, Dan, 36n5
McMenamin, Dianna, 188, 189
McMenamin, Mark, 188, 189

McNeley, James Kale, 314n4
Melville, Herman, 61, 63, 68, 148
memory, 13, 31, 76, 105–107, 109, 111, 209; biosemiotic, 57; bodily; 103; collective, 166–167; of landscape, place, 105–106
Mentz, Steve, 116, 128n3, 192, 314n2
Merchant, Carolyn, 25
Merkur, Daniel, 304
Merleau-Ponty, Maurice, 17n9, 43, 82, 83
Merrick, John, 216
metaphysics, 51, 70, 79n6, 131, 271, 278
meteorology, 114, 116, 117, 129n8, 178, 203n7
Metz, Simon, 216
Michaels, Walter Benn, 42
microbiome, 3, 191. *See also* bacterium, bacteria; fungus, fungi
Middleton, W. E. Knowles, 116
mind, 2, 3, 4, 5, 7, 27, 32, 37, 48, 50n6, 51–61, 66, 68, 69, 71, 78, 79n3, 82, 102, 143, 206, 208, 222, 223, 251n6, 255, 257, 266, 291, 293, 297, 298, 299, 314n5; bodymind, 29, 36n4, 105, 107, 112; as consciousness, 302; creative, 12, 51, 54; ecology of, 10, 54; mind-body relation, 50n6, 55, 304; mind-matter dualism, 3, 22, 44, 223, 234; of place, 13, 105–106; wind-mind, 303–304, 306, 311. *See also* body, bodies; Cartesian dualism; subject
mindfulness (Buddhism), 291, 293, 295, 297–298. See also *Vipassana* (Buddhism, insight or mindfulness)
Mitchell, R. W., 148
Mitchell, W. J. T., 238
Mitman, Gregg, 148
modeling (as a semiotic process) 142, 146–154
modernism, modernity, modern, 2, 13, 14, 17n7, 17n9, 22, 36n2, 37, 41, 48, 57, 59, 61, 64, 65, 69, 70, 78, 79n6, 83, 109, 122, 126, 129n18, 134, 153, 200, 240, 253, 254, 259, 261, 264, 267, 283, 286, 287, 301, 304; early, 116, 118, 129n8, 139n11; of poetry, 81, 273; of science, 72–74, 78, 79n5. *See also* postmodernism, postmodern
moha (Buddhism, delusion), 292, 298
Molero, Jeronimo, *196*
monism, 79n1, 243, 251n6
monkey, 190, 205, 215–218
Monsanto, 203n7
Montrose, Louis, 138n2
Moore, Charles, 198–200
Moore, Marianne, 61
Morante, Elsa, 108
more-than-human, 1–5, 16, 16n4, 17n5, 22, 30,

35, 58, 63, 64, 71, 81, 89, 104, 107, 131, 284, 288, 300n3, 311. *See also* nature(s); nonhuman
Morrison, Toni, 60
Mortimer-Sandilands, Catriona. *See* Sandilands, Catriona
Morton, Timothy, 15, 28, 29, 80, 91, 93, 178, 184, 270, 272, 288, 290n3
Muir, John, 299
Murray, Gilbert, 132

Nachträglichkeit (Freud), 77
Nagel, Thomas, 67–69, 79n1
Naipaul, V. S., 179
Najagneq, 304
narrative, narrativity, x, 1, 5–8, 11, 12, 16, 16n3, 17n8, 21, 26, 28–35, 52, 57, 58, 72, 75–77, 83, 88, 98, 103–107, 109, 111–112, 115, 125, 128, 135–138, 138n1, 138n3, 146, 149, 188, 196, 223, 233, 262, 296, 312; Aboriginal, 284, 285; cosmological, 258; cultural, 292, 299; of ecophobia, 132; embodied, 131; emergences, 8, 112; environmental, 184; material, of matter, 8, 9, 13, 52, 130; of the mind, 298; site of, 255; of suffering, 294, 297; of trans-corporeality, 228
narrative agency. *See* agency
NASA, 68
Native American (people), 259, 292
natura naturans, natura naturata, 286. *See also* Spinoza, Baruch
naturalism, 240
nature(s), 12, 21–23, 34, 38, 43, 49, 61, 62, 64, 67–70, 78, 79n5, 80–81, 83, 85–86, 106–108, 116, 120–121, 123, 125–127, 134, 140n11, 141, 148, 150, 174–175, 178, 182, 185n4, 202, 223, 225, 240, 245, 252n10, 255–257, 263, 278, 284, 286, 293, 296, 299, 305, 309, 314n8; and agency, 24–25; agency of, 108, 131, 138n2; in biosemiotics, 16n2, 71, 73–74, 142, 154n9; bodies and, 253; bodily, 1, 2, 8, 13, 21, 53, 56, 84, 89, 292; and culture, x, 3, 5, 6, 9, 10, 27, 35, 36n3, 51, 55–57, 60, 61, 63, 65–66, 72, 87, 145, 183, 213–214, 261, 266, 283, 297; and ecophobia, 135, 138n1; eloquence of, 29, 139n5; forces of, 132, 304; in Goethe, 80–94; human, 3, 16, 30, 58, 188, 190–191, 266; law of, 244; material, 1, 52, 80; nature-culture, naturecultures, 5, 27, 36, 107, 267n4; *Naturphilosophie,* 288; nonhuman, 3, 16, 30, 58, 215–216, 267n2; of ocean, 191; of plastic, 194; and rights, 254; of shit, 177; Spinoza's *natura naturans* and *natura naturata,* 286; wild, 61–62; writing, 16n5, 87. *See also deus sive natura;* ecology

Navajo (people). *See* Dineh or Navajo (people)
Na'vi, 257–258, 263–265
neonicotinoid. *See* pesticides
Newman, Barnett, 78
Newton, Isaac, 85–86, 88, 93n1, 94n7
Nietzsche, Friedrich, 79n6, 278
nihilism, 73, 79n6, 278
Nilch'i (Navajo, Holy Wind), 305
Niño El-Hania, Charbel, 71
Nixon, Rob, 11, 136
no-self (Buddhism, *anatta*), 16, 267n6, 291, 293, 294, 295, 298
Noble, Denis, 77
Noble Eightfold Path (Buddhism), 292
nominalism, 72, 74
nonhuman: agency, 15, 35, 130, 135, 137, 283; animals, 132, 142, 146, 148, 153, 215–217, 296; bodies, 38, 104, 246, 289; creativity, 53; forms, 2, 7, 52; human-nonhuman, 9, 25, 27, 62, 255; landscape, 124; natures, 3, 26, 27, 30, 57, 58, 65, 69, 145, 215, 267n2; relations, 35; vitalities, 240. *See also* animal; more-than-human; posthumanism, posthuman
nonhuman turn, 240
nuclear: age, 223, 228; bomb, 200, 234, 236; reactor, 32, 226–228
Núñez Cataschunga, James, 257

object, xi, 4, 8, 9, 24, 26, 27, 30, 34, 39, 46, 61, 70n4, 81, 85, 87, 89, 90, 104, 105, 106, 123, 133, 135, 144, 148, 154n4, 154n6, 159, 167, 170n3, 184, 193, 195, 198, 199, 203nn6–7, 207, 223, 244, 251n1, 251n4, 273, 274, 277, 283, 285, 298; autonomous, 115; benign, 193, 198, 200; body as, 169n1; constituents of nature as, 22; demonized, 63, 196; dynamical, 143, 154n5; inanimate, 196; material, 42, 142–143, 145, 152, 177, 222, 236; meaning-generating, 72; natural, environmental, 143, 144, 146, 149, 239, 246; rainbow as, 126; semiotic, 77–78, 145; static, 207; subject-object split, dualism, 22, 26, 34, 80, 87, 116, 119. *See also* subject
object-oriented-ontology (OOO), 10, 15, 193, 202, 203n8, 240, 278, 288
Oceans, 150, 186, 188, 190, 192, 194, 197, 198
Odling-Smee, F. John, 150
Oh, Jea Sophia, 290n5
Oldenburg, Henry, 129n11
onto-epistemology, onto-epistemological, 26, 55, 223, 283, 293
ontology, 3, 9, 12, 21, 27, 34, 47, 49, 101, 103, 131,

158, 160, 169, 266, 293; agential-realist, 26; ecological, 82–83; flat, 39; human, 130; new materialist, 288; object-oriented, 10, 15, 193; relational, 22, 288
onto-tale, 52, 285
ontotheology. *See* theology
Oppermann, Serpil, x, xii, xiinn1–2, 12, 17n5, 17n8, 22, 25, 31, 84, 130, 138n3, 139, 193, 238, 253, 255, 257, 266, 267n2, 290n1, 292
oppression, 6, 138, 164, 292, 294. *See also* ableism; justice; racism; sexism; speciesism
organism: biological, 3, 24, 30, 41, 43–44, 53, 55, 61, 68, 72, 76, 78, 102, 106, 131, 141–143, 147, 150–153, 196, 200, 257, 303, 312; complex, 77; land as, 189–191; living, 5, 142, 145–146, 148–149, 200, 304; mobile, 81; multicellular, 33, 71, 76; non-human, 72, 257
organization, 4, 43–45, 48, 57, 75, 76; activist, 195; autopoietic, 46; biological, 151; political, 268n11; self-organization, 37, 40, 42, 44, 47, 53, 56; semiotic, 153; social, 40, 49, 115
Origen, 74
other, otherness, 12, 31, 34, 35, 55, 58, 85, 130, 217. *See also* alterity
Ovid, 110

"Pachamama" (Mother Earth), 254, 256. *See also* "Sachamama" (Source of Life, Source of Light)
Packer, Laurence, 170n5
Pagel, Walter, 239, 243, 246, 251n1, 251n5, 251n9
Pahl, Katrin, 243, 251
pain, 13, 14, 130–137, 162, 206, 208–209, 297, 298, 300n4
Pali (language of the Buddha), 291
Palmer, Lauren, 200
Palmers, Vanya, 278
panpsychism, 285–287, 289, 290n1. *See also* Mathews, Freya
Papanja (Buddhism, proliferation), 297
Paracelsus (byname of Philippus Aureolus Theophrastus Bombastus von Hohenheim), 15, 239–241, 243–246, 251n1, 251nn3–4, 252n9
Parker, Pat, 209
Parkhurst, Ferdinando, 239, 243, 251n3
Parlati, Marilena, 17n10
Parthenope, 97, 109, 110
Past, Elena Margarita, 113n6
Paticcasamuppāda (Buddhism), 291. *See* dependent origination (Buddhism, *paticcasamuppāda*)
patriarchy, 214; heteropatriarchy, 293

Patton, Kimberley C., 202n3
Paul III, pope, 267n2
PCB (polychlorinated biphenyl), 292
Peirce, Charles Sanders, 54, 67, 70, 142, 143
performativity, 29, 33, 283
pesticides, 160, 204, 208; neonicotinoid, 160, 164. *See also* pollution, pollutants
Peters, Katrin, 197, *198*
phenomena, 1, 3–5, 7, 9–10, 22, 26, 44, 52, 53, 55, 62, 65, 88, 101, 106, 146, 151, 160, 223, 224, 251n1, 254, 263, 278, 285, 303; atmospheric, 116, 120, 125; biological, 71; saturated, 274; semiotic, 152; social, 40, 103
phenomenology, 15, 198; bodily, 17n9, 43, 172; eco-phenomenology, 105
Phillips, Dana, 3, 11, 14
philosophy, 15, 59, 116, 117, 251n3, 251n7, 260, 287, 289; Buddhist, 292, 295; Daoist, 286; of Kant, 271, 273, 276; natural, 103; object-oriented, 240; process, 24; of science, 68, 73, 172; semiotic, 70, 71, 73, 74, 79n6, 142–143, 145; vital-materialist, 115; of Whitehead, 288, 290n2
Phoenician (people), 309
Phoenix, 60
photography, 224, 230, 238. *See also* art; landscape
Pickering, Andrew, 10, 28, 123, 133, 185n5, 222, 223, 238, 291. *See also* mangle
Pjatigorskij, Aleksander, 151
place, xi, 5, 9, 30, 36n6, 81, 97, 98, 101, 103, 110–112, 166, 179, 183, 232, 236, 249, 256, 269, 273, 302, 306; of bees, 166–167, 169; and body, 3, 11; and ecocriticism, 17; ecology of, 104, 184; local, 64, 194; meeting, 279; and memory, 103; "middle," 6; mind and, 13, 105–106, 299; natural, 90; nature as, 80, 87; ocean as, 192; and photography, 221–222, 225, 229; poetics of, 287; restoration of, 211; savage, 60; spirituality of, 284; and stories, 312–313
plastic, 14, 41, 139n6, 152, 179, 186, 188, 193, 194–202, 203n9, 236, 258. *See also* pollution, pollutants
Plato, 57–58, 309
Pliny, 116
Plotinus, 94n8
Plumwood, Val, 34, 35, 84, 284–285
plutonium, 181, 226, 228
Poinsot, John, 74
Polanyi, Michael, 72
politics, 6, 11, 50n5, 56, 106, 109, 158, 159–160, 163, 168, 169n1, 189, 194, 233, 248, 254, 260, 262, 263, 266, 284; bee, 14, 164, 169, 170n10; bee-human,

157; cosmopolitics, 264, 267; of cure, 14, 204, 206, 208–210; disability, 207–208, 215; of gender, 10; identity, 295; of matter, 14; multispecies, cross-species, 159, 165, 169. *See also* biopolitics

pollution, pollutants, 6, 8, 14, 90–91, 110, 173, 207, 262; fracking, 89; global, 11; military, 210, 212; persistent organic pollutants (POPs), 194; plastic, 186–188, 194–195, 197. *See also* chemicals; contamination; dioxin; plastic; toxins; trans-corporeal, trans-corporeality; waste

Popper, Karl, 69, 72, 79n5

porosity, 5, 13, 82, 97, 100–106, 111–112; porousness, 191. *See also* viscous porosity

postcolonial, postcolonialism, 14, 16n5, 128, 177, 179, 183, 260, 290n5; excremental, 177, 183. *See also* colonial, colonialism

posthumanism, posthuman, 10, 12, 17n5, 17n8, 21, 82–83, 84, 109, 131, 184, 187, 190, 193, 283, 297, 300n3; aqueous, 191; ecological, 13, 80, 82–84, 88–89, 92–93. *See also* cyborg; humanism; more than-human; nonhuman

Postlethwaite, Pete, 138n1

postmodernism, postmodern, 4, 12, 26, 27, 28, 36n2, 38, 55, 59, 65, 83, 84, 92, 118, 139n5, 143, 181, 236, 283, 286; ecological, 10, 12, 17n8, 21–25, 27–28, 31, 34, 35n1, 84. *See also* modernism, modernity, modern

posture, 15, 239, 241, 245–249, 251n4; of nonchalance, 15, 246, 248, 250, 252n10; of side-curved head, 246, 247, 250

Praeger, Dave, 178–179

pragmaticism, pragmatism, 67, 181

Preston, Claire, 161

Prigogine, Ilya, 34, 44

primate, 216

proliferation (Buddhism). *See Papanja* (Buddhism, proliferation)

Prometheus, 60

Protagoras, 276

protein, 53, 68

psychology, 59; evolutionary, 71. *See also* ecopsychology

Pynchon, Thomas, 174, 175, 177, 183

quantum physics, 2, 27, 45, 49, 72, 87, 137, 222, 267; double slit experiment, 33; Higgs field, 278; quantum mechanical field theories, 23, 100. *See also* atom; Barad, Karen; Bohm, David; Bohr, Niels; intra-action

queer, queerness, x, 107, 109, 113n5, 133, 208, 213, 214, 267, 278, 299

Queiroz, João, 71

Quigley, Peter, 139n5

racism, 23, 183; scientific, 216. *See also* oppression

radioactivity, 222, 225–228, 234

Raffles, Hugh, 162, 170n8

Rancière, Jacques, 157–159

Rasmussen, Knud, 304, 314n3

realism, 25, 71, 74, 142; biosemiotic, 12, 67; speculative, 193, 203n8. *See also* agential realism

Rebrovick, Tripp, 251

reductionism, 67, 68, 276, 285

reenchantment, x, 12, 23–24, 27, 28, 31, 35n1, 36n1. *See also* disenchantment; postmodernism, postmodern

reflexivity, self-reflexivity, 37, 46, 48

relation, relationship, x, 4, 7, 11, 12, 22, 24, 25, 29, 34, 35, 37, 41, 46, 48, 49, 51, 54, 65, 70, 73–74, 76, 78, 81, 90, 92, 105, 107, 115, 116, 118, 120, 125–127, 130, 131, 135, 138, 140n11, 141–149, 151, 169, 175, 208, 222, 244, 249, 250, 252, 257, 258, 261, 264, 266, 269, 271, 273–275, 278, 288, 292–293, 295–296, 305–306, 312, 314n6; bee-human, 157, 160, 163, 164–167; biopolitical, 159–160; culture-nature, 57; ethical, 35, 256; internal, 23, 24, 27, 29, 34; interrelations, 2, 56, 106, 161, 167, 285, 286, 299; mind-body, 55; mind-matter, 60, 66; semiotic, 152, 154n6, 158

relationality, x, 21, 22, 23, 26, 27, 28, 55, 83–84, 87, 106, 193, 195, 294

religion, 56, 123, 245, 248, 283, 287, 290, 291. *See also* animism; spirit

Renaissance, 59, 100, 129n7

res extensa, res cogitans, 74. *See also* Descartes, René

response-ability, 34, 35, 159

responsibility, 17n6, 39, 90, 135, 190, 192, 195, 200, 237, 284, 292, 294. *See also* ethics

restoration, 210–214, 287; bodily, 207–208; of health, 206, 213; of prairie ecosystem, 14, 204, 213, 214–215

Ricoeur, Paul, 70, 79n2

Riegl, Alois, 251n7

Rigby, Kate, 6, 11, 16, 81, 91, 288, 290n1, 290n4, 292, 297, 298

risk, 5, 12, 119, 221; society, 80, 187, 193, 194

RNA, 32

Roberts, Callum, 186, 202n5

Roe, Thomas, Sir, 120

Rolston, Holmston, III, 139n6

Rosch, Eleanor, 44, 102

Rose, Deborah Bird, 267n5, 284
Rosen, Robert, 147
Rothko, Mark, 270
Rouse, Joseph, 10
Ruach (Hebrew, divine wind), 307, 309
Rudd, Gillian, 116
Runa (people), 255

"Sachamama" (Source of Life, Source of Light), 256, 257, 261. *See also* bioluminescence; "Pachamama" (Mother Earth)
Safina, Carl, 188
Sagan, Carl, 277
Sagan, Dorion, 94n5
Sander, Emmanuel, 70
Sandilands, Catriona, 10, 14, 105, 106, 139n5
Santiago School, 45
Sapir, Edward, 254
Sapp, Jan, 68
Satterfield, Terre, 136
Saussure, Ferdinand de, 71
Scarry, Elaine, 133
Schauder, Stephan, 32–33
Schelling, Friedrich, 82, 288, 290n4
Schiller, Friedrich, 36n1, 132
Schopenhauer, Arthur, 274
Seamon, David, 94n6
Sebeok. Thomas, A., 71, 142, 146, 147, 154nn7–8
Secondary revision (Freud). See *Nachträglichkeit* (Freud)
secularism, 283
Seeley, Thomas, 161, 163, 170n10
Segal, Zindel V., 297
self, 38, 45, 63, 64, 92, 211, 246, 267n6, 285, 288, 291, 292, 293, 294, 298; embodied, embedded, 35, 136; human, 9, 12, 61, 131, 133, 134, 136, 191, 245; material, 187, 192, 293; no-self, 16, 267n6, 291, 293, 294, 295, 298; poetic, 58, 60, 62; self-other, 87. *See also* subject
semiosis, 53, 70, 74, 79n6, 255, 266; cultural, 73; web of, 71. *See also* biosemiotics; ecosemiotics; semiotic niche; sign
semiosphere, 5. *See also* biosemiotics; ecosemiotics; semiosis; semiotic niche; sign; zoosemitics
semiotic niche, 141. *See also* biosemiotics; ecosemiotics; semiosis; semiosphere; sign
Serres, Michel, 114–115, 118–121, 123, 125, 128, 129n14
Setta-Silva, Edileusa, 263
sexism, 23, 133, 139n10. *See also* oppression
sexuality, 103, 185n2; queer, 109, 133. *See also* gender, gendering

Shakespeare, William, 60, 129n16, 130, 132, 314n2
Shapiro, James A. 68
Shay, Nick, 65
Sheets-Johnstone, Maxine, 69
Shelley, Percy Bysshe, 60, 132
Shintani, Laura, 77
Shiprock, 314n4
shit. *See* excrement
Shubin, Neil, 188, 189
Shukin, Nicole, 159
Siegel, Taggart, 160
sign, 1, 4, 5, 13, 21, 24, 27, 30, 53, 60, 67, 72, 74, 79n6, 98, 106, 108, 126, 141, 143–149, 152–153, 154n3, 154nn5–7, 157, 162, 169n2, 216, 239; iconic, 70, 79n2; process, 16n2, 145–146, 257; systems, 150. *See also* biosemiotics; ecosemiotics; semiosis; semiosphere; semiotic niche
Sila (Inuit, intelligence of the air), 303, 304
Silkwood, Karen, 228
Simard, Suzanne, 36n5
Simmer-Brown, Judith, 295
Simpson, Homer, 172, 181
Simpson, James, 74
Slovic, Scott, 16n5, 17nn5–6, 136
Snow, Elvira, 216
Snow, Jenny Lee, 216
social systems theory, 12, 45, 49, 56
sociology, 2
Sontag, Deborah, 241
Sontag, Susan, 238
Soyinka, Wole (pseud. of Akinwande Oluwole-Soyinka), 177
speciesism, 23, 297. *See also* oppression; racism
speculative realism. *See* realism
Spinoza, Baruch, 48, 243, 251n6, 285–286. See also *deus sive natura;* immanence, immanent; nature(s); ontotheology; substance
spirit, 58, 97, 110, 186, 253, 256, 261, 266, 283, 306, 314n5; as ancestors, 307; ecology, 291, 302, 304; Hebraic, 314n6; spiritual, 74, 129n10, 165, 229, 245, 291, 292, 294–295, 297, 300n1
spirituality, 15–16, 131, 283–284, 287–289, 292, 293, 295, 297; ecospirituality, 284, 288, 290–291. *See also* religion
Spretnak, Charlene, 22–23, 25
Spuybroek, Lars, 241
Stanley, John, 296
Starr, Alison, 200, *201*
Steiner, George, 132
Stengers, Isabel, 314n10
Stewart, Kathleen, 251n8

Stewart, John, 49n1
Stewart, Rob, 186
Stockman, Vivian, 212
Storm, Theodor, 81
Strabo, 105
Stratton-Porter, Gene, 165
structuralism, 76
subject, 4, 24, 26, 59, 62, 81, 82, 84, 90, 105, 135, 142, 147, 149, 159, 162, 169n1, 170n3, 176, 202n2, 222, 250, 294, 300n4; autonomous, 115; biopolitical, 158, 160; ethical, 35; human, 3, 8, 9, 23, 37, 139nn5–6, 187, 240, 261, 277, 297; local, 259; nonhuman, 78, 266; political, 158; semiotic, 149; social, 34; subject-object splits, dualism, 22, 26, 34, 80, 87, 116, 119; subjectivity, 5, 23, 265, 293. *See also* Cartesian dualism; object; self
substance, x, 3, 4, 10, 26, 32, 34, 36n7, 42, 45, 79n5, 84, 87, 91, 92, 98, 108, 110, 111, 114, 121, 131, 177, 187, 188, 192, 193, 199, 202, 202n3, 203n6, 228, 243, 251n6, 251n9, 286, 302; chemical, 52, 80, 83, 151, 173; human-made, 152; material, 101, 178; toxic, 7, 23, 83; xenobiotic, 29, 194
suffering (Buddhism). See *Dukka* (Buddhism, suffering)
Sullivan, Heather I., 3, 11, 13, 17n9, 44, 93n2
surrealism, 110
sustainability, 193, 228, 285
Sutton, John, 113n3
Swimme, Brian, 30–31
sympathy, 239–252; as agent, 240
system, ix, 6, 24, 33, 35, 42; in cascade, 29, 119; closed, open, 44; discursive, 9; human, 21; living, 3, 34, 43, 53, 75; self-sustaining, 207, 213. *See also* autopoiesis

Tanha (Buddhism, craving), 292
Tartu-Moscow semiotic school, 147
Taubes, Susan Anima, 73
Taylor, Astra, 210
Taylor, Sunaura, 210, 216
TCE (trichloroethylene), 210
Teasdale, John D., 297
"temporarily able-bodied persons" (TABs), 208
Tenzel, Andreas, 243
Terry, Edward, 120
text, textuality, x, 7, 9, 14, 17n9, 21, 23, 28, 34, 41, 43, 55–57, 59–66, 70, 111, 115, 116, 118, 131, 138n2, 141, 143, 146, 151, 154n8, 236, 238, 255, 257, 271, 273, 287, 309, 311, 314n3; bodies as, 98, 111; imaginative, 51; literary, 2, 10, 12, 59, 61, 65, 66, 79n7, 157, 165, 169; material, 6, 11, 104, 139n5; matter as, x, 6, 17n8, 29, 42, 52; as semiotic object, 77; textual-semiotic, 54
theology, 38, 79n6, 131, 239, 288; ecotheology, 288–289, 290n5; medieval, 72; negative, 289, 290n5; ontotheology, 276, 278; reformation, 73; semiotic, 69, 70, 74; transcendental, 110. *See also* deep incarnation (ecotheology); *deus sive natura*
Thévenot, Melchisédech, 118, 120, 123, 125
thing: power, 194, 195, 203n8; theory, 10, 193, 203n8, 238
Thomas Aquinas, 73. *See also* Aquinas, Thomas
Thompson, Evan, 44, 102
Thompson, Jerry L., 230
Tilley, Christopher, 135
Tondl, Ladislav, 146, 147
Tooby, John, 71
toof (*ignimbrite campana*), 98, 100
toxins, 3, 5, 92, 188, 194, 196, 198, 210, 212, 223; antitoxin movements, 193. *See also* pollution, pollutants
transcendentalism, transcendental, 3, 58, 79n6, 110
trans-corporeal, trans-corporeality, 25, 84, 92, 93, 101, 103, 110–111, 113n2, 139nn5–6, 172, 294, 297; concept of, 293; ecological intuitions of, 299; narratives of, 228, 236, 284, 291; at sea, 186–203, 223. *See also* Alaimo, Stacy, body, contamination, corporeal
Truman, Harry, 37
Tsing, Anna, 160, 267n5
Tuana, Nancy, 10, 101, 103, 106, 131, 133, 138n2, 203n9, 288, 290n2, 291
Tucker, Mary Evelyn, 30–31
Turner, J. Scott, 150
Turner, Terence S., 75–77
Turrell, James, 15, 269–278

Uexküll, Jakob von, 54, 74, 141, 142, 147, 149, 169
Uexküll, Thure von, 146
Ulanowicz, Robert E., 70
Umiker-Sebeok, Jean, 71
Umwelt (semiotic environment), 53. *See also* Uexküll, Jakob von
United Nations Food and Agricultural Organization (FAO), 297
Universal Declaration on the Rights of Mother Earth, 254, 260
uranium, 32, 208
Uzendoski, Michael, 256, 260

value, 36n6, 38, 135–136, 138n1, 144, 165, 168, 169n2, 174, 209, 215, 250, 254, 292; of ecosystems, 193; educational, 133; environmental, 145; ethical, 55; fact and, 9; intrinsic, 22, 39; philosophical, 138. *See also* ethics
Van der Tuin, Iris, 3, 16n1, 31
Van Rompay, Thomas J., 251n4
Varela, Francisco, 12, 40, 43–45, 54, 102
vegetarianism, 296
Velardi, Claudio, 98
Venter, Craig, 192
Verner, Samuel P., 216
vertebrates, 24, 162, 189
Vesalius, Andreas, 139n11
Vico, Giambattista, 76
Vidal, John, 254
Vipassana (Buddhism, insight or mindfulness), 293
virus, 1, 106, 179, 191
viscous porosity, 203n9, 291. *See also* porosity
vitality, vitalism, ix, 12, 21, 22, 25, 26, 27, 29, 30, 33, 38, 161, 193, 244, 248, 251n6, 284, 308
Vivieros de Castro, Eduardo, 261, 266
Von Hohenheim, Philippus Aureolus. *See* Paracelsus (byname of Philippus Aureolus Theophrastus Bombastus von Hohenheim)

Walls, Laura Dassow, 253, 254, 255, 257, 266, 267n2
war, 185n1, 203n10, 209, 212, 236, 237, 246; Cold War, 64–65, 229; First Gulf War, 179; Spanish-American War, 176; warfare, 292; World War II, 100, 108, 174, 175, 226, 233
Warwick, Anderson, 176, 183
waste, 8, 11, 14, 32, 64, 65, 90, 111, 173, 174, 178–179, 183, 184, 185n4, 186–188, 200, 202n3; garbage, 181, 182, 184, 186, 197–199, 202n3; litter, 152, 166, 229, 243, 244; radioactive, 152; rubbish, xi, 182; wasteland, 61, 229. *See also* contamination; pollution, pollutants
water, 36n5, 39, 60, 63, 76, 83, 85, 92, 115, 117, 121, 122 125, 144, 145, 176, 180–181, 184, 190, 192, 198, 199, 204, 211, 215, 231, 234, 262, 275, 292, 307, 312, 313n2; ecosystems, 151; freshwater, 262; groundwater, 32, 178, 210; saltwater, 188, 189; seawater, 122, 188; streamwater, 313; underwater, 100; waterscape, 124, 126; watershed, 215; waterways, 124, 198, 287
Weber, Max, 35n1
Weinryb, Ittai, 251
Wells, Patrick, 170n6
Wenner, Adrian, 170n6

Westling, Louise, 17n9, 57, 82, 83
Wheeler, John A., 33
Wheeler, Wendy, 4, 5, 11, 12, 31, 36n4, 53–54
White, Daniel R., 25
Whitehead, Alfred N., 79n5, 274, 288, 290n2, 313n8
Whitman, Walt, 15, 61, 240–241, 244–250, 251n1, 251n7, 252n12; "A Song of the Rolling Earth," 246, 248; *Leaves of Grass*, 250; "Song of Myself," 61–62, 240, 244–245, 246–247, 250
Whitty, Julia, 188, 189, 190
Wiener, Norbert, 69
wilderness, 87, 173, 221
Wilhelm, Maria, 257, 265, 267n9
Wilkie, Laurie A., 113n3
William of Newburgh, x, xi, xiin4
William of Ockham, 73
Williams, G. 297
Williams, William Carlos, 61, 273
Williamson, Robert G., 307
Wilson, Edward O., 71
wind, 52, 60, 117, 120, 122, 134, 150, 230, 232, 274, 301, 303–307, 309, 311–313, 314nn4–6; Wind's Child, Dark Wind, Glossy Wind, Rolling Darkess, Revolving Wind, 306. *See also* air; atmosphere; *Nilch'i* (Navajo, Holy Wind); *Ruach* (Hebrew, divine wind)
Winterson, Jeanette, 299
Witherspoon, Gary, 306
Wolfe, Cary, 10, 82
Wood, Michael, 78
wood wide web, 257
Woolf, Virginia, 57
Worringer, Wilhelm, 251n7
wu wei, 287. *See also* Lau Tzu

Yaeger, Patricia, 17n10
Yakumama, 262
Yarrow, Thomas, 113n3
Yates, Julian, 128
yoga, 245, 291
Yupik (people), 303

Zajonc, Arthur, 93n1, 94n6
Zapf, Hubert, 12, 51, 79n7
Zeus, 41
Zimmermann, Michael E., 25
Žižek, Slavoj, 179, 185n4
zoo, 216. *See also* Barnum, P. T.
zoosemiotic, 14, 71, 147. *See also* biosemiotics; ecosemiotics
Zoroaster, 113n5

CPSIA information can be obtained at www.ICGtesting.com
Printed in the USA
LVOW03s1327021214

416726LV00009B/18/P

9 780253 013989